T0361217

MERCANTILIST THEORY AND PRACTICE:
THE HISTORY OF BRITISH MERCANTILISM

# CONTENTS OF THE EDITION

*Reasons Humbly Offer'd to the Honourable House of Commons by the Tobacco and Wine Merchants* ([1700?])

Charles Davenant, *An Essay upon the Probable Methods of Making a People Gainers in the Ballance of Trade* (1699)

*Truth is but Truth, as it is Timed!* (1719)

*A Ballance for Merchants and Mariners* (1719)

[David Bindon], *A Letter from a Merchant who has left off Trade to a Member of Parliament* (1738)

Volume 3: The Colonial System

[Richard Eburne], *A Plaine Path-Way to Plantations* (1624)

Balthasar Gerbier, *A Sommary Description* (1660)

*An Answer of the Company of Royal Adventurers of England Trading into Africa* (1667)

*News from New-England* (1676)

Arthur Dobbs, *An Essay on the Trade and Improvement of Ireland* (1729–31)

*Representation of the Board of Trade Relating to ... his Majesty's Plantations in America* (1733–4)

[Malachy Postlethwayt], *The African Trade, the Great Pillar and Support of the British Plantation Trade in America* (1745)

*The Case of the Importation of Bar-Iron from our own Colonies of North America* (1756)

William Knox, *The Interest of the Merchants and Manufacturers of Great-Britain, in the Present Contest with the Colonies* (1775)

Josiah Child, Charles Davenant and William Wood, *Select Dissertations on Colonies and Plantations* (1775)

Volume 4: The Industrial Interest and the Employment of the Poor

Peter Chamberlen, *The Poor Mans Advocate, or Englands Samaritan* (1649)

Henry Robinson, *The Office of Addresses and Encounters* (1650)

Richard Haines, *A Model of Government for the Good of the Poor and the Wealth of the Nation* (1678)

Richard Haines, *England's Weal and Prosperity Proposed* (1681)

*A Discourse upon the Necessity of Encouraging Mechanic Industry* (1690)

[John Pollexfen], *England and East-India Inconsistent in their Manufactures* (1697)

# MERCANTILIST THEORY AND PRACTICE:

# THE HISTORY OF BRITISH MERCANTILISM

*Editor*
Lars Magnusson

Volume 1
Trade, Growth and State Interest

Routledge
Taylor & Francis Group

LONDON AND NEW YORK

First published 2008 by Pickering & Chatto (Publishers) Limited

Published 2016 by Routledge
2 Park Square, Milton Park, Abingdon, Oxon OX14 4RN
711 Third Avenue, New York, NY 10017, USA

*Routledge is an imprint of the Taylor & Francis Group, an informa business*

© Taylor & Francis 2008
© Lars Magnusson editorial material 2008

BRITISH LIBRARY CATALOGUING IN PUBLICATION DATA

Mercantilist theory and practice: the history of British mercantilism
1. Mercantile system – Great Britain – History – 17th century – Sources 2. Mercantile system – Great Britain – History – 18th century – Sources I. Magnusson,
Lars, 1952–
330.1'513'0941

ISBN-13: 978-1-85196-927-2 (set)

Typeset by Pickering & Chatto (Publishers) Limited

# CONTENTS

# GENERAL INTRODUCTION

A group of writers roughly existed between the late sixteenth and the middle of the eighteenth centuries who published pamphlets and tracts on economic issues, especially regarding (international) trade, money, finance and beneficial governance. The great economist Joseph Schumpeter called them the 'consultant administrators'. They were state bureaucrats, merchants, politicians and swindlers; men of different trades and ranking. We find them all over Europe during the so-called early modern period, from Spain to northern Scandinavia. The economics they formulated belong, according to Schumpeter, to the family of 'quasi-systems'.[1] This meant that what they wrote was to some extent coherent and systematic. Moreover, the consultant administrators often formulated analytical principles upon which they based their views and recommendations. According to Schumpeter the 'honors of this literature' with regard to analytical quality and sharp insights go to English businessmen and civil servants, although the first person within this group he credits with composing a scientific treatise was an Italian from Calabria, Antonio Serra. Without doubt, their analytical premises and principles were not always explicitly or very clearly formulated. Still Schumpeter viewed this literature as important for the development of analytical economics and therefore for the emergence of classical political economy.[2]

Few historians of economic thought and doctrines have treated the consultant administrators particularly generously. More often they have been described as mere practical men who formulated unsystematic recommendations and views mainly in order to pursue their own (economical and political) interests. They were rent-seekers who formulated the standpoint of specific interest groups, merchants, manufacturers, state officials and politicians.[3] However, this view is biased as there is in principle no reason to believe that economic writers of this age were more prone to holding partisan views based on economic or political interest than, for example, during our own time. Certainly we can almost always

1 J. A. Schumpeter, *A History of Economic Analysis* (London: George Allen & Unwin, 1972), pp. 143–4.
2 Ibid., pp. 194–5.
3 See for example R. B. Ekelund and R. D. Tollison, *Politicized Economies. Monarchy, Monopoly and Mercantilism* (College Station, TX: Texas A. & M. University Press, 1997).

identify great analytical minds who reflect upon the nature of their own (economic) times and hence contribute to the development of economic science. Then as now we can also find hoards of writers who earn a living by propounding sensational theories, or who publish texts with a specific political bias from the point of view of a direct special interest. However, we cannot naively presuppose that interest and/or political bias completely rule out the possibility of formulating analytical propositions of great scientific potential. Such coincidents happened then as they happen today.

As has been amply demonstrated by modern research, many of the most brilliant writers in, for example, England during the seventeenth and early eighteenth centuries – such as Josiah Child, Charles Davenant, John Locke and Nicholas Barbon – made important contributions to 'the 1690s boom' in economic thinking (according to Terence Hutchison's formulation) which Adam Smith and the classical school could build upon.[4] Such writers were by no means disinterested observers taking no part in public life or in the creation of their own private riches. Josiah Child, for example, was the director of the East India Company and died one of the richest men in England, while Nicholas Barbon emerged as a *nouveau riche*, making a fortune on building speculation after the great London fire of 1666. This did not hinder them from formulating ideas and principles of analytical value. More precisely these men helped to formulate a view of the economy as a general system of (market) relations which only could be understood against the backdrop of a general supply and demand theory of price formation. Without doubt, this was a revolutionary move without which it is hard to conceive the tremendous development of economic science which has occurred during the last two hundred years.

To some extent Schumpeter himself contributed to this less favourable view of the consultant administrators. He begins his discussion of them by emphasizing that '... this literature is not a logical or historical unit'. Moreover, those who wrote it, '... unlike the philosophers of natural law, form no homogenous group'. The link between them is instead that they '... discussed immediate practical problems of economic policy, and these problems were the problems of the rising National State'.[5] This is certainly accurate and we will return to this later. However, to say that the consultant administrators did not formulate a coherent theoretical system (as did for example the eighteenth-century French Physiocratic school) does not mean that they were unable to think in a coherent manner or that they were merely 'practical' as opposite to 'theoretical'.

4    See T. Hutchison, *Before Adam Smith. The Emergence of Political Economy 1662–1776* (Oxford: Polity Press, 1988), pp. 56–7. See also L. Magnusson, *Mercantilism. The Shaping of an Economic Language* (London: Routledge, 1994), pp. 116–17.
5    Schumpeter, *A History of Economic Analysis*, p. 143.

* * *

The rise of early modern states in the form of strong monarchies formulates the historical context of the consultant administrators and their thinking. Moreover, this state-making process was carried out in a competitive struggle for power and influence. Since the late medieval period it was well understood that an economically strong country (or monarch) also implied a powerful political and military position. Such thinking was a distinctive force behind what has been called 'fiscal' imperialism; an activity carried out by many medieval as well as early modern rulers and dynasties up until the eighteenth century. By capturing more land the income of a state would rise as a consequence of more peasants paying dues and rents to the crown. However, economic strength was also – and exceedingly so – interpreted as being based upon the whims of the marketplaces; upon the international competition over trade and trade routes. It was often held by contemporaries that a country which could capture important trade routes would have the upper hand in times of military conflict and political power struggles. Moreover, during the seventeenth century a view increasingly emerged among rulers that it was most favourable to establish an industry at home in order to work up raw materials instead of sending them out to foreign lands. By doing this many more hands could be employed and there were great profits to be made by industrious manufacturers and clever merchants. Also, through taxes and duties of different kinds the coffers of the state would be better provided with money, according to a view which dominated most minds in western Europe from the end of the seventeenth century.

The discussion of the relationship between economic means and political power goes back at least to the Florentine political thinkers of the Renaissance period, including of course the most famous of them, Niccolo Machiavelli. As is well known the civic humanist version of republicanism was a broad tradition which dealt with the role of patrotism and other republican values for a well-governed and virtuous state.[6] It is a mistake only to emphasize the practical content of the seventeenth-century discussion on economic issues in general and foreign trade in particular. Hence, it is also unfruitful to think of these discussions as mere reflections of as special merchant interest.[7] In fact many of the authors – including the British – propounded their special interests within an idiom which at least partly dealt with political principles and the reason of the state. Especially in *Discorsi* and *Il principe* Machiavelli had set out to illustrate how a virtuous state could be preserved and developed in a new historical conjecture,

---

6  The obvious source here is J. G. A. Pocock, *The Machiavellian Moment. Florentine Political Thought and the Atlantic Republican Tradition* (Princeton, NJ: Princeton University Press, 1975).

7  A special variant of this is J. Oldham Appleby, *Economic Thought and Ideology in Seventeenth Century England* (Princeton, NJ: Princeton University Press, 1978). For these matters, see also Magnusson, *Mercantilism*, chs 1 and 3.

the rise of modern princes. This theme was developed during the sixteenth century by, among many others, the Italian Giovanni Botero and even before that by the great French thinker Jean Bodin. Especially in Botero's *Della Ragion di stato*, from 1589 the important role of international trade and foreign competition for the power of the polity (kingdom or republic) was discussed in detail. Machiavelli had specifically emphasized the role of economic expansion for the increasing power of the prince – achieved either through military expeditions or trade monopolies, but also by successful open competition.[8]

Without doubt, the position of a specific state in the international competitive struggle for power and influence is a key for understanding the writings of the consultant administrators in their particular countries. In Naples Antonio Serra would ponder over how a small nation without its own resources in silver and gold would be able to survive and even gain from this fact. He wrote a tract on this subject published in 1613 where he suggested that a small state like Naples would have to export in order to cover the importation of necessities and luxuries as well as the importation of money (silver). In turn this meant that Naples had to develop a 'favourable balance of trade' in goods and it should be the task of the prince to fulfil this crucial task, for example by creating manufactures. Serra's considerations on the necessity of a favourable balance of trade became a much discussed topic later on, not least in England in the seventeenth century.[9]

In Spain during the late sixteenth and most of the seventeenth century, a lack of silver and gold was not the main problem at all. On the contrary, by coercion such resources were amply provided for by the Spanish imperial forces and shipped over from the Americas under the protection of a potent navy. However, by the end of the sixteenth century it was well known that this bullion had not only brought riches to Spain, but that it had brought with it serious problems.[10] Already in 1556 Martin de Azpilcueata (and only later on Jean Bodin in France) formulated the famous so-called quantity theory of money. What would happen if there was such a great inflow of silver and gold was that money would fall and goods rise in value. Hence the so-called price revolution was a well-known phenomena among contemporary Europeans. When the price level increased in Spain this meant that domestic wares became more expensive and imports cheaper. As a consequence domestic industries as well as agriculture suffered from cheap foreign competition. In Spain state officials like Luis Ortiz in the 1580s, controller of the public finance, struggled hard to find remedies for

---

8   For a recent interpretation of Botero as an 'economist', see M. Senellart, *Machiavélisme et raison d'Etat* (Paris: Presses Universitaires de France, 1989).

9   On Serra, see for example Hutchison, *Before Adam Smith*, pp. 19–20.

10   See C. Perrotta, 'Early Spanish Mercantilism: the First Analysis of Underdevelopment', in L. Magnusson (ed.), *Mercantilist Economics* (Boston, MA: Kluwer, 1993), pp. 17–58.

this problem. He came up with a classical and seemingly timeless proposition: to prevent Spaniards from exporting their money and from buying foreign goods. In the seventeenth century Geronomi de Ustariz and others would develop this into a fully-fledged system of protection and import-substitution. The state must subsidize and by all means try to develop a domestic industry and manufactures, they advised.[11]

In contrast to Spain, the French monarchy in the sixteenth century was not so involved in international economic rivalries. Bloody civil war and internal conflicts were more the matter of the day here. However, the beginning of the seventeenth century saw the emergence of economic nationalism also in this country. Around the turn of the century the *valet du chambre* to King Henri IV, Berthélemy Laffemas, published a number of tracts in which he promoted the establishment of manufactures in France in order to avoid 'unnecessary' imports. According to Laffemas the problem was that France sold its raw materials too cheaply in order to buy foreign goods. In a more aggressive tone some decades later his message was reinforced by the writer Antoine de Montchretien; this French patriot with a strong disdain for foreign influence was in fact the first to use the concept of 'political economy'. For Montchretien the very concept 'political economy' presupposed strong protectionist measures taken by a dirigiste state. He was strongly propounding the thesis that political and military power went along with economic development and modernization at home. Later on during the seventeenth century this would form the backbone of the so-called Colbert system. For Jean Baptiste Colbert the truth behind the principle of developing resources and a manufacturing sector at home showed itself in the quite successful wars which France fought with England and the Dutch republic. At the same time France fought vigorously to develop its foreign trade, not least to bring home gold and silver.[12]

France was a large country which after the period of civil war at the beginning of the seventeenth century was able to establish a powerful monarchy with an absolutist stance. From the middle of the seventeenth century it was able to compete successfully with the other great European powers. This was not the case with the bulk of the small German states. With the exception of the free trading ports – most of them once belonging to the mighty *Hansa Verband* (the Hanseatic League) – German states and principalities were less involved in foreign trade. A particular German prince or ruler would rely mainly on internal resources for his power and income. Hence we should not be surprised to find that German consultant administrators were mainly interested in extending the tax base of their realms either through increasing the tax burden of their citizens (the extensive strategy) or by developing agriculture as well as introducing a bet-

---

11  Ibid., pp. 22–3.
12  Magnusson, *Mercantilism*, pp. 176–7.

ter regulative order concerning trade and handicrafts (the intensive strategy). In the German states therefore a literature emerged from the seventeenth century which has been proposed as a 'mercantilism' with a difference, the *sonderweg* doctrine of 'cameralism'. It particularly discussed taxation and how beneficial policies could be introduced in order to increase the population (more tax payers and soldiers), improving agriculture and developing trade and industry. When the first chairs in economics were inaugurated in Prussia and other German lands in the beginning of the 1720s (the first in Europe in fact) it was supposed that the professors should teach 'useful' subjects such as *Policey* (good government), economy (private and public householding) and cameralism (basically taxation and other sources of income for the ruler).[13]

* * *

According to most orthodox interpretations, it was on the basis of what the consultant administrators did and wrote that it is possible to identify a specific system of 'mercantilism'. Schumpeter for example treats 'mercantilism' as a more or less English version of this literature and economic thinking. It was a discourse concentrating specifically on foreign trade issues and in particular on how foreign trade might improve the situation of the English commonweal; to increase its wealth and power. This focus is not particularly awkward given the geopolitical position of England during the seventeenth and eighteenth centuries. As we will see, this literature is perhaps best understood as a response to the growing possibilities and also problems that became increasingly visible during this era of escalating international competition and trade wars.

To what extent 'mercantilism' is really a 'system' or 'school' of economic thinking and literature has been a hotly debated issue ever since Adam Smith formulated his viewpoint on the 'mercantile system' in 1776. The bulk of what is commonly known as 'mercantilist literature' appeared in Britain from the 1620s up until the middle of the eighteenth century. Among the best-known English 'mercantilist' writers we find Thomas Mun and Edward Misselden in the 1620s, while James Steuart's *Principles of Political Oeconomy* (1767) is conventionally thought of as the last major 'mercantilist' work. The concept 'mercantilism' first appeared in print in the Marquis de Mirabeau's *Philosophie Rurale* in 1763 as *systeme mercantile*. In France during this period the concept was utilized in order to describe an economic policy regime characterized by direct state intervention in order to protect domestic merchants and manufacturers in accordance with seventeenth-century Colbertism. However, the main creator of 'the mer-

---

13  On cameralism, see K. Tribe, *Strategies of Economic Order: German Economic Discourse 1750–1950* (Cambridge: Cambridge University Press, 1995), or his earlier *Governing Economy. The Reformation of German Economic Discussion 1750–1840* (Cambridge: Cambridge University Press, 1988).

cantile system' was Adam Smith. According to Smith the core of the mercantile system – 'the commercial system' – consisted of the popular folly of confusing wealth with money. Given the practical orientation of the mercantilist writers they proposed one general principle: that a country must export more than it imports, leading to an net inflow of bullion, the so-called 'positive balance of trade theory'.[14]

The main architect of the mercantile system of economic thinking, according to Adam Smith, was the English economic writer and tradesman Thomas Mun. Smith argued that behind the 'mercantilistic' policy formulations stood a special interest which utilized the idea of a positive balance of trade in order to propagate a protective trade policy in general, including duties on imports, tariffs, bounties, etc. According to Smith the mercantile system implied a giant conspiracy on behalf of master manufacturers and merchants in order to skin the public and the consumers: 'It cannot be very difficult to determine who have been the contrivers of this whole mercantile system; not the consumers, we may believe, whose interest has been entirely neglected; but the producers whose interest has been so carefully attended to; and among this latter class our merchants and manufacturers have been by far the principal architects'.[15] From Smith onwards the view of the mercantile system as dirigisme (particularly export and import protection) in order for the state to support a special interest with the aid of the ideology of the positive balance of trade developed into its present status as *the* canonical interpretation of seventeenth- and eighteenth-century economic thinking and writing. After David Hume had made his specie-flow theory public in 1750, arguing that the favourable balance theory was an intellectual error (a net inflow of bullion must certainly mean a relative rise in prices which through the export and import mechanism will tend to correct itself ), it was only for Adam Smith to draw the conclusion that the argument for protection and against free trade in general was based on a mere intellectual mistake.

This viewpoint was contested by the German historical school a century later, which identified mercantilism as a rational expression of nation-building during the early modern period. According to Gustav Schmoller, *Merkantilismus* was the policy of unity and centralization pursued especially by the rulers of Brandenburg-Prussia during the seventeenth and eighteenth centuries. Hence also mercantilism expressed the economic interest of the state and viewed economic wealth as a rational means to achieve political power. The much debated balance of trade theory was perhaps misguided as a general analytical tool. However, Hume's argument relied upon the belief that markets forces were really at work and the quantity of money theory was applicable to more distant times.

14  Magnusson, *Mercantilism*, ch. 1.
15  A. Smith, *An Inquiry into the Nature and Causes of the Wealth of Nations* (Oxford: Oxford University Press, 1976), Book IV, ch. viii, p. 661.

Given the war-like situation of the early modern period in Europe this could not be taken for granted, he believed. In this particular situation the adoption of protectionism, infant industry tariffs and even restrictions regarding the export of money would have been the perfect rational choice at the time.[16]

In the 1930s an attempt to straddle these two very different definitions of mercantilism was made by the Swedish economic historian Eli Heckscher. In his 1931 book *Mercantilism* he attempted to present mercantilism as a system of economic thought and economic policy as well as a broader school of social thought.[17] Hence he agreed with Adam Smith that the balance of trade theory at the core of the mercantilist 'doctrine' was a mere folly of the mind. However, Heckscher also regarded mercantilism as a system of economic policy. And as such its logic was – as the historical economists emphasized – nation- or rather state-making. Hence, with the aim of pursuing the goal of national power, the mercantilists developed a number of nationalist economic policy tools, including tariffs. Hence, the British Navigation Acts as well as the establishment of national standards of weights and measurements, a national monetary system and other innovations, could be viewed as the outcome of the same mercantilist policies. Lastly, Heckscher also detected a specific 'materialist' or indeed cynical world view behind much of what the 'mercantilists' wrote regarding the necessity of poverty in the early modern economies as well as the role of workers as mere instruments of the rich and powerful (see further the Introduction to Volume 4 of this collection).[18]

It is not easy to grasp in Heckscher's synthesis how the concepts of mercantilism as a system of economic theory and policy-making and a social system of thought relate to each other. By some (for example Jacob Viner) Heckscher was, unfairly no doubt, interpreted as a follower of Gustav Schmoller.[19] Another response came in the heated scholarly discussion which took place over mercantilism in the 1950s and 60s. In 1939 A. V. Judges had vigorously rejected the notion of a particular mercantilist doctrine or system.[20] Mercantilsm had neither a common theoretical core nor any priests to defend the gospel, he stated. His rejection of 'mercantilism' as a coherent system was later taken up by a number of British economic historians. For example D. C. Coleman outrightly denounced the usefulness of mercantilism both as a description of economic policy and of

16  Tribe, *Strategies of Economic Order*, pp. 1ff.

17  On Heckscher's mercantilism, see L. Magnusson, 'Eli Heckscher and his Mercantilism Today', in R. Findlay et al. (eds), *Eli Heckscher, International Trade, and Economic History* (Cambridge, MA: MIT Press, 2006), pp. 231–6.

18  E. F. Heckscher, *Mercantilism*, 2 vols (London: Routledge, 1994).

19  J. Viner, 'Review of Heckscher's Mercantilism', *Economic History Review*, 1st series (1935), p. 100.

20  A. V. Judges, 'The Idea of a Mercantile State', *Transactions of the Royal Historical Society*, 4th series, 21 (1939), pp. 41–70.

economic theory; it was 'a red herring of historiography'.[21] Its main problem was that it gave a false unity to disparate events and ideas. Hence mercantilism was not a school of economic thinking and doctrine as for example the Physiocratic school of the eighteenth century.[22]

Since 1960s the scholarly debate has basically repeated these standpoints. It is probably fair to say that most modern scholars judge that it is correct to stress that mercantilism was not a finished system or coherent doctrine in the nineteenth- and twentieth-century sense. However, while 'mercantilistic views' mainly appeared in pamphlets which dealt with economic and political issues of the day, this does not necessarily imply that economic writers during the seventeenth and early eighteenth centuries composed economic texts without some common aims, views and shared concepts in order to make intelligible the complex world of economic phenomena – this was as we saw basically Schumpeter's view on the matter. Hence, it is perhaps better to perceive that the mercantilist writers shared a common vocabulary to argue for specific political and economic viewpoints. On the other hand, Coleman et al. were certainly right when they stressed that commentators such as Schmoller and Heckscher overemphasized the systematic character of mercantilism as a coherent system both of economic ideas and economic policy more or less directly stemming from these doctrines.

However, now as well as in the past the discussion of mercantilism is entangled within a broader political discussion, especially regarding Adam Smith's classical system and the pros and cons of free trade. Hence those who challenge free-trade liberalism and the theory of comparative advantages in particular have always found parts of the mercantilist 'doctrine' useful – an obvious example here is of course John Maynard Keynes.[23] Moreover, the left has often regarded at least some parts of 'mercantilism' (protectionism and dirigisme) as illuminating the process of development and underdevelopment as a backdrop of economic globalization.[24] Several scholars have insisted that mercantilist ideas were inspired by the same kind of basic arguments propounded during the nineteenth century, emphasizing the role of import-substitution as a means for underdeveloped countries to become more developed and ultimately rich. On the other hand, when Chico-inspired economists like Robert Ekelund and Robert Tollison have more recently developed their interpretation of mercantilism as a 'system of rent-seeking', it is of course Adam Smith's interpretative framework which is once again put on the frontline. According to such an analysis mercantilism

21  D. C. Coleman (ed.), *Revisions in Mercantilism* (London: Methuen, 1969), p. 117.

22  See contributions by Judges, Coleman and others in ibid.

23  Keynes's positive views on mercantilism appeared in his *General Theory of Employment, Interest and Money* (London: Macmillan, 1936), pp. 333–4.

24  For example see C. Perrotta, 'Is the Mercantilist Theory of the Favourable Balance of Trade Really Erroneous?', *History of Political Economy*, 23:2 (1991), pp. 301–36.

is depicted as a system of economic policies with the aim of protecting special interests.[25]

However, such ideologies do not take us very far in disentangling what the consultant administrators of the early modern era really wanted to say and for what purpose. Moreover, they invite us towards anachronistic interpretations of the history of economic thinking and writing. What I would like to argue for instead is a historical reading of what 'mercantilism' was and how it should be interpreted. Above all it should be judged in its specific historical context. Hopefully, this collection of texts will provide further arguments for the choice of this more fruitful (and historically respectful) approach.[26]

* * *

The late twentieth century is not the first time in history when the rapid increase of international trade – globalization – seems to threaten the very fabric of historically stable state formations and polities founded upon a matrix of conflicting/collaborating elites and power groups. Today there are discussions dealing with the how the nation state will be able to survive intensified globalization in the form of trade and capital flows, off-shoring and other phenomena. A common fear is that fierce global competition will destroy the very fabric and the legitimacy of modern welfare countries in particular, as the nation state seems unable to deliver what it once could. In the face of increased globalization modern polities experience a dilemma: if they applaud global competition too enthusiastically they may have to face an increasing lack of legitimacy for their institutions. Or if they try to protect themselves from globalization this might force them to develop populist, protectionist and even (in the worst case) xenophobic policies.

It is perhaps of no consolation that fears of increased international trade and globalization have been sensed many times before in history. However, with a backdrop of rapidly increased international trade and financial activities at the end of the nineteenth century, the 1880s saw the emergence of protectionism and eventually the formation of the social state. Without any doubt, increased global competition during the second half of the nineteenth century and the establishment of informal economic empires led to the formation of new political coalitions in the different states which supported the reason of the state as a

---

25  Ekelund and Tollison, *Politicized Economies*, p. 87 and passim.

26  Without doubt, such an historical approach will once again be found useless by Ekelund and Tollison (see their attack on 'the historians' in ibid., ch. 1). However, to put texts in historical context by trying to understand them on their own merits does not have to exclude other readings. This was, for example, noted by Schumpeter when he talked about the difference between an 'analytical' approach and a wider 'visionary' aspect in writing the history of economics. It is obvious that he thought that both of these approaches were most legitimate and useful. See Schumpeter, *A History of Economic Analysis*, pp. 3–4.

leading formula both in its international and domestic policies. Industrial power and informal empire – especially the free-trade imperialism of Great Britain – endangered the political stability of a European order which had been established in Vienna in 1815 and again after the political reaction which followed 1848.

The texts included in the current collection, *Mercantilist Theory and Practice: The History of British Mercantilism*, deal specifically with British responses in the seventeenth and eighteenth centuries to the problems of increased economic internationalization, trade competition, warfare, national glory and political strength. As we have seen, these texts belong to a broader strand of literature and it is clear that British reactions to problems of fierce competition and state-building by economic means were not the same as those of other European countries. To the eye of a Spanish imperialist or an Italian patriot who lived in one of those tiny city states which seemed to give little hope of national glory, the possibilities and problems of globalization looked very different indeed. In the British case we would expect writers to be especially interested in the role of foreign trade in order to make a state powerful and rich. It is more than probable that writers from this country with regard to international political affairs would emphasize the importance of the global marketplace and the pivotal role of what David Hume in the middle of the eighteenth century called 'jealousy of Trade'.[27]

In England during the seventeenth and early eighteenth centuries this jealousy was very much focused upon Holland. In the Dutch republics, with Amsterdam as the centre, something was established at the beginning of the seventeenth century which the great French economic historian Fernand Braudel baptized a 'world economy'.[28] Hence Amsterdam became the centre of financial and trade activities stretching its arms around the globe. It was the fabulous fortunes the merchants of Amsterdam were able to collect which struck the world with wonder and gave rise to the 'embarrassment of riches', according to Simon Schama.[29] The other European powers watched with wonder how this tiny republic, hardly yet recovered from a bloody war of liberation against the Habsburgs, had risen very rapidly at the beginning of the seventeenth century to prosperity and power. Most impressive, according to foreign contemporary observers, was that this tiny tract of land was able to house such a plentiful population. As a great population was increasingly perceived as a cornerstone of political power and military strength, the achievement of the Dutch republic was looked upon with respect and as an example to copy. In the first place, most argued that it

27  Discussed at length in I. Hont, *Jealousy of Trade. International Competition and the Nation-State in Historical Perspective* (Cambridge, MA: Belknap Press of Harvard University Press, 2005).

28  F. Braudel, *Civilization and Capitalism 15th–18th Century*, 3 vols (London: Fontana Press, 1985), vol. 3, pp. 1ff.

29  S. Schama, *The Embarrassment of Riches* (Berkeley, CA: University of California Press, 1988).

was not because of an exceptionally productive agriculture that this nation had grown from rags to riches.[30] Instead, it was commonly agreed that it was trade and industry which had brought the Dutch republic to its present wealth in men and power. For observers such as William Temple in the 1670s it seemed clear that '... that no Country can be found either in this present Age, or upon record of any Story, where so vast a Trade has been managed, as in the narrow compass of the Four Maritime Provinces of this Commonwealth'. He continued 'Nor has Holland grown rich by any Native Commodities, but by force of Industry; By improvements and Manufacture of all Foreign growths; By being the general Magazine of Europe, and furnishing all parts with whatever the market wants or invites'.[31]

First, according to Temple, the Dutch had emerged as successful tradesmen because of their sound political institutions – their 'Constitutions and orders'. Hailing the republic's free constitution he stated: '... as Trade cannot Arise without mutual trust among Private Men; so it cannot grow or thrive, to any great degree, without a confidence both of Publick and Private Safety, and consequently a trust in Government, from an opinion of its Strength, Wisdom and Justice ...'.[32] Furthermore, the liberal Dutch constitution admitted and encouraged the immigration of nonconformist Dissenters. Many able traders and skilled manufacturers were able as a result to establish themselves in the Dutch lands. This in turn provided an important precondition for an open and competitive commercial atmosphere. Further, such mercantilist writers who were inclined to speak in favour of freer trade – not so uncommon as we would expect[33] – alleged that a higher degree of economic freedom was an important factor behind Holland's rise to prosperity.

What the Dutch case seemed to illustrate more than anything else was that increased international trade was the foundation upon which military strength and national power could be built. At the same time national power was regarded as a precondition for the accumulation and preservation of wealth. Hence, as was often stated in contemporary discourses, 'trade' tended to 'follow power'. Historical accounts have shown, according to the very influential writer from this period Charles Davenant, that trade was first entertained '... by little states

30  For an illustrative example, see what Sir William Petty wrote about the 'Dutch miracle' in *The Economic Writings of Sir William Petty* (1899), ed. C. Hull (New York: Augustus M. Kelley 1986), p. 250.

31  W. Temple, *Observations upon the United Provinces of the Netherlands* (1673; Cambridge: Cambridge University Press, 1932), pp. 128–9.

32  Ibid., p. 131.

33  See Henry Robinson, *England's Safety, in Trades Encrease* (1641) and *Briefe Considerations, Concerning the Advancement of Trade and Navigation* (1649), this volume, pp. 93–174; Henry Parker, *Of a Free Trade* (1648), Volume 2 of this collection, pp. 1–46; and Charles Davenant, *An Essay upon the Probable Methods of Making a People Gainers in the Ballance of Trade* (1699), Volume 2 of this collection, pp. 157–292.

that were surrounded by neighbours in strength much superior to them'. Due to a lack of national power small countries were often attacked by greater nations and as a result their commerce had withered away: '... one battle swept away what had been gathered by the industry of many ages'.[34] Thus trade necessitated power – but at the same time power was a function of plenty and trade.

Contemporary seventeenth-century observers in England and elsewhere contemplated different answers to the Dutch miracle. One way to react was to say that the Dutch had snatched the trade of other countries through ruthless competition, but also admittedly through stubborn and hard work, parsimony and a public spirit.[35] Hence the English merchant and writer Thomas Mun in the 1620s emphasized how the Dutch had been able to out-compete the English herring fishermen and had ousted them from the North Sea. It was on this basis that the Dutch monopoly of the trade between the Baltic and the North seas had been developed during the early seventeenth century, according to Mun.[36] Another explanation was proposed by writers such as William Temple – for a while British ambassador in Holland. Temple especially emphasized the wealth-bringing effects of specialization and the division of labour. Trade was not a zero-sum game but created instead spirals of increased demand which in turn stimulated even more trade. A country of tradesmen is much richer than a country of farmers, he noted. Moreover, a trading country can host many more citizens than an agricultural one. A dense population is thus a sign of riches, and will at the same stimulate increased demand and more riches.[37]

The rise of Holland, its riches and its ability to develop a prosperous international trade most certainly led to envy. Amsterdam's role as the entrepot of international commerce and financial activities was looked upon with great suspicion by the powers of Europe, including France and England. Its attempts to establish a commercial empire in Asia and in the Americas also drew the envy of the great powers. Hence the phase of globalization which occurred in the seventeenth century and even more so in the next century stimulated reactions similar to those felt in the nineteenth century, and for that matter also in our contemporary society. Increased international trade and globalization was perceived as a threat to the established international political order. It was also taken to have

34 C. Davenant, *Discourse on the Public Revenues and on Trade, Part III* (London, 1698), in *The Political and Commercial Works of that Celebrated Writer Charles D'Avevant*, 5 vols (London: R. Horsfield, 1771), vol. 1, p. 350.

35 See for example J. Child, *A New Discourse on Trade* (1693), in L. Magnusson (ed.), *Mercantilism*, Critical Concepts in the History of Economics, 4 vols (London: Routledge, 1995), vol. 3, pp. 17–18.

36 T. Mun, *England's Treasure by Forraign Trade* (1664), in Magnusson (ed.), *Mercantilism*, vol. 1, pp. 136–7.

37 Temple, *Observations upon the United Provinces of the Netherlands*, pp. 128–9.

detrimental effects on the internal affairs of states, as well as to endanger established power relations and social structures.

As Istvan Hont has shown recently, the eighteenth-century discussions between economic pamphleteers and writers such as Charles Davenant, John Pollexfen and John Martyn from the 1690s onwards must be seen as different reactions to the important issue of how increased price competition on the world market ought to be tackled by Great Britain (similar to the present discussion on the effects of so-called off-shoring).[38] Could a wealthy country with high wages really compete with cheap imports from the low-wage countries? As a Tory free trader (the phrase was coined by the economic historian W. J. Ashley more than a hundred years ago)[39] and free-trade imperialist, Charles Davenant looked upon the future of Britain as the entrepot of cheap calicoes and other wares from India and other formal or informal British colonies and plantations. According to Davenant the upkeep of an economic empire was a necessary precondition for British wealth and power. Through the profits from reselling, shipping, serving as a financial intermediary and by working up Indian wares which could be sold to other European countries with great gain, Davenant thought that Britain could develop its wealth and power (see further the Introduction to Volume 4 of this collection).[40] However, another reaction (also easy to relate to contemporary debates) was to say that Britain would gain more by protecting itself from the inflow of cheap wares and by what have subsequently been recognized as import-substituting activities, i.e. developing domestic industries which would employ a multitude of poor labourers. As Hont has clearly shown, a third response during the eighteenth century was to develop the argument that the inflow of cheap products was not a problem as long as the rich country with higher wages increased its productivity in order to sell wares more cheaply than others.[41] The latter was of course the road perhaps first suggested by John Martyn, but later on men such as Josiah Tucker, David Hume and Adam Smith followed in his path. This was the response that would win the day in the long run. Through David Ricardo, Robert Torrens and others this suggestion was developed to become part and parcel of the modern theory of comparative advantage.

However, discussions in England on how to react to increased international trade and globalization started much earlier, during the seventeenth century. In many of these discussions the East India Company was in the forefront of public controversy and therefore commented upon in tracts and pamphlets. Hence already in Mun's first published tract, *A Discourse of Trade* (1621), we

---

38  Hont, *Jealousy of Trade*, ch. 2.

39  W. J. Ashley, 'The Tory Origin of Free Trade Policy', in his *Surveys: Historic and Economic* (London: Longman, 1900).

40  C. Davenant, *An Essay Upon the East India Trade* (1696), in Magnusson, *Mercantilism*, vol. 1, p. 221.

41  Hont, *Jealousy of Trade*, pp. 246–7.

learn that the reason why this author defend the East India trade was because it 'does not consume, but rather greatly increase the generall stocke and Treasure of this realme'.[42] Hence it is in the interest of the state to increase its trade with foreign lands. Already here the relation between economic expansion (or growth) and the state interest is clearly spelled out. Moreover, Mun here put down a principle which had been common parlance in many political tracts and treatises since the sixteenth century – and which is clearly visible in the Florentine tradition – namely that 'the trade of Merchandize is not onely that laudable practize whereby the entercourse of nations is so worthily performed but also (as I may terme it) the verie Touchstone of a kingdomes propertie'.[43] In the same manner Mun's best-known tract, *England's Treasure by Forraign Trade* (printed in 1664 but written almost four decades earlier) is a patriotic piece which in vitriolic language defended the English reason of state against the intrusion of Dutch merchants and fishermen. Here Mun talks about the 'love and service of our Country' and calls the merchant the 'steward of the Kingdom's stock' – he recognizes that 'private gain ... may ever accompany the publique good'. He hails the merchant for his cunning, knowledge and patriotic virtues which are essential for the prosperity of the realm.[44] Certainly, Mun was no radical republican – although he must have learnt a lot about Italian history as he for many years sailed to Genoa – but instead a truthful servant of the British kingdom. However, in this he follows the tradition from Machiavelli who – as John Pocock emphasized so long ago – transformed early Florentine republicanism into an outright support of the new prince.[45] Mun admires Venice and particularly Genoa for being Aristocratic republics, but senses that in a democratic republic (Florence during its 'democratic' rule of *Falconieri* Piero Soderini) there is an overarching danger that liberty and government 'might be changed into the Servitude'. In such a republic – and this is of course a distinct echo of Machiavelli in particular – private men are ready with the help of the public treasure to 'spend their lives in defence of their own Soveraignty'. But the common good seems to be best preserved in a kingdom where the prince defends 'the distinction between the *meum & thum*'. Against the Dutch Muns speaks as a true defender of British interests: '... there are no people in Christendome who do not more undermine, hurt, and eclipse us daily in our Navigation and trades, both abroad and at home.'[46] And although there are Dutch settlers in England 'certainly they are not of us, no not they who are born and bred here in our own Countrey, for

---

42  T. Mun, *A Discourse of Trade*, in Magnusson (ed.), *Mercantilism*, vol. 1, p. 49.
43  Ibid.
44  Mun, *England's Treasure by Forraign Trade*, p. 49.
45  See Pocock, *The Machiavellian Moment*.
46  Mun, *England's Treasure by Forraign Trade*, pp. 120–1.

still they will be Dutch, not having so much as one drop of the English bloud in their hearts'.[47]

Hence we should not be at all surprised that during the seventeenth century in England – as in the following century – the threat of foreign competition, international trade and globalization was discussed in the context of state interest and patriotism. The 'jealousy of trade' of which Hume spoke of was to a large extent the application of the reason of the state to international trade.[48] This was as much a theme in seventeenth-century discussions as in the eighteenth century.

* * *

An important question has been raised over and over again in the lengthy discussion on 'mercantilism', from A. V. Judges to D. C. Coleman and sometimes still today: whether within the term 'mercantilism' we can find a coherent set of principles or doctrines. To some extent it is not possible to solve this issue as there is no common understanding of what constitutes a 'doctrine' or a set of 'economic principles'. Neither does this collection of works from the seventeenth and eighteenth centuries solve this puzzle for us. The texts presented here are not the most original or the best-written contributions to this literature – rather they constitute the mediocrity of 'mainstream' forgotten or half-known authors (with some exceptions such as Josiah Child, Charles Davenant and Josiah Tucker). But by examining these lesser-known texts something else seems to appear. From this material we can get a glimpse of the richness of the economic and political discussions that were carried out in Britain during the period from the Elizabethan age up until the middle of the eighteenth century. With regard to these discussions we can without doubt identify a number of contingencies and patterns. Economics can surely never be settled once and for all with generally accepted blackboard theories. By examining the texts presented in this collection we can listen to authors who varied in their opinions and argued with each other. They discussed issues such as how to construct a system of foreign trade which was most beneficial for the nation (something we still do today). They argued over colonies and the employment of the poor (which is still done today). They were of course far behind present-day economists in technical brilliance and mathematical rigour. However, they were at least as observant of the current hopes and plights of their economic world – something which (some) modern economists have tended to forget when replacing relevance with technical precision and perfection.

---

47  Ibid., p. 141.
48  Hont, *Jealousy of Trade*, p. 13.

# WORKS CITED

Ashley, W. J., *Surveys: Historic and Economic* (London: Longman, 1900).

Atkins, S. H., 'Certain of Sir Thomas More's Epigrams Translated by Stanihurst', *Modern Language Review*, 26:3 (July 1931), pp. 338–40.

Beer, M., *Early British Economists* (London: Allen & Unwin, 1938).

Berg, M., *The Age of Manufactures, 1700–1820: Industry, Innovation and Work in Britain* (London: Routledge, 1994).

Braudel, F., *Civilization and Capitalism 15th–18th Century*, 3 vols (London: Fontana Press, 1985).

Cary, J., *An Essay Towards Regulating the Trade and Employing the Poor* (London: Sam Mabbat, 1719).

Chaudhuri, K. N., *The English East India Company: The Study of an Early Joint-Stock Company* (London: Cass, 1965).

Coats, A. W., 'Changing Attitudes to Labour in the Mid-Eighteenth Century', in A. W. Coats, *On the History of Economic Thought*, British and American Economic Essays, vol. 1 (London and New York: Routledge, 1992), pp. 63–84.

Coleman, D. C. (ed.), *Revisions in Mercantilism* (London: Methuen, 1969).

Cunningham, W., *The Growth of English Industry and Commerce*, 2 vols (1903; New York: Augustus M. Kelley, 1968), vol. 2: The Mercantile System.

Davenant, C., *The Political and Commercial Works of that Celebrated Writer Charles D'Avevant*, 5 vols (London: R. Horsfield, 1771).

Delcourt, A., *La France et Les Etablissements Français au Senegal entre 1713 et 1763* (Dakar: Mémoires Ifan, 1952).

Drake, J. D., *King Philip's War in New England, 1675–1676* (Amherst, MA: University of Massachusetts Press, 1999).

Ekelund, R. B., and R. D. Tollison, *Politicized Economies. Monarchy, Monopoly and Mercantilism* (College Station, TX: Texas A. & M. University Press, 1997).

Fortrey, S., *England's Interest and Improvement* (London, 1673).

Freedman, J. S., 'The Career and Writings of Bartholomew Keckermann (d. 1609)', *Proceedings of the American Philosophical Society*, 141:3 (September 1997), pp. 305–64.

Furniss, E., *The Position of the Laborer in a System of Nationalism* (1920; New York: Augustus M. Kelley, 1965).

Gee, J., *The Trade and Navigation of Great Britain Considered* (London, 1729).

Gould, J. D., 'The Trade Crisis of the Early 1620s and English Economic Thought', *Journal of Economic History*, 15:2 (1953), pp. 121–33.

Heckscher, E. F., *Mercantilism*, 2 vols (London: Routledge, 1994).

Hertz, G. B., 'The English Silk Industry in the Eighteenth Century', *English Historical Review*, 24:96 (October 1909), pp. 710–27.

Hinton, R. W. K., *The Eastland Trade and the Common Weal in the Seventeenth Century* (Cambridge: Cambridge University Press, 1959).

Hont, I., *Jealousy of Trade. International Competition and the Nation-State in Historical Perspective* (Cambridge, MA: Belknap Press of Harvard University Press, 2005).

Hutchison, T., *Before Adam Smith. The Emergence of Political Economy 1662–1776* (Oxford: Polity Press, 1988).

Johnson, E. A., *Predecessors to Adam Smith* (New York: Prentice and Hall, 1937).

Judges, A. V., 'The Idea of a Mercantile State', *Transactions of the Royal Historical Society*, 4th series, 21 (1939), pp. 41–70.

Keynes, J. M., *General Theory of Employment, Interest and Money* (London: Macmillan, 1936).

King, C., *The British Merchant or Commerce Preserv'd*, 3 vols (1721; New York: Augustus M. Kelley, 1968).

Lawson, P., *The East India Company. A History* (London and New York: Longman, 1993).

Lipson, E., *The Economic History of England*, 3 vols (London: A. & C. Black, 1929–34).

McCulloch, J. R. (ed.), *Classical Writings on Economics*, 6 vols (London: William Pickering, 1995).

Magnusson, L., *Mercantilism. The Shaping of an Economic Language* (London: Routledge, 1994).

— (ed.), *Mercantilism*, Critical Concepts in the History of Economics, 4 vols (London: Routledge, 1995).

—, *The Tradition of Free Trade* (London: Routledge, 2004).

—, 'Eli Heckscher and his Mercantilism Today', in R. Findlay et al. (eds), *Eli Heckscher, International Trade, and Economic History* (Cambridge, MA: MIT Press, 2006), pp. 231–6.

Martyn, H., *Considerations upon the East-India Trade* (London: A. and J. Churchill, 1701).

O'Brien, P., 'European Economic Development: the Contribution of the Periphery', *Economic History Review*, 2nd series, 35:1 (1982), pp. 1–18.

Oldham Appleby, J., *Economic Thought and Ideology in Seventeenth Century England* (Princeton, NJ: Princeton University Press, 1978).

*Oxford Dictionary of National Biography* (Oxford: Oxford University Press, 2004).

*Palgrave's Dictionary of Political Economy*, ed. H. Higgs, 3 vols (London and New York: Macmillan, 1894).

Perrotta, C., 'Is the Mercantilist Theory of the Favourable Balance of Trade Really Erroneous?', *History of Political Economy*, 23:2 (1991), pp. 301–36

—, 'Early Spanish Mercantilism: the First Analysis of Underdevelopment', in L. Magnusson (ed.), *Mercantilist Economics* (Boston, MA: Kluwer, 1993), pp. 17–58.

Petty, W., *The Economic Writings of Sir William Petty* (1899), ed. C. Hull (New York: Augustus M. Kelley 1986).

Pocock, J. G. A., *The Machiavellian Moment. Florentine Political Thought and the Atlantic Republican Tradition* (Princeton, NJ: Princeton University Press, 1975).

Pomeranz, K., *The Great Divergence. China, Europe and the Making of the Modern World Economy* (Princeton, NJ: Princeton University Press, 2000).

Postlethwayt, M., *Britain's Commercial Interest Explained and Improved*, 2 vols (1757; New York: Augustus M. Kelley, 1968).

Ramsay, G. D., 'Clothworkers, Merchants Adventurers and Richard Hakluyt', *English Historical Review*, 92:364 (July 1977), pp. 504–21.

Schama, S., *The Embarrassment of Riches* (Berkeley, CA: University of California Press, 1988).

Schumpeter, J. A., *A History of Economic Analysis* (London: George Allen & Unwin, 1972).

Semmel, B., *The Rise of Free Trade Imperialism. Classical Political Economy, the Empire of Free Trade and Imperialism 1750–1850* (Cambridge: Cambridge University Press, 1970).

Senellart, M., *Machiavélisme et raison d'État* (Paris: Presses Universitaires de France, 1989).

Shelton, G., *Dean Trucker and Eighteenth-Century Economic and Political Thought* (New York: St Martin's Press, 1981).

Smith, A., *An Inquiry into the Nature and Causes of the Wealth of Nations* (Oxford: Oxford University Press, 1976).

Steuart, J., *The Works, Political, Metaphysical, and Chronological, of the Late Sir James Steuart of Coltness, Bart*, 6 vols (London: T. Cadell, 1805).

Supple, B., *Commercial Crisis and Change in England 1600–1642* (Cambridge: Cambridge University Press, 1959).

Temple, W., *Observations upon the United Provinces of the Netherlands* (1673; Cambridge: Cambridge University Press, 1932).

Thomas, P. J., *Mercantilism and the East India Trade* (1926; London: Frank Cass, 1963).

Tribe, K., *Governing Economy. The Reformation of German Economic Discussion 1750–1840* (Cambridge: Cambridge University Press, 1988).

—, *Strategies of Economic Order: German Economic Discourse 1750–1950* (Cambridge: Cambridge University Press, 1995).

Viner, J., 'English Theories of Foreign Trade before Adam Smith, I–II', *Journal of Political Economy*, 38 (1930), pp. 249–301, 404–57.

—, 'Review of Heckscher's Mercantilism', *Economic History Review*, 1st series (1935), p. 100.

Wadell, D. A. G., 'Charles Davenant (1656–1714) – A Biographical Sketch', *Economic History Review*, 2nd series, 2 (1958–9), pp. 179–88.

Walker, D. A., 'Virginia Tobacco Suring the Reign of the Early Stuarts: A Case Study of Mercantilist Theories, Practice and Results', in L. Magnusson (ed.), *Mercantilist Economics* (Boston, MA: Kluwer, 1993), pp. 143–71.

Ward, G. F., 'The Early History of the Merchants Staplers', *English Historical Review*, 33:131 (July 1918), pp. 297–319.

Watt, R., *Bibliotheca Britannica: or, A General Index to British and Foreign Literature*, 4 vols (Edinburgh and London: A. Constable and Company, 1824).

Wilson, C., *England's Apprenticeship, 1603–1763* (London: Longmans, 1984).

Wren, M. C., 'The Disputed Elections in London in 1641', *English Historical Review*, 64:250 (January 1949), pp. 34–52.

# INTRODUCTION

In England at the beginning of the seventeenth century, according to the economic historian Charles Wilson, '[g]overnments, administrations and merchants were fumbling their way towards a new and aggressive conception of a mercantile economy, protectionist, self-sufficient, exclusive'.[1] Without doubt this had a background in the increasing importance for England of its foreign trade which was felt everywhere in the context of the remarkable economic upsurge taking place in Europe during the latter half of the sixteenth century. England had of course been an important trading nation since the high middle ages. Of special importance was her overseas trade, with raw materials such as wool, tin and leather being sent to north European ports. Unfinished wool cloth was probably the single most important English export commodity from the middle of the sixteenth century – mainly to Holland and Flanders. Antwerp was the main customer of English cloth until it was sacked by Spanish troops in 1576 and much of this trade moved over to the Dutch city of Middleburg at the end of the century. Much of the trade in unfinished cloth was carried out on a monopolist basis by the chartered company of the Merchant Adventurers. After a less than successful start with the famous Alderman Cockaynes project from 1613 – an ambitious but failed large-scale scheme to form a new company which would sell dyed and finished cloth to Europe to challenge the Merchant Adventurers' monopoly (which may in fact have decided the failure of the project) – this commodity nevertheless became an increasingly important export. As a consequence English wool producers became increasingly involved in bitter competition with other cloth-producing districts and countries in northern Europe.[2]

It is against this background of expanding foreign trade that the English state from the late sixteenth century began to take an increasing active interest in the affairs of merchants. According to William Cunningham, we can sense rising

1 C. Wilson, *England's Apprenticeship, 1603–1763* (London: Longmans, 1984), p. 40.
2 See especially the seminal work by B. Supple, *Commercial Crisis and Change in England 1600–1642* (Cambridge: Cambridge University Press, 1959); and J. D. Gould, 'The Trade Crisis of the Early 1620s and English Economic Thought', *Journal of Economic History*, 15:2 (1953), pp. 121–33.

'national sentiments in regard to sea power' during this period.[3] Even before this date foreign trade was well regulated in England. The famous Statute of Employment from 1390 for example stipulated that exactly what each merchant carried away in monies should be returned by the same merchant. For Eli Heckscher this Statute was a standard example of a typical 'mercantilist' policy with the aim of hindering the export of valuable goods (including silver and gold) – but it was surely only one of many regulations concerning foreign trade at work during the late medieval period.[4]

It was also the same William Cunningham who more than a hundred years ago formulated the viewpoint – common among most British economic historians ever since – on the relationship between the naval power of England and her foreign trade. Despite constitutional and other changes he believed that England held a steady course aiming at maritime supremacy during the whole period of the 'mercantile system' which according to Cunningham can be roughly dated to between the middle of the sixteenth up to the middle of the eighteenth century (at least).[5] This relationship between naval ambition and foreign trade worked in both directions. The quest for maritime supremacy had direct economic consequences, but in turn the economic and foreign trade relations influenced the direction of naval and international power politics in England. In Elizabethan times the policy was mainly defensive. The fear was of an imperialistic Spain; of invasion and increased maritime dominance by the Spanish Empire in the North and Baltic seas. That the Spanish kingdom could be a threat to vital economic interest such as the transportation of cloth to north European ports was shown by the sacking of Antwerp in 1576 and the beginning of the Dutch war of liberation. However, during the seventeenth century England's naval power became aware of another threat: the Dutch republic and its amazingly rapid rise as a leading trading star. Elizabeth's successors invested much precious gold and silver in the navy and sought to stimulate shipbuilders to put more sails to sea. The distinction between warships and civil tonnage at this time was rather slim as any ship could easily be equipped with guns and soldiers (this was how the great Armada had been defeated); hence the Crown also stimulated private ship owners and trading companies to build ships. The launching of charted companies with specific privileges for trade with, for example, the East and West Indies and Africa from around 1600 onwards must also be seen as a consequence of such a policy. Much of the regulation during this time was of a passive kind (which Heckscher baptized as a 'policy of provision' to distinguish it from a

---

3    W. Cunningham, *The Growth of English Industry and Commerce*, 2 vols (1903; New York: Augustus M. Kelley, 1968), vol. 2: The Mercantile System.

4    E. F. Heckscher, *Mercantilism*, 2 vols (London: Routledge, 1994), vol. 2, p. 297.

5    Cunningham, *The Growth of English Industry and Commerce*, vol. 2.

later more active 'mercantilist' type of policy)[6] which aimed to keep important wares within the country which could be of crucial importance during wartime, including foodstuffs. On such items there was an outright export ban. This was also the case with timber, hemp, sailcloth and other necessary items for the royal fleet.

However, from the early seventeenth century there was a certain shift of priorities. Gradually maritime policies became even more active and aggressive. The quest to challenge the Dutch led directly to the establishment of the 'Navigation' policy. Its general aim was to replace foreign merchants and ships with English ones; hence only English merchants and ships should have the right to carry English domestic produce to and from foreign ports. To engage in competition with the Dutch as well as what was left of the Hanseatic merchants in the North and Baltic seas became a top priority. However, the aim of navigation policies was also more directly aggressive: protected by a great naval and commercial fleet it should be possible to snatch at least some parts of the profitable trade carried out especially by Dutch merchants to distant Asia and America. It was especially from the 1620s that such policies were actively developed.[7] Perhaps the most powerful of such regulations were the Navigation Acts of 1651 and 1660 (amended in 1673 and 1696). The first of these acts was put to parliament after the attempt to create a political alliance with the Dutch had failed. The idea for an alliance must be seen – as Charles Wilson has noted – as a direct consequence of the trade and industrial crisis which broke out in 1649 and especially hit the cloth and textile industry.[8]

However, the first period of trade and industrial crisis in which this emerging visible hand of the state was tested occurred in the 1620s and is immediately connected to the establishment of the favourable balance of trade doctrine.[9] The export of cloth fell dramatically, many clothiers were brought to the verge of bankruptcy and unemployment in the textile areas became epidemic. Distress was common and the authorities feared 'disturbances' and widespread begging and stealing: 'The Unemployed went in groups to the houses of the rich, demanding food and money, and seized provisions in the market place', one contemporary eyewitness reported.[10] In 1622 the Privy Council commented upon a petition presented '... by the clothiers of the county of Suffolk and Essex complaining that they were disabled from going forward in their trade by reason of

---

6    Heckscher, *Mercantilism*, vol. 1, pp. 80–1.

7    Cunningham, *The Growth of English Industry and Commerce*, vol. 2, p. 14.

8    Wilson, *England's Apprenticeship*, p. 62.

9    E. Lipson, *The Economic History of England*, 3 vols (London: A. & C. Black, 1929–34), vol. 3, p. 305.

10    Ibid., vol. 3, p. 306.

the great quantity of cloths lying upon their hands for which they could find no utterance or vent'.[11]

As a consequence of the crisis a number of royal committees were appointed in order to find remedies. Contemporaries mainly interpreted the cause of the crisis as 'a want of money' originating from either too much bullion being exported or too little minting going on at the Royal Mint. Modern interpreters would perhaps rather emphasize the trade and monetary chaos set in train by the Thirty Years War on the European continent (to which much of the English export was destined) as well as the loss of foreign markets due to the same circumstances. However, this explanation of the true nature of the crisis was already hinted at by leading merchants such as Thomas Mun and Edward Misselden, who were members of the royal committees. While others tended to see the malady as an unfavourable exchange caused by manipulations against English monies by Dutch and Jewish money dealers, Mun and Misselden argued instead that the problem was not the exchange rate itself but what caused it to fall, namely the unfavourable balance of trade in real wares and stocks. Whenever a country imports more than it exports the exchange rate must fall as there is a greater demand for foreign money or bills of exchange. Money and bills of exchange are commodities whose prices are regulated in the same manner as other commodities: through the mechanism of supply and demand.[12]

In this discussion especially Mun claimed that, in order to prosper, a country must export more than it imports. This gives rise to an inflow of money which – if it is traded – increases the stock of the commonwealth. Further, a country must direct its trade so that it exports manufactured goods and imports raw materials to work up. Indeed, he says '... our wealth might be a rare discourse for all Christendome to admire and fear, if we would but add Art and Nature, our labour to our natural means'.[13] Explicitly aimed for an English public, this message had an aggressive tone, especially directed against Dutch commercial interests. The control over important trades such as the 'fishing of herrings, Ling and Cod ... would be sooner decided by swords, than with words', he warned (most prophetically as war between Holland and England broke out soon thereafter).[14]

Indeed the message seemed clear cut. The 1620s crisis could only be remedied by more exports and a more aggressive trade policy, implying that England would be able to grab a larger share of the international trade. For such policies – including for example the Navigation Acts – the unfavourable balance of

11   Cited from L. Magnusson, *Mercantilism. The Shaping of an Economic Language* (London: Routledge, 1994), p. 62.

12   For details, see ibid., ch. 3.

13   Mun, *England's Treasure by Forraign Trade* (1664), in L. Magnusson (ed.), *Mercantilism*, Critical Concepts in the History of Economics, 4 vols (London: Routledge, 1995), vol. I, p. 73.

14   Ibid., p. 137.

trade idea became an important excuse. It was the new market situation – and especially the increasing challenge from Dutch merchants – which more than anything else gave rise to what later generations have tended to name the 'mercantilist' doctrine.

\* \* \*

What has been described above is the historical context of the famous so-called 'favourable balance of trade' theory which has puzzled interpreters ever since Adam Smith gave it status as the leading theoretical principle of the mercantilist school. Without doubt it can be interpreted in a number of different ways. Perhaps Max Beer has come closest to a historical understanding of it. He suggests in his *Early British Economists* (1938) that the crux of this 'doctrine' was the idea that more money was needed in circulation: 'a struggle for liquid assets'.[15] Hence, an often repeated worry of seventeenth-century economic writers in England was that a shortage of money would curtail economic development. For England this was especially problematic as it had no silver or gold mines of its own – according to Antonio Serra the situation was the same in Naples.[16] The solution to this dilemma was an importation of money from abroad. As bullion could only be obtained in exchange for goods a country without gold and silver would have to export more wares than it could import from its trading partners. This would lead to a net inflow of monies, which would remedy the situation. Hence the kingdom's stock would be enlarged in wares, and it would have to pay less in kind for its imports.

Certainly, English writers in the seventeenth century did not believe that money (gold or silver) was identical with wealth. During this time King Midas was regarded as the mere fool he undoubtedly was. For example in 1699 Charles Davenant wrote: 'Gold and Silver are indeed the Measure of Trade, but that the Spring and Original of it, in all nations is the Natural or Artificial Product of the Country; that is to say, what their Land or what their Labour and Industry produces'.[17] The majority of writers from Thomas Mun and Edward Misselden in the 1620s by and large agreed with this statement. Some of them might have added that to have abundance of money in the country was of great importance for economic progress and the wealth of the nation, but this did not imply that money was identical with wealth. Rather, most at the time argued that a net inflow of money was a barometer which signalled whether a nation won or lost in its trade with other countries. Others said that abundant money helped to speed up intercourse in the marketplace and to stimulate growth and development. Thus,

---

15  M. Beer, *Early British Economists* (London: Allen & Unwin, 1938), pp. 188–9.
16  See the General Introduction, above, p. xiv.
17  C. Davenant, *An Essay Upon the Probable Methods of Making a People Gainers in the Balance of Trade* (1699), in Volume 2 of this edition, p. 270.

a net inflow of money could be a means to procure wealth, but wealth itself was always the result of production and consumption.

Another interpretation was suggested by J. D. Gould some forty years ago.[18] It is clear that many English writers, including Thomas Mun, were well aware of both the quantity theory of money and the existence of demand elasticity. Against this background it is perhaps peculiar – and this in particular puzzled Jacob Viner[19] – that contemporaries did not draw the logical conclusion that an inflow of money could not be obtained over a long period, as an increase of prices would lead to less foreign demand (in accordance with the specie-flow mechanism later developed by Hume). However, as Gould argues, Mun and others could have interpreted the contemporary situation in a different manner: that a net surplus of inflowing money would not effect export prices if it was necessary in order to organize a greater volume of trade. According to Gould such an argument might have made sense in the context of the undeveloped credit institutions existing at the time.

However, regardless of which interpretation we give the favourable balance of trade theory, it is clear that this theory had been abandoned in its simple form by most writers by the end of the seventeenth century. Some critical voices argued that the principle was impractical as a policy goal as it was impossible to account for a trade surplus in quantitative terms. Others found problems on more theoretical grounds – i.e. directly or indirectly admitting to the premise later known as the specie-flow argument. Instead, from the 1690s writers such as Josiah Child, Charles Davenant and Nicholas Barbon developed a new idea which has been called the theory of 'foreign-paid incomes', the 'labour balance of trade theory' or the 'export of work' theory.[20] Instead of holding on to the dogma that a country should receive an inflow of bullion through the balance of trade, these authors stressed that a country should export products with as much value-added content as possible and import as little of such products as they could. The more manufactured goods were exported the more income would accrue to England, they thought. The profit would come from the fact that the buyer – Spain, Portugal or other countries – would not only pay England for its raw materials but also for its labourers. Such a 'labour balance theory' – which found its most mature statement with James Steuart in the 1760s[21] – is related to the simple 'bullionist' idea that an inflow of money makes the country rich. It

---

18  J. D. Gould, 'The Trade Crisis of the Early 1620s and English Economic Thought'.

19  J. Viner, 'English Theories of Foreign Trade before Adam Smith, I–II', *Journal of Political Economy*, 38 (1930), pp. 249–301, 404–57.

20  The first to explicitly draw attention to this was E. A. Johnson, *Predecessors to Adam Smith* (New York: Prentice and Hall, 1937).

21  J. Steuart, *An Inquiry into the Principles of Political Economy*, in J. Steuart, *The Works, Political, Metaphysical, and Chronological, of the Late Sir James Steuart of Coltness, Bart*, 6 vols (London: T. Cadell, 1805), vol. 1.

certainly served as an excuse both for high duties on the import of manufactured wares and for subsidies to infant manufactures. Without doubt, such views were – and still are – used to argue in favour of industrial protection. In their modern version we often call these arguments import-substitution theories. Let the foreigners buy our worked-up commodities while we buy their cheaper wares. This means that they pay for the employment of our labourers! To a large extent this reaction must be seen against the backdrop of the intensified rivalry of the major trading countries from the end of the seventeenth century and onwards. It was a reaction to increased globalization interpreted as intensified competition on world markets. As Istvan Hont has recently shown, increased protectionism was certainly not the only reaction which this historical conjecture triggered off.[22] But at least at the beginning of the eighteenth century in Britain this became the most dominant voice when it came to actual policies being made.

\* \* \*

In most of the texts in this volume the relationship between foreign trade and state power is discussed from different angles. During much of this time the Dutch republic was regarded as the main trade rival of England – hence the establishment of the Navigation Acts in the middle of the seventeenth century as well as the three Dutch-English wars fought during roughly the same period. However, at the end of the seventeenth century Holland was replaced by France as the main fear and trade enemy. Under the auspices of the Colbert system France had gained both political and economical force. Basically using a strategy of import substitution, it used its resources to develop many new manufactures. In the late seventeenth century there was a general complaint in England that it lost in its trade with France. In a pamphlet written by Samuel Fortrey in 1673 we hear of the '... vast sums of money the French yearly delude us of; either by such commodities as we may as well have of our own, or else by such others, as we might as well in great part be without'. Among the latter Fortrey lists sixteen categories of French imports that should be avoided. Among them we find luxuries such as velvets, silk, serges, hats, feathers, girdels, hatbands, fans and perfumed gloves as well as linen cloth from Britanny and iron-wares from Auvergne.[23]

The fear of an 'underweight' in the trade between France and England rose to its climax at the beginning of the eighteenth century. After the signing of the Utrecht peace treaty with France in 1713 a heated debate broke out between its defenders and those who critized it for being too lenient to French trade interests. The writer Daniel Defoe was hired by the Tory government to defend the treaty while the Whig critique came from a group of economic writers pub-

---

22  See I. Hont, *Jealousy of Trade. International Competition and the Nation-State in Historical Perspective* (Cambridge, MA: Belknap Press of Harvard University Press, 2005).

23  S. Fortrey, *England's Interest and Improvement* (London, 1673), pp. 22–3.

lishing their own periodical, *The British Merchant*. In this journal Theodore Janssen published his 'General Maxims of Trade' which vividly illustrates the protectionist outlook of this group. According to Janssen a number of trades were unfavourable for a country, specifically: 1) a trade which brings in 'mere Luxury and Pleasure'; 2) a trade which hinders the consumption of the domestic produce; and 3) a trade which 'supplies the same goods as we manufacture'.[24] Without doubt this was a view which would dominate much of the discussion during the next half century.

24  Janssen's piece appears in C. King, *The British Merchant or Commerce Preserv'd*, 3 vols (1721; New York: Augustus M. Kelley, 1968), see vol. 1, pp. 4–5.

# THOMAS MILLES

Thomas Milles, *The Customers Replie. Or Second Apologie. That is to say, an Aunswer to a Confused Treatise of Publicke Commerce, Printed and Dispersed at Midlebourghe and London, in Favour of the Private Society of Merchants-Adventurers* (London: James Roberts, 1604). Bodleian Library, University of Oxford, shelfmark MS Bodl. 913 (1).

Thomas Milles, *The Custumers Alphabet and Primer. Conteining, their Creede or Beliefe in the True Doctrine of Christian Religion* (n.p., 1608). Bodleian Library, University of Oxford, shelfmark MS Bodl. 913 (2).

Thomas Milles (1550–*c.* 1626), customs officer and antiquary, was born in Ashford, Kent, and entered public service about 1570. Among other services he was employed by Sir Francis Walsingham as an agent between England and Scotland in 1585. After assisting in the negotiations on the treaty of Berwick in 1586 he was offered the lucrative post of Customer of Sandwich, which included powers to unravel plots against custom houses, such as intercepting foreign agents. Milles held this post until 1623 when he retired, thus fitting very well with Schumpeter's description of an English consultant administrator. He devoted his late years to writing economic treaties on trade, trading companies and the practice of customs farming. He protested against the abolition of the 'old staples' and was a fierce enemy of what he saw as the monopolist practices of the Merchant Adventurers in the exporting of unwrought cloth. As a bailiff of Sandwich he opposed the monopoly of London and defended the rights of outport towns. His main work was *The Customers Apologie* (London: n.p., 1601). This work was followed by several others including the two reproduced here. Milles also published an attack on the practice of farming out customs in *A Caution Against Extremity by Farmers* (n.p., 1606).[1]

---

1 For further information, see the entry on Milles by John Whyman in *Oxford Dictionary of National Biography* (Oxford: Oxford University Press, 2004).

THE
# CVSTOMERS
## *REPLIE.*

*O R*
## SECOND APOLOGIE.

That is to fay,
### An Aunſwer to a confuſed
Treatiſe of Publicke Commerce,
printed and diſperſed at Midlebourghe
*and London, in fauour of the priuate Society*
of *M E R C H A N T S-A D V E N-*
*T V R E R S.*

### *By a more ſerious Diſcourſe*
of E X C H A N G E *in Mer-*
*chandiſe, and Merchandiſing*
EXCHANGE.

Written for vnderſtanding Readers onely, in fauour of all loyall Merchants, and for the aduancing of
*T R A F F I C K in E N G-*
*L A N D.*

### AT LONDON,
¶ Printed by *Iames Roberts*, dwelling in
Barbican. 1 6 0 4.

# TO THE RIGHT HONO-
## RABLE THE LORD *BVCKHVRST*,
L. High Treaſurer of England. The Lord *Henrie*
*Howard*, L. Warden of the Cinq-Ports : and the Lord *Cecill* of
*Eſenden*, Principall Secretarie of Eſtate to the Kings Maieſtie,
and of his Highneſſe moſt honourable
Priuie-Counſell.

HE NVMBER IS BVT
*ſmall, (at leaſt not very great) of men ſo*
*ſenceleſſe or weake of iudgement, but gene-*
*rall inconveniences they readily ſee, and*
*can eaſily diſcerne. Notwithſtanding, to*
*find out the grounds of publique harmes,*
*and the meanes how to cure them, is a ſtu-*
*die ſo intricate, & a practiſe ſo dangerous,*
*that wary men hold it ſafer to prouide for*
*priuate eaſe (in regard of the times) then to buſie theyr wits for anie*
common-good.

*But how aduiſed ſoeuer, and reſpectiuely wiſe in this kinde, the*
*moſt ſort ſeeme to be, as wiſhing onely that all might goe well, though*
*not long of themſelues : fewe or none are found of ſo ſtill a temper, as*
*not to complaine, when publique greefes worke theyr owne ſencible*
*ſmart.*

*Such then as by long and extraordinary patience ſupping vp theyr*
*priuate wrongs, haue endeuoured to giue way to the ſtreame of publick*
*contumelies, in hope of better dayes : muſt needes be excuſed if com-*
*pelld at the laſt by lawleſſe neceſsitie, to referre euents to GODS*
*prouidence, in diſcharge of their Duties to* Him, *their* Prince, *and*
Country, *they vndertake the defence of their owne reputations in a*
*Cauſe publicke and generall. The rather, when as without purpoſe of*
*offence towards any, their Intentions appeare, to giue onely a reaſon of*
*ſuch Diſorders in their preſent Functions, as for want of ſerious In-*
*ſpection, or true Information, haue hetherto by Iealouſie and miſcon-*

A 3 *ceit,*

# THE EPISTLE.

*eeit, yeelded matter and occasions from time to time of their speciall
Disgraces and obloquie.*

   *Such and none other, was the drift and scope of a late Discourse
of the present Estate of Customes, not so publiquely printed, as priuately directed* To the Graue and godly wise in highest Authoritie, *by the Title and Inscription of* THE CVSTO-
MERS APOLOGIE.

   But. Pro captu Lectoris habent sua fata Libelli. *For the booke
being written for vnderstanding Readers, and so digested, that by
reading alone, without passion or partialitie, such might be their own
and onely Iudges; hath notwithstanding, by the* Ignorant *beene lately censured, and strangly mistaken. Vainely striuing to commend &
make good that within Booke, which neuer was in question: and ma-
liciously vrging some things without Booke, that neuer were meant by
words nor writing to be defended. But with such successe as still be-
falls* Folly, *who delighting to see her owne shadow daunce, hath not
the grace to conceale her owne shame.*

    ¶ *About such time as by the goodnes of* GOD, *the light of the
Gospell beganne to lay open the Errors of Superstition in these parts of
the world, and by the hands of our* Soueraignes *to disperce them in
this Kingdome: many Questions were mooued to vphold sundry
poynts of the Popish religion; but none so hotly disputed for the time,
as that which they terme the* Sacrament of the Alter, *and* Pray-
ing to Saints. *Whereof amongst others, a certaine young Scholler
more confident then wise, hauing vndertaken a serious Defence: as
one sicke of loue with the thing he had begotten, and ambiciously affecting the publishing of it; entreated a learned friend of his, & well-
minded to the Cause, to read it ouer. The request was performed.
But looking for Arguments fitting the Question, When nothing was
found but a needlesse labour, to approoue and maintaine by the* Catholick CREEDE, That IESVS CHRIST, was the true
SONNE of GOD, very GOD, and very MAN that redee-
med the Worlde: *And that there was also a* COMMVNION
OF SAINTS. *The Booke was returned without applaude, or shew
of satisfaction.*

   RIGHT HONORABLE. *Such hath beene of late yeeres,
the successe of a like learned Writer, who printing,* A Treatise of
publique Commerce, *in fauour of the priuate Societie of the* Merchants-Aduenturers, *hath with much a-doe, and a heape of sillie
words, (farre vnfitting the grauitie of his Theame) endeuoured to*
*perswade*

## Dedicatorie.

*perſwade his Readers,* That Trafficke rightly ordered, is the honor of Kings, and proſperitie of Kingdomes : *And that Merchants in that reſpect,* were to be cheriſhed , fauoured, and encouraged in all Common-wealths. *Quia* VITA CIVILIS IN SOCIETATE POSITA EST, SOCIETAS AVTEM IN IMPERIO ET COMMERCIO. :

*It is ſtrange to obſerue,what ſtrong apprehentions are able to worke in weake mens braines. For as a plaine ſimple man was ſometimes perſwaded, that if* Pontius Pilate *had not beene a Saint,the Apoſtles would neuer haue ſuffered his Name to ſtand in the* Creede *: ſo this* Treatiſe-Writer , *by a ſtrong imagination of the* Merchant-Adventurers *extraordinary deſerts : ſeeing the admirable effects of the golden bleſſings of England, by turning* Creekes *into* Ports , *ioyning* Ports *vnto* Townes, *rayſing* Townes *into* Cities , *and enriching whole Countries with* Artificers and Trades, Marriners & Shipping. *Applauding withall, theyr ſinguler happines , and great good fortunes,to haue the managing thereof within themſelues. Commending their* * *dexterities, in* diſpoſing , diuerting , deuiding, mincing,abridging, reſtrayning, *and laſtly* confining *the* Store and Staple *thereof within the Walles of ſome oue two Townes for beſt aduantage in* * Forraine Countries , *culloured with the Title of their ſpeciall* Mart-Townes. *And aboue all things extolling their excellent wits, and abſolute cunnings, in moulding Lawes by meere Diſcretion, to hold all men vnder, and themſelues aboue. Onely for ſending or ſayling croſſe the Seas from Coaſt to Coaſt , without haZard of their Perſons, or loſſe of their Goods more then vſuall & ordinary. And for wearing* * Chaines of gold about their Necks, Caps and greene Feathers, Hats and white Feathers , Buskins of purple Veluet , guilt Rapiers, Daggers , Bridles , Stirrops, Spurres, *and ſuch like ,* at Tryumphs, *and* publique meetings. *But ſpecially for* feeding, maintayning , *and* ſetting * thouſands *on worke* beyond-Seas, *when God knowes the wants, & heares the cryes at home : would faine perſwade others, (beeing bound to ad-mire them himſelfe,) That their* Gouernour *is for Skill the* * PI-LOT, *for Grauitie the* Iudge , *and for Wiſedome the* Oracle *of all orderly* Commerce . *Their priuate* * DECREES, *aboue* COMMON LAVVES, *and* FORRAINE-TREATISE. *Theyr particuler* * SYNODES, *aboue* GENERALL COVNSAILES, *and their* * SOCIETY *a* COMMVNION OF SAINTS. *Pronouncing all that diſlike, diſtaſte, or diſtruſt their* Doctrine, *for* ENTER-LOPERS. *That is to*
*ſay,*

Read the Treatiſe printed at Midleburgh, anno. 1 6 0 1.

* The Merchants Aduenturers, boaſt themſelues to bee able to make and diuert a Trade,at their pleaſures. Page, 23.

* Marke this well by the way,for heerein lyes hid, The Pot of Roſes.

* Page,154.155.156.

* At Antwerpe. 20000.
About Antwerpe, 30000.
In Flaunders, 60000.
Page, 24.

* Pontius.

* Talmud.

* Synhedry.

* Synagogue.

## THE EPISTLE.

say, * Scismaticks, Hereticks, *and* Infidels *, vnworthy to breath Common-ayre, or liue in any Common-Wealth. Concluding strongly withall, That these* Men *thus put in trust with the credite and Creame of the Kingdome,* (our Cloth,) *must needes bee holden more loyall to their* Prince, *more seruiceable to the* State, *more welcome to their* Neighbours, *and therefore more to be honoured, then any other* Men, *with a Name aboue all Names,* of MER-CHANTS-ADVENTVRERS.

*With this and such like stuffe the Booke beeing confusedly fraught,* (cuius contrarium verißimum est,) *might well haue beene suffered to haue dyed in the birth, if withall it had not beene mingled with aßertions of obloquy & vntruthes against* CVSTOMERS *of the* Out-Ports of the Realme.

CVSTOMERS. *A kinde of Creatures capable of Religion aswell as Reason: free Men by birth, and of best education. Men euery way happy, saue in their Names and Callings: and in nothing more wretched then in the Places of their Functions*. The Out-Ports of the Realme. *O holy* LONDON! *Men I say, that being by the curious eye of the Law,* Chosen of the best, *and placed in the ranke* of the most sufficient *that Wisedome can finde, or choise afford; would faine retaine the reputations, if not of* Saints, *yet at the least of* Christians, *and plaine* honest Men.

*To let it therefore in some sort appeare, that it is not enough for Men affecting their owne good & credits by* Traffick, *to value theyr worths by disgracing of others; and that by such kind of Imputations & Shifts, as none but* Merchants (*perhaps themselues that thus byte and whine,*) *onely or most vsually commit, and is not in the* Customers *power to preuent or amend: that which ensueth, hath beene wrung from them by way of further Defence. For though it might be said, That to answere all priuate oppositions were fruitleße, and to no end: yet least he that runnes alone, should still thinke himselfe foremost: to satisfie* Wisedome *and* Authoritie *it selfe, I haue beene prouoked (by words & writings) out of other Mens labours and former experience, (as by way of witnes) to make good that for* Traffick, *which the* Apologie *before did but tenderly touch, and briefelie set downe.*

*Besides. Not to shew the decay of those Effects which both maintaine* Customers *Credits, and giue Eßence to their Functions, by the occasions of the Ecclyps in their* Cause Efficient: *were wittingly to betray the generall good of all Men, & worthily to set down in perpetuall obloquy. And publique slaunders are not washt off but by*
*publique*

---

Marginal notes:

* All English, Christian, & loyall Merchants, Crucifige.

London the onely Port of England, all other Ports are counted but Out-Ports, to London.

The Law is as carefull in the choise of a Customer, as of a Shriefe of the Shiere.

Customers are no Prophets; to geße by the Goods, of what Nation the Owner is, it beeing a mysterie among Merchants, to lend hands, and culloure one anothers dealing.

The Treatise hath beene twice printed at Midleburge and London, and dedicated to the Lord Cecill.

# DEDICATORIE.

*publicke Defence.*

For TRAFFICK *therefore* : Cuſtomers *beeing bound, and bold to contend, the aduancement whereof, like Hony in Hiues, increaſeth Cuſtomes.* ＊Not that Commerce, which children aſ-ſoone as theyr tongues are at liberty doe ſeaſon their ſports by: Nor that which Weomen among themſelues doe chop and change by : *But that* TRAFFICK *whoſe Lawes at the Standart of Equitie, wey out Order, (not by priuate Diſcretion, nor partiall Affeſtion) but by the weight of generall Iuſtice. Whoſe* Merchants *are Perſons all euery where Loyall and friendly. Whoſe* Ports *&* Staples *at home,*Markets *&* Marts *at home & abroade, are places for acceſſe conueniently eaſie, and for ſafety generally free. And whoſe* Merchandiſe, *for Matter honeſt, for* Vſe *profitable, by* Nature *admirable, and by* Art *made amiable, is at all handes vendible onely for the* Goodnes.

*That* TRAFFICK, *I ſay, whoſe diuine Elixar* Goodneſſe, *the quinteſſence of* Nature *and* Art *applied to* Materialls, *breedes* Miſteries *in*Trades, *turnes* Trades *into* Mettals, *and all* Mettals *into pure Siluer, and fine Golde. The reſtauring power whereof, eaſing all griefes in Sores, ſuppling all Sores in diſeaſes, and curing all Diſeaſes in particular* Members, *holdes the whole Bodies of*Kingdomes *in health. Laſtlie : That* TRAFFICK *which concernes* Kings *and* Kingdomes, *whoſe ſeate is euery where the* Soueraignes *boſome. Whoſe voyce well tuned, is the harmonie of the* World, *To whom* Courts *and* Countries *owe fealtie and homage, the meaneſt* Subieſts *feeling her care, & the greateſt* Princes *ſubieſt to her prouidence. Whom both* Noble *and* vnnoble *admire, as the* Nurſſe *of all their earthly honors, proſperities, peace and ioy. To the end, I ſay, that by other mens complaints, as well as* Cuſtomers, *the world may ſee how hunted, reſtrained, monopoliſed, and ill beholden, that* TRAFFICK *is & hath been to all* priuate Societies. *In the Fore-Ranck whereof I ſet the* ＊HAVNCES, *(that beeing but* Subieſts *a part and a ſunder vnder ſeuerall* Soueraignes *; yet combined together, dare conteſt with* Princes : ) *and theſe our* MERCHANTS-ADVENTVRERS, *as her two moſt wayward and wrangling children. Who preferring particuler* Decrees *before generall*Treatiſe *and*Lawes, *& with publick weapons maintayning contentions for priuate wrongs ; in ſteed of*Order *pretended, breede nothing but complaints at home, confuſions within themſelues, endleſſe troubles to graue* Counſailes *at* Counſaile-Tables, *and vnkind Iarres betweene* Kingdomes, States, Allies, *and*

＊ The childiſh commendation of *Trafficke*, by the *Treatiſe-writer.* Page. 3.

＊ This is heere added, onely that the *Treatiſe-writer* might examine the grounds of his ovvne folly or frenzie in taxing Cuſtomers as friends to the *Haunces,* by ſpeaking againſt his *Merchants-Aduenturers.* To whom, as to *Subieſts,* onely for their *Soueraignes* ſake, they wiſh all kindnes and loue, but reuerence neyther as *abſolute Princes.*

## The Epistle.

*and forraine* Neighbour-friendes.

   *Leauing therefore the* Treatise-Writer *to beleeue still in the* Creede, *whose Articles are certainely most holy and true, though* Pontius Pilates *Name stand for no Saint :* And the Merchants-Adventvrers *to the Story of* Isis. *Whose Image of gold it was that men so admired, in all places where it came, and not the beautie of the Beast that bare it. I referre your Wisedomes and Honourable patience, to the* Counter-Treatise *following : beeing a plaine Demonstration of that Canker of* Commerce, Merchandising-Exchange. *I say a cleere detection of that Contempt of* Lawes, *Disdaine of* Equity, *Scorne of publique* Magistrates, *Dishonour of* Princes, *and Mysterie of Iniquitie. And a liuely Description of that* \* Monster *of* Creete, *deuouring as it were by yeerely tribute, the bodies of* Men, & *soules of* Christians. *His hatching and broode, his Muces* & *haunts, his Practise and* Shifts, *his Shape and* Name, *vnder the Title of* Merchandizing-Exchange. *The* Laborinth *of whose inextricable Errors, none may safelie enter, & whose* Person *none can encounter and quell, but fatall* Thesevs, *assisted by the thred of addresse and Counsaile of* Ariadne. *A worke sometimes proiected to giue light vnto others, but happily reserued to honour your* Lordships *and these our dayes withall.*

   *And since the case of* Customers *stands so farre preiudged, that euen theyr Cryes seeme but Ecchoes in the* \* Deserts, *round about the* Plaines, *neere the* FORREST OF SHIFTS, *the sound whereof most men passe by but heare not, many heare but vnderstand not, some few vnderstand but regard not, and no man pitties. And that their painful Apologies are left to the* Ignorant, *to prostitute publiquely, and turne into Sinne ; whilst they sit still in silence, like* Barnes *so ding'd that they dare not greit : Let* Experience *tell* IELOVSIE *how she torments* Traffick, *by clogging her* \* Seruice *with swarms of such Instrumēts as loue her Customs, but as Rats do loue Cheese. And let* Nature *tell* SVSPITION *howe* Traffick *appeales. That whilst her* \*Hovses *as Places infected, or haunted with Sprites, are either abandond, or by Extremities made subiect to Shifts : The* Free-will Offerings. *The Effects of* Loyaltie. *The* True-loue-knots, *knit betweene* Subiects & Prince. *And Tokens of* \* Affection *(religiously moued in* Minds, *admiring the glorious* OBIECT *of their owne welfare* & Good) *from the harts of her* Merchants, *humbly presented to* Soueraigne Dignitie, *and to None other due. Become now set to sale. As if*

*franck-*

\**VSVRIE.*

*1565.*

\* *Ovt-Ports.*

\* *Custome seruice.*

\* *Custome houses.*

\* *Customer.*

# DEDICATORIE.

*franck-harted* Loue, *& true-louing* Loyalty (*the* Homage *of* Sub-iects, *and* Honor *of* KINGS.) *Were* Thinges *transferrent from that* Prerogatiue *which giues them life and* Beeing. *Or sub-iect to* Exchange. *Or vendible for* Money. *Or fit for* *FAR-MORS. *Drying* TRAFFICK *thus from the Lyme-kill to the Cole-pit : euery way decaying her* PORTS, *& disgracing her* Seruaunts.

* The Farming out of Customes, offensiue to Nature: and vnto Traf-fick meerely *Heterocli-ton.*
*Et* Licentijs *sumus omnes deteriores.*

*But as inveterate* Errors, *hold still their aduantage, and are ne-uer ouerthrowne, till from* Signes *vnto* Causes, *by* Effects *it appeare how the Worlde in Matter of* TRAFFICK *hath beene abused, o-uer-ruled, and ouer-seene : So when* TRVTH, *the Daughter of* TIME, *by practise and proofe shall be brought to light, then shall* Ignorance *and* Impudencie *stand both confounded, &* IELO-SIE *herselfe see that in* Customers *vertue is not vice.*

*For if it be true that* Truth *hath sworne,* Customers *haue writ-ten, &* Experience *confirmes. To wit : That looke what the* Soule *is to the ontward actions of the* Body, *in ordering each Member, so as to* Nature *seemes fittest for the good of the whole* Man : *the same is* TRAFFICK *in disposing* Mysteries *and* Trades *to the behoofe of the* Common-Wealth. *The* *DAY-STARRE *is risen, and the* *DAVVNING *appeares, which giuing life to our* Hopes, *makes vs breath out thus much, and say : The time may come, when this hartie zeale of ours to our* SOVERAIGNES *honour, and his* Peoples *happines, may be better regarded, and deserue not onely thanks and good words, but make all men confesse themselues* (Merchants *at least) to owe as much to these weake endeuours of* CVSTOMERS, *euen those of the despised* Out-Ports *of this* Realme, *I say not as one* Port, *one* Towne, *or one* Citty *of* Lon-don, *but many* Ports, *many* Townes, *and many* Citties *like* Lon-don, *and all their wealth besides are worth, some few* priuate, parti-culer, *and* preuenting Persons *excepted. The* Censure *whereof I most humbly submit to* Iudgement *and* Wisedome, *with this* Caution *& finall* Conclusion. *That* TRVTH *lyes deepe, and few there are that vndertake the toyle to delue till they finde her. And though* Publique *harmes & priuate* Disgaces *to men of my Cal-ling, haue singled me foorth, and pressed mee forward to worke thus alone, for the* Common-good *; the burden whereof makes mee cry aloude : I must confesse, that in these* Apologies, *and forced* Defen-ces, (*accusing no man, for that was the Deuils part from the begin-ning, nor at warre with any but* Sinne *and* Dishonestie) Nil magis in Votis nec habui, nec habeo, quam vt inter plures, aliquos
inveniam

* The King.
* The Prince.

## THE EPISTLE.

ínveniam, qui de iftis judicare queant. Iudicare autem non poffunt nifi vtcunque Literati, aut Rerum vfu periti. Ex hijs fatis mihj pauci Lectores, fat erit fi vel vnus : *In Appealing there-fore to the* G R A V E S T *and* W I S E S T *in* H I G H E S T A V-T H O R I T Y. *I haue thought it meeteft & fafeft for triple refpects, to prefent* my felfe, *and my poore* feruice , *to your* honorable Lordfhips, *by whofe fpeciall fauours next* G O D *and my* SOVERAIGNE, *I am that I am, and fo defire to be knowne.*
(∵)

Your L L: by feuerall Duties.

deuotedly bound.

*Tho: Milles.*

# THE CHAPTERS CON-
## *tayning the matter handled in this*
### TREATISE.

B.                              A

# The Contents.

¶ An *Abridgement* of the ſpeciall Inconueniences to this Realme of England, handled in the foreſayd tenth Chapter.

¶ A generall Concluſion.

---

ꙅ A Pre-

Page, 1

## A TREATISE
## Of EXCHANGE in *Merchandise,*
### and *Merchandising* EXCHANGE.

## ¶ A Preface or Introduction to the
### Matter handled in the Treatise
### of EXCHANGE.
### (∵)

ALl things whatsoeuer tend naturally to some *End.
Which* End *beeing the* Perfection *of that for which
it worketh, is onely attaind vnto by apt & fit* Meanes.
*That which appoynts & moderates* fitnes *& Forme
in working, is termed a* Law : *by which, as by* Rules,
*the World and all things therein are distinguisht and stinted. Which
Limitation is both the* Perfection *and* Preseruation *of the Things
themselues.* Measure *therefore working by* Proportions, *is the way
to* Perfection. *And since nothing doth perrish, but through the* too
much *or too little of that, the due proportioned* Measure *whereof
dooth giue* Perfection ; Measure *is also the* Preseruation *of all
Things. For to* Proportions, Excesse *and* Defects *are* opposites.
Iustice *then beeing the foreconceiued* End *of all Actions, is prescri-
bed and perfitted by* Lawes , *and preserued by* Measures . *Which
beeing the Heauenly charge of Earthly Princes; sets foorth & lymits
their* Soueraignties *& Prerogatiues sacred & royall, otherwise (in
regard of their humane Substances and qualities) transcēdent . For
it is said,* They are Gods *in regard of* Iustice , *but theyr* Persons
*shall die like Men.* Iustice *is* Distributiue *or* Commutatiue.
Commutatiue Iustice *encludeth* Traffick. *The end of* Traffick *is*
Equalitie *in supplying Necessities,* vt quod vspiam nascitur Boni
id apud omnes affluat : *eyther by bartring wares for wares, or by
some Midds or* Meanes *certaine and indifferent to preuent* Aduantage.

*The* End *therefore in* Traffick *beeing* Equitie , *and the vse* Exchange ; *the* Measure *is by publicke Consent of all Nations called*
Money. *And as the* Standart *of all kind of* Measures *for generall*
Iustice *like* Vrim *and* Thummim *is the* Princes charge onely : *gi-*
*uing*

**Page. 2.**          Of EXCHANGE in Merchandife,

*uing thereby* Weight *and* Content, Length *and* Breadth *to all*
Proportions : *So the coyning of* Money *and the valuation thereof,*
*being a* Meafure *of principall Excellency and peculiar to* Trafficke,
*is immediatly,* Vni foli et femper, *an effentiall part of* Soueraigne
Authority. *Out of which Premiffes ,* this *muft be concluded . That*
*either to coyne* Money *, or being coyned to alter the true* Valuation
*thereof, in what kind foeuer ; is in* Subiectes *whofoeuer , when and*
*wherefoeuer , to prefume vpon the Maieftie of* Soueraigne Princes,
*to prophane the Sacred Seate of* Iuftice, *to contemne publicke* Authority, *and in* Trafficke *to preuent and peruert all* order *and* E-
quity. *A Capitall finne againft God and Nature.*

> ¶ Thus much only being added by way of *Preface ,* by
> the Cuftomers of the Out-Ports , who for the *Effectes* fake
> are euery way bound to aduance the *Caufe :* That which
> followes of the *Matter* and vfe of *Trafficke ,* is proper to
> Merchants. Heare therfore a loyall Marchants experience,
> writing in his owne Stile and Phrafe of *Exchange* in *Mar-*
> *chandife,* and *Marchandifing* Exchange, in Order as follow-
> eth.
>
>                     *Tractent Fabrilia Fabri.*

---

C H A P.  I.

¶ *The Antiquitie, neceffity, and vfe of Lawfull* Exchange,
*and a Defcription thereof.*

T Is Apparant To Svch As
are converfant in Records of tyme and olde
Wryters, that the exercife of *Exchange* is a
thing of greateft antiquitie: borne with *Traf-*
*fick* it felfe, and as it feemeth , begate the firft
Names and Titles of thofe which are called
in Latine, *Numularii , Argentarii,* and *Coly-*
*bifta,* that is to fay, publique and common Exchangers , and
Commutors of Bullyon, ftrange and forraine coynes to all maner of Strangers , for the lawfull and currant money of thofe
Countryes and Common-wealths , where the faid *Exchange*
was *proportioned* and *authorifed* by the Princes & Gouernors of
the fame.

And becaufe the Office of *Exchanging,* and curtefie of lending money in a Common-wealth , after an eafie & tollerable
                                              reckoning,

## and Merchandifing *Exchange*.

reckoning, is very neceffary and expedient. The olde Ciuill Lawes did graunt and permit to this honeft kind of *Exchange*, a certaine rate in the hundred by the yeere, for th'intereft of fuch mony as was lent to fuch as had neede.

And a certaine exercife and vfe of the fame was fometime allowed and admitted in England, as when the Tables of *Exchange* were fet vp, & erected in diuers Townes thereof, in the time of King *Edward* the third, and other Kings raignes fucceeding him.

The *Exchangers* & Keepers of which Tables, did change to all manner of Forraine Marchants and Strangers, which reforted thether : afwell Bullion, as all forraine coynes and Moneies which they brought thether for the currant Money of the Realme, according to the Princes iuft valuation thereof.

And this manner of *Exchange*, feemeth alfo to be the firft occafion of the erecting of thofe fhops of *Exchange*, which at this day bee called in Spaine and Italy *Cambios* and *Bancos*, which at the firft inftitution of them were appointed for great fafegarde, and commoditie of fuch as had Money, for that they might without danger lay into the fayd *Cambios* and *Banckes* (as it were *in Depofito*) what fums of Money they would, for the which the Cambiadors and Bankars would be anfwerable, as for a thing depofited, and committed to their cuftody, and would alfo make payments thereof, according to the order of the fayd Depofitor. Which farther did vfe to *change* Siluer for Gold, and all manner of forraine coyne and Money, for the lawfull and currant Money of thofe Countryes, and that according to the lawfull valuation of the fame. And moreouer, by thefe Cambiadors or Bankars, fometime there was wayes and meanes taken, to make *Exchange* of Money, from one Country to another : for fuch as had occafion for to trauell and paffe Countryes. Likewife according to the iuft and publique valuation of fuch coyne and Monies, the reward and falary of Cambiadors for their labors and paines in keeping Money, *Exchanging* white Money for Gold, or forraine coynes for the lawfull and currant Money of Spaine, within this thirty yeeres, was not aboue two and a halfe in the thoufand, for the fpace of on Faire, which commonly endureth there fix weekes, and this intereft and gaines amounteth not aboue three in the hundred for the whole yeere.

This

Page. 4,          ## Of EXCHANGE in Marchandiſe,

This manner of *Exchange* is not onely to be ſuffered & permitted in a Common-wealth : but as it appeareth, very neceſſary, expedient, and commodious to the ſame : not onely for
the exchanging of Bullyon and coynes within the ſelfe ſame
Realme and Common-wealth : but alſo for the paſſing of
Money from one Country to another, for ſuch as haue affaires
to trauell Countries as the Embaſſadors of Princes do : wherby be diuers perrils auoyded that they ſhould runne in, carrying of ready Money about them. So that the ſayd *Exchange* be
not practiſed of ſuch as traffick Merchandiſe, and will imploy
theyr money ſo exchanged againe in wares and commodities
to be returned into theyr owne Coumtrey. For to all ſuch the
ſayd *Exchange* was alwayes prohibited in England , as a thing
diſcommodious and pernicious, both to the Prince and Common-wealth, as may appeare by diuers Acts of Parliament,
prouided to that end.

EXCHANGE          ¶ *Exchange* therfore is a certaine lawfull kind of commutati-
deſcribed.        on and changing of Money, appointed by the publick authority of a Common-wealth, eyther for the changing of Bullyon
ſtrange and forraine coynes brought thither, according to ſuch
valuation as the ſayd Bullyon and coynes haue, or be eſteemed
at, by the common authority of the ſame Common-wealth
and Country.

Or elſe it is a certaine meanes, for the commutation and exchanging of Money from one Realme or Country to another,
according to the iuſt and lawfull valuation of Money priced &
ſet foorth by the publicke authority of ſuch Countries and
Realmes.

### CHAP. II.
*How Merchants haue deuiſed and introduced another
kind of Exchange.*

BVT vnder the coullor and pretence of this lawfull *Exchange* and commutation of Money , Merchants of late
yeeres haue deuiſed and brought vp another manner of
*Exchange* of coyne : to the which they doe alſo commonly giue this plaine and ſimple name , *Exchanging* : vvhen
indeed it is not ſo, but a meere fæneration, and a making a ware
and merchandize of Money : for that in the ſame, and by the
ſame they buy and ſell, rayſe and abate the price of Money, as
                                                        well

and Merchandifing *Exchange*.

well as they doe rayfe and abate the price of any other vvare &
Merchandizes they traffick in. Wherefore it is not to be called
fimply *Exchange*, but properly and aptly to be called the *Mer-chandizing of Money*.

Yet becaufe that through the practife and pollicy of Merchants, fpecially trading & frequenting the Marts of *Antwerpe*,
and the Fayres of *Lions*, for the paffing of Money from place
to place by the fame, which alfo is done after a certaine fort and
kind of exchanging and commuting of Money, it may conueniently be called & haue the name of *Merchandizing Exchange*.
Forafmuch as Money paffed and exchanged after this way and
manner, muft be payd againe according to the conditions and
compacts taken and agreed vpon with the Merchants, for the
price & valuation therof : and not according to the iuft & lawfull valuation it hath by any publicke Authority of that Common-wealth, which is author of the fayd Money : the vvhich
temerarius alteration of publick coynes & monyes, is the principall foundation of the fayd *Exchange*; and of the gaines and
lucar proceeding of the fame : for the loue & greedines wherof, the other lawfull *Exchange* is exiled and expelled both out
of Spaine and Italie; and through the frequenting therecf, the
trade of Merchandife is corrupted in all Countries, and fpecially in England, by the bufie practifing thereof of Merchants
betweene Antwerpe and England, which haue brought many
inconveniences vnto this Common-wealth, & be thereby the
onely Authors, why all manner of wares and Merchandizes
beare fuch excefsiue prices as they doe at this day within the
Realme, as heereafter fhall be declared, by the opening of certaine circumftances effentially appertayning to the fame *Exchange*, without the which it can neither be vnderftood nor
practifed; and fo fhall it euidently appeare, that all th'inormi-
ties difordering the prices of all manner of things vendible in
the Common-wealth, haue theyr originall from thence.

### Chap. III.
*The Compacts and Conditions commonly agreed vpon in*
Merchandifing Exchange.

Irft, the taker and Receiuer of Money by this *Exchange*,
muft compound & agree with the Deliuerer of the fame,
at what *diftance* of *time* the fayde Money fhall be payde a-
againe

**Page.6.**      Of EXCHANGE in Merchandiſe,

gaine in a forraine Country or Citty appointed for the payment thereof, for there bee three kindes of diuerſities, and
Diſtances of time moſt commonly in vſe at this day amongſt
*Merchants*, for the repayment of ſuch Money as is taken and
deliuered by this *Exchange*.

Secondly, the taker and Receiuor of Money by this *Exchange*, muſt compound and agree with the Deliuerer thereof,
to make payment againe in the forraine Country, according
as the ſame Money receiued is valued by the *Merchants*, to
bee worth in the currant Money of the ſame forraine Country, and according to the price and valuation the ſayd currant
Mony hath in this their *Merchandiſing Exchange*, and not after
the Princes iuſt valuation of the ſame Money.

C H A P. IIII.

*The Termes of Art proper to* Marchandiſing Exchange,
*by diuerſities of* Times, *and Diſtances
of* Place.

*At ſight.*      THe firſt kind of diuerſity, *Merchants* call the taking and
deliuering of Money *at ſight*, the cuſtome wherof in this
*Exchange* & commutation, cōpelleth the Receiuor of the
Money vpon a litle Scedule or Bill, containing the ſumme &
value of the forraine coyne and Money, which muſt be payd
againe to the vſe of the Deliuerer, immediatly as the ſaid Scedule & Bill ſhall be ſhewed and preſented by the Deliuerer or
his Factor, to the Factor or Seruant of the ſaid taker and Receiuor of Money, or els to his owne ſelfe.

The ſecond, is to take and deliuer Money by or at *Vſance*,
and the cuſtome of this diuerſity compelleth the taker of Money by this *Exchange*, vppon his Bill or Scedule to pay the value thereof againe in forraine coyne or Money, at the end of
one month next immediatly ended, after the firſt daie of the
making of the *Exchange*, in the Towne or Citty appointed
thereunto in the ſayd Scedule: either by himſelfe, his Factor or
Seruant.

*Vſance.*      This ſpace of time of one month, is limited for this ſecond
Diſtance of time in this *Marchandiſing Exchange*, called *Vſance*,
betweene *London* and *Antwerp*, and other Marting Townes
there-abouts, by the Bankers and *Exchangers* of the ſame *Exchange*.

The

and Merchandifing *Exchange.* Page,7.

The third is called *Double Vfance*, by the vfe and cuſtome *Double*
whereof, the Taker and Receiuer of Money by the fame *Ex-.Vfance.*
*change*, is compelled by his Bill or Scedule, to pay the value;
thereof againe in forraine Money at the end of two months
next, immediatly ending after the day that the Money was
firſt taken vp by *Exchange*, either by himfelfe, Factor, or Seruant, in the place appointed and affigned thereunto by the
fayd Scedule.

And heere is to be noted, that thefe two latter Diſtances of
time, be made longer and fhorter for the payment of Money
taken vp by the fame, after the diuerfitie of any of the fayd two
kindes, according to the Diſtance of the Places, for the which
the fay *Exchange* is or fhall be made at any time.

### Chap. V.

*The Diuerfitie of Prices of Money currant in* Merchandiſing
Exchange, *according to the Diſtances of* Place, *and*
*difference of* Times.

Like as the time and fpaces limited to euery diuerfity and
Diſtance of time & place, of this *Merchandifing Exchange*,
differ and vary one from another, betweene *England* and
*Antwerp*, and other Marting Townes thereabouts : fo hath
th'englifh pound paffed by this *Exchange*, betweene the one
Country and the other, at diuers and fundry prices, differing
one from another, according to the time it is *Exchanged* for,
from the one place to the other.

Firſt, the price of the Englifh pound *Exchanged at fight*, differeth from the fame pound valued by any Prince or publicke
authoritie, ordinarily *foure* or *fiue pence* in the pound.

Secondly, the price of th'englifh pound *Exchanged* for *V-*
*fance*, differeth from the fame pound deliuered, and taken for
fight, ordinarily *fiue* or *fix pence* in the pound.

Thirdly, the price of the fame pound taken and *Exchanged*
for *Double Vfance*, differeth from the pound by *Vfance*, vi. or
vii. *pence* : fo that an Englifh pound *Exchanged* by this laſt diſtance of time, differeth in price from a pound taken vp by the
firſt difference of time, xii. or xiii *pence* in the fayd pound.

Many other diuerfities, as well of Times as of Money, be and
may be practifed & exercifed in this *Merchandifing Exchange :*
Whereof to difcourfe perticularly, were too long and tedious ;
forfomuch as this briefe declaration of thefe diuerfities before

C.

**Page,8.**          Of EXCHANGE in Marchandife,

fore recited, may fuffife not onely for the perceiuing and vnderftanding of the fame: but alfo for all other that be, or may
be practifed in the fayd *Merchandifing Exchange*, for as thefe
three prices differ proportionally one from another, according
to the rate and diftance of time: fo doe all other prices therof,
according to the proportion of time they bee paffed for.

Chap. VI.

*The manner of rayfing the valuation of Money in*
Merchandifing Exchange.

FOrafmuch as the iuft and lawfull valuation of Money cannot maintaine this fubtill *Merchandifing Exchange*, euerie
peece of Gold, and great peece of Siluer, fet forth & currant in any Common-wealth, is alwaies of more valuation after that it is currant Money in this forefaide *Exchange*, by two
pence, foure pence, or fixe pence in a peece, more or leffe, according to the quantity and fubftance it is of, then it is by the
Princes, and publick authority of the Countrey where it was
firft coyned.

Which pollicie in rayfing of Money, is cheefely practifed
of the Bankers of Antwerpe, to allure Merchants of all other
parts to bring thither ready Money, and therefore make they
the coynes of all other Countries, more woorth with them,
then in any other Country els, although they be not fo allowed
and excepted by the authoritie of theyr Countrey. Yet being
thus valued by them, they be made the common currant Money to buy and fell all manner of wares & Merchandizes there
trafficked, and the way to paffe and practife theyr *Exchange*
with.

And becaufe they will not haue the Princes Lawful Money
to be the meane to buy & fell all things with, they compound
in all their Contracts, Bargaines and *Exchanges*, to haue the
payments made in this theyr Inuented Money, which they
call, *Currant Money in Merchandize*: And furthermore, by
this licentious libertie that they vfurpe in prifing, and valewing
all Princes Money, they make many forts of Money currant a-
mongft them, which common Authority doth not permit nor
allow to be payable nor currant in the Countrey. Whereby
they haue greatly increafed and aduanced the trade and con-
courfe of *Merchants* in thofe parts and Countryes: notwithftanding,

and Merchandising *Exchange.*

standing,therewithall hath proceeded the greatest occasion, of the excessiue prices which raigneth vpō wares,Merchandizes, and commodities, in all Countryes at this day.

## Chap. VII.
### *The difference betweene the Lawfull* Exchange, *and Merchandising* Exchange.

IN the *Exchange* which before is called tollerable and lawfull *Exchange*, the price and valuation set foorth by publick authority, is chiefely to be considered and regarded in the Money *Exchanged* thereby, to the end that a iust & equall payment, may bee made againe thereof to the Party that deliuereth his Money by the sayd *Exchange*.

As for example, if the Ambassador of a Prince had neede of 100. li. English to be payd him at Antwerp, and would deliuer his 100. li. in London, to haue the iust value thereof payd him againe in Flemish Money, at his or the comming of his letter to Antwerp.

Heere is to be considered onely, what and how much the English pound is worth Flemish, by the Princes valuation of those parties,the valuation whereof is at the least xxii. shillings and vi. pence Flemish, after which valuation the hundred pound English shall make Flemish 112. li. 10. sh. Likewise, if he would haue a 100. Crownes of the sun, payd him in *Paris* in Fraunce, for the value thereof deliuered in *London* by the *Exchange*, forsomuch as it is knowne, that the French crowne is valued in England at vi. sh. English; & in Fraunce it is valued by the Prince at 50. sous ; now vi. sh. in Enlish after 2. sous and a halfe for the English grot, amounteth to 45. sous in the crowne, so that a hundred crownes amounteth to 4500.sous in French, and after the French valuation of the crowne, they amount to 5000. sous, so that for a hundred crownes at the value thereof deliuered in England by this lawfull *Exchange,* he ought to receiue in Fraunce, 111. crownes, 5. sous, as hee doth at Antwerp for his 100. li. a 112. li. 10. st. Flemish : and this *Exchange* may be made without the Merchants three diuersities and *distances of time*, very well, truly, and iustly, because neither party seeketh to buy and sell Money thereby, but to commute and *Exchange* it, according to the iust value giuen to the same, by the Princes and common authorities of both

Coun.

## Of EXCHANGE in Merchandiſe,

Countryes. So that neither the Taker nor Deliuerer ſhall haue any more or leſſe, then that is due to them, although the Deliuerer of the Money do tarry, or be contented to tarry 15. or 20. dayes for the receite of his Money, the Receiuor receiueth no domage nor hinderance thereby, but rather commoditie and profit, nor yet the Deliuerer, if hee haue his Money to ſerue his purpoſe at the time appointed, ſo that heere is no neceſſitie of intereſt to be payd to any partie for the forbearing of Money.

And ſurely this was onely the vſe and cuſtome of the *Exchange* at the firſt beginning thereof, to the which if it were reſtored againe, the Princes Embaſſadors of England, lying in Fraunce and in other places ſhould not leeſe, 7. or 8. in the hundred, for two or three months ſpace, in taking vp of Mony for Parris, to be payd againe at Antwerp, and from thence at *London* by *Merchandiſing Exchange*, to doe their Prince and Country ſeruice, but ſhould rather be gainers by the lawfull and honeſt *Exchange*, as reaſon and conſcience declareth they ſhould bee. And yet notwithſtanding might the *Banker* and *Cambiador* be allowed for his paines and labour, for the receiuing and paying of the Money, ſomewhat after the olde manner of Spaine and Italy, which is after the rate, of three in the hundred for the yeere, and ſo ſhould he not be euill payd therfore, nor yet the Payer and Deliuerer of the Money by *Exchange* ouer burdened and charged, as they be now a dayes eaten out of houſe and home by *Merchandiſing Exchang*, if onely this lawfull *Exchange* were reſtored againe, for the paſſing of Money from Country to Country.

Contrariwiſe, in this corrupt and crafty *Exchange*, and commutation of Money, the ſayd publicke valuation of Money is altogether neglected, ſecluded, and put out of minde, and only the price and valuation, that Money hath giuen to it by meere chaunce in the ſame *Exchange*, conſidered and paſſed vpon: and ſo neither can equallity nor indifferency be obſerued in the payment againe of the Money, taken and deliuered by the ſame *Exchange*, but that one of the parties muſt be burthened thereby, nipped and oppreſſed, for that it is bought & ſold at lower and higher prices then it ought to haue by publick authoritie, according to the pleaſure of *Merchants* ſeeking lucar and gaines thereby. As for example, if one in London would haue a hundred crownes paid him in Parris by that *Exchange*,

and Merchandifing *Exchange.*

*change,* firft, at his deliuering in London of his 100. crownes, he muft compound & agree with him he maketh his *Exchange* withall, how much Englifh Money hee fhall deliuer in London, for euery French-crowne to be payd in Parris againe : for the Princes valuation will not ferue, but hee muft agree vpon a new price of Englifh Money for the faid crownes : fo where it is worth in England by the Princes valuation but vj. fhillings, the *Exchanger* will haue fixe fhillings foure pence, or fix pence, or peraduenture a noble, according as the occafion of *Time* ferueth for euery crowne to be paid in Parris, and fometimes more.

So that, where by equitie and confcience, which is knowne by the Princes and publicke valuation of the crowne, the Deliuerer of the Money in England, fhould receiue for his hundred crownes deliuered in England, a hundred and eleuen crownes and fiue fous at Parris, he now by this *Merchants Exchange,* fhall receiue at the moft not aboue 105. crownes, or 102 crownes, and fometime leffe then the hundred crownes. So that by this one example, appeareth fufficiently what a difference it is to paffe Money by the Lawfull *Exchange,* which is ruled and ordered by the ftable & conftant price giuen to Money by publick Authoritie, and by this other fallible *Exchange,* depending onely vpon the alterable price of Money, giuen after the inftable affection of couetous Merchants.

## Chap. VIII.
### *The firft ftanding* Bankes *and* Pillars *of* Merchandifing Exchange. *And a Defcription thereof.*

THE firft & principall piller of all, may *Rome* moft worthily be taken and reputed, where fuch great rapine, auarice, and other filthines is fo in common vfe, that it is figured in the Scriptures by the Beaft and Harlot, with vvhom all the Princes, Merchants, & rich men of the Earth haue committed abhomination, and of whom they haue learned the loue of Money, that is, Idolatry : Whofe Antichriftian Princes and Gouernours, by reafon of the Anates, and other great tributes exacted, fpecially of the Ecclefiafticall perfons of all other Realmes, inuented this Commutation and *Exchange,* as the moft expedient and commodious meane for the conueying of their reuenewes vnto them ; fo that the holy Fathers be-

*Vfury firft hatched in Rome.*

C 3                    ganne

Page,12.                Of EXCHANGE in Marchandife,

ganne firft in the Babilonicall *Rome*, the erection of a ftanding
Banck for the Traffick and *Merchandifing Exchange*, by which
meanes it hath euer fince beene in exercife, for the tranfporting of Money as a ware and *Merchandize*, by the miniftery of
*Merchants*, from all places of Chriftendome to the Citty of
*Rome,* Rome. Vnto the which in continuance, the fayd *Merchants* being fo delighted with that trade, haue deuifed to adioyne three
other Citties for *Standing Bancks*, and Pillers of the fame *Ex-*
*change,*as *Venice*, *Lyons*, and *Antwerpe* : Which foure places, be
*Venice,* therefore called *Standing-Bancks*, becaufe the Exchangers and
*Lyons,* Bankers thereof, doe exercife the fame *Exchange* publiquely,
*Antwerp.* and haue their open fhops for the fame purpofe at this day in
all the faid Townes ; and moreouer, they haue as it were fome
kind of Warrant, Liberties, and Preuiledges, from the Superi-
our Powers of the fame Townes, for the more fure and fafe
Traffick therein.

By which Preuiledges, (at the leaft in thefe other three Citties) vnder the pretence and couller to be lawfull *Exchangers*,
and honeft Merchants, all honeft trade of Merchandize is corrupted throughout all the Townes & Regions of *Europe* : but
fpecially in England, all manner of wares and Merchandifes, &
other commodities of the Realme, be growne thereby to exceffiue prices ; from whence alfo fpring daily more and more
abufes and abfurdities, in the Trades and manner of all forts of
Occupiers throughout all Chriftendome.

*The Difcription of*        Therefore *Merchandifing Exchange*, is an vnlawfull com-
*Merchandifing*        mutation of Money made betweene parties, vppon certaine
*Exchange.*        fubtill compacts & conditions for the paffing of Money from
one Country to another, according to the priuate valuation
giuen by *Merchants* and Banckars, to the coynes and Monies
of all Princes and common Wealths ; deuifed and inuented of
them, only for their priuate benefit, and gaine, to the confufion of all good order in *Merchandifing*, and the corruption of
all honeft occupying and Traffick in any common Wealth.

CHAP. IX.
*Three Practifes, and fiue Abufes hurtfull and pernicious to all*
*Common-wealths by* Merchandifing
Exchange.

Firft

and Merchandifing *Exchange*. Page,13.

Irft, Merchants doe make thereby all Princes coynes and Moneys, to be as wares and Merchandifes, buying and felling the fame for more and leſſe price, as well as any other kind of ware and Merchandife they traffick in, contrary to the nature of Money, and alfo the Lawes and Ordinances of all Princes and Common-wealths, by whofe authority onely, coynes of Money ought to haue theyr price and valuation, and that vnalterable, for the preferuing of an *Equitie* in all thinges vendible in the Countries and Common-wealths.

Secondly, Merchants do vfe by that meanes to ferue theyr turnes of Money from one Country to another, therewith to buy wares and Merchandifes: by which pollicie, they hinder Princes and Common-wealthes, of fuch toles and cuftoms as they fhould pay to them, vpon theyr wares and commodities that they would bring and convey into their Dominions and Countries to doe theyr feate with, if this Merchandifing of Money were not: whereby alfo many Merchants do coullour the conueying of ready Money out of the Realme of England. And fpecially it is a great let, impediment & hinderance to the bringing in of Bullyon into this Realme, which all forraine Merchants were wont to doe, when the commodities of the Realme were vented & vttered at *Callice*, or at the *Staple townes* within England, before the two *Societies* of Englifh Merchants began to vfurpe fuch Liberties for the Traffick, as they pretend at this day to enioy by lawfull Authority.

Thirdly, Merchants at this day doe practife to buy and fell onely according to the price and valuation that Money hath, by the diforder of this *Merchandifing-Exchange*: and doe omit and paffe ouer the iuft and lawfull valuation of Money giuen, and fet foorth in euery Country by the Prince and common authority thereof; Money beeing the onely meane to preferue a mediocritie and an *equalitie* in the prices of all things vendible, in any Countrey or Common-wealth, and fo haue they beene the occafion why the prices and eftimation of all manner of wares and commodities be fo excefsiuely inhaunced & rifen in the Realme of England at this day.

¶ 1. Firft, by the occafion of this *Exchange*, many perfons *Vfury.* in diuers places, be fore intangled and wrapped in & with heauie burdens, byting, and *inextricable Vfuries*.

2. Second-

### Of EXCHANGE in Merchandife,

2. Secondly, it caufeth the Traffick, with the vfe & cuftome of borrowing and lending of Money in a Common-wealth, to be hard, deere, and fcant, which is a very neceffary and expedient thing to be liberally, frankly, and freely vfed.

3. Thirdly, it giueth occafion to all maner of Occupiers, although they follow no iuft and lawfull trade of Merchandize, to fet theyr prices of their Wares after fuch fort and rate, that theyr gaines thereby may paffe and exceede, not onely *fix* and *eight* in the hundred, but alfo *twelue*, for a fmall time.

4. Fourthly, vnder the cullour therof, not only the *Bankars* of Antwerp, and Lyons, with fuch like Vfurers, openly, and by profeffion practifing Vfury, doe exceede the Limits of all honeft and lawfull intereft, in letting or lending out their Money, but alfo all other couetous Perfons, hauing Money by them, by the example of thefe *Exchaungers*, either publickly, or priuily, either openly or fecretly, feeke the meanes and wayes, to put out their Money for the like gaines, pretending and alledging for their excufe, that they put and let out their Money, in company with thefe *Exchanging Merchants* and open Vfurers, vpon common gaine.

5. Fiftly, many *Merchants*, efpecially fuch as haue growen to great wealth and riches, be and haue beene by this meanes allured and entifed, to giue ouer and neglect all manner of honeft trade of *Merchandize*, and buying and felling, whereby they haue beene and might be profitable and commodious to there common Wealth : and to followe this filthy, vnlawfull, and too farre exceeding gaine and lucar of practifing wicked Vfurary, chopping and changing of Money, and all for the hope they conceiue thereby, to obtaine and get both a more abundant and certaine gaines, and that alfo with leffe labor, charges, perrill and aduenture.

### Chap. X.

*How & by whom the practifing of the* Merchandifing Exchange, *is the Caufe of all* exceffiue prices *in Commodities & things vendible : to the preuenting and peruerting of all lawfull* Traffick *and orderly* Dealing *within the Realme and Common-wealth of England.*

THe neceffity of conferuing an equallity in contracts of buying and felling, and a fit meanes for the exportations, and importations, of things neceffary and commodious
for

## and Merchandifing *Exchange.*

for a Common Wealth, hath caufed all wife & politick Rulers of Regions and Countries, to iudge the vfe of coyned Money, figned with fome publick *figures*, *notes*, and *carreƈts*, to be the moſt conuenient thing that could be deuifed. In like manner hath it beene iudged, and thought no leffe expedient and neceffary, by all fuch wife and experienced Men, that the fame coynes and Money ſhould haue their *indication*, *valuation*, *price*, and *eftimation*, onely by publick Rulers & common authoritie of euery Common Wealth : from the which no priuate Perſon, Order, or Societie in the fame, may or ought to ſwarue or vary, nor alter, vnder capitall paine. Forfomuch as the fayd publick valuation, is as it were the effentiall part, whereby any kinde of matter, fubſtance, or mettall, is receiued and accepted for Money, and for a lawful meane to buy & fell withall, in euery well ordered Common Wealth. And whereas the valuation of this common, and lawfull meane of price, is not well knowen, or not worthily accepted, ſtraightly & duly obferued, of all manner of Perſons, Societies, and Orders, there doth experience teach, that thereof followeth confuſion and diforder, with exceffiue and immoderate prices in the commutations of all things Vendible in the Common Wealth.

As for example, when a Prince or Ruler of any Country, doth decry and difalow any kinde of coyne and Money, which he hath fuffered before time to be currant, at a certaine price and valuation throughout his Realme, the fame coyne immediatly as it is fo decried, lefeth the eftimation it had before, and is of no value to buy any kinde of ware with, amongſt all the common people of the fame Realme ; fo that few or none will receiue the fayd Money for any manner of ware, though one would offer it at much lower price then it was before currant for : and if it chaunce any doe bargaine to take it, they will raife and inhance the price of the wares they vtter, much aboue the ordinary price thereof, & all becaufe it lacketh their Princes and common valuation of their Country. In like manner do the common people of all Countries, efteeme forraine, ſtrange, and vnknowne coynes brought vnto them, not valued by the common authority of their Country, how fine and pure foeuer the matter or mettall of them be, onely (as is fayd before) for lacking the publick valuation of the Country. Wherby it is apparant, that the Princes and publick valuation of Money,

D.

Page,16.          Of EXCHANGE in Marchandife,

ney, is of fo great efficacy and authority, in euery ciuill Common Wealth, that not only it maketh it a meane to buy things withall, but alfo it preferueth a moderation, equallity, and indifferency in the prices of all things, fo bought and fold betweene party and party. Therefore is the fayd valuation folemly, and (as a man may fay) religioufly to be kept and obferued of all manner of forts of perfons in a Common Wealth. And the Alterars & Changers of the fame by their priuate authority, are worthily to be reprehended and reproued, how craftily and fubtilly foeuer they doe it, for the manifold inconueniences they thereby bring into their Country : With a number of which, the Common Wealth of England, is fore troubled at this day , through the frequent practifing of *Merchandifing Exchange*, by the two *Societies* of *Merchants Staplerers* and *Aduenturers* of England, betweene their owne Country, and the Marting Townes of Flanders, with flights , crafts, and fubtilties : continually thereby altering the price and valuation of their Princes coyne; by the occafion whereof, all manner of wares and commodities only fold in the Realme of England, be brought and grow to fuch inordinate and exceffiue prices, as they beare at this Day : for the proofe of the premiffes, this reafon may be firft made.

Afore this *MerchandiZing Exchange* was practifed by the Englifh Merchants *Staplers* and *Aduenturers*, betweene the Marting-Townes of Flaunders, Brabant, & their owne Country, in the trafficke of Merchandife to and fro, no perfon complained vpon any manner of Merchandize, or commoditie of the Realme, nor of forraine Realmes brought into England, did at any time grow or arife to inordinate or excefsiue prices: yet were the commodities of the Realme abundantly & plentifully, yea , more liberally exported and tranfported into all forraine Countries, then at this day . But there were not in thofe dayes fo many forraine wares brought in againe into the Realme, as be at this day. For from the raigne of the famous King *Edward* the third, in whofe dayes the trade of Merchandize began cheefely to be exercifed in England, vnto the end of *Edward* the fourth, which is the fpace of aboue 150. yeeres, Acts of Parliament were prouided, thereby forcing all maner of men that occupied and fold the wares and commodities of the Realme to forraine Merchants, to raife and keepe vp the prices of them, and penalties layd vppon thofe which went a-
bout

and Merchandiſing *Exchange*.          Pge,17.

bout to diminiſh and bring downe the prices of them.

And in all this ſpace of time, not onely *Wooll* and *Felles*,
were Staple wares at *Callice*, and other *Staple-townes*, in England, and at length, *Broad-clothes* tranſported into Flaunders,
and Brabant ; but all other manner of commodities of the
Realme, as *Leather, Lead, Tinne, Butter*, and *Cheeſe*, were *Staple-
wares*, and *freelie* ( onely paying the Kings cuſtome for them)
carryed & exported *out of the Realme* into all forraine Realmes.
But ſithence theſe two Societies of Engliſh *Marting-Merchants*, practiſing the *Merchandiſing Exchange*, haue made the
exporting and tranſporting of the commodities and Merchandizes of the Realme, to the Staple of *Callice*,& Marting-townes
of Brabant, a priuate trade to themſelues, the Princes of this
Realme haue beene conſtrained to reſtraine and prohibite, not
onely the going out of certaine of the aforeſaid commodities
of the Realme ; but alſo haue beene compelled to ſtudie and
deuiſe meanes by Acts of Parliament, to bring & keep downe
the prices, as well of the commodities of the Realme : as of all
forraine Realmes. Therfore it muſt needes be concluded, that
*Merchandizing Exchange*, and the practiſing thereof, is the occaſion of this great inconueniencie and Miſchiefe raigning in
the Common-wealth of England. By the reaſon whereof, all
things be growne to exceſſiue prices.

Alſo, ſince theſe two afore-ſaide Companies of Engliſh
Merchants vſurped theſe Liberties and Priuiledges to themſelues, that the one of them ſhould tranſport only Staple wares
to the Staple of *Callice*, and the other Broad-clothes, with ſuch
other Commodities, vnto the *Marting-Townes* of Brabant,
the moſt part of all the good Townes of the Realme of England haue decayed and come to ruine, which partly hath come
to paſſe, by the reaſon that many kinde of Artificers, which
were wont to inhabite the ſaid Townes, maintaine and make
thē proſperous by ſuch artificialls as they made there : by the
meanes of theſe two fraternities of *Marting-Merchants* be vtterly deſtroyed & conſumed, for that they were not able at length
to liue by their arts and labours, theſe fore-ſaid Merchants deuiſing and cauſing the like Artificials as the ſaid Artificers made
in England, to be made in forraine Countries, and were by
them brought and tranſported into England, and ſold better
cheape ſome-what, & lower priced then thoſe of Engliſh making might be aforded. Thorough which occaſion, the Eng-

*Margin notes:*

Staples wont to be al-
wayes in England, and
not beyond Seas.

Free tranſportation of
home Commodities, na-
turall for Traffick, & beneficiall for the Cōmon-
Wealth.

Note, Staple-Townes
beeing called Mart-
Townes, began the de-
cay of Trades & Townes
in England.

D 2                                     liſh

## Of EXCHANGE in Merchandife,

lifh Artificers in continuance were worne out, becaufe none
were brought vp vnder other, to follow their faid Art & workmanfhip , that they exercifed , forfomuch as they perceiued, that they fhould not be able to liue by fuch kind of labour
in time to come; becaufe the forraine workmanfhip was more
regarded, and fooner bought then theirs. Partly alfo they haue
beene the deftruction, decay, and ruine of the faid Townes, by
taking away the trade of the Staple from the faid Townes, for
the vtterance of the commodities of the Realme, which for the
moft part of all the time, from *Edward* the third , to the end of

**Staple Townes alwaies within England, made the Realme full of Traf-ficke.** *Edward* the fourth, were kept in good Townes of England, or
at leaft fhipped from them when the Staple was kept at *Callice*,
by the occafion wherof, there was fo great refort of people vnto the faid Townes, that thereby they were enriched, and daily
profpered and flourifhed. Where fince, for lacke of like refort
and trafficke, and the deftruction of the forefaid Artificers, they
be altogethers ruinous and decayed, and neuer like to be reftored, fo long as thefe Merchants enioy theyr vfurped liberties.

Moreouer, fince thefe two Societies of Englifh Merchants,
vfurped vnto them the priuate exportations of the commodities of the Realme, the liberall, vfuall, and daily bringing in

**The hindrance of bring-ing in of Bullyon.** of Bullyon into the Realme by forraine Merchants out of all
forraine Realmes, to buy the commodities of England, hath
decayed and ceafed; and feuere and great punifhments and penalties be prouided by the Princes of fuch forraine Realmes, a-
gainft all them which fhall attempt the conueying of any fuch
things out of theyr Realmes into England : Where in times
paffed, they moft gladly fuffered and concented vnto it, for that
it was openly knowne, to all Princes and Rulers of Common-
wealths in Chriftendome, that what kinde of Merchant foe-

**Staples euer kept within England.** uer, reforted *into England to the Staple-Townes* , for the buying
and carrying away of the commodities & Merchandifes there-
of, were bound by the Acts and orders of the Realme, to pay
for them at the faid Staples, in ready gold and filuer afore their
departure from thence ; as may appeare by diuers Acts made
in diuers Kings dayes, from *Edward* the third, vnto the end of
*Edward* the fourth : and therefore at that time were all Princes
well contented, to fuffer their Merchants to carry their coynes
and Bullyon into England.

Which manner of Traffick, continued betweene England
and all other Realmes, till that thefe Merchants became to be
                                                                    a pri-

and Merchandiſing *Exchange.*

a priuate Society, and ſo vvithin a while after, compounded &
agreed with the Merchants of Holland,Zeland,Brabant, Flanders, and other Countries there-abouts, which were the buyers of the Staple-wares,to receiue their Money for ſuch Staple-
wares, as the ſayd Staplers ſold them at *Callice*, in Flemiſh
Money, at the Marting Townes of their owne Countries, rating, ſetting,and valuing the Engliſh pound, at a certaine ſtin-
ted price of Flemiſh Money, for euer thereafter to bee payed
vnto them, after the ſaid price ; which was a drift driuen of the
ſayd Staplers of England, to bring to paſſe this *Exchanging*
Traffick, to the intent they might make the returne of their
Money, from thence into England by *Merchandiſing Exchange* : whereby they made a reckoning, much more to their
priuate gaines and lucar, then to be payed in ready Money at
the Staples of *Callice*, or any place of England, according to
the olde cuſtome, although that manner of payment was
much more beneficiall, and commodious for the common
Wealth of the whole Realme, which they paſſed not vppon,
neither yet doe, ſo they may gaine and get Money.

And thus the faire Lady *Merchandiſing Exchange*, enticed
and allured the *Merchants Aduenturers* of England, to procure
themſelues in fraternitie, and to ſeeke meanes to plant their
*Marting Townes* in a forraine Realme and Country, for the vt- Townes, *a deceptio Vi-*
terance of the commodities of the Realme, becauſe they might *ſus*, to turne all Traf-
make their returne and imployments, from thence into Eng- fick beyond Seas, to
lang, by the reckoning of Money currant in the ſayd *Merchan-* the ruine of England.
*diſing Exchange* . And by this meanes, ceaſed and ended the
franck and free bringing in of Money, & Bullion into England
by forraine and ſtrange *Merchants*, after the Engliſh *Merchants*
had nuſſeled themſelues in the *Marting Townes* beyonde the
Sea, ſo that now a dayes, no Money or Bullion is brought into
England by *Merchants*, but ſecretly, and as it were, by ſtealth,
and for the reſpect of priuate gaines and profite, which they
finde thereby, after the reckoning they make thereof, by cur-
rantnes of Money in their *Merchandiſing Exchange.*

Item, when it pleaſed that famous Prince, King *Henry* the *Henry the eight.*
eight, vpon good conſiderations and purpoſes , and for the
great benefite of his people, and common Wealth, to aug-
ment and increaſe the valuation and price of his coyne and
Money, throughout all his Realme, within a little proceſſe
and countinuance of time after, it chanced by the malice and
wickednes

wickednes of men, such a quantity of currupt, and drossy
coyne of Money, to bee brought into the Realme out of forraine Countryes, by the Ministery of *Merchants* : (as it hath
beene supposed, thought, and gathered by certaine cercum-
stances) which Money being currant, as well as the true and
lawfull Money, amongst all manner of persons within the
Realme, by the reason of the likenes of the fashion, and forme
that it had with the true and lawfull Money, caused many inconueniences to rise therby at lenght, to the whole Common
Wealth : for such a meruailous desire and hastynes, entred into all kinde of Occupiers, by the lothsomnes and hatred they
conceiued of the sayd Drosse coyne, to bestow it vppon one
thing or other, that thereupon beganne to grow some disorder of prices in all wares and commodities, sold in this Kingdome : which being first perceiued by the Graue, and Father-
ly Gouernors of the Realme, in the raigne of blessed King *Edward* the sixt, they consulted together for the deuising of some
wayes to be taken, to auoyde the said disorder so begunne and
sprung. And the best meanes for that purpose was thought by
their wisdomes, to be the deminishing, of all the white currant coyne and Money of the Realme : intending by that
meanes at the length, to haue vtterly banished from thence all
such counterfeited coyne, taking leisure withall study & care,
to doe it with as much ease, and as little losse to euery State &
condition as could be deuised. But before this their godly and
most lawdable purpose, could be brought to effect, when it
was yet but in talke and consultation, and onely a rumor bruted and spred abroade that such a decry of Money should be ;

The *Merchants Aduen-
terers*, priuate shift to
preuent the Princes pur-
pose for the common
good.

The *Merchants Aduenturers* prepared withall speed possible,
Armour and defence against the losse, which they feared their
State should fall into thereby, when indeede euery person of
the Realme, ought to haue borne with a very good will the
sayd losse, for the redressing of the sayd disorder so sprung vp
in the Realme, in the prices of all things, bought and sold betweene party and party : according as the prudent and wise
Counsellors of the Kings Maiesty, had deuised and purposed
to haue brought to passe, and as the rest of all States of the
Realme would haue yeelded vnto : if the *Merchants Aduenturers*, had beene destitute of their *Exchange*. But greedy lucar
and priuate gaine, coulde not suffer their couetous harts to
beare any little losse at that present, though it should in the end
haue

and Merchandifing *Exchange.* Page,21.

haue turned to the common benefit of all the Realme. And fo forfooth without further helpe, they vfed the pollicy of *Merchandifing Exchange*, their practife wherein was as it were, to difualue and decry the price, of the Englifh pound in currant Money by the fame *Exchange*: for the paffing of Money therby betweene England, and their *Marting-Townes*. Which pound had beene currant amongft them, two and fro in the fayd *Exchange*, vntill that time, betweene 26. fh. and 30. fh. Flemifh, but then fodainely they decried and difualued it to 16. and 17. fh. Flemifh ; and at length, to 13. fh. Flemifh, before the alteration of the coyne was proclaimed : by the which occafion, the prices of all forraine wares and *Merchandizes*, rofe exceffiuely in England, as of neceffity they muft, for the leffe Flemifh Money is allowed for the Englifh pound at the *Marting-Townes*, at the other fide the Sea in their fourefayd *Exchange*, the dearer and the higher prices muft all that Country wares beare, bought there to bee tranfported into England, which for the refpect of the bafe price of th'englifh Money, muft needes be fold after the like rate in England. For whereas before vntill that time, the Englifh pound had beene worth at the fayd *Marting-Townes*, at leaft, 26. ff. Flemifh, then by this abafing of the *Exchange*, 26. ff. Flemifh was brought to bee worth at the end, 40. ff. Englifh, becaufe the fayd Englifh pound was no more in value, but 13. ff. Flemifh, in their *Merchandifing Exchange*, by which meanes the thing that coft but 13. fh. Flemifh, was fold betweene 20, and 26. ff. Englifh, in England : which manners of Sales, muft needes caufe all manner of Flemifh wares to beare exceffiue and inordinate prices there, which immoderate prices of ftrange and forraine wares, were fufficient caufe to be alledged, why all the commodities of England, did firft arife to fuch prices as they doe ftill beare, euen at this day : becaufe fo great a quantity, of the fayd Flanders wares were brought thether, and bee in fo great vfe, fo much bought and fpent, of all manner of forts of perfons in England.

Yet notwithftanding, the faid Flemifh wares were not the next and principall caufe, that the Englifh commodities did fo rife and exceed in price : but rather the two Companies of Englifh Merchants, the *Staplers* & *Aduenturers*, for they made fo gainefull reckoning at their Marting-Townes, by returning home theyr Money by *Merchandifing Exchange*, that they paft

not

## Of EXCHANGE in Marchandife,

not what price they gaue and paid for the commodities of the Realme in England; for the *Staplers* made aboue 28.fs. Flemifh of euery pound Englifh they folde theyr wares and Merchandizes for, by an old compofition taken betweene them and the Merchants of thofe parts, by the which manner of reckoning, they got aboue 60. in the hundred in England.

The like reckonings made the *Merchants Aduenturers*, by the fales of theyr commodities, although theyr gaines were not fo certaine, becaufe they had no fuch compofition with the Merchants of thofe parts, as the *Staplers* had. Yet fold they after fuch rate, that they made of euery Englifh pound, betweene 26. and 28. fhillings Flemifh, all the while the *Exchange*

*Admirable Vfury, after the rate of 400. pound, or 500. pound, made of 100. pound in one yeere.* came from thence, betweene 16. and 18. fh. for the Englifh pound. And fo amounteth theyr gaines to aboue 50. and 60. in the 100. for a Moneths fpace, or at the moft, for the fpace of one Mart, making and returning home theyr Money by their *Exchange.* During the time of which *Exchange*, there was fuch a fpeedy and quicke trafficke betweene England and the Marting-Townes, and all for the loue of this lucar & great gaines, that no commoditie in England tranfportable for thofe parts, could lye by them vnbought. And this meanes and practife of the two Companies of Merchants, in following the Trafficke & *Merchandifing Exchange*, was the principall caufe, why both forraine wares, and Englifh, grew to fuch excefsiue prices in England. For when all other forts and conditions of perfons of the Realme, perceiued, that the bettering and amending of the coine of Mony of the Realme, was nothing efteemed amongft the Merchants, but rather leffe regarded, as though it had bin leffe in value then it was before, forfomuch as they daily encreafed the price of the wares they brought from the Marting-Townes to be fold in England: All other States likewife, beganne to paffe and fet nothing by it, and fo rather couited to beftow it rafhly and vnaduifedly in one thing or other, what price fo euer things did beare, then difcreetly and warily to forefee and looke afore-hand, how they might beftow it, for the bringing downe of the immoderate prices that euery thing was growne vnto, becaufe they were perfwaded, that the faid Englifh coyne, was no more worth then the *Exchanging Merchants* valued it at. In fo much, that the Clothiers which came to *Blackwell-hall*, fet theyr pices on their Clothes, according as they learned of the Merchants the price of Money came

from

and Merchandiſing *Exchange.* Page;23.

from the *Marting-Townes* in their *Merchandiſing Exchange* into England, and not according to the valuation thereof giuen & proclaimed by their Prince. So that Merchants brought all men to follow theyr bow, as concerning the eſtimation of Engliſh Money, where they in the meane ſeaſon, paſſed not what they gaue in England for the Commodities thereof, though they ſold them to no profit at the Marts, becauſe the returning of the Money from the Marting-townes by theyr *Merchandiſing Exchange,* was ſo profitable and gainefull vnto them, during this baſe and low price of *Exchange.*

*Merchants gouerne the Common-wealth.*

Likewiſe, whereas the Queenes Maieſtie, by the aduice of her prudent and graue Counſellers, mooued with great loue, zeale and pitty towards all ſtates of perſons, but ſpecially towards the poorer ſort, oppreſſed and burthened with the exceſſiue prices of all things vendible within her Graces realme, which ſprung and roſe (as the common fame went) by the occaſion of the Droſſy and monſtrous Baſe-Money, currant and ſet forth, or at the leaſt way, permitted to be currant and ſet foorth, by her Graces predeceſſors throughout the Realme : like a moſt godly and louing Princeſſe, hath taken away and aboliſhed, all the ſaid courſe and Droſſy Money & coyne, and for it reſtored as fine ſiluer coyne, as euer was currant in the Realme before, or rather finer; hoping, meaning, and intending thereby, to haue taken away there-with, the corrupneſſe and droſſines of prices, which likewiſe all thinges ſold in her Maieſties Realme at that time was corrupted with : As without doubt (if no ſubtill pollicie had come betweene, to haue letted and ſtopped her Graces wholeſome purpoſe therein) it would haue effected. For ſome likelihood thereof began a little while to appeare, by the falling of the prices of victuall at the Markets, when it was firſt noiſed and bruted abroade, that by a certaine day appointed and limited, no Money but ſuch as was of fine Siluer, or Gold, ſet forth by her Maieſty, or by her Graces Predeceſſors, ſhould be paiable or currant thereafter, within the Realme : and that all the droſſy coyne, ſhould be brought to her Mint of London, where euery man ſhould receiue for the ſame pure and fine Siluer Money of her Graces coyne : whereat all perſons much reioyced, although for the preſent euery ſtate of the Realme knew they ſhould receiue a loſſe thereby. Yet the conſideration of the benefit that was to come therafter, perſwaded them to beare the preſent loſſe with

ELIZABETH.

E. **a** good

Page,24.          Of E XCHANGE in Merchandiſe,

a good will. But heere blind couetouſneſſe, with greedy gaine
and lucar raigning in the *Marting-Merchants*, ſtirred vp theyr
wits to practiſe their old ſubtill pollicie for the ſauing of theyr
ſtate from loſſe,which was to bring downe and abaſe the Engliſh pound in their *Merchandiſing Exchange*, for the returning
home of theyr Money into England from their *Marting-townes*
at the other ſide the Sea; and as they did before, in the bleſſed
time of King *Edward*, ſo now at the firſt bruite and rumour of
this Queenes moſt noble and euer praiſeable enterpriſe, they
cauſed the price of her pound of Money to be valued in theyr
*Exchange* but at 16. and 17. ſs. Flemiſh : by which occaſion, as
it came to paſſe before at other reformations of Monies , the
prices of all thoſe Countrey commodities, and alſo of all other
forraine Nations and Countries, did not onely keepe theyr
old exceſſiue and deere prices in England , but did rather encreaſe and waxe higher, and ſo did likewiſe the commodities
of the Realme follow after, not onely becauſe forraine wares
did ſo, but ſpecially for the haſtines men made to beſtow their
Money vpon them, by the examples of the *Merchants Aduenturers*, who ſpared not to buy all manner of wares tranſporta-
ble beyond the Sea, at what price ſoeuer was demaunded for
thē, for that this returning home of Money by *Exchange*,made
them great gayners, and would be a way & meane, if the worſt
fell, to keepe and ſaue them from all loſſe and danger in the fall
of the Money, which all other ſtates and conditions hauing
theyr traffick within the Realme, looked to haue ſuſtained and
borne by the reformation of the ſaid Money , which theſe
*Merchants Aduenturers* did prouide to auoyde, through this
theyr peculier traffick and practiſe,by toſſing and turning their
Money, betweene England and their *Marting-Townes*, by the
ſayd *Merchandiſing Exchange*.

For although the commodities of the Realme, which they
tranſported to the *Marts*, roſe from 4. li. to 6. li. and 7. li. Engliſh, yet might they ſell them at the *Marts*, as good cheape as e-
uer they did, and be greater gainers then in times paſt. For ſo
much, as though cuſtomably they did make afore times 30. &
34. ſs. Flemiſh of a pound Engliſh in theyr ſales , after which
rate,they made 6. and 7. pound, 8. ſs. Flemiſh, of 4. li. Engliſh,
and ſo 150. pound, and 160. li. Flemiſh , of a 100. li. Engliſh,
yet becauſe they returned theyr Money by *Exchange* at that
time after 28. ſs. and 30.ſs. or 32.ſs. Flemiſh for the Engliſh
                                                              pound,

### and Merchandifing *Exchange*.

pound, theyr gaines paſſed not aboue 13. in the hundred.
Where now felling their commodities at the ſaid prices of 6. &
7. li. Flemiſh, though they paid alſo for them ſo much in England of Engliſh Money, (after which reckoning they did or do
make of 100. li. Engliſh, but 100. Flemiſh ) yet returning home
their Money, after this reckoning and low *Exchange* of 16. and
17. ſs. Flemiſh for the Engliſh pound, they got betweene 17. &
25. in the hundred, notwithſtanding they ſold not vnder 24. &
26. ſs. Flemiſh for the pound Engliſh during the ſaid lowe *Exchange :* after which rate, although they made but 120. & 130.
li. Flemiſh of their 100. li. Engliſh, yet made they in England
at the returne of their Money, by the foreſaid low *Exchange,* a-
boue 150. and 160. li. Engliſh of their 100. li. tranſported firſt
from thence to the Marts. By which manner of reckoning,
theyr gaines roſe to aboue 50. and 60. in the 100. for the ſpace
of one Mart. And ſo by this policy of *Merchandiſing Exchange,*
Merchants Aduenturers haue not only ſaued themſelues at all
falls of Mony paſſed in England, & haue hindred the Queenes
Maieſties purpoſe, for the bringing downe of the exceſſiue pri-   *Note.*
ces of things, in the vtter aboliſhing of all the droſſy & corrupt
Money in the Realme : but there-withall , they haue beene e-
uermore the occaſion and Authors of the diſorder , and of the
rayſing of all manner of wares and commodities in the Realme
more and more, to ſuch exceſſiue and inordinate price, as eyther they haue borne or doe beare at this day ; neither is there
any other kinde of State or Perſons in the Realme, that eyther
could haue deuiſed, or els that went about to fruſtrate her Maieſties purpoſes, in reducing all the baſe coynes to ſo pure or
fine ſubſtance or matter , but onely theſe *Merchants Aduenturers,* by the practiſe of their *fraudulent Exchange :* for all other
maner of perſons of the Realme, would gladly haue borne the
loſſe of the Money, according to the Queenes Maieſties meaning, becauſe they perceiued, that they ſhould thereby thereafter ſaue more for the buying of things at moderate and reaſonable prices, then they ſhould loſe by the reformation of the
coyne ; for the cauſe beeing taken away of thoſe exceſſiue prices (which was as all men ſaide, the droſſy and baſe coyne and
Money of the Realme) the effect which proceedeth thereof,
muſt needs alſo haue ceaſed and vaniſhed away . But ſeeing it
hath not ſo come to paſſe, men muſt needes ſay and confeſſe,
that ſome other ſubtiltie and policie, beſides the foreſaid droſſy

Page, 26. ## Of EXCHANGE in Merchandife,

*Merchandifing Ex-*
*change.*

coyne, hath caufed this inordinate prices, which is *Merchan-difing Exchange* ; practifed by *Merchants Aduenturers*, as is heretofore proued.

I т в м , the fame practifing of *Merchandifing Exchange*, is the meanes whereby all things doth continew deere , and at high prices ftill in England : for like as is before declared, the *Merchants Aduenturers* , for their owne priuate lucar & gaine, by the pollicy thereof, caufed all things in the Realme to rife to immoderate and exceffiue prices : altering the valuation of the Englifh pound, without reafon or equity , by difualuing, and bringing downe the prices thereof, farre vnder the value it ought to haue had in the fayd *Exchange* : which pollicy they inuented, at the fall of the Money , to preuent the loffe their State and Company fhould haue receiued thereby.

So after the fall was proclaimed in England , for the loue of the like priuate gaines and lucar which they had tafted of fo fweetely at the fame time , euer fince they haue kept the price vnder the fumme of Money it ought to bee worth in the fame *Exchange*, and thus paffing and returning their Money in-to England vniuftly and without equity , they ftay all man-ner of wares and commodities, at the vnreafonable and ex-ceffiue prices they firft brought them to , or rather doe raife them higher.

For neuer fince the Queenes Maieftie , reduced all the cor-rupt coyne of the Realme to pure and fine Siluer , the price of the Englifh pound hath come from the *Marting-Townes* into England, aboue 22. ff. 2. pence Flemifh, at Vfance by the fayd *Exchange*, where before till the firft fall was noifed in England, the coyne being moft droffy and corrupt, the price of the fayd pound came from thence betweene, 26. and 28. ff. Flemifh. To the which price the fayd *Merchants* , fhould doe their en-deuour to bring it againe , rather then as they doe, keepe it at fo vile a price, and farre vnder the price that it is efteemed, and valued to be worth, in valued Money of that Country, fet foorth by the Prince thereof, forafmuch as all the Money of the Realme, is now fo fine and pure. But greedy lucar hath no

*Mark well the vfe and*
*aduantage which the*
*Marchants Aduenturers,*
*make of their fpeciall*
*Mart Townes, beyond*
*the Seas, to the good of*
*their Country.*

reafon , which caufeth that both the *Merchants Aduenturers* of England, and alfo the *Merchants* of the *Marting-Townes*, doe (as it were) by a confpiracy betweene them , keepe the value of the Englifh pound, at fo vniuft and vile price in their *Mer-chandifing Exchange* ; for by reafon thereof, doe the *Merchants*

of

and Merchandifing *Exchange*.

of thofe parts fell there wares to Englifh *Merchants* , for meruailous much more gaines,then euer they did before,and buy
the commodities of England againe of them as good cheape,
as euer they did at any time before : likewife the fayd *Merchants* of England, gaine and get much more then euery they
did , whether they make imployments of their Money home
in wares , or in Money by *Exchange* from the *Marting-
Townes*.

Therefore it appeareth, that as this bafe, vile, and low price
of the Englifh pound , in their *Merchandifing Exchange*, did
raife at the firft, all manner of wares and commodities, to immoderate & exceffiue prices in England : fo by the fame *Merchants*,hauing gathered fo fweete and pleafant gaines,doe they
ftay and keepe them at thofe fayd immoderate , and exceffiue
prices, from the which there will no way be found to remoue
them, fo long as the *Merchants* may liberally at their pleafure,
vnder-price the Queenes Maiefties coyne of England, in their
*Exchange* : and fo trade and Traffick therewith,betweene England, and the fayd *Marting-Townes* , becaufe of the great commoditie, gaine , and profit the *Merchants* of both Countries
receiue by the fame.

Moreouer, the Queenes Maieftie of England , receiueth
great loffe and dammage at the *Merchants* hands, by taking or
prouiding Money of them by this their *Merchandifing Exchange* , according as they practife it now a dayes : for where
the *Merchants Aduenturers* , and *Staplers* of England, efteeme
the Englifh pound in their *Merchandifing Exchange*, not aboue
22.ff. 6. pence Flemifh, from London to Antwerp, at *Vfance*,
yet is not that the true and iuft valuation it ought to haue in
currant Money of the fayd *Exchange* , forfomuch as by the
publick valuation of that Country Money, proclaymed by
the commandement of the Prince, anno. 1559. the Englifh
pound of Money is efteemed to be worth, of the fame valued
Money, 22. ff. 6. pence Flemifh at leaft, which valewed Money is better by 6.pence, and 12.pence in a pound , then the
currant Money by *Exchange*.

So then , when one deliuereth Money in London by *Merchandifing Exchange*, to be payd againe at Antwerp , *at fight*,
he ought to receiue there for his Englifh pound of Money, at
the leaft, 23. ff. Flemifh, of this *Exchanging* Money , and after
the Order of *Merchants*,in the fayd *Exchange*, if it be deliuered

E 3                                                                    for

Page,28.          Of E X C H A N G E in Marchandife,

for *Vfance*, he ought to receiue 23. fh.6. pence Flemifh.

Neither can the *Merchants* giue any good reafon, why the price of the Englifh pound in their *Exchange*, fhould be efteemed at this day but at 22.fh. 6. pence, feeing it is no leffe worth in the valued Money of the fayd Country.

For after their olde Order of their *Exchange*, when the Englifh pound was valued in thofe parties to bee worth 26. fh. 8. pence Flemifh of the Princes Money, the fayd pound in currunt Money of that *Exchange*, was worth 28. fh. fo that then their was 4. Grotes of *Exchanging* Money allowed more to the Englifh pound at the leaft, then of valued Money, yea moft commonly it came from thence into England, by their *Exchange* at 30.fh. Flemifh, and fomtime at 34.fh. of the fayd Money, & from hence it went at a more and higher price in their fayd *Exchange*.

Therefore according to the proportion of the prices of Money then, and now at this day : the price of the Englifh pound from hence ought not to bee vnder 23. fh. 10. pence, & from hence at 24.fh. 4. pence, for from hence by the Order of *Exchange*, vnto the *Marting-Townes*, the price of the fayd pound is higher and more worth, then from thence hether commonly, by 6. pence Flemifh.

Wherefore if truth and equity were vfed in this *Merchandifing Exchange*, or if the forefayd Englifh *Merchants* frequented the *Marting-Townes* beyond the Sea, for the preferment of the Common Wealth of their Country, and not rather altogether for their owne priuate gaines and lucar, they would neuer maintaine this piraticall *Exchange*, that they practife now a dayes, efteeming the Englifh pound to be leffe worth of their *Exchanging* Money, then the Prince alloweth it to be worth of his valued Money, which was neuer feene before thefe dayes.

For feeing their *Exchanging* Money is worfe by 6. pence & 12. pence in a pound, then the Princes valued Money, why fhould not more thereof bee giuen and allowed for the Englifh pound, then of valued Money according as it hath beene accuftomed, to bee euer heere before when the Prince of that Country allowed 26. fh. 8. pence of his valued Money for the Englifh pound.

Therefore that the Queenes Maieftie, might be exonerated of fo great loffe, when her affaires doe require the forefayd
meane

## and Merchandiſing *Exchange*. Page,29.

meane to prouide Money, and to the end ſome way of reformation, might alſo be prouided for the redreſſing of the exceſſiue prices, that ſpecially all forraine wares be ſold for in England: the foreſayd *Merchants Staplers* and *Aduenturers*, would
bee by ſome order compelled to bring the Engliſh pound, to
this aforeſayd iuſt price & valuation, it ought to haue in their
vniuſt and polling *Exchange*, & then ſhall they bring the Sales
of their commodities, at the *Marting Townes* to be ſold at 26.
and 27. ſſ. Flemiſh, and vpwards for the Engliſh pound: for
the Sales of their wares muſt bee 2. ſh. in a pound aboue the
price it hath in their *Merchandiſing Exchange*, or els ſhall they
make no reckoning to liue by.

And ſo after this reckoning, raiſing the price of their *Exchange*, ſhall they be able to ſell in England, and afford all forraine commodities, 25. in the hundred better cheape, and vnder the price they ſell them now a dayes: which reckoning
ſhall induce ſome manner of reformation, in the diſordinate
prices which all wares beare at this day, to the great eaſe of all
the Common Wealth.

After the ſame ſort, when the ſayd *Marting-Merchants* venture into Spaine, although they can deuiſe no ſuch way and
meanes to practiſe their *Exchange* thether, as they doe to there
*Marting-Townes*, yet by the example thereof, they occupy in
that Country as ſubtill practiſe, and as iniurious, and hurtfull to
the Common Wealth of their Country, as their *Exchange*.

For when they beſtow xx. Nobles in the commodities of
England, to be tranſported into Spaine, at the comming thether withall, they make not their reckoning to ſell their wares,
to make their Engliſh Money good againe in Spaniſh Money,
that is, to make of euery Engliſh Noble 15. *Rialls* of plate, and
of euery 5. ſh. Engliſh. 11. *Rialls*, or a ſingle Ducate of Spaine,
which were to make of euery pounds worth of Engliſh wares,
4. Ducates in Spaniſh Money: but they make their reckoning
to ſel their wares there, as the Ducates were valued in England,
when the coyne and Money of England was moſt baſe and
droſſy, after the reckoning they make of an Engliſh Noble, but.
11. *Rialls* or a ſingle Ducate in Spaine.

So where they ſhould ſell the 20. Nobles Engliſh, for 26. or
27. Ducats Spaniſh, if they were profitable *Merchants* for their
Country, with ſome gaines towards their charges, they content themſelues now a dayes, rather then faile, to make of the
20. Nobles

**Page,30.**        Of EXCHANGE in Matchandiſe,

20. Nobles Engliſh, but 20. Ducats Spaniſh, and ſo turne the matter cleane contrary, deuiſing afore-hand at their returning home into England, to make by the Sales of ſuch Spaniſh wares as they bring into England, not onely 20. Nobles Engliſh, of 20. Ducats Spaniſh, but within theſe few yeeres they haue priced Spaniſh wares after ſuch ſort, that they haue ☞ made of euery Spaniſh ſingle Ducate, betweene 8. and 10. ſh. Engliſh.

Which vnreaſonable reckoning they were moſt diligent to make, when the Engliſh pound was moſt vily priced in their *Merchandiſing Exchange* : and that was alwayes at ſuch time as when either the Queenes Maieſtie that now is, or any of her ☞ prodeceſſors : were moſt ſtudious by the aboliſhing of the ſayd droſſy and baſe coyne then currant, to haue brought downe the exceſſiue prices by their ſubtilty, raiſed vpon all things in England.

For at ſuch times, the ſaid *Marting Mearchants* haue alwayes thought beſt and moſt fitteſt to take occaſion to raiſe, and enhaunce the prices of all manner of things in their owne Country, to the entent thereby to decline and auoyde the loſſe that ſhould be borne by the reformation of the coyne & Money, and therewithall did they venture moſt buſily, their owne Country commodities into Spaine, in greater number then euer they were wount to doe before, and all becauſe of this new manner of reckoning, to make of euery Spaniſh Ducate 8. or 10. ſh. Engliſh, in the Sales of thoſe Country wares.

Through which occaſion, they haue alſo raiſed the commodities of that Country, to double and treble the price that euer they were wont to be ſold for in Spaine : inſomuch, that the wiſe and diſcreete men of that Country, wiſh that the *Mar-* *Note,* *ting Merchants* might be kept from the trade of that Country, two or three yeeres together, for then they ſay that the Wines of thoſe Partes, would not bee much more worth then the caske they be put in : And ſo likewiſe of Oyles, and other commodities thereof which now be vnreaſonable deere : and yet doe they ſell their owne Country commodities in that Country, not only as baſely and low priced as euer they did ꞏ but al *Note.* ſo haue brought them to bee in no regarde or eſtimation throughout all the country, where they haue brought all thoſe Country wares to bee ſold in England, for thrice as much as a foretimes they were wount to be ſold in England, which be

vnreaſonable

and Merchandifing *Exchange.* Page,31.
vnreafonable and exceffiue prices.

Yet can they not well fell them vnder thofe prices to be any gayners, they leefe fo much in the Sales of their owne commodities which they fell in thofe parts, although they needed not to doe fo, if they kept any *Merchantlike* Order in the tranfporting of their commodities into thofe parts: and in the Sales thereof at their comming thether, as other *Merchants* of the Realme haue done in times paft, when they made euer reckoning to make in the Sales of their commodities in that Country, 15. Rialls of plate of euery Englifh Nobles worth of ware they brought thether, which gaines is fufficient towards the charges.

So might wife and difcreete *Merchants* doe now at this day, as well as they which were wife in times paft did ; for the commodities of England, be as neceffary and commodious for * This Treatife was writthe Country at this day as euer they were before, and therfore ten about the time of the would they giue for them * as much Money as euer they did, Colloquy of Bruges, whereof I *poore* and *plaine* W R I T E R of this *Treatife*, haue aunis, 1564. et 1565. had good experience, *euen in thefe dayes.*

---

## An *Abridgement* of the fpeciall Inconueniences to *this Realme of England, handled in the forefayd tenth Chapter.*

FIrft, that from tranfporting of the *Store,* and tranflating of the *Staples* (fometimes held at *Callice* and other *good Townes* in *England*) to priuat *Mart-Townes* in *Forraine Countries,* hath proceeded the principall occafion of the ruine and decay of moft of the *Ports, Hauens, Townes,* and *Cittles* of this Realme, & the ouerthrow of fundry Artificers and Trades dwelling within them, moft neceffary to haue beene maintained for the generall good of the Common-Wealth, and fpeciall reliefe of the poore.

Secondly, That *Merchants* by the Vnderpricing of the coyne of this Realme in there *Merchandifing Exchange,* at their priuat *Mart-Townes,* haue beene the impediment, that neither the Queenes Maieftie, nor her Predeceffors, could bring to effect the thing which they went about, by reforming and refining the droffy and lothfome coyne, and Money currant in

F. the

Page.32.

### Of EXCHANGE in Merchandiſe, the Realme.

Thirdly, the ſayd *Merchants*, by the practiſing of their *Merchandiſing Exchange*, were the originall cauſe why all manner of wares, *Merchandizes*, and commodities, as well of the Realme of England, as of all other forraine Realmes, riſe to huge, immoderate, and exceſſiue prices.

Fourthly, that all the excellent and neceſſary commodities of England, bee vnprofitably exported and tranſported into forraine Countries at this day, forſomuch as by the occaſion of their *Merchandiſing Exchange*, they bee better cheape ſolde abroade, then they coſt in England; to the great diſorder, and hinderance of the Common-Wealth.

Fiftly, the Queenes Maieſtie is greatly defrauded by the ſayd *Exchange*, when her Maieſties affaires doe conſtraine her to prouide Money by that meanes at the foreſayd *Merchants* hands, (contrary to the truth and valution of her owne coyne) and ſo likewiſe be her Ambaſſadors, ſent in her Maieſties affaires and meſſages into any forraine Realme, when ſoeuer they haue neede to prouide Money by the ſayd *Exchange*.

Sixtly, by the practiſing of the ſayd *Exchange*, all manner of Gold and Siluer is continually conuaied, carried, and tranſported out of the Realme, and is the let and impediment, why neither Bullyon of Gold or Siluer, is ſo liberally and freely brought into the ſame as in times paſt it hath beene.

Seauenthly & laſtly, the ſayd *Exchange* cauſeth, through the vile, baſe, and vntrue valuation the foreſayd *Merchants* keepe the Engliſh pound at in their foreſayd *Exchange*, being ſo farre vnder the price it ought to haue; that theſe immoderate and exceſſiue prices, which they haue brought all things to be ſold at in England, cannot be diminiſhed, brought downe, or mittigated, to moderate, reaſonable, and indefferent prices.

———————————

and Merchandiſing *Exchange.* Page.33.

## *A generall Concluſion.*

THis Treatiſe *thus ended, hath for warrant and Credite theſe foure Circumſtances : probability of* Reaſon, *plaines of* Stile, *ſpeciall* Experience , *and* Time *of writing . From whence this* Concluſion *beeing drawne, is heereunto added. That* KINGS *and* KINGDOMS *are heauenly* Relatiues. *And* TRVTH *hath ſaid it, That the Deſire of* Money, *is the roote of all* Euill, *& that* Couetouſnes *is flat* Idolatry . *Which ſtanding moſt true, it followes by Conſequence , that* MERCHANDISING EX-CHANGE *is that* Laborinth *of Errors & priuate* Practiſe, *whereby (though* KINGS *weare* Crownes, *& ſeem abſolutely to raigne) particuler* BANKERS, *priuate* SOCIETIES *of* Merchants, *& Couetuous Perſons, (whoſe End is* Priuate gayne*)are able to ſuſpend their* Counſailes, *& controle their* Pollicies: *offering euen* Bountie *to* KINGS, *the Fountaines of* Goodnes, *& lending* Mony *to* Soueraigne STATES *and* EMPERORS *themſelues , that onely can make* Coyne, *and ſhould haue to giue largely , and lende vnto others . Thus making* KINGS *to be* Subiects, *and* VAS-SALLES *to be* Kings. *Such hath been the ſtrength of that Staine and Stay of* Pietie, *that contempt of* Iuſtice, *that ſeede of* Diſſention, *that world of* Warres, *and Art of* Witch-craft, VSVRIE. *Such is and will be the power thereof at all occaſions : till* KINGS *and* COVNSAILERS *take their owne Charge in hand , and (next to* RELIGION *that ſanctifies all ) relieue & maintaine the* Nurſe *of* IVSTICE, *that rectifies all. To wit,* free-borne TRAFFICK, *I meane in* ENGLAND, *and* Engliſh TRAFFICK.

*In Magnis voluiſſe ſat eſt, ſunt cætera* DIVVM.

*1.Tim.6.15.*
*Coloſſ. 3. 5.*

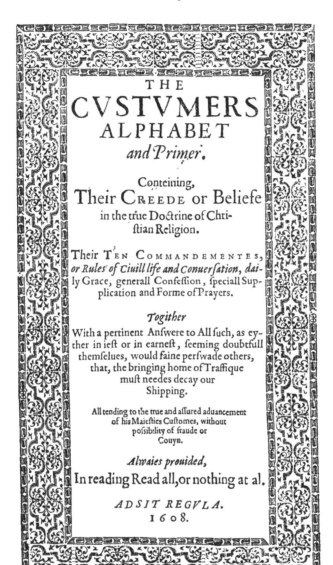

THE
# CVSTVMERS
ALPHABET
*and Primer.*

Conteining,
Their CREEDE or Beliefe
in the true Doctrine of Chri-
ſtian Religion.

Their TEN COMMANDEMENTES,
*or Rules of Ciuill life and Conuerſation,* daily Grace, generall Confeſſion, ſpeciall Sup-
plication and Forme of Prayers.

*Togither*

With a pertinent Anſwere to All ſuch, as eyther in ieſt or in earneſt, ſeeming doubtfull
themſelues, would faine perſwade others,
that, the bringing home of Traffique
muſt needes decay our
Shipping.

All tending to the true and aſſured aduancement
of his Maieſties Cuſtomes, without
poſſibility of fraude or
Couyn.

*Alwaies prouided,*
In reading Read all, or nothing at al.

*ADSIT REGVLA.*
1608.

# A

## A

a. e. i. o. u.

✠ b. c. d. f. g. h. k. l. m. n. p. q. r. s.
t. w. x. z. &per se. Con, per se.
title, title, Est, Amen.

1. 2. 3. 4. 5. 6. 7. 8. 9. 10.

# TO THE RIGHT HO-
## NORABLE MY SPECIAL GOOD
LLL: *THOMAS* BARON OF *BVCKHVRST*,
Earle of *Dorfet*, and *Lord-Treafurer* of England. *Henrie*
Lord *Howard* of *Marnehill*, Earle of *Northampton*, & Lord-
Warden of the *Cinq-Ports*. And *Robert* Baron of *Effen-*
*den*, Vicount *Cranbourne*, Earle of *Salifbury*, and Principall Secre-
tarie of State to the K I N G s Maieftie. All Knights of the
moft Noble Order of the G A R T E R, and Lords of his
Highneffe moft Honourable
*Preuy-Counfell.*

 *Y Dutie and Seruice to you honorable*
*L.L.L. euery way humbly premifed:*
*I haue thought it good to prefent the*
*fame with the loyall Endeuours of a*
*willing mind, though feeble wit, and*
*weaker brayne; the Argument I con-*
*feffe being of a higher pitch and grea-*
*ter compaffe, then I did imagine whē*
*I tooke it in hand.*

*Hazard at the firft did much difcourage me, & in the mids,*
*by Friendes I had been diffwaded in regard of the paines, but for*
*th'*Enthoufiafme *ftill founding in mine eares.*

    " Ton Ame ne doibt, ta flamme eft fi diuine, &c.
*Thy Soule is fo befet by vowes that are deuine,*
*Thou fhalt not tread amiffe, why fhould thy hart decline'?*
*By whofe perfwafion whē I had but begun, my Confcience thrnft*
*me forward, and thus preuailed at laft.*

    " Ie veulx qu'un. bel ofer, &c.
*Then dangers ftand afide, tis* G o o D N E s *calls me to it,*
*If ought doe put me by, t'is* W i s D o m s *hand fhall do it.*

*My ftayes befides were thefe : That* T R v T H *was all my*
*Ground, which as* Time *did fuggeft,* Experience *ftill fup-*
*plyd. My Pen* O P O R T E T *made, and was euer apt to mend :*
*But* O R D E R *gaue the* Forme, *which I moft of all fufpected,*

A 2. *and*

## THE EPISTLE.

*and ſaw ſome cauſe to doubt , till* PRAYER *in concluſion did
vndertake to perfect or perſwade the beſt. So that if the* Forme
*for the plaineneſſe may paſſe without offence , the* Matter *for im
portance may perhaps deſerue a double and treble reading.*

The Matter *indeed is* TRAFFICK, *I meane our freeborne*
Traffick, *that Nurſe of* IVSTICE *which feedes vs all , and
(heere handled* ab Effectis,*) containes thoſe very* CVSTVMS
*for which the* Schollers *in all the* Free-ſchooles, *of our* SOVE-
RAIGNES *daily* Tributes , *haue ſo long beene ſubiect to bayting and beating : and for which my ſelfe , of late ſo graciouſly
chidden, was forſt (by ſpeciall commaund,) to ſpell againe my
Letters, and con this* PRIMER.

*Now be it what it may be , as your* WISDOMS *ſhall
eſteeme, and as* GOD *ſhall giue ſucceſſe , (to whom the Glorie
of* All *in* All *is due,) three principall reaſons haue moou'd me to
preſent it to your* LLL: *view, in the names of All the reſt. The*
FIRST, *beſides his* knowledge *and ſufficiencie of ſkill, by eminencie and* Place *hath ſpeciall* Experience *to iudge of what I
write. The* SECOND, *keepes the Keyes of all thoſe verie*
Potts *that lymits out my Charge, for whoſe ſakes indeede reci-
proke Loue did inſtant me to write. And the* THIRD *was the
meanes to make me firſt a* Cuſtumer, *when I had giuen it ouer
and little thought vppon it. For theſe regards (I ſay) and treble reſpects, (mine Ends beeing no wayes priuat, myne Intentions alwaies Loyall, diſclayming no mans Perſon, but Sinne and
Diſhoneſtie,) I held it meeteſt and ſafeſt , to preſent my* Selfe,
*and the Fruites of all my Vowes, to your L L L: mylde Cenſures
and Protections. By whoſe ſpeciall Fauouts, as I am but what I
am, ſo I deſire but to be knowne*

Your L L L: by ſeuerall Duties
deuotedly bound


*Tho: Milles.*

To the G R A V E S T and G O D L I E-
VV I S E *in Higheſt Authority.*
( ⸫ )

**Gentleman,** a friend , and a louer of
learning, comming into a Free-Schoole,
where diuers young Schollers were learning their Grammers, deſirous to feele
how they thry ude at their Bookes by ſome familiar
Queſtion, demaunded , (their Huiſhers ſtanding
by) *VVhen an Engliſh is giuen to be made into Latine,*
*whats firſt to be done ?* The aunſwer is eaſie: namelie,
*To ſeeke out the Principall Verbe :* yet all ſtoode ſilent
and halfe amazed, till (\* **one**) at the laſt, (the Queſtion repeated, and he vrged to ſay , *VVhat was to be*
*done*) replyed; **No harme ſir I hope, at leaſt,**
**that I wote of.** Which the **Gentleman** taking in very good part, ſuſpecting rather ignorance
in the Huiſhers, then want of wit in the Scholler, departed ſmyling.

Moſt **Reuerend**, and **Right Honourable,**
This Queſtion and Aunſwere, includeth the ſtate of
all the Students in the Free-Schooles of *our Soue-*
*raignes Cuſtumes,* where ſuch as the Teachers be, ſuch
are the Schollers. There is a reaſon for all thinges.
And the reaſon heereof is not ſo much , for want of

B. wit,

## *The* CVSTVMERS

wit, in the Learners; **To deale iuſtly betweene the Prince and the people,** which in this kinde of Doctrine is the *Principall Verbe,* as in their angry and haſtie Huiſhers, who while the *Graue-Maiſters* and *Moderators* of the Schooles, were diſtracted, and buſied in the ſtudy and practiſe of higheſt poynts of Learning, haue vſed no Method, but beating the Schollers.

" *Qui paria eſſe volunt peccata. Ipſique laborant*
" *Cum ventum ad verum eſt, Senſus moreſque repugnant,*
" *Atque ( ipſa* VTILITAS,*) Iuſti prope mater & Æqui.*

" That make all faults alike, yet they themſelues are dome,
" When Truth in queſtion falls, each finger ſeemes a thorne,
" And *(Profits-*ſelfe) empaird, whence *Iuſt* & *Right* ſhould come.

Which kinde of Diſcipline diſcouraging all men, and driuing many good wits from the Schoole, to the ſecrete iniury of the whole Common-wealth; forcde me to my Booke, and as well as I could, to *Analiſe* my leſſon, meaning therby with the fore-ſaid playne Scholler, **No harme at all.** Such therefore as it was, I did briefely ſet forth in a \* *Diſcourſe* then following. The matter whereof partly drawne from mine owne patience and experience, & partly obſerued and learned from others: the Forme vvas meerely mine owne, and had for my warrant the Rules of my Grammer.

\* The CVSTOMERS Apologie.

And ſince *Thinges are then well done, when thinges are well taken;* to cleare and acquite me from partiall clamor, and the ſinne of preſumtion; I ſhewd, That the Will applyant to Reaſon, was guiltleſſe of paſsion, and Nature ouer-borne appeales to Neceſsitie. *Quæ quod cogit, ipſa, ſolet vtiq; defendere.* For hard in deede,

## Alphabet *and* Primer.

deede, and aboue meafure extreame fhould theyr cafes feeme, that ftill fubiect to beating, might neyther bemoane themfelues, nor bee fuffered to cry. And fo much the rather, when as (**ſo farre as I wot of**) in all thofe Complaints, there was nothing concluded nor included, at leaft intended thereby, but a naturall Defence of an honeft reputation in that kind of Calling, which the Law it felfe in great wifedome hath layde out, and referued **for men of the beſt ſort onely**, and a dutifull zeale to find out thereby *The principall Verbe.*

---

¶ Thus farre forth, & in thefe very words, hauing fometimes vndertaken a priuate Defence in a Caufe of importance both publique and Generall, and finding our groanes & heauy Complaints are vanifhed like founds, and valued but as *Ecchoes* in the * *Deferts* and *Playnes*, neere the Forrest Of Shifts, and Wildernes Of Sin. Which whilft fome went by, they heard not, fome heard, but vnderftood not, fome few vnderftanding, regarded not, and none did pitty : I held it then beft (like a barne fo dingd that I durft no longer griet) to fup vp my griefes with filence.

But when I perceiued, that though I fate ftill, the caufe it felfe daily did grow worfe & worfe : & remembred withall my * vow to my Patron and Founder of our Schooles, at my firft admiffion : in difcharge of my dutie, which in this refpect I owe to my God, to my Prince and my Country, I once more refolued to fpeake with my penne, and examine all my former writings, not as by way of *Genefis* to prefcribe a new Arte to our Graue & Wife Maifters, for that were prefumption in the higheft degree : nor as by *Analſis* to conteft with the Doctrine and Method of our feuereft Huifhers, for that were but humour & indefcretion : but whilft *others* of higher Formes, and farre better learning diftrufting theyr Schooles, remooued theyr feates to a furer ftanding, as a poore Scholler defirous to learne and thriue at my Booke, to fpell out my *Primer* by the very letters and poynts of my leffon. That fo redeeming the time, I might beft giue way to the ftreame of difgraces in hope of better dayes now comming: remembring withall, that *Errors* haue no beeing but in abfence of *Truth.* And howfoeuer *Errors* paft haue multiplyed themfelues, the Ages fucceeding muft reforme as they may, & as there is a reafon, fo God hath appointed a time for all things, for *Dies dat confilium.*

B 2                                         Con-

* Cuftomers are fworne at theyr firft admiffion, to doe their endeuous to deale iuftly betvveen the Prince and the People.

¶ Learned Sir *Henry Billingſley*, fometimes Cuftomer of London. ¶ Worthy Sir *Thomas Ridgeway*, Cuftomer of Exeter and Dartmouth. Novve Treafurer of Ireland.

## The CVSTVMERS

* The KING.
* The PRINCE,

Confidering therefore the reuolutions nowe paſt, and preſent diſpoſition of theſe our happy dayes, the * *Day-ſtar* beeing riſen, and the * *Dawning* in our eyes, reuiues our dull ſpirits, ads life to our hopes, and makes Vs breathe out yet this much & ſay, that the time may come, when this hartie zeale of ours to our Soueraignes honour, and his Peoples happines, may be better regarded, and deſerue not onely thanks and good words, but make

* *Sandwich.*
* *Norton-Court.*

all men confeſſe and acknowledge themſelues, as much indebted to theſe weake indeuours of ours, euen from an * Out-Port in the Deſart, & humble * Cottage of this Laud, as all their wealths are or can be made worth : And the Ages to come, find ſomthing at leaſt to muſe and to maruaile at ignorances paſt, when it ſhall plainely appeare by demonſtratiue reaſons, and no wandering Diſcourſe, that in poore Cuſtomers Truth was neuer *Error*, nor Vertue Vice, as the World hath beene told, and ſo long borne in hand. For can they but ſee, they ſhall learne to ſpell, & by ioyning their Letters, both reade and diſcerne (beſides other mattets,) that 1 𝕻𝖚𝖇𝖑𝖎𝖈𝖆𝖓𝖘 and 2 𝕾𝖎𝖓𝖓𝖊𝖗𝖘, are ſeuerall words, & imply a diſtinction both of manners and men, and were it, or might it be that Docible Perſons were but ſuffered to learne, 𝕻𝖚𝖇𝖑𝖎𝖈𝖆𝖓𝖘 could & would teach 𝕾𝖎𝖓𝖓𝖊𝖗𝖘 to be like themſelues : not *Saints* nor *Hypocrites*, but firſt humble Chriſtians, and then plaine honeſt men.

1 CVSTVMERS.
2 SEARCHERS and
    WAITERS.

### 𝕴𝖓 𝖒𝖞 𝖇𝖊𝖌𝖎𝖓𝖓𝖎𝖓𝖌 𝖙𝖍𝖊𝖗𝖊𝖋𝖔𝖗𝖊 𝕲𝖔𝖉 𝖇𝖊 𝖒𝖞 𝖘𝖕𝖊𝖊𝖉𝖊.

*A Ioue principium Muſæ Iouis omnia plena.*

Great **A**

¶ GOD Alſufficient, *Alpha* and *Omega*, onely Wiſe, and eternally Iuſt, without precedent or patterne, out of Confuſion firſt drew Perfection, and at the end of his Worke, delighted to behold that all he had made was ſo like himſelfe, *Valdè Bona*, exceeding good.

Little A.

The laſt of all was MAN, the Image of himſelfe, his *Microcoſmus, Chiefe D'oeunre*, Maiſter-peece, & modell of Perfection. In whom, and by whom, direct, & make vſe of all the reſt. But pride by preſumption perſwading diſobedience, Man became ſeduced, and by *the leaſt part of his truſt*, bewraying his whole Corruption, in ſteed of bleſing was worthily accurſt, both in him & his, had not *Wiſedome* herſelfe, out of loue and affection ſo belayed his fall, that the Word which made all of nothing, was the meanes to reſtore all from nothing, and GOD became a MAN. A miracle of miracles, and myſterie to muſe on, but not to expreſſe : whereby the greateſt loſer, hath made the greateſt gaine.

As the motiue of the Worke was the Creators onely Will, the meanes his Word, the way his Wiſedom, the meaſure *Æquum et Bonū*, bounds of his owne Iuſtice : So the abſolute perfection, &

end

## ALPHABET *and* PRIMER.

end of all, was his preſeruing and boundleſſe mercy, (the Prerogatiue of *Deitie,*) for the Creature to admire on, as his Creators infinite honour, and owne eternall happines.

Now, whatſoeuer *Nature* could afford, or *Man* thus reſtored was able to poſſeſſe, is Gods free gyft from all beginning. That as a Lord peramount, his honoꝛ & ſeuice might iuſtly be known to all his Tennants by ſpeciall duties, and thankfull acknowledgements of their eaſie Rents, and ſo rich a Fee-farme.

The titles of his Tenures are RELIGION and IVSTICE, the one maintaines his peculiar honour and perſonall Rights, the other, effects of *Loue* & *Loyalty*, for his Tennants mutuall good: the Lawes, Cuſtomes and Doctrine whereof, pend by his Spirit, and drawne from the eſſence of heauenly *Deitie*, are ſo concurrent; that to perfect our happines, where both of theſe are not, there can be neither Ɪ and therefore Comparatiuely vſed in this our Leſſon, ſhal both ſanctifie our wits, bleſſe our endeuours, & illuſtrate each other.

*Qui per alium facit, per ſemetipſum facit.* Gods immediat Ꞧ Rents,    Ꞧ *Prayers & Thankſgiuin*
God himſelfe expects and receiues at our hands, ſuch is our Tenure: the ꝛ reſt he accepts, being faithfully payd to his Stewards    ꝛ *Tythes and Tributes.*
and Vicegerents. In which reſpect we ſtand alſo bound to reuerence and admire the tranſcendent reſpects of Soueraigne ſublumitie in earthly States, by theyr *Attributes* & *Tributes*, as GODS ·
among men.

The *Attributes* of power in earthly Princes, are their PREHE-    𝕻ꝛe𝕳eminence.
MINENCE and their PREROGATIVE, (*Iuſtice* and *Mercie*) the    PRＥRＯGAＴIＶＥ.
two ſacred Titles of Diuine Soueraigntie: the one ſets forth the
Dignities of their *Perſons* and *Places*, the other tranſcends to the
motions of their mindes.

The firſt is that *Storge*, and naturall inclination to *Equitie* and *Iuſtice*, that diſtributing bread to the meaneſt of their Subiects, entendeth at leaſt that all ſhould enioy their *Birthrights*, to the generall Treaties of Entercouſe abroade, and Common Lavves at home, to grow vp thereby to liue to theyr ſeruice & the Common-wealth.

By the other, out of meere *Loue* and *Affection* it may well beſeeme them, to ſtande gracious to ſome more then all the reſt, euen beyond the boundes of *Iuſtice*, and yet doe no wrong.

The firſt ſhewes them but from their Seates of *Iuſtice* & height of *Dignities* aboue other men.

The latter beyond the Thrones of Kings, extolls their *Perſons* higher then themſelues, as more then the ſonnes of mortall men.

Theſe then are no *Synonimas* (in our dymme ſights and vveake Conceits) but words of diſtinct reſpects, & of Chiefeſt reuerence,    *Cat' exochen.*
the blending whereof, hath bredde in the World ſuch dangerous Contempts and Capitall Errors, as no Power but the Higheſt, no

             C.                     Wiſedome

## *The* Cᴠꜱᴛᴠᴍᴇʀꜱ

Wifedome but the Graueft, may or can reforme. To whó therefore in all obedience wee proftrately referre them. Onelie in the firft wee fpy the fame forme of Caraĉters, as in the Alphabet of our Letters. But in the other, (beeing a *Hyeroglificke* aboue our reach or Learning) wee heare the full found of all thofe vovvels, that giue life to our Mutes, & muft direĉt our fpelling in the Title of our *Tributes* : the fcope of Loyaltie, and nowe our fpeciall Leffon.

**Pꝛeheminence.**

Pʀᴇʀᴏɢᴀᴛɪᴠᴇ.
Whereof reade more in the Defcription of (Trafficke) hereafter.

¶ Leauing therfore the Rights of *Religion* to thofe learned Diuines, that both by life and doĉtrine, direĉting the way by *Fayth* and *Good-workes* how to winne Heauen, teach vs that *Faith* alone in the Aĉtion of fauing, is the Caufe of Saluation ; but in the Partie faued, both muft concur together. And not to thofe *deftructiue* Doĉtors, that to build vp theyr Church, blow vp Commonweales : and by Loofenes of lyfe, and Traditions of Men, to aduaunce themfelues, rob Gᴏᴅ of his honour. Nor thefe *diftractiue* Teachers, that to Reforme our Church, difturbe our Kingdome ; and prepofterouſly propounding fuch fancies of Perfeĉtion as no reafon can reach to, nor themfelues expreffe, preferring Sacrifice before Obedience, difpence with *Charitie* to pleafe felues, & obtrude vpon Gᴏᴅ more then he requires. Affuring our felues, that to all whó his Spirit doth make Repentant, Gᴏᴅ by Cʜʀɪꜱᴛ, is and will be a moft gracious Gᴏᴅ, and a louing Father. But Gᴏᴅ without Cʜʀɪꜱᴛ is a confuming fire.

¶ Cuftomers Creede & Beleefe, and Articles of Religion

Not Popifh.

Nor Precife.

But the Catholick, Apoftolick, & Chriftian Fayth, now truely taught, freely profeſed, and conftantly defended, in the Churches of England, Scotland & Ireland:

This (I fay) we leaue to thofe facred Diuines that worke obedience in Subieĉts by the rules of Confcience ; and admiring the bleffednes of thefe our dayes, pray for our *Princes* and *Prelates*, & all that vphold or haue but a will to further this our truly *Catholicke* and *Chriftian Religion*.

¶ Leauing alfo the Duties of all our *diftributiue Iuftice*, to thofe moft Woórthy and moft Honourable Perfons, that poffeffing our Courts, by Mᴇᴠᴍ and Tᴠᴠᴍ, difcerne and decyde the Cafes and Queftions of fpeciall Right , and of generall Reafon, as well betwcene Subieĉt and ᵇ Subieĉt, as the Soueraigne and his ᶜ Vaffalls, by the Lawes and Statutes , or peculiar Cuftomes, caft in the ᵈ Mould of Wifedome in our owne Land ; or moderate Extreames by ᶠ Confcience among Men. And to the Graueft & Wifeft in ᵍ higheft Authoritie, that to maintaine the Good by cenfuring the Euill, *Sic irafcuntur, vt vitia tantū perimant feruatis hominibus, atque ita traĉtatis vt veri boni neceffariò fiant : quantumḗ, damni antea dederint, in reliqua vita refarcire queant* . And to thofe Heroicall ʰ Cenfors of merit and valour, that beeing moft *Noble* themfelues, to decyde the Doubts, and determine the Queftions of reputation & worth in all the Degrees of our *Natiue* Right , and *Datiue* Honour, fo maintaine our Credits, *Vt quum Prædia, Feuda et Poffeffiones, paĉtis et tranfaĉtionibus obnoxia : Iu-*

The Decalogue of our Courts of Iuftice, whereto Cuftomers frame the Rules of their Ciuill lyfe and conuerfation in England.

  ᵇ
ɪ Cᴏᴍᴍᴏɴ-Pʟᴇᴀꜱ.
  ᶜ
ᴢ Kings-Bᴇɴᴄʜ, and Court of Wardes.
  ᵈ
ᴣ Pᴀʀʟɪᴀᴍᴇɴᴛ.
  ᶠ
ᴄ Cʜᴀᴠɴᴄᴇʀʏ, & Court of Requefts.
  ᵍ
ꜱ Sᴛᴀʀ-ᴄʜᴀᴍʙᴇʀ, & Counfell-Table.
  ʰ
ᶠ The high Coneftable and

*riu-*

## ALPHABET *and* PRIMER.

*ris-Communis, et forenſibus procellis agitentur :* NOBILITAS *interea,* | Earle-Marſhalls Court of CHI-
*ſolis Regibus beneficiaria, Inſtitutis heroicis, et familiaribus ita acquieſ-* | VALRY.
*cit.* That

    " *Per proauos numerantur aui, ſemperque renata*
    " *Nobilitate virent, et prolem Fata ſequntur.*
    " *Continuum propria ſeruantia lege tenorem.*

    **k**

And to thoſe learned Ciuilians, that *per ﬁﬁquum et Bonum* , ſo | 7 ADMIRALTIE.
belay the publique peace of our **k** Seas, and our **l** Land, that by | **l**
dooing vs Iuſtice, our Neighbours take no wrong. | 8 ARCHES.

    Theſe parts (I ſay) of diſtributiue *Iuſtice,* we gladly referre to | **a** *Matter.*
thoſe worthy Iudges that ſit in our Courts, and by Law & Con- | **e** *Place.*
ſcience protecting our **a** *Liuings* , our **e** *Liberties,* our **i** *Liues,* our | **i** *Perſons.*
**o** *Honour,* & our **u** *Peace* ; doe iuſtly deſerue all Grace frō our So- | **o** *Order.*
ueraigne, and all loue at his handes . Theſe are the GRAVE- | **u** *End.*
MAISTERS & Moderators of our Schooles, that by the Rules | Our **Maiſters.**
of our Bookes, examine our Leſſons.

    The **Prince** hath his Courts apart, for **m** *Publique* Reuenewes | **m**
and **n** *Priuate* Expences : where Accountants are taught for the | 9 EXCHECKER.
moſt part, by Court-Rowles & Court-Rules, grounded on Preſi- | **n**
dents , Examples , or elſe Diſcretion . Thoſe firſt are our | 10 GREENECLOTH.
**Huiſhers.** | Our **Huſhiers.**

    The Comfort is great where Men dwell in houſes, whoſe foun-
dation is layd on aſſured grounds. In which regard wee *poore*
**p** *Schollers,* want words to expreſſe our Ioyes and Conceites, of | **p**
the bleſsings of GOD in theſe our dayes, for the ſtayes of *Reli-* | Cuſtomers.
*gion* and *diſtributiue Iuſtice.* Were thoſe *Patrons* of Honour whom
*Mercury* ſhould ſerue, by APOLLO but found out : & the roofes
of our *Schooles* made wind-tight and water-tight in the breaches
& wants of **q** *Commutatiue Right* : We (I ſay) with all thoſe that | **q**
ſerue in the **r** Temples of Concord, and **ſ** Altars of Truth, would | Trafficke.
make verſes in prayſe of our PRINCES and PEERES , and ſing | **r**
*Alleluiah* to the great GOD of Heauen. | Staples.

    The Commutatiue part then that ſeemes moſt out of frame, | **ſ**
now falling out, and fitted for our Leſſon, we are by our Letters | Mynts.
to ſpel out the words that belong to the Titles of our PATRONS | **t**.
**t w x z** Tributes. Wherin our mild *Moderators* vouchſafe to ſtand | Cuſtomes.
by vs, helpe our dym eye-ſights, ſupport our weake wits, & di- | **w** ⎰ **x** Tonnage
rect our ſhaking hands. And Chriſtes ✠ be my ſpeede, and the | Subſidies ⎱ and
holy Ghoſt. | **z** Pondage.

―――――――――

    ¶ The Nature of all Things that conſiſt in Action, is beſt ſeen
and valued by the eminencie of the Obiect whereon it workes,
and End whereto it tends.

    The higheſt Obiect (next GOD and *Religion,*) is the Maie-
ſtie of our SOVERAIGNE, and Good of our Country, there
beeing no Action more dutifull then to amplifie the honour of
                C ι                    the

## *The* CVSTVMERS

the *One*, and procure the profperitie of the *Other* · nor any more odious, then wittingly or willingly to empayre the Meanes, mutually meant for the maintenaunce of Either.

It followes then by confequence, at all hands agreed on, that to maintaine the Princes Reuenewes, and to further the profperitie and peace of his People, is (or ought to be) the fpeciall care of euery Mans beft Endeuour.

The Duties which G o d hath layd out, and for his honor referued, by the words of his Law were double onely, and of two feuerall kindes, daily *Sacrifices* and *Oblations* of Free-will. The one proceeding, from the ordinary Obferuaunce that giues the formall diftinction betweene the *Creature* and the CREATOR. The other demonftrates that francknes of *Loue* and cheerefull *Deuotion*, that ought to proceede from the harts of his owne and peculiar People.

Nowe that which *Deitie* demaunds by the Lawes of *Religion*, within his Church to be honored by, doth hold as a confequence for earthly Princes within their Kingdoms to raife their Tributes by. Like Obiects, like Ends, *Maieftie*, and *Loue*, by two forts of Duties, *Neceffitie* and *Free-will*. The One muft fubfift, the Other cannot be bound. Giue therefore as vnto G o d himfelfe that which is G o d s ; fo vnto *Cafar*, that is due to *Cafar*.

Thus Cuftomes that grow by *Trafficke*, are due to our K i n g, and are no fmall nor idle Portions in the Body of his Reuenews. But as in *Religion* and the feruice of G o d, there is nothing hath more difturbed the Confcience, nor diftracted Mens minds, then a mifvnderftanding, and diuerfity in conceits, of the true fence and vfe of the word (*Church*,) fo fares it with Traffick about the Tearmes and vfe of *Cuftomes*.

*Church* and *Cuftomes*, wordes that are too generally taken : and fo mifvnderftoode.

For though *Cuftomes* (in this kinde) doe currantly runne, and be vfually taken for all kinde of Duties that acrue to the King on things Barterable or Vendible, by way of Marchandife crofing the Seas, either Outward or Inward, (for from Port to Port both Land & Seas are naturally free) yet it hath a peculiar fence, a fpeciall vfe and proper fignification, implying eyther thofe ancient *Staple-Rights*, on Wooll, Wooll-fells, Tinne, Lead & Lether, &c. called *Great* and *Grand Cuftomes*, outward ; or the three pence on the pound, payd onely by Strangers , by the name of *Petty-Cuftomes*.

Grand C v s t o m s,

Petite C v s t o m s.

All Titles befides (of this kind) howfoeuer they be called, or generally comprifed and ftiled *Cuftomes* , are notwithftanding, diftinguifhed from them by fpeciall Names , and different vfes, as *Subfidies*, or *Aydes*. And thofe alfo fubdiuided into *Tonnage* & *Pondage*.

Subfidies { Tonnage and Pondage.

The vfe and end of C v s t o m s.

The firft (properly, and indeede onely to be called Cuftomes) by wifedome layd out from all beginning , is *Ius Coronæ*, an Inheritance

## Alphabet *and* Primer.

heritance of the Crowne, the *preemption* in Trafficke, and *pro-* *tection* of Traffick, beeing two Essentiall partes of that personall · *Preeminence*, and locall *Dignitie*, which fundamentally our Kings haue claimed, and for defence of the Kingdome, and safe passage at Seas, iustly may challenge. As consisting (to our Weake vn-derstandings) of the chiefest Materialls our State affoords, to to draw in *Bullion* by. And in that respect holden for their *Ar-* *tificiall Mynes* of Gold & Siluer, to maintaine the Pulses of our Soueraignes *Mynts*, whose *Exchange* of Money, as a Fountaine for abundance, ought to fixe and guide the true valuations of all Things besides. For as the Standarts of all Weights & Measures for generall Iustice, are the Soueraignes Treasure and peculiar charge, & the coyning of Monies theyr onely (*Hoc age*,) so their Coynage, a worke for Matter & Forme of principall Worth, & theyr *Exchange* a Mysterie of heauenly skill, by equalitie and proportions *certaine* and *indifferent*, are the Sterne and Compasse to steere all courses right.

    The later called *Subsidies*, are offred vp at Parliaments, on things subiect to Restraints by Proclamations for speciall Causes and different vse, and in that regard giuen sometimes but on this Thing, sometimes but at that Port, and some-times *Ad Tempus* onelie. Though now for all Things, at all Ports, and for terme of our Soueraignes lyfe, as vrgent Necessity, or publique Vtilitie, for the Freedome of *Trafficke*, and behoofe of the *Ports* haue see-med to require; Due likewise in their kinds and turnes for reci-prock Ends. The *Body* beeing by G O D and *Nature*, so bound to serue and maintaine the *Head*, as the *Head* is ordained to gouerne and defend all the *Members*.

    Thus *Customes* are those artificiall duties that our Kings must haue, and Necessity hath layd on *Trafficke* by our *Staple Comerce*, to supply theyr naturall defects, and wants of *Bullion*.

    And *Subsidies* are those naturall respects which *Loue* is desirous and *Loyaltie* doth offer, by *Trafficke* to honour our Soueraignes by (besides theyr auncient *Customes*,) that by all Meanes, and at all hands *Maiestie* may be seene, and *Soueraigntie* subsist.

    These are all the Titles of our Commutatiue Tributes, by the Lawes of our Schooles, the bounds of our Lessons, and Alpha-bet of our Letters. Yet is there a third, called *Impostes*, or *Impo-* *sitions*, whose Heteroclite vse, and conuertible sound, wee know not how to spell: for beeing but the *Genus* to the former two, & held for a *Species* of some other Duty in our weake conceits, hath decciued many.

    For whereas *Maiestie* must, may & can but subsist; what *Ado-* *ration* and *Tythes* are to G O D, the same are *Customes* & *Subsidies* to his *Lieuetenants*. And beyond the bounds which Wisedome pre-scribes for the practise of *Truth*, Discretion may hunt, but shall
**D.**                                        find

*Marginal notes:*
*Bullion.*
*Staples.*
*Mynts.*
*Exchange.*
*Weights & Measure.*
*Generall Iustice.*

The Vse and End of the Subsidie
of *Tonnage* and *Pondage.*

*Impostes* or *Impositions,*

## *The* CVSTVMERS

find nought faue *Error*. For what exccedes, is but *Poperie* in the
Church, and in Policie, deuices to difturbe *Common-weales*.

What refts then but this, that *Omne minimum inimica Natura, &
Omne nimium vertitur in vitium*. Enough makes a feaft, but abufes
marre all, whereof we muft alfo fpell fome-thinges hereafter.

*Impoftes* then by the Rules of our Bookes, and Letters of our
Leffons, are eyther the *Cuftoms* wee fpoke of, and thofe *Cuftoms
Impofitions*, that to maintaine the Effence of Maieftie, Neceffitie
found out : Or thofe *Subfidies* afore-faid, that Marchants by *Trafficke* doe franckly and willingly *impofe* vppon themfelues : or els
in our *Natura Brevium*, no where to be found.

Italian Gouernments, and the
Difcords of the Netherlands. But as *Aliquid Boni propter Vicinum Bonum*, fo *Multum mali
propter vicinum Malum*. Our Neighbours fower Grapes haue fet
our teeth on edge. For by their examples, drawne (as they call
it) from their Princes *Prerogatiues*, but would fay *Preheminence*, if
they vnderftqode themfelues. *Impofitions* are made Taxes vppon
Marchandife, befides the duties aboue-fayde : not fo much by
Statutes or Treaties of Entercourfe, as by a kinde of difcretion,
which wanting place and vfe in the ftudie of our Cuftomes, haue
likewife no part in the honourable ends thereby propounded and
intended. For beeing as they are, Effe&s of vnknowne Caufes,
of Matter vncertaine, and of forme no wayes fitting the Mould
of our free Commerce, all men refufe to argue thereof, to define,

The Popes ambitious Taxes on
our Clergy, impouerifhing the
Realme by exhaufting our Treafure, made our Kings draw on the
Barrons warres, to fupply theyr
pouerty & wants, vpõ the People.

Impofitions doe but ayme at Order, and the preferuation of our
Shypping by gueffe.

Shipping of neceffity to be main-
tayned. to deuide, or to bring them into Queftion. The rather for that,
beeing in theyr nature irregular and litigious, they haue beene
occafions of much vnreft and diforders in former times, efpecially
in the firft and fecond ages of our Kings, till *Magna Charta* compounded fuch griefes. And albeit the vfe of them fince might
happily ayme at the beating backe of fome Forraine idle Cómo-
dities, brought in and obtruded vpon vs by Strangers, to the hinderance of our Trafficke in Trades, & decay of our Ports in Mariners and Shipping, which the wifedome of our State muft alwayes maintaine : yet gathering withall vppon the naturall and
free-borne Subie&ts, they repyne thereat, as men willing to obey,
but not able to difcerne betweene the difpofitions of States, and
changes of Tymes, & fo is a fpeciall ground of all our Diforders.
The Subie& ftill appealing to the pofitiue Lawes of our owne
free *Trafficke*, as their generall Inheritance, and Strangers vrging
theyr *Treaties* and mutuall *Contra&ts*.

The Ends of *Impofitions*, are Dif-
order of *Trafficke*. Thefe *Impofts* of difcretion or ftrayned *Preheminence*, ( if wee
terme them right) haue likewife begotten fome other *Impofitions*,
of bafer Nature, and more dangerous Effe&ts, whereby that facred Word of Wifedome, and higheft power, ( our Soueraignes
*Prerogatiue*,) is vnreuerently proftituted, and many wayes pro-
phaned. For, beeing fometimes pleafed, (as well may befeeme
them) out of meere loue and affe&tion, in publique reftraints, by
                  fpeciall

# ALPHABET *and* PRIMER.

speciall fauours to make some of their Seruants more happy then their fellowes; the same by sales and transactions, transmuted or transferred, is a meanes to make Subiects from hand to hand, to racke and *impose*, euen vpon & among themselues. When indeed and in truth, the (*Grace*) looseth *Beeing*, both in Matter, Forme, and Vse, vppon the first *Exchange*. For when Fauourites get suits vnfitting theyr Callings, or vse them not themselues: it is but Witchcraft and Sorcery that all such intend, as by Leases or Purchase for priuate gaine, thinke PRINCES *Prerogatiues*, eyther vendible for Money, or subiect to Exchange. Such *Impost-Maisters* Religion hath accurst, theyr Money therefore and themselues, (without Repentance) must perish both together.

*Wine, Beere, Coales, &c. And whatsoeuer in this kinde is eyther solde or put ouer to a second or third hand for Money.*

These *Imposts* we take it, (vnder our *Graue-Maisters* correction) are but Romish *Peter-pence*, and *Italian-Inuentions*, where theyr PRINCES *Preheminence*, and forst kinde of *Dignities*, haue little other Subsistence: Beeing therfore but borrowed, they may well be sent home. *England* was neuer any vassall to *Rome*, and hath or may haue (beeing but rightly vsed) enough of her owne.

*Simones-Magi.*

*Acts. Capit: 8. ver: 20.*

But *ô fortunatos Anglos bona si sua norint!* For the Maiestie of our *Customes* somtimes so admired, seeme now like Anticke *Medalls*, that reteyning but their sound, haue lost themselues in theyr Value and Vse, both of Matter and Forme.

*Trafficke ill beholden to all such English Gentlemen as trauailing for experience, make the Imposition of Italy a fit precedent for the gouernment of England, vvhen they come home.*

Thus our *Wooll*, (some-times the wonder of the Worlde,) are now the *Trophees* of strange Lands, and signes of our shame, and turned into Cloth, our Cloth into nothing; at least nothing lesse then *Bullion*. And the Rates vppon *Wooll*, first grounded by Statutes, layd on Cloth by *Discretion*, not iustly discerning the reason of our *Customes* in the Vse of the *One*, and End of the *Other*.

*Our Golden-Flees, the Trophee of the House of Bu gundy.*

*Our Cloth become confiscable beyond Seas, or by speciall fauour returnable vpon vs.*

Our basest *Fell-wooll* of Shorlings, the refuse of the rest, and sweepings of our *Staples*, (neuer vsed in Cloth,) is by our kindest * Neighbours, in a new kinde of Drapery, made the glorie of our *Wolls*, and credite of our Kingdome, and might be made a Patterne to reforme all our Clothing, and recouer our *Bullion*.

Our *Fells* & our *Leather* forsake vs by Licenses. GOD knowes why, where, how or whether, but without returne of *Bullion*.

Our *Tyn* and our *Leade*, so lately well recouered, seemes now againe layd vp in Huxters handling, and might haue beene a sure and speciall helpe to haue drawne in *Bullion*.

*\* The Duch-Church at Sandwich, who flying the tyranny of Body and Conscience at home, admitted to refresh themselues but with our English ayre, layd the first foundation of true making of Bayes, Sayes, & Sarges there. (Trades neuer vnderstoode of vs before,) till abuses elswhere ouer-whelmed them with others, with an Imposition that well-neere breakes theyr harts: yet hold they still theyr first innocencie, and maintaine the credite of that Townes-Seale, both for Number, Weight, and Measure, in all parts of the World.*

Our *Pettit-Customs*, onely seeme still to holde their owne, but with vncertaine *Byas*, since *Lex Mercatoria* became obsolete, and to vs vnknowne.

*Lex Mercatoria.*

In steede of all which, our *Returnes* (for the most part) beeing but toys and *Tabacco*, Bells or Bables, of things *needlesse* or *bootelesse,*

## *The* Cvstvmers

*leſſe*, doe ſhew how Strangers for better wares, can fat vs vp with
pryde, or fodder vs with folly.

Our *Subſidies* that ſometimes were ſo fewe, ſo eaſie, ſo louing-
ly offred, ſo graciouſly accepted, and ſo willingly payde, as the
*Cuſtomes* haue ſayled, are become the Subiects of *Extremitie*, euen
to the tything of our ſmalleſt Mynt and Comin. And our ſweet
*Nurſe* and *Miſtreſſe*, Traffick, diſtempered and diſtreſt with
dangerous fits of a hot burning Feauer. Not farre from Frenſie;
which wee poore *Schollers* cannot but ſee, and (what ere betyde
vs) bewayle and lament; and before our *Graueſt* and *Wiſeſt Phyſi-
tians*, proſtrate our ſelues for remedy. And I among the reſt, as

the *Apothecaries Boy*, that for bringing but one \* *Pill* to preuent
the laſt acceſſe, was ſo ſhent for my labour. The *Symptome* and
*Cryſis* of whoſe diſeaſe will beſt appeare in our Leſſon nowe following.

---

¶ The faſhion and face of our *Cuſtomes* beeing thus layd open,
theyr Vſe by practiſe but once made knowne, would enflame the
world with admiration and loue of the ſpeciall Bleſſings & Prudence of our Land; the Zeale whereof onely hath preuented all
our Studies, almoſt conſumde our ſelues, and yet is the motiue of
all our beſt Endeuours.

*Cuſtomes* therefore and *Subſidies*, both depending on *Trafficke*,
as Effects that riſe and fall with theyr efficient Cauſe: the rayſing
of *Trafficke* like Hony in Hyues, muſt needes increaſe eyther.

Trafficke! O the compaſſe and profunditie of this one &
onely word (*Trafficke*,) more fit for *Wiſedome* to ſtudy, and *Elo-
quence* to vtter, then our weake braynes to ſpell. In which regard we cannot but bewayle the loſſe and want of thoſe worthy
Wits of older tymes, that to tune the whole World, wrote Volumes on this Theme.

The three Bookes of Sibilla, ſo well preſerued, ſo deerely
bought, and carfully kept by *Tarquine* the *Elder*, are long ſince by
*Stilico* that Traytor, blowne vp, burnt and gone.

> *Ne tantùm Patryſ ſaun et Prodstor Armis,*
> *Sancta* Sybillinæ *fata cremauit Opis.*

But, ô, thoſe *Acroamata*, and pryuate Inſtructions of kingly
Doctrine! ſo grauely diſcuſſed, ſo attentiuely heard, and richlie
rewarded with Talents of Gold, are eyther forgotten, beyond
our hearing, or out of our reach.

And *Tully De Republica*. A Booke able to make a Wiſe-man
in one dayes reading, (as ſome beleeue and write) ſo carefullie
ſought for, both farre and neere by our late *Cardinall Poole*, hath
not yet been ſeene, except the *Amalthean Vatican* of our newe
ᵒ Tarqvinivs Priscvs haue happily found it out, whoſe
care, coſt, and loue to Learning, in the Kingdom of the *Muſes*,
deſerues

# ALPHABET *and* PRIMER.

deſerues a Golden Crowne : yet this is our côfort, that the light they ſaw by, was but beames of this *Sunne*, their *Enthouſiaſme*, but motions of this *Good Spirit*, and their cleereſt water ſet from the ſtreames of this flowing *Fountaine*, that runnes ſo franckly, and may ſerue our Turne.

For T R A F F I C K E is but a free Bartering, or buying & ſelling of 1 Vendible Wares. At 2 Markets côuenient. By 3 Marchants, Subiects, or Strangers. According to the 4 Rules of Reciprocke Commerce. Generally intending 5 Honour to Princes, and Proſperitie to Common-wealthes.

And here at the firſt view appeare all our fiue Vowells, in fiue Wordes, that teach vs all to ſpell, and make vs all to ſpeake ; to wit, a M A T T E R, as *Vendible Wares*. e P L A C E, *Markets conue-nient*. i P E R S O N S, *Marchants, Subiects or Strangers*. o O R D E R, *Rules of Reciprocke Commerce*. And u E N D, *Honour to Princes*, and *Proſperitie to* v *Comm̄on-v-wealthes*.

The firſt wee call **a**. The ſecond ſtands for **e**. The third **i**. The fourth is **o**. The fift ſtands for **u**. And (**u**. S I R S.) And **u**. *My Lords*. **w**. *And all*.

Heere were ſit ſtaying to admire on the Maieſtie of thoſe two wordes of Power, P R E H E M I N E N S and P R E R O G A T I U E. Whereof the firſt hath two of our Vowels for P E R S O N S and P L A C E, but the laſt contaynes them all. But wee muſt not play too much with the beauty of thoſe Letters : Let vs fall to our Bookes, and ſpell out our Leſſon.

¶ In the condition of the **Matter** layde out for *Trafficke*, what euer it be, *Goodnes* more or leſſe makes it firſt Vendible, as reſpected for the *goodnes* onely, and ſo fit for Trades.

¶ In the **Places**, conueniencie at home or abroade ; eaſineſſe of acceſſe by Sea or by Land, & freedome with ſafetie : for *Matter* and *Perſons* is onely regarded in all Marts and Markets.

¶ In the qualitie of Marchants **Perſons** whoſoeuer they be, *Subiect* or *Stranger*, *Loyaltie* and *Alliance* onely makes their *Traffick* auowed. For with knowne Traytors, or open Enemies, the Law admits no Commerce.

¶ The beſt Rules for **Order** to direct *Trafficke* by, are thoſe that beeing preciſely ſquared out, to the *Generalitie*, *Certaintie*, and *Indifferencie* of the *Lawes* of our Land, and forraine *Contracts*, admit no particular, partiall, nor doubtfull deceit, iniury, nor diſturbance to *Matter*, *Perſons*, nor *Place*.

¶ The **End** of all *Trafficke*, is *Honour* to Princes, and *Proſperity* to their Kingdoms ; whoſe policie and gouernment, religious and Iuſt, muſt needes be formed to their Patterne D E I T I E, by the *Obiect* of *Goodnes*, and end in *Peace*.

But all Goodnes is needfull : *Trafficke* therfore in regard of the Vſe of *Goodnes*, muſt needes be generall. For looke what the

E.　　　　　　　　　Soule

**u**　　　　　　**u**
The K I N G and P R I N C E.
**u**
The C O V N S A I L E.
**w**
The Common-wealth.

**e. i.**

**a. e. i. o. u.**

**a.**
¶ M A T T E R, muſt be vendible.

**e.**
¶ P L A C E conuenient for Marts and Markets.

**i.**
¶ P E R S O N S, fit to Traffick.

**o.**
¶ O R D E R in Commerce.

**u.**
¶ E N D of Trafficke.

## *The* CVSTVMERS

Soule is to the outward Actions of the Body, in ordering each
Member, so as Nature finds fit for the good of the whole *Man*:
such is *Trafficke*, in disposing Mysteries & Trades, to the behoofe
of the whole *Common-wealth*. A consideration in no part of Ciuill
Gouernment to be neglected, much lesse in this great *Cause* of
*Customes*.

GOODNES therefore, as the life of the Soule, to perfect our
*Trafficke*, both in *Matter, Place, Persons, Order* & *End*, is the scope
of our Studie, and length of our Lessons. That in *Trafficke*, as in
all things, it may at last appeare, that *Finis coronat Opus*.

Thus *Customes* from *Trafficke* haue their first Essens & beeing,
and by it increase, to the *Honour* of Princes, and *Prosperitie* of Cō-
mon-weales. For *Trafficke* then it is that we *Customers* contend, &
stand bound to contest what euer betyde vs, vntill shee be relie-
ued by the Cordialls of *Goodnes*. Which now falling out, & fitted
for our Lesson, let vs play the *good Schollers*, and ply our Bookes
well, to spell out *Goodnes*, that some *Good-Man* at last, may get
vs leaue to play.

---

*Eusebius*

¶ *In regimine Ciuitatis. In Republica gubernanda, et in Orbis*
" *Imperio, minimum est quod possunt homines: In Causa vero Reli-*
" *gionis multo minus. Magna, Magnus perficit DEVS.*

He whose onely *will*, and absolute *Power* could worke so well,
that all hee made became exceeding *Good*, to his owne eternall
Glory, and Mans immortall Blisse: GOD I say, GOD I meane,
& GOD the third time, though ONCE for all. Whom onelie to
know, is euerlasting Life, and Ioy but to heare and make mention of his Name, beeing a law to himselfe; of his owne Perfection, doth likewise perfect all he *wills* or *doth*. His *Goodnes* beeing
the Forme of all thinges, from which to swarue is to returne to
Nothing, and which in him as the Fountaine we must admire, &
most affect and desire in our selues.

GOODNES then is the glorious center of DEITIE it selfe, frō
whence all Circumferences both in Heauen and Earth, deriue not
onely Essence, but happines in *Beeing*.

From hence it is, that out of Learning and Zeale to Religious
Rights, some godly-disposed, haue seemed to obserue a kind of
*Trafficke*, and free Commerce, betweene the *Throne* of Heauen,
and the *Church* vpon Earth, by Doctrine & Prayer for the vse of
*Goodnes*. All heauenly Inspirings downeward, and all holie De-
sires vpwards, beeing as *Angels* or *Marchants*, betweene GOD
and vs. That as his Doctrine doth teach vs our supreame *Truth*:
so our Prayers might confesse him our soueraigne *Good*. But this
height and depth of *Goodnes* we leaue to Diuines. The length &
breadth thereof, must lay forth our Lesson, by giuing GOD his
Honour,

# ALPHABET *and* PRIMER.

Honour, and our Soueraigne K I N G his Right. For *Cælum Cælorum sibi ipsi assumens Terram dedit filijs hominum*.

**As therefoze at first we pzaybe God foz our speede, So now in Goodnes, God graunt we pzoceede.**

*Tu mihi summe Opifex rerum Cor fingitio purum
Et Recti inspira renouatum pectore amorem.
Os mihi tute aperi, Tu dirige labra loquentis
Vt Tibi promerita persoluant laudis honores.*

---

¶ We haue speld already how our *Customes* and *Subsidies* liue & die with *Trafficke*, as Effects that follow theyr Efficient Cause. In which respect, first *Trades* and *Tradesmen* must be sought for, made of, and at all hands nourisht. Then *Marchants* of all sorts, must be kindly entreated, and by freedome encouraged in euery Common-wealth.

All *Trafficke* is either *Outward* and *Inward*, of Things bredde at home, or set from abroad: and three things there are, that by the Spirit of *Goodnes*, giues it three degrees of lyfe, and thrice-happy beeing. Viz. **Commodities, Money,** and **Exchange.**

**Commodities.**

The first, as the B O D Y, vphelde the World in the infancie of *Trafficke*, by bartering Good-things for Good-things, to supply Necessities, till *Fraude* came in.

**Money.**

The second, as the S O V L E in the Body, beeing a weight of supreame woorth, to maintaine Equalitie, and preuent Aduantage by cósent of Nations, first made Good-thinges vendible.

*Olim. Cum non esset Monetæ vsus, nec aliud Merx, aliud pretium dicereter: pro temporú rerumǿ ratione, vtilia vtilibus permutabant homines. Sed ob difficultatem contrahentium electa est Materia, cuius publica et perpetua estimatio, premutationum difficultatibus æquabilitate quantitatis subueniret.*

**Exchange.**

The third, as the S P I R I T in the *Soule*, is seated euery where in the Soueraignes owne bosome, to direct and controll by iust proportions of length and breadth, weight & content, the truth, worth, and vse of *Goodnes*, both in Money, and all Things els.

*Kata panta.
Regula Veritatis.*

The first, whilst *Goodnes* in plaine dealing lay open to all vses alike, knew not the Titles of Kings nor Kingdomes.

*Kat'auto.
Regula Iustitiæ.*
*Ius monetæ proprium est Principis et inter Regalia Magna censetur.*

The second, is the right hand of *Iustice*, which crowning Kings, first layde the foundation of that preheminent Dignitie, that shewes the difference and distinction of Soueraignes and Subiects.

The third, is that forme of *Maiestie*, and transcendent Power, that of Mortall-Men, makes Gods on Earth.

*Kath'olou Proton.
Regula sapientiæ vel ordinis.*

Thus in *Trafficke*, *Commodities* both Barterable and Vendible, by Trades and Mysteries are layd out for Subiects. **Money** as the *weight* to value the woorth, and **Exchange** the *Measure*, to sette forth the vse of *Goodnes* by, belongs onely to P R I N C E S, the sacred Ministers of heauenly Iustice; Each supporting other by mutuall supplyes for Reciprocke Ends. The P R I N C E graciously be-

*Post ipsam Legem nil æque vtile est ac necessariú Reipub: vt Númorú vsus. Proinde Grecis Nomos merito appellatur. Quasi dicas gubernandi Regula. Vel gubernaculum.*

## *The* CVSTVMERS

ly beholding the *prosperity* and *wealth* of his loyall *Subiects,* as the onely Mirror of his owne Greatnes and Honor. And the *Subiects* religiously admiring the *Maiestie* of their *Soueraigne,* as the glorious Obiect of their *Welfare* and *Good.*

And thus it appeares by the course of our spelling, set poynts of our Lesson,& lynes of this our *Primer.* That our Kings Trade is *Coyning,* and his Mysterie is *Exchange.* His ★ *Right* therefore, *vni, soli, et semper.* By the rules of all *Truth,* all *Iustice* and all *Order* must be Gold and Siluer, Materialls of *Bullion.*

* The KINGS *Proprium* and peculiar *Right.*

¶ The motyue of this worke, was a naturall defence of poore despised and contemned *Customers;* by whose disgrace the *King* receiues such losse, and the *State* more wrong. But the mayne dryft & Scope of all, is an orderly aduancing of our Soueraignes Reuenewes in his duties of Customes, that so many haue vndertaken, and so few haue set forward. Wherein all that hath beene said, might passe but for conceit, and contemplatiue discourse, without the hand of some Ministeriall function.

The motyue of this ALPHABET, and mayne dryft of this PRIMER,

*Customes* therefore beeing Effects of that great Cause vvhose Actions are conuersant about no meaner Obiects then the Soueraignes *Honour,* and Subiects *happinesse,* requires Collectors of choyse respect, and absolute trust: Men truly Religious and honest in deede, as *Customers* are euery way entended to be.

And such were they some-times reputed, till Neglect in theyr Choyce, and Contempt of theyr Persons, made *Ielousie* begin to suspect their endeuours, whilst *Ignorance* and *Impudencie* in countenaunce and maintenaunce supplanted their Credites. First by *Controllers,* then *Superuisors,* and lastly by *Farmers,* and *Vndertakers,* besides *Searchers* and *Wayters* God knowes how many.

I come therefore now to speake of that Function which vnderlying the charge of so great a trust, none should obtrude on at aduenture, or vndertake in iest, but such as Nature hath fitted, & Authoritie admitted in lawfull manner. For how-soeuer the Name of *Customers* seeme now out of fauour, as the Obiects of Disgrace, and publique Slaunder; the curious eye of the Lawe (still constant in his choyce,) call them kindly by their Names, and culls them all as curiously forth, (as Shriefes in their Shieres) " from among the best and most sufficient, that Wisedome can " find, or choyce affoord, as men most fit to attend vpon *Trafficke,* and in collecting *Customes,* most likely of all others, To deale iustly betweene the Prince and People. Giue therefore cheerefully, collect vprightly, and aunswere truly, as vnto GOD himselfe, all his due honour, in *Oblations* and *Tythes:* so to our KING, all his due *homages,* in the Rights of his *Customes,* and loyall *Supplyes.* Deale (I say) iustly betweene the Prince and the People.

The *Customers* onely knowne to the Lawe.

The intention of the Lawe in choosing *Customers.*

HOC

## ALPHABET *and* PRIMER.

### *HOC OPVS, HIC LABOR EST.*

This is the *Dyapazon* of all our *Muficke*, and full compaffe of that Song wherein each muft hold apart; heere therefore paufe a while, that all may fing together.

For great hath beene the care from time to time, & the inuentions fundry, that haue beene vndertaken, for the aduauncing, collecting, & true aunfwering, of all fuch duties as grow in this kind. But as in the State of a naturall Body, thofe difeafes proue of moft dangerous confequence, that are of longeft breeding, & furtheft from cure, whofe pulfe is neuer felt, nor Symptoma knowne; fo hath it long fared with this Argument of *Cuftomes*. Wherein fometimes about the Caufe it felfe, (*Trafficke*) vvhether free-borne or no, then about the *Matter*, without difference or diftinction of *Art* or *Nature*, *Outward* ot *Inward*, *Abundance* or *Want*, *Dutie* or *Free-will*. And laftly about the Forme of theyr orderly directing, collecting, and true anfwering how to ftoppe the courfe of *Errors*, and currant of *Abufes*, is become the greateft pretended care at leaft and moft ferious Queftion.

For information and Reformation whereof, how-foeuer the Confcience of my Calling vnder his facred *Maieftie*, & fpeciall dutie befides, as his Highneffe fworne Seruaunt, haue fingled me forth, and preft me ftill forward, by one occafion or other. *Quo fato nefcio, fed non fine Numine*, as my hope and comfort is, firft by 1 *A Generall Apollogie*: thē a fecond 2 *Replyes*, & 3 *The true vfe of Port Bands*: & laftly, *A Priuate* 4 *Caution*, againft the Farming out of *Subfidies*, vnder the name of *Cuftomes*, to prefume thus with my penne, but to wifh and further; I euer concluded that none but the *Graueft* and *Wifeft* in higheft Authoritie, might promife and performe it: Before whom now beeing fo lately commaunded to fpeake, I may not, I cannot, I dare not hold my peace.

All humble refpect of Dutie therefore, & proftrate Reuerence premifed, I proceede with my Leffon, and build on our Defence vpon my firft Religious and reafonable grounds.

1 Againft Informers of all forts.
2 Againft priuate Societies.
3 A Treatife worth the reading.
4 The Satisfaction of the offence conceiued againft that *Caution*, was the occafion of cafting all the reft into this new Mowld, called,
5 *The Cuftomers* ALPHABET & PRIMER.

---

RELIGION and IVSTICE, are the fundamentall ftayes of all States and Kingdoms, the one by fanctifying, the other by affuring the perpetuities of all tranquilitie of Minds and earthly Honours. *Iuftice* beeing *Diftributiue* and *Commutatiue*; the *Commutatiue* part includeth *Trafficke*.

There was a time when the Chriftian world was all fet on fire, deuided by Difputes, and diftracted in Opinions, about the *Catholicke-Church*, and fome poynts of *Truth* in the doctrine of *Religion*: But the GOD of Heauen be praifed, it hath found the beft footing in thefe our dayes & Kingdoms that the world doth affoord, and his hand in our *Soueraigne* and *his*, for euer vphold it.

The true Catholick and Chriftian Religion, as foundly taught, & as freely profeffed in England, Scotland and Ireland at this day, as in any priuate or publicke part of the World.

F.                              The

## *The* CVSTVMERS

*Vppon the compounding of the Difcordes in the Netherlands.*

The like feemes now (I fay, euen now) to offer it felfe about the Vfe & Ends of our free-borne *Trafficke*, that Nurfe of Iuftice which feedes vs *All*. The priuate peruerting of whofe generall Intention to publicke *Good*, hath much difturbed our fpeciall Bliffe, and giues occafion of this Alphabet or Primer.

*Trafficke* then, beeing the hand that layès out all men theyr Worke, prouides all men theyr Foode, and payes all men theyr Fees, ought at all handes to be ferioufly fupported, that fo fupports vs all; and her willing Difturbers, and witting Peruerters, held as Enemies to *Order*, that is to fay, to *God* and *Nature*.

And fince in all Actions, the fafeft path to walke in, and fureft rule to guide our felues by, is to follow *Nature*, the patterne layd out by the God of *Order*: the way from *Error* to *Truth*, & from *Confufion* to *Perfection*, muft be by proportions, vntill we come to that *End*, which is able and fufficient to perfect and preferue all our worldly happines. *Meafure* therefore muft fit at the Sterne, and by fteddy proportions, cunne and fteere this our Shippe of *Trafficke* thorow all the ftormes of Extremities and dangers of Shyfts, to our long-defired Port.

As the beauty of Nature is Order, fo the way to Order is Number more or leffe, to auoyde the Rocks and Sands of *Exceffe* and *Defect*. **Exchange** therefore without all exceptions, muft lay the foundation, and abfolute ground of all our Endeuours, to this intended Redreffe.

*The Writer heereof, alluding to his owne trouble for the Caution hee wrote againft the Farming out of Subfidies, vnder the name of Cuftome, fets forth vvithall a true Idea of Trafficke, by fayning a Shyppe (called the Harry-Bonaduenture,) fraught with pitch, tarre, maftes, falt and oyle, and good ftore of Bullion: that after a long voyage, in her returne homewards to the Iland of Exchange, meetes with a dangerous ftorme in the Narrow-Seas, and doubting the Goodyn-fands, falls in with the Forelands, cafts Ankor in the Downes, and there ryding all Windes to death, puts in at laft to Sandwich-Hauen. Where finding neither Staple nor Staple-wares, (fometimes held there, and fithence at Canterbury adioyning) of Fleece-wooll, Broad-clothes, Tyn, Lead, nor Leather. &c barters her Commodities for Bayes, Sayes, and other Duch newe Drapery there. And in Exchange for her Bullion, befpeakes Kentifh Broade-clothes againft her next returne: Prouided, they be made & warranted by the Rules of Sandwich Bayes, and Seale of that Towne onely, and none other.*

**Exchange**! haue we fpyde out *Exchange*? Then haile Maifters, Marriners, and Mates at all hands: Call vp our loyall Marchants, true Patriots, Enterlopers and all, and be of good cheere. Relay well the Bowlyne, keepe your tacklins tight and fure. Aloofe aloofe with the Maine for feare of the *Goodwines*. I feeme to fee our Iland, for the Fore-lands appeare. CASTOR and POLLVX cóming both together, did boade vs good-lucke. Our Barke is ftrong enough to beare out her leakes. Our Loade-ftone proues good, and our Compaffe is true, therefore aloofe (I fay) with the Maine, by this Cape of *Good-hope*, to the Harbor of Safetie, and Hauen of all our Reft. For *Reliquis tantum Sinus eft et Statio malefida Carinis.*

Now, all thinges confift of Matter and Forme, *et Forma dat effe rei*: the Matter beeing Weight, and Meafure the Forme, are fitted and efteemed by their *End* and *Obiect*, GOODNES. All *Goodnes* is eyther by Nature or by Art. And as in *Goodnes* there is a pro-

# ALPHABET *and* PRIMER.

.a proportion to fit with the *Matter* wherein it confifteth : So in *Omnis Forma infunditur fecundum*
·*Trades*, the bleffing of G O D by Nature, and the benefit of Indu- *meritùm Materiæ.*
ftry by Art, is more or leffe admired, to the fpeciall reputation &
profit of thofe *Perfons* , and thofe *Places* that firft affoord them.

According to thefe grounds of the three things in *Trafficke* before layd downe, as *Money* for the Matter, a Weight of greateft
worth, and for the Forme, a worke of royall efteeme : So *Ex-*
*change*, a Meafure of rareft perfection, and Myftery of heauenlie
skill, fitting none but Soueraigne States and Kings, muft ftint the
values, and guide the proportions of *Goodnes* , in all Materialls
befides. But all *Goodnes* is needfull. *Exchange* therefore, as the
Spirit in the Soule, to perfect our *Trafficke*, by the Fountaines of
1 *Bullion*, and ftore of Princes 2 *Coyne*, in refpect of the vfe there-   1 *Staples.*
of, ought to be generall. Forafmuch as the *good* intended there-   2 *Mynts.*
by, is fo due to all, as cannot be difturbed or reftrained to anie,
without diforder and confufion , for *Omne Bonum, eft fui diffufi-*
*uum⌐.*

This I fay then, is that treble-twifted thred, twyned by louing
and loyall **Ariadne**, to guide our fatall T H E S E V S by, thorowe
all the Mues and Mazes of that *Labyrinth* of Errors, (*Marchan-*
*dizing Exchange*,) to free and redeeme the Bodies of Men , and
Soules of Chriftians, from the yeerely, monthly , and daily deuouring Iawes of that Monfter of *Creete*, and Bawde of *Bankers*,
(**Vfury**,) to the rayfing againe, and perfect vniting of *Religion* &
*Iuftice*, that Mercy and Truth among Men, may fit kindly together, and Righteoufnes and Peace may kiffe each other.

Thus all things in Nature doe tend to perfection by the Rules
of *Order* , and degrees of *Goodnes :* but the vfe makes all. For
*Quò mihi Fortuna fi non conceditur vti ?*

The vfe of *Mettalls*, both Gold and Siluer, as cheefeft materialls for Princes *Coyne*, is in this refpect fo vrgently needfull, that
where *Nature* fayles, *Art* muft make good : in which regard, the
want of Mynes in this Kingdome, hath beene euer fupplyed by
forraine *Bullion,* and auncient *Cuftomes.*

The want of *Coyne* in the Princes Treafurie , fhewes defect of
*Naturall Mynes*, or neglect of artificiall Supplyes, whereof *Bulli-*   *Cudendæ monetæ Ius proprium eft*
*on* is chiefeft. Neither is it enough, fit, nor conuenient, that bee-   *Principis et inde publicæ fiunt.*
ing prouided, or brought to the Mynt, (the publicke pulfe and
hart of *Trafficke*,) priuate Subiects prefume to coyne it for themfelues : leaft thereby Kings become feruaunts to their owne Vaffalls, and conftrained to borrow that fhould be apt to lend . A
courfe in Nature both miferable and prepofterous. For what harder condition , then to fee *Clothiers* compeld to worke out other
mens *Wooll*, for a fhred in the end of the felfe-fame cloth ? Yet
this is worfe. For where all Trades are valued by, and vented for
Money, this makes Coyne both difvalue & fell it felfe. O *hyfteron*
F 2                               *proteron.*

## *The* Cvstvmers

*proteron*, & ground of all Diforder. If K I N G s aboue themfelues haue none but G o d, that only makes *homage* ioyne *honor* to their Crownes, and feeing their feruice doth yeelde them reward, all others below them beeing proftrate at their feete, the names of Wages and Fees, is too bafe for Soueraignes from beneath them to receiue : and for Subiects to offer, prepofterous, perfumptuous, and euery way prophane.

If then the Type of Princes be their Thrones and Dignitie ; if the Obiect of their Actions, (next the glory of that *Deitie* whom they reprefent,) be their owne greatnes & honour ; if Marchants buy and fell *Goodnes* but for theyr owne auaile ; what greater gaine then for Subiects to attaine to their Soueraignes *Dignitie* ? And what harder eftate, then to fee Kings fet aworke, and waged by their Seruants ?

*Conftantinus Magnus, ne aliter quam fancte et legitime hoc regale vteretur : effigiem fuam nummu fic infculpi voluit, vt hominis Deu flexis genibus invocantis prae fe ferret. Moneta aute dicta quod moneat ne quid fraudu in Materia figno vel pondere fiat.*

If the Law pronounce it death, (and that moft worthilie) to counterfet Princes Coynes, by what meanes foeuer ; vvhat can expiat that finne of Prefumption, that as it were with their owne Hands and Stampes, vfurpe their *Preheminence*, and difturbe their *Exchange* ?

In a word, let the hart by the lyuer, receiue his tinctured *Chylus*, by his owne mouth and ftomacke, and the blood with the Spirits fhall fill all the vaines. And if Nature haue taught all men to affect the generall *Good* by particular Trades, and appoynted each Trade his proper Materialls by the helpe and vfe of Money, leaue *Bullion* for Princes, and the World can vvant no Coyne ; the eafie courfe and recourfe of whofe *Exchange*, fhall fet all things in tune, and ferue all Mens turnes.

But to compare things by contraries, will beft illuftrate either. Wee all cry out of *Couetyfe* and *Priuate-gaine*, as good reafon, for G o d himfelfe hath pronounced it the roote of all Euill, and the loue of Money to be flat Idolatry. Which being bad in *Subiects*, muft needes be worft in *Kings :* How great then muft our happines appeare, to haue *Bounty* it felfe come dwell among vs ? And what hartie remorfe ought it to moue to *fome* him and his, abridged or depriued of the principall meanes to practife theyr vertues ?

Great therefore, greater, and greateft of all, muft theyr Accounts be to G o d and *Nature*, that prepofteroufly peruerting his proper Materialls, turne his beft helps for *Bullion* to their priuate aduantage ? to the intollerable difturbance both of Court & Country, and almoft vnrecouerable wrong to the King and his Crowne. Wherein *Cuftomers* wanting wordes to fet out theyr griefes, haue made fignes with their * pennes. And yet ceafe not by Prayer to groane in this manner.

*\* The fecond Reply, or Treatife of Exchange. &c.*

D **that**

# ALPHABET *and* PRIMER.

𝕺 that our Tongues oꝛ Pennes could but expꝛeſſe,
𝕺ꝛ had the gift to make Men vnderſtand
Thoſe great Effects of ſacred happines
Exchange (alone) would woꝛke, by *Prince* and *Counſells* hand :
*Religious Iuſtice* ſhould then ſo bleſſe our Land,
   That Men on Earth might ſee by this *Idea* made,
   What Heauen it ſelfe doth boade in this our Kingly Trade.
So farre off, are *Cuſtomers* from guile in this behalfe.

¶ Now ſee but what is paſt,& ſo put all together,to heare what words they ſpell.

That, **Goodnes** (whoſe Standerd is D E I T I E,) applyed to the actiue perfections of *Commutatiue Right* , by the rules of our Booke, and ſcope of our Leſſon, is a beautifull aſpect, and bene-ficiall influence of Heauenly Beatitude, in the operations of Na-ture and Art, (which in Greeke is vnderſtoode by *Calocagathia*.) Sanctifying and aſſuring the formall Eſſence of all happy Beings: For *Bono ſuo conſtant Omnia*.

*Kaloca'gathia,* id eſt, *Aequum et Bonum, Honeſtum et Vtile :* Beauty and Bountie, Profit & Pleaſure.

And G O D ſawe that all hee had made was exceeding *Good*.

That **Bullion** or **Billion,** is a worde of Art , giuen to the ele-mentall perfections of purenes and finenes in the ſolide Commo-dities of Gold and Siluer, layd out by nature at the Standert of T R V T H, to fixe the proportions of *Good, Better*, and *Beſt* in, for the eaſier extention of *Goodnes* , by vendible *Commerce:* For, as *Omne Bonum eſt ſui diffuſiuum,* ſo *Quantò communius eò melius*.

*Deprehenſum a peritioribus eſt, in Mundi creatione, principē Deum Arithmeticā eſſe vſum, Geometriā stem ac Muſica, ſiquidē Arithmetica ratione compacta connexaque creduntur Elementa : Geometria vero Fi-guras effinxit vt inde firmitatem conſeque-renter, ſtabilitatem ac prō Natura vi mo-bilitatem. Proportiones adnexxit Muſicæ ne terra plus in terreno ſentiretur Elemento, quam Aqua in Aqueo, et in aereo aeru et Igni in ignea Natura: nec Elementorum vllum omnino, in aliud reſolui vlla ratione quiret . Proinde, quum audis a D E O eſſe vniuerſa in numero creata et pondere ac menſura : intellige ad Arithmeticam Nu-merum reſerri, pondus ad Muſicam ad Ge-ometraum vero Menſura adiectum Nomen. Quippe aſtringente grauitatem leuitate cō-fouentur omnia ſulciuūturque : in meditullio namque, ignea poteſtate cohibetur Terra, ſed et huic ignu innititur. Ita profacto eſt, Magnitudo Exquiſitiſſimi, nec laudas vn-quam pro dignitate Operu, necnon late pa-tens vu et motus, admirabilem Opificu præ ſe fert potentiam . Diſpoſitio vero excul-tiſſima, mirificam oſtentat Sapientiā, Vſus vero ad optimū vbiq; cōducens latius exu-birantem nobu ingerit bonitatem. Proinde ſummi Platonici vniuerſum hoc velut au-guſtiſſimam Dei ſtatuam eximie venerati ſunt. Et que in eo cæteris Maieſtate Natura præſtare videntur, tanquam Idearum cer-tiōra Simulachra. Cælij Rodigini, Lib. 1. Cap. 2.*

That *Money* or *Coyne*, is a figured proportion of *Number* and *Weight*, layd out by Art at the Standerd of I V S T I C E to weigh the *degrees* of *Goodnes* by, in all thinges vendible; *Vt quod vſpiam naſcitur Boni, id apud omnes affluat*. The woorth whereof, none but Soueraine-wiſdome can iuſtly value or equalize , and abſolute Authoritie ſtampe and make currant: becauſe, *Omne quod efficit Tale, id ipſum eſſe magis Tale oportet*.

And. That **Exchange** (whoſe Standerd is E Q V I T I E,) is that Rule in *pollicie* and gouernment of *State*, which ſencibly demon-ſtrates thoſe heauenly Effects of *Power* & *Wiſedome* that D E I T I E imparts to mortall *Gods*, and *Counſailes* on Earth, by meanes of Money, to maintaine the worth, and ſhewe the true vſe of all Things in *Trafficke*, by their proper Obiects, & peculiar Ends.

That as **Goodnes** Diuinely ſublimated , becomes onely fixt in **Bullion:** and **Bullion** onely coynd, deuides the proportions of *Good, Better*, and *Beſt*, reciuing life in it ſelfe from Soueraine Eſſence, becomes currant withall, through all the parts of ven-dible *Commerce:* to ſhew the preheminent potencie that P R I N-c E S haue aboue their *Subiects:* So **Exchange** meaſuring propor-tions in Gold and Siluer by weights of *more* or *leſſe*,to vphold the iuſt value, and maintaine the true vſe of *Goodneſſe* , as well of all things in *Trafficke*,by Coyne,as in Coyne it ſelfe ; ſets forth their
   G.                      ſinguler

## *The* CVSTVMERS

finguler *Care, Prouidence, Prudence* and *Wiſedome*.

The orderly practiſe whereof being outwardly obſerued, conſiſts in the ready exchange of currant Coyne, purged and prepared by the fire of their Mynts, for dead or droſſie *Bullion*, layde

\* That is to ſay, Wares ſo cenſured at the *Staples* before they come to the Ports to croſſe the Seas, as vpon the honour of the Kingdom, and creditte of the Perſons & Places that firſt affoorde them, are made as vendible without all poſſibilitie of fraude or deceit frō the Seller to the Buyer, as are our *Sandwich* Bayes. &c.

downe at the Altars of their publick Temples, for \* *Stapled-Commodities*, as the word it ſelfe both ſpells and imports. But the myſterie of this Art, is quietly conueyd in the lending and loanes of currant Coyne to ſuch as want, vpon equall termes of H o m a g e and T r v s t. The End of *Money* being to make all things vendible, by equalitie of worth, and value of it ſelfe, for the quicker diſpatch and aduauncement of *Trafficke*: and the *Ends* of *Trafficke* the Soueraignes *honour*, the Kidgdomes *peace*, and the Subiects *wealth*. Thus mouing and diſpoſing all mens Endeuours, by willing Courſes, and perpetuall Motions, to ſerue and worke for O n e, and that O n e made able to maintaine the *Syntheſis*, and protect the freedome of *Trafficke*, by fitting all Mens turnes.

And thus is *Trafficke* made the true and aſſured practiſe of that

*¶ Lapis Phyloſophicus.*

*myſticall Phyloſophy*, wherein ſo many wits haue ſpent theſelues, & blowne the coales in vaine; whoſe heauenly *Elixar*, (*Goodnes*,) the Quinteſſence *of Nature* and *Art*, by Diuine ſublimation applyde to Materialls, breedes Myſteries in Trades, and purging all droſſe of deceit from Trades, turnes Trades into Mettalls, and all Mettalls into pure Siluer, and fine Gold.

*¶ Vniuerſalis Medecina.*

And **Exchange** becomes that *Cordiall preſeruatiue*, which eaſing all griefes and ſores, ſuppling all ſores in diſeaſes, and curing all diſeaſes in particuler Members, holds the whole Body of Kingdomes in health. The ſacred Rules whereof, as no prophane Couetyſe could euer comprehend, nor confident Empericke attaine to practiſe; ſo none of priuate Diſcretion, or partiall Affection, may preſume to alter or controll, as being a Doctrine peculiar to the *Graueſt* and *Wiſeſt* in higheſt Authoritie, and for P r i n c e s themſelues.

Of *Trafficke* then, by Nature ſo admirable, and by Art made ſo amiable, thus wonderfully wrought, & orderly taught by Rules of T r v t h, I v s t i c e & E q v i t y, what can be leſſe ſaid, then, that her Doctrine is Heauenly, and fit for none but *Kings*, and *Counſaile-Tables*, her ſeate beeing euery-where the Soueraignes owne Boſome. Whoſe voyce well tunde, is the harmonie of the World; to whom both Courts and Countryes owe *Fealtie* & *Homage*: the meaneſt Subiect feeling her Care, and the greateſt Princes ſubiect to her Prouidence; whom both Noble and Vnnoble admire, and loue as the Nurſe and Protectreſſe of all their earthly *Honours, Proſperities, Peace* and *Ioy*.

Since G o o d n e s then is that purging Fire, that ſent from Heauen, can onely purifie from droſſe of Deceit, all the Materialls prepared and preſented at the ſanctified Altars of publique

Com-

## Alphabet *and* Primer.

Commerce, to make *Kings* adored, & *Subiects* happy : And Gold and Siluer, of all folide *Bodies*, the apteft and fureft for generall behoofe to fixe this *Goodnes* in : No maruaile at all, if all men, admiring the *Beautie* and *Bounty* of the One and the Other, fo ferioufly affect them as their chiefeft Treafure.

But admit it were graunted, that fome One Man alone might become poffeffed of all the Gold which the world doth côtaine, and of all the Siluer that Nature affoordes; or each Man as much as his hart could wifh, yet the fame vncoynd, would prooue but idle or comberfome, for want of publicke vfe. For though *Goodneffe* by DEITIE vniuerfally infufed, and in *Bullion* fixed by publicke confent, be fufficient for worth to fet foorth it felfe, yet till *Soueraigntie* by Wifedome appoynt out their vfe, & Power make them Currant; euen *Coyne* is not Coyne, and hath no life at all, but refts a weight of maffy Mould, and fenceleffe *Beeing*. VVoe woorth then all thofe PROMETHEY, that for priuate refpects, fteale this Heauenly-fire, frô the holy 1 Altars of *Vnity* & *Truth*, and in contempt of *Maieftie*, rob and engroffe the publicke ftore of our 2 *Temples* of *Iuftice*. And all thofe NADABS and ABIHVES, that offering ftrange fire, from prophane Altars of priuie 3 *Prefumption*, feeke to poyfon our *Trafficke*, and all parts of *Commerce*.

*Vt mundo Natura Curfum. Soli Lumen et Aqua fluxum, fic gratiã Auro.*

1 Mynts, by Coyning for themfelues.

2 Staples, by Monopolies.

3 Counterfetters of Coyne.

**Money** in a Kingdome, beeing the fame that Blood is in the *Body*, and all Allayes but humors. For when the Standerd of *Goodnes* in Gold and Siluer, is vnfteddily fixt, & *Money* in weight vnconftantly Coynd, & for vfe vnwoorthily Currant, as all *Commodities* befides, become deerer and deerer; that is to fay, of more efteeme then *Money* it felfe : So the People of that Kingdome, grow troubled, and vnquiet within themfelues, according to the bafenes of the Coyne when it is perceiued.

That KING then that puts in his *Coyne* much *Bullion*, and little *Allay*, makes Himfelfe powerfully admyred, his Nobles refpectiuely honoured, and his Commons obediently diligent, and all Men willing to raife themfelues by their Induftries and Trades, holding their times well fpent, and labours well employed, for fuch Money as they beleeue and find to be perfect Treafure.

Contrariwife, he that puts much *Allay* to little *Bullion*, makes *Maieftie* it felfe, contemptibly weake; the *Nobles*, neglectedly defpifed; and the *Commôns*, ftubbornly careleffe, to worke for that, they find afore-hand and know, not woorth their labour. The onely way to Reputation and Wealth, beeing left to *Religious Tillage* and *Honeft Grafing*. *Victus* & *Veftitus* being euerie Mans want. Neceffity vpholding the eftimation of their *Commodities* far aboue *Bafe-Money*, whilft all men feeke to them, & they almoft to no man.

And as a fteddy Standerd, and ftore of Coyne in the Princes

Trea-

## *The* CVSTVMERS

Treaſury, makes all things els cheape, holds Trades in requeſt, ſhewes Kings to be powerfull, and Subieꜩ wealthy: ſo, as the *Standerd* falls vncertaine, and Money engroſt into priuate handes, all things grow deere, the King becomes weake, and his Subieꜩ poore, whilſt Coyne it ſelfe by **Uſurp** in *Marchandizing Exchange*, eates out Induſtry and Trades; and *Marchandizing Marchants* by MONOPOLIES, conſpyre to ſtrangle *Trafficke*. Examples hereof may be *Edw:* 3. 1338. at his going to conquer *France*. And *Edw.* 4. ouerwhelmed by warres at home.

*Marchandizing Exchange.*

MONOPOLYES.

For **Money** is not regarded for the Name-ſake, but for weight of true worth, and vſe of currant value. King *Henry* the 3. in his pound, or xx. s. of currant Siluer coyne, put xij. ounces ſterling. Which then was, and yet is worth an ounce of fine Gold, and ſo was payd his Rent. *Edw:* 4. rayſd that ounce to fortie ſhillings, which hee found but at foure Nobles. And *Edw:* 6. receiued no more in eyght pounds-rent of Siluer coyne, then xij. ounces ſterling; and ſo loſt to himſelfe & his Nobility ſeauen parts of their Reuenewes, the Land beeing the ſame it was in *Hen:* 3. time, & not rayſed in proportion; which theyr Tenants euer found.

The way to retayne *Gold* and *Siluer* within a Kingdome, and draw more vnto it, is to hold a perfeꜩ and ſteddy Standerd at home, & call all Forraine-coynes currant, one penny in an ounce of Siluer, and xij. pence in Gold aboue their owne. But aboue all that can be ſaid, or any way deuiſed, maintaine the Springhead, (*Trafficke*,) and when all wants are ſupplyed, the waſt will ſeeme needfull, or at leaſt not much regarded.

*Trafficke,* a more aſſured meanes to ſupply our King with *Bullion,* then the Mynes of INDIA.

And thus is Gold and Siluer (the ſeates of *fixed Goodnes,*) fitlie *ab effeꜩis,* called *King* & *Queene* of the world, in making Kings as powerfull in their Thrones, to proteꜩ their Subieꜩ both by Sea and Land, & diſpoſe of *Trafficke* within their Kingdoms, as GOD by *Goodnes,* in *Number, Weight,* & *Meaſure,* firſt made the world, and ſtill doth guide the ſame. Each KING beeing an *Idea* of DEITIE it ſelfe, ſo much excelling in *Preheminence* of power for his *Perſon* and *Place,* and in *Prerogatiue* of wiſedome for *Affeꜩion* and *Loue,* by how much they endeuour, to expreſſe in themſelues, and extend vnto others, the Charaꜩers of their *Maieſtie,* & Titles of their *Glory,* (IVSTICE and MERCY,) in the true vſe of *Coyne.*

*Auro et Argento, Quid non?* hauing GOD and a good cauſe to friend.

But theſe *Mathematicks* are *Acroamaticall,* fit for ALEXANDER the great, and ARISTOTLE the wiſe, to walke & diſcourſe of, *Horis matutinis in Gymnaſio Lyceo,* by then ſelues all alone, and not for vs to ſpeake of, or ſpell. Neither had we thus preſumed (deſpiſed as we are) from our deſolate *Schooles,* and lowly *Cottages,* to ſteppe into the Court, and enter the Mazes of theſe ſacred grounds, but to beate downe and preuent the dangerous *Suggeſtions* of Imaginary Doꜩrine, and *Legerte de maine* wherwith ſome

*The onely cauſe of publiſhing heereof in this ſort.*

Specula-

## Alphabet *and* Primer.

Speculatiue Men, rifen vp in our time, bewitch all they meete; and (were it but poffible,) would feduce the Wife: who feuering themfelues from the *Body* of our Commerce, and wandering out of fight, to keepe all men ftill vnder, & themfelues aboue, would perfwade the world, that *Trafficke* of herfelfe is a perillous byting beaft; and that to bring her home to her owne Creekes & Ports, muft needes deftroy all our Sheepe in *Cotfall*, and decay all our Shypping on *Cheuiat-hills*, and *Barham-downes*: which Affertion of theirs, fo ftrangely vndertaken, and ftifly maintained, if neyther fond nor falfe, yet is it but as true, as the building and raifing of *Tenterden-fteeple*, was the ruine and decay of our *Sandwich-Hauen*, whom Land and Seas haue fet fome 30. miles afunder. For confutation whereof, this place and time requires that fomthing now be faid to fatisfie the Wife, though I muft confeffe the eafines is fuch, that how to difpute it in any ferious manner, I cannot well deuife.

¶ All Affertions whatfoeuer, that fall within the compaffe of humaine Difcourfe, are made and maintained eyther by pregnancie of Wit, cleerenes of Reafon, or demonftratiue Experience, (for againft Diuine Reuelations wee meane not to difpute,) the Minde confulting ftill with memory, and fancies Conceits. In which refpect it is, that *Imagination* is truly termed the Storehoufe of Wit, Memories Seate, and Fancies Pallace. By meanes whereof, as the pulfe deelares beft how the hart doth worke; fo the thoughts of our Mindes, to purpofe good or bad, doe foonft bewray themfelues.

Vppon this Anuile then we will begin to ftrike, and entering this Clofet, demaund of thefe affured and confident Difputers, fo boldly contefting againft all Commers, that the bringing home of *Trafficke*, muft needes decay our Shipping; whether their wits in fo deeming, be within them or without them. If they aunfwere, Within them, as likely they will: then they, (without their wits,) muft needes be diftracted, franticke, or mad. And who is able *cum ratione infanire*? And if to mend themfelues, they confeffe theyr wits to be without them, then muft they ftand as witleffe, their Conceits beeing but Dreames, and their Dreames but Fancies.

But let their wits alone, and leaue them to their fancies, till they finde one the other, for perhaps they fee more reafon then their Wits can deuife, or Conceits can vtter; I aske them then, (as men that would feeme at leaft to vnderftand thefelues;) whether by this (our *Shipping*,) they meane Ships of *Burden*, or Ships of *Defence*, or both, or neither? <sub></sub>

All Shyps are eyther for Burden or Defence.

If they fay Shyps of *Burden*. How fhould fancy or frenfie, by Difcourfe of Wit or Reafon, maintaine a Conceit, and perfwade it vnto others, which Experience in the Ports doth dailie condemne,

H. demne,

## *The* CVSTVMERS

demne, and demonftratly controll? Complayning ftill for want of Keyes, Docks, and Wharfes to build on. Not of *Matter*, but of *Place*, where *Trafficke* once doth come, and but vnmaske her face.

And fhould we thinke it poffible, that fhe which hath had the power to turne *Creekes* into *Ports*, adde *Ports* vnto *Townes*, rayfe *Townes* into *Citties*, and enrich whole *Countries* with *Artificers* & *Trades*, *Marriners* and *Shipping*, with our Neighbours abroad in leffe then 50. yeeres, fhould proue fo idle, nay hurtfull now at home. *Trafficke* is the Chariot, & *Shypping* are the Wheeles that beare our glorious L I G H T, and is that *Body* fhadowleffe that neuer wants the S V N N E.

*Ships carry Trafficke, as wheeles doe the Chariot. And Traffick the triumphant Coach that beares the Glory of our K I N G the Worlde round about.*

But ftill they feeme to mutter much, and mufe among themfelues, framing Conclufions without the bounds of Reafon, or due regard of all our former premiffes, to fee if feare with fancie may perfwade the Wife. That if *Trafficke* be reftored, and Strangers compeld to feeke her heere at home; it is not vnlikely, but to ferue their Turnes, they will come prouided with Shypping of their owne. And then what? Forfooth, though *Trafficke* make vs rich (as no queftion but fhee will,) what bootes our Wealth, when *Inuafion* or *Pyracie* may rob vs of our ftore?

To which I aunfwere thus. Let Saylers tend their Tacklings, their Maifters whiftle, and Captaines high commaund: Bring home our *Staples*, and C A S T O R and P O L L V X the G O D S of our Seas, made able and powerfull to warrant our *Trafficke*, skilfull P A L I N V R V S that fits at our Helme, obferuing our Compaffe, will fafely guide our *Courfe*, and direct all our *Shypping*. *Protecti-on* and *Direction* beeing effentiall parts of that *Preheminent, Dig-nitie*, and facred *Prerogatiue* our K I N G s haue euer had, *Experience* hath confirmed, and our *Counfells* may challenge.

*The Nauy-Royall before Sluse, 1340. And before Callais, 1588.*

This care and feare therefore comes too neere our Sterne, importing a diftruft of the prouidence and prudence of our Land, and fauors of Prefumption, or fome-thing worfe.

*Blafphemie.*

Thefe curious cafters beyond the Moone, would goe further if they durft, and enquire how G O D can hold the Sky, & keepe the Sunne from falling: Or what hee did before the World vvas made.

But admit it that affection and loue to *Trafficke*, (*ne quid afperi-us*,) haue made them fearefull of others good, and iealous of their owne; I wifh the to beware how they come too neere the *Helme* for touching the *Rudder*. For what got P R O M E T H E V S for his Sky-ftolne fire at laft, from the wheeles of this Chariot, when the fimple *Satyre* for kiffing it in kindneffe onely, found it burnt his lyppes?

Leauing therefore all thofe *Holy* grounds, and *Cordialls* of G O O D N E S to our facred I D E A S of *Maieftie* and *Wifedome*, that

beeing

# ALPHABET *and* PRIMER.

beeing *Best* themselues, must needes be *Good* to others, but specially *Trafficke*, whose heauy Spirits, so tumbled & so tost by *Embargoes* abroad, and *Extremities* at home, desirous of some rest; reposing her selfe at their sanctified feete, giues vs likewise leaue to returne to our Bookes, and spell out our Lesson.

Now our Lessons are her *Tributes* and personall *Rights*, vvhich Necessity doth call for, and Free-will doth offer: namely, *Customes* and *Subsidies*, but chiefely *Customes*, which onely & alone could we once be taught distinctly but to read, would ease all our *Griefes*, increase all our * *Fees*, and pay for all her Phisicke. For *Customes* then, lets now apply our selues, and spell our Letters.

* This is meant by the OVT-PORTS onely.

*Customes* (I say,) but not such *Customes* as conquering *Romans* deuised, and imposed vpon the stubburne and stifnecked *Iewes*, whose Tributes were Cursses of Diuine *Iustice*, to keepe them vnder. Whose * *Publicans* became *Christians* themselues, and taught the foundations of *Religion* to others, though their *Searchers* by nature became *Harpyes*, and their *Wayters* by profession, were euery way *Sinners*.

IVDEA.

* S. MATTHEVV, sometimes a *Publican*.

Nor such *Customes* as *Tyranny* doth inuent, and daily impose vpon enthralled *Subiects*, to stand on, and raise it selfe by.

ITALIE.

Nor such as tumultuous *Warres* haue made our Neigbours deuise, and impose among and vpon themselues, to defend theyr liues and their liberties by.

NETHER-LANDS.

But such *Customes*, as mildnes and mercy to relieue our Neighbours, our Allies, and our Friendes, the Wisedome of our Land hath inuested our KINGS, to maintaine the *Maiestie* of our Kingdome by.

Such *Customes* as demonstratiuely shewing the Reall possession, & Actuall protection, our *Soueraignes* hold of euery Mans welth, leaue notwithstanding to euery Subiect his *Meum* and *Tuum*, and full vse of his owne.

Lastly, such *Customes*, as like easie *Quit-rents* of a fertile *Fee-farme*, shew the power of the *Lord*, and greatnes of the *Mannor*, the defrauding whereof, doth worthily forfet all possession and protection of the immediat *Free-holder*.

For *Customes* of themselues, and properly taken, are but easie payments of a *Currant-Money*, to Customers at their e *Ports*, by i *Marchants*, Subiects or Strangers, for such *Stapled* Commodities, as o *Orderly* bought, and for Number, Weight, & Measure, sufficiently censured, before they crosse the Seas; with the *Staple* Seale, and speciall Certificate come warranted thether; for our Soueraignes u *Honor*, and Countries credit.

a. e. i. o. u.

And heere now who sees not in a very fewe wordes but thus put together, the full vse and sound of all our fiue Vowells, for *Matter*, *Place*, *Persons*, *Order*, and *End*, that the *Ports* and the *Staples* ralate each to other.

H 2                                        But

## *The* CVSTVMERS

But as the *Steward* of a *Mannor*, that sits to hold a Court, wanting the Rolls and autenticke Records of his Lords Reuenewes, can neither call the *Tennants* diftinctly by their Names, demaund their *Quit-rents*, nor vnderftand their Homage, how each doth bound his Fee, or hold his owne : fo fares it with *Cuftomers*. For beeing tyde to their Ports by carefull attendance, for difcharge of their Bonds and peculiar truft : Their wares without warrant, and their *Staples* out of fight, from whence their worke fhould come. Their Vowels all difplaced, their Mutes are dombe, and Liquids iarre. For without ʊ Sɪʀs, and ʊ my *Lordes*, ʊ hath no found, to fpeake or fpell out 𝕮𝖚𝖘𝖙𝖚𝖒𝖊𝖘 : and all for lacke of 𝕾𝖙𝖆𝖕𝖑𝖊𝖘.

ʊ ʊ ʊ
𝕮 𝕰 𝖒 𝖘.

*Trafficke*, fubiect to the *Syncope*, or great fwounding which heere is defcribed, and the remedies.

𝕾𝖙𝖆𝖕𝖑𝖊𝖘! Now fee fee my Lords, for Gods fake fee, how *Traffick* falls a weeping, her pulfe is weake, & her Spirits fayle, her face is pale and wan, at the name and found of *Staples*, the want wherof fo wounds her Soule, that her hart is fet on bleeding ; yet côfort her ftill, & hold her vpright to keepe her from deadly fwouning : and fpeake her fayre, that fhe doe not defpayre of the Cordialls in your onely keeping.

Tell her kindly withall, *Primatio præfupponit habitum*, for neuer man yet was fo continually ficke, whofe health hath not had a *Beeing* : and the difproportioned difpofition of Confufion it felfe, dooth argue an intention, and poffibilite of Order. Therefore fpeake my good Lords, to reuiue all her fpirits, for your wordes are full of power ; yea fpeake aloude (I fay) & affure her you will belay all her *Staples*. Yea, fpeake you, and you (Sɪʀs) for your *Bullion* fake, for that is your right, and no mans but yours, by the Rules of all *Truth*, and fixed *Goodnes*. For your Mynts fake, for that is your *Honor*, and no mans but yours by the Rules of *Iuftice*. For your *Exchange* fake, for that is your *Glory*, and no mans but yours by the Rules of *Equality* ; and for your *Cuftomes* fake, for that is your profit, and no mans but yours, by the Rules of *Iuftice* and *Equitie*, fo fhall *Honeftum* and *Vtile* concurre both together : *Honeftie* being euermore the height and type of *Honour*, & publicke *Vtilitie*, the Mother of *Iuft* and *Right*, for each mans good and gaine. Say not you can reftore them, for that fhee knowes already, but fay you will doe it, and then fhe will beleeue you. And wee your poore *Schollers*, loyall *Subiects* and *Seruaunts*, wil euery way attend you with all our beft endeuours. Or els farwell fweet *Trafficke*, and fo farewell *Cuftomes*, yea farewell *Iuftice* : nay farewell *Religion*, and then farewell *All*. So farre off are *Cuftomers* from guilt alfo in this behalfe.

*Quicquid enim Iuftum, id etiam vtile cenfent fummi Philofophi, itemque quod honeftum id effe Iuftum. Ex quo efficitur, vt quicquid honeftū fit, idem fit vtile. Cice: offic: lib: 2.*

But alas poore *Cuftomers*, who doth harken to your cryes, or beleeue your Reports ? Who fhall weigh your zeale, to our *Soueraignes* Honour, and his *Peoples* Good, or care for your Endeuors ? Yet be not difmaid ; *In magnis voluiffe fat eft, fint catera Diuū.*

Stand

# ALPHABET *and* PRIMER.

Stand ſtill but awhile, and let G O D himſelfe alone. What though inveterate Errors of ages that are paſt haue multiplyed themſelues, and now ſeeme to muſter againſt our happy dayes: our D A Y S T A R R E that is riſen, and D A VV N I N G in our eyes, will in good time diſperſe them, or amend them as they may, and take but thus much onwards. That *Ignorance* hath beene e-uery way the Mother but of *Errors*, of whom came *Miſchiefes*, and of ſuch our *Inconveniences*, which though they threat *Confu-ſion*, yet tell vs notwithſtanding, there is a way to *Order*, that leades vs to *perfection*, as *Truth* by the Cauſes of *Truth* ſhal come but to be knowne.

KING.
PRINCE.

Now *Truth* indeede lyes deepe, and the danger ſuch in dig-ing, that no man hath the patience to delue vntill they find her: & I am to too weake (* alas,) to worke her out alone. O that WISDOME therfore which onely can diſcloſe thē, would make men admire thoſe glorious Titles of *Iuſtice* and *Mercy*, (Em-blemes of *Truth*,) that the Volumes in her *Cabinet*, and *Treaſu-rie* containes ! Then ſhould wee learne the Rules and proporti-ons of Numbers, Weights, and Meaſures. The vſe of *Staples* in former times, how they were kept, and whether they be gone. Then ſhould wee ſee thoſe wonderfull effects of our *Loadſtones* at home, that haue wrought ſuch miracles in other forraine Lands, and Nations from abroad, bringing *Bullion* in amaine, make our * *Pulſes* to beat in moe places thē one. And we poore Schollers made confident in our *Cuſtomes*, without poſſibilltie of fraude, cauſe of diſtruſt, or feare of *blame*.

* The Wryter almoſt tyred & out of hart, referres the *Truth* of all, to the Records of the K: *Treaſury* in his *Exchequer*, for Weights & Mea-ſures, *Staple* Accounts & Orders.

* *Myntes*.

In the meane time, ſith no men can pipe well that want their vpper lyps, conſequence concludes it, and *Truth* makes it good, that as no *Church* hath no *Tythes*, and no *Court* no *Quit-rents* ; ſo no *Staples* no *Cuſtomes*. Whereby *Neceſſity* ouertaken, beeing put to her ſhyfts, makes bold with *Free-will*, and to ayde P R E-HEMINENCE, tranſcending to PREROGATIVE, turnes Cu-ſtomes into Subſidies of Tonnage and Pondage, as if P R E HE-MINENCE and PREROGATIVE were meerely *Synonimas*, and meant but one thing ; and bounded *Iuſtice* that layes out all our Rights, were that boundleſſe *Mercy* that makes vs all to liue ; and *Mercy* it ſelfe, but a word of prophaneneſſe, or ſome ordina-rie thing.

Cuſtomes in England, or in Engliſh *Trafficke*, alwayes preſuppoſe our *Staples*, and liue and dye or follow thē, as Effects their proper Cauſes.

The blending or miſtaking of *Pre-rogatiue* for *Preheminence*, a dange-rous meanes to prophane the So-ueraine effects and reuerence of Mercy in Kings.

Thus whilſt our *Graue Maiſters* & *Moderators* of our *Schooles* haue been buſied and diſtracted in the ſtudie and practiſe of the higher poynts of learning our *Staples* beeing ſtolne, tranſmuted and tranſplanted, our *Cuſtomes* are confounded : and wee poore Schollers ſtill tyde to our *Stakes*, ſeeme fitte for nothing but bea-ting and bayting. Hence grew the grounds of all our *Diſorders*, the breaches of our *Schooles*, and our * *Nurſes* deadly ſickneſſe, that threatned all our Ruines : had not *Wiſedome* frō aboue, out

Marchants by Societies monopoli-zing our *Staple* Commodities, and Royall wares, baue found the way to Staple them ſtill beyond Seas, & ſo confounding both our *Cuſtomes* & diuerting all our *Bullion*, fill the Realme with baſer or more need-leſſe matter in their returnes.

* *Trafficke*.

of

## *The* CVSTVMERS

of *loue* and *affection* so belayde our falls , that the power of that WORD which made vs first of nothing, became the meanes to redeeme vs all from nothing; and \*BOVNTIE it selfe hath laid the foundation, (and begun at the least) to become the MAN: whereby our ioyes may be great , and by so much the greater, by how much our greatest losse (as all men thought) is like to become our greatest gaine.

\*KING.

The comfort that Cuſtomers cō-ceiue of the King and Prince.

Our comforts then growing from our *Soueraignes* owne PER-SON, and our hopes aboue hopes, from the power of his WORD; whose naturall ſtorge to *Iuſtice* and *Right* beeing euery vvay good, their *affections* also free, and *loue* without end : Lets heere reſt awhile , and ſetling our ſelues , both thinke and thanke *God*, and learne to ſay *Grace*, that *Grace* in diſgrace may pitty our caſes among the reſt, and raiſe our poore credites from im-pudent Ignorance, inſolent Pride , and ſhameleſſe Diſdaine : ſaying ;

The Cuſtomers daily Grace.

> As God by his Goodnes and Truth did direct vs,
>      whoſe mercy endures for euer,
> So his Grace and his fauour vouchſafe to protect vs,
>      for his mercy endures for euer.
> That our Traffick by Staples in temper againe,
>      for his mercy endures for euer,
> Our Ports with their Cuſtomes may chaūt it amaine
>      that his mercy endures for euer.

---

Thus farre by poynting and ſpelling in this ALPHABET and PRIMER our weakenes hath attaynd to reſolue and read out. That the right of Kings beeing *Bullion*, their Honour theyr *Coyne*, theyr Glory their *Exchange*, and *Cuſtomes*, their Homage and honeſt gayne : ſhewes that *Maieſtie* is preheminent and may well be ſeene, and that *Soueraigne Prerogatiue* may likewiſe ſubſiſt. But our PATRONE being robd of his *Staples*, ſpoyld of his *Bullion*, and wanting the *Cuſtomes* ſhould growe from his ſtore ; his *Mynts* all decayed, & almoſt out of worke, is forſt to ſeeke ayde by *Subſidies, Impoſitions, Impoſts, Lones* of his owne for intereſt, and Marchants *Supplyes*. Aye mee alas, and woe is me therefore.

*Tranſitio* from Cuſtomes to Sub-ſidies by a *Simile*, ſetting forth the oddes and difference of eyther.

There's a *Place* in this Land where a great Man doth dwell, in whoſe beautifull Garden a ſtately *Fountaine* ſtands, in the vſe and rayſing whereof, it ſeemes that Art contends with Nature, and both conſpire together. The *Spring* by plentifull *ſtreames*, through Pypes and Quills ſeruing all the *Ceſternes* of the *Te-nants* adioyning, with a power in priuate, to ſtoppe or let out at pleaſure. By tract of time, corruptions abroad, or neglect at
            home

# Alphabet *and* Primer.

home the *Spring* becomes perverted, the *ſtreames* runne waſt, or the *Fountaine's* out of frame, that the Lord of the ſoyle, vvho ſhould releeue others, by the bountie of his owne, wanting water himſelfe, craues ayde of the *Tenants*, whoſe *Ceſternes* containe no more of themſelues then his currant afforded & Conduct controld. His wants at the firſt are gladly ſupplyed. But the ofter the worſe ; for in theſe Elements of life and vitall ſubſiſtence, *Religion* bids *Reaſon* prouide firſt for *Nature*, & be next herſelfe. Diſtreſſes beeing dangerous, if not deadly, when the blood is retracted, and the *Hart* wants his owne.

This muſt helpe for a time (till our *Staples* be found) by *Meum* and *Tuum*, betweene *Cuſtomes* and *Subſidies*,) to compare and demonſtrate, for want of the One, the vſe of the other.

But heere lets pauſe awhile, the better to ioyne our Letters together, and miſtruſting our ſelues, craue ayde of our *Maiſters* and *Myld-Moderators*: that hauing eyes which can ſee, they may helpe vs to ſpell, and eares that can heare, they may harken how we reade, & make vs vnderſtand. 1. Firſt, how it comes to paſſe, that our *Staples* beeing diſſolued or tranſplanted out of ſight (from whence all our *Homagers* were ſometimes vvont to come) and our *Cuſtomes* retaining the leaſt part of themſelues, beſides their voyce & ſound ; all Tytles notwithſtanding ſeeme dyde with their Tincture, and drownd as it were, with the *Eccho* of their Name. 2. And in calling for our *Subſidies*, where & how to find out the *Principall verbe*.

As in the two ſacred words of higheſt power, aforeſaid: ſo in the blending & miſtaking of *Cuſtomes* for *Subſidies*, Traffick is diſordered, & Cuſtomers being diſgraced, hūbly craue that the worlde might be ſatisfied, and theſelues better taught.

All Tributes couered vnder the title of Cuſtomes confuſedly.

For whilſt our *Staples* were at home, & ioyned to our *Ports*, or ſo neere together, that each might anſwere other, our *Loade-ſtones* drew in *Bullion*, for our *Mynts* at hand to coyne : and wee reading in our * *Rentalls* as well in *value* as in *quality* & *quantitie*, what our *Marchants* there had bought, could call iuſtly for our Cuſtomes before they croſt the Seas, without fraude or covyn, or other Booke of Rates. But in our *Pondage* and *Tonnage*, we know not how to reade or ſpell, and therefore ſeeke to learne. For,

The way how to collect Cuſtome confidently and truly.

* The Staple-Certificats & Cuſtomers-Entries, were certaine Controlements each to other, without Bookes of Rates. The way to receiue Subſidies by Bookes of Rates, different frō that of Cuſtomes, and more partiall and vncertaine,

*Horatius.*

> " *Haud Natura poteſt Iuſto ſecernere iniquum,*
> " *Diuidit vt bona diuerſis, fugienda petendis :*
> " *Nec vincet ratio hoc tantundem vt peccet. Idemq,*
> " *Qui teneros Caules alieni fregerit horti*
> " *Et qui nocturnus Diuum ſacra legerit.* ( A D S I T
> " R E G V L A) *peccatis quæ pœnas irroget æquas,*
> " *Ne ſcutica dignum horribili ſectere flagello.*

It is not our weake ſtrength alone can ſtay
Or hold the Skales of *Good* & *Ill* vpright :
Nor is that *Reaſon* good that makes all one by day,
To crop a Neighbors garden-*leekes*, & rob a Church by night :

## *The* CVSTVMERS

A RVLE muſt guide the whole to keep the parts from ſwaruing,
And puniſh faults in euery one according to deſeruing.

     And not to thinke that euery ſlippe,
     Like deadly-Sinne deſerues a whippe.

    For : If *Soueraigne Dignitie* be that ſacred *Obiect* which *true-louing Loyaltie* is apt to admire, and ſeckes to honour with *naturall reſpects*, (ſuch as all *Subſidies* are or ought to be) who can be capable of ſo great a glory, by perſonall Right, but *ſelfe-ſubſiſting Maieſtie?* and who can accept of ſo great affection, but the eye of *Grace?*

    If theſe our *Subſidies* of *Tonnage* and *Pondage*, be thoſe *naturall reſpects* which loue is deſirous that loyaltie ſhould offer, to honour our *Soueraigne* and *Patrone* onely by, beſides his Cuſtoms, who can impoſe thē but Loues owne *affection?* who can eſteeme them but the hand of *Mercy?* and what can encreaſe them but *cheerefull alacritie* in the Giuers mind?

    Laſtly. If *Tonnage* and *Pondage* be thoſe *honourable Effectes* of affectionate Loyaltie which Marchants tranſcending their other duties, with *ioy* preſent and *Mercy* takes. Who ſhall direct and dilate their proportions by *Number*, *Weight*, & *Meaſure*, for the mutuall behoofe of *Loue* and *Grace?* VVho I ſay, can teach vs this part of our Leſſon, but the graueſt and Wiſeſt, and wiſedome from the Higheſt? namely, **howe to deale Iuſtlie betwéene the Prince and the People?**

    For *cheerefulneſſe* and *alacritie*, inducements vnto *Grace*, the hart & Eſſence of all our *Aydes*, (as coldneſſe in affection makes preſents little worth) whilſt we ſought to further, and by often repetition at all hands to encreaſe to our *Patrons* honor and his Peoples good, that *Honeſtum* and *Vtile* might ſtill keepe together, by the rules of *Right* and *Reaſon:* Wee are checkt and controuled by *Court-rolles* and *Court-rules*, and made to beleeue that *Honeſtie* in this caſe hath naught to doe with *Profit*. Diſcretion commaunding the moſt for the King; as if *Honour* heere were booteleſſe, or ſome idle thing: and that *publique Vtilitie* were meant by *priuate Gaine*. We conteſt in nothing, but euerie way willing and deſirous for to learne, our *harmeleſſe diſpoſitions* are ſcornd and deſpiſed; our *Truth* is held for *Errour*, our *Vertue Vice*. And for crying but A D S I T  R E G V L A, wee are dingd ſo like Barnes that we dare not greit. And thus with the grounds of our former Diſorders, began the degrees of all our Diſgraces; which the ſequell now ſhall ſhewe.

---

    ¶ As in all other Functions, ſo in this of *Cuſtomers*, three things there are to warrant the Calling, but without the fourth none can ſubſiſt. For beſide, the authoritie of our firſt Inſtitu-
tion,

*[marginal notes, left column:]*

*Hoc autem de quo nunc agimus, id ipſum eſt quod vtile appellatur, in quo verbo lapſa cōſuetudo deflexit deuia. Eoq́; ſenſam deducta eſt, vt honeſtatem ab vtilite ſecernens honeſtum aliquid conſtituerit quod non ſit vtile, et vtile quod non ſit honeſtum qua, nulla pernicies maior vita hominis poſuit afferri.* Cicero offic: Lib: 2.

The mylde diſcretion of *Cuſtomers* to aduaunce *Subſidies* by, deſpiſed.

1.

## Alphabet *and* Primer.

tion, that giues vs power to be dooing in this kind. The Ports
and Places allotted for Boundes that lymit our seruice. And the
diligent performance which in this respect the greatnes of our
trust doth exact and import: There is Countenaunce & maintenaunce to be fitted to our Charge, which in this regarde we
deserue & may require. For the Oxe is not muzeled that trea-
deth out the Corne. *Religion* sayes. And *Iustice* hath appointed,
that the daily Labourer be truly payd his hyre. But *Nos non no-
bis indificamus Aues.* We serue at the Altar both daily & houre-
ly, and yet are held vnworthy to breathe or liue thereby. For
besides the penurie of such Fees and Rewards as our Functions
deserue, and our charges require ; our fare beeing slender, and
our drinke very skant ; we dip but our dishes in our Neighbors
*Cesternes* to quench our thirst, and at Noone in his garden crop
a few of his *Leekes*, with his owne consent, to keepe vs frõ star-
ving : And this addes oyle to the fire of our Furnace ; heere lies
the gall of all our bitternesse : Our breathes are saide to infect
with their sent, and poyson the ayre.

This is our horrrrible Sinne, our Sacriledge, or Burglarie at
least. As if *We* heereby, & none but *Wee* , had spoyld the *Kings
Staples*, stolne away his *Bullion*, conceald his *Customes* , and at
Midnight robd a Church. Of all this *Ignorance* but accusing,
our *Huishers* bynde vs hand and foote, and *Iealousie* torments vs
with a kinde of *Controller*. Whose skill can no wayes helpe vs,
for his Letters are those Characters that wee would spell to
read ; and *Actum agere*, the scope of all his Lesson.

This *Man* at the first seemes doubly diligent, till *Experience*
makes him wise, beeing proude of his Name, and content with
the ease of his Place and credite ; but his belly wanting eares, he
betakes him boldly to a Bed of *Onyons*, and spares our Neighbours *Leekes*.

Now *Leekes* and *Onyons* thus meeting together , and increasing the smel to our further disgrace, and onely blame, made an
easie way to our late *Supervisors* , and theyr *Factious Retinewe*.
Whose rules of *Extremity* in hunting for Profit , and reforming
our Schooles disorder and Abuses, so perfumed our Ports by eating *Garlicke*, that *Honor* and *Honestie* became both amazed, and
remooud theyr Seates.

These at the first made a glorious shewe like the Moone at
full, yet prooud but *Commets*, for men to gaze on as they hung
in the Ayre , and their greatest Letters but *Cyphers* in August
when they came to the spelling. For stuffing our *Houses* vvith
swarmes of such Instruments as loue our Tributs but as Rats
doe loue Cheese, so bewitchd poore *Trafficke* by Sorcerie,
and shyfts, that as our Ports became abandoned, like places infected or haunted with Spirits : All our *Free-will offerings, effectes*

　　　　　K.　　　　　　　　　　　of

*(marginal notes:)*

2.

3.

4.

Controlers.

All mens errors and faults, still layd
on the *Customers*.
*Quousq̃, tandẽ audebunt dicere, quic-
quam vtile quod non sit honestũ? nul-
lam enim pestẽ maiorem dixerim vitæ
et societati hominum posse contingere
quam eorum opinio qui ista distraxe-
rint.* Offic: Lib: 3.

The 4. *Supervisors* that vndertake
to correct Magnificat in the *Out-
Ports*.

*Trafficke* first bewitcht: And

The *Out-Ports*, first abandoned.

## The CVSTVMERS

of *Loyaltie*; the true-*loue-knots* knit betweene *Subiects* & *Prince*, and *tokens* of *affection* (religiously moou'd in mindes, admyring the glorious *Obiect* of their welfare and good) from the harts of Marchants : humbly presented to Soueraigne *Dignitie*, and to

*The Subsidies of Tonnage & Pondage farmed out.*

man els due ; *Au plus offrant* beeing set to sale, were thrust at last into Huxters handling. These, some call *particular Farmers*, some *Farmers generall*, some *Vndertakers* with *Farmers*, not so much of *Customes*, as they would pretend, as of the *Subsidies* afore said, called *Tonnage* and *Pondage*.

*Qui male agunt oderunt Lucem.*

*Farmers.*
*Vndertakers.*

The first sort of these, may be seene and knowne. The latter, neither seene nor knowne in publique sort, as *Publicans* be, haue yet their meetings and appointments together. And possessing the body, vndertake by meanes to purge the blood, and purifie the Spirits of our weake, diseased and distracted *Trafficke*: some by *Tabacco*, and some by a *worse* and *viler* thing. *Cuius Camarinam*, I dare not stirre without pardon and reuerence, first humbly sought, and duly premised, *Ne nauceam ciem*.

*The Refiners of Gold and Siluer in London.*

It is strange I confesse for men to behold what Art dooth & can doe with the meanest materialls that nature affords, when she *vndertakes* to worke ; for I haue sometimes seene good and pure *Bullion* both drawne and refined from the durt and dust whereon the workemen stood : but these clense by water, and then purge by fire, and their working may be seene.

*The Duch new Drapery of Bayes, Sayes, &c, first deuised in Sandwich, and from thence learned and set vp elswhere within the Realme.*

*The only Patterne of a free Staple.*

Nay, I haue often admired, and with ioy beheld the store of currant coyne in fine siluer and pure gold, that sometimes was drawne frō the shorlings of our Fells, the refuse of our woolles, and sweepings of our *Staples*, by the industry of *Art*, and helpe of fire and water. But these *Vndertakers* are *Artists* indeed, that attend vpon theyr *Trades*, and concurre in their labour ; theyr dooings are seene, their Persons knowne, their worke squard out by the Standard of Truth, and their Wares made vendible, onely by degrees of Goodnes.

*Lex Veritatis.*

These *Artists* worke in Gods Name, whose *Elixar Goodnes*, by the misterie of their Trades, turnes their worke into Mettalls, and their Mettalls into *Bullion*, to serue our publique Myntes, that Marchants at their *Ports* may haue to pay their *Tributes* before they passe the Seas in ready currant Coyne, by the rules of *Iustice*.

*Lex Iusticiæ.*

*Lex Sapientiæ et ordinis.*
*Besides the Kings & townes Seales, they haue 3. Seales to distinguish the worth of euery mans wares and worke, and that which deserues not the worst Seale, is cut into peeces, or put by to be amended, as being no wayes vendible at home nor abroade.*

These are our skilfull Workmen, whose orderly proceedings for the vse of Goodnes, by the waights of Iustice, and skales of Truth, giuing euery man his Right, to *Good, Better* and *Best*, in the value of his worke, by the warrant of their S E A L E S, makes *Deity* in nature to be generally adored, and *Industry* in Art to be more or lesse admired, to the speciall praise and profit of those *Persons* and *Places* that first or last affoord them.

These

# ALPHABET *and* PRIMER.

Thefe are our *honeſt Sacriſtaines*, and fure friendes to *Trafficke*, fit for our Altars of *Vnity* and *Truth*, whoſe religious affections to the practiſe of Iuſtice, ſo bleſſe their Endeuours, that all men admiring the *Beautie* and *Bounty* of their Induſtries and worke, deſire to poſſeſſe them before Gold & Siluer, to our *Soueraignes* great *Honour*, and his *Peoples* ſpeciall *wealth*.

Theſe deale not with our Cuſtomes, nor obtrude vppon our Subſidies, but teaching the way how to find out the one; and with allacritie how to pay the other, attend on *Honeſtum & Vtile* ſtill together : O that our *Fleeſe-wooll* were thus vndertaken, & our *Broad-clothes* but made and dreſt in this manner!

Laſtly: Theſe I ſay, and none but theſe, (for all theyr followers elſwhere, haue fayld in their Rules, and crazd their credit,) are the childrens children of our former holy Prieſtes, that firſt found out the *Pit* in this *Deſert* of our Land, wherein ſo long a goe the * *Fire* was hid that ſanctified all our Tributes, and with the muddy moyſture onely that therein they found, (as our Sun did lately ſhine,) drew downe that heauenly heat which warmd our frozen *Trafficke*, and would reuiue our *Staples*, if WISDOME ſaw it good,) euen when the *Pit* was dry, and to all mens knowledge the *Fire* was ſpent and gone.

But theſe *Farming Vndertakers*, or *vndertaking Farmers*, ſeeme men of other skill, & different profeſſions : who drawing their Doctrine frō *Tritemius Abbas Steganographia*, and *de Portas* learned workes, of their priuate Experience, haue altered all our Rules of *Honeſtum* and *Vtile*, to *Lucri bonus odor ex re qualibet*, and made an Art of *Trafficke*, to purge her ſpirits by, and refine her Tributes, from all the vertuous vices & vicious vertues of *Leekes, Onyons*, and *Garlicke :* by a kind of diſtillation & ſtrange * *Limbecke* of their owne.

Now 1. how theſe men worke. 2. What men they are. 3. Frō whence their doctrine comes. And 4. whereto it tendes, are curious Queſtions, and may be worth the ſpelling.

For if heauenly *Goodnes* be the life of *Trafficke* , from whence as *Trades* doe ſwarue they turne againe to Nothing. And *Golde* and *Siluer* our choſen Materialls, by true proportions to fix this *Goodnes* in, as we haue learnd to ſpell : Then worke not theſe in *Gods Name*, like plaine-meaning Men, but as confident , careleſſe, and therefore dangerous *Empericks*, that ſhunne the Rules of *Truth*, who finding our *Trades* all ſubiect to *Monopolies*, and apt to be contracted, bring all our *Miſteries* to be pounded in one *Morter*, and there ſo ſqueiſe the Braines of *Trafficke* , and refine her *Tributes :* that our *Ports* beeing once confounded as well as our *Staples, Honour* might doe them Homage; and publique *Vtilitie* become their priuate gaine.

If *Currant Coyne* the Soule of *Trafficke*, and our Soueraignes

K. 2. onely

---

*Margin notes:*

They haue 12. ſworne men (beſides vnder officers,) that as Iudges examine each mans worke before it paſſe the Seales : who being skilfull in all the Trades that belong to theyr Drapery, are impartiall Cenſurers of all Defaults, aſwell in ſpinning, weauing, fulling, and dying, as working, for the Buyers behoofe, euen to the mulct, and recompence of a thred and a farthing.

The *Staples of Kent* in E: 1. E: 2. & *Edward* 3. time, kept at *Sandwich* and *Canterb:* (where nowe they of the Duch Church dwell,) was remooued firſt for 15. yeres to *Bridges*, & after placed at *Calice*, the loſſe wherof, being now 50. yeeres ſince, would draw on a ſpeciall Diſcourſe beſides this PRIMER.

* *Read the ſecond of the Machab: chap:* 1.

An *Antitheſis* between the former *Vndertakers* of *Sandwich*, and thoſe now of *London*, *Tritemias Abbas de occulta philoſophia*, *Ioannes Baptiſta de Porta: De furtiuis literarum Notis* .

* Theyr new Booke of Rates.

1
2
3
4

1 How they worke:

## *The* Cvstvmers

onely *Trade*, be thofe proportions of Number and Weight to buy & fell by that makes *Goodnes* vendible for all our behoofes. Then are thefe Vndertaking-Farmers, *Marchants*, that (Tradeleffe themfelues) liue by buying and felling, and fo by buying to fell againe : that rayfing all their profits from others Trades and paynes, are bound to pay their homage before they paffe our *Ports*, with purpofe to tranfport our *Goodnes* croffe the Seas. And therefore made by Name incapable and incompatible to vndertake our Functions, or deale with our Tributes. As men fpecially forbidden by the Statute-lawes and wifdome of our Land, to obtrude vpon our *Cuftomes* : much leffe our Subfidies of *Tonnage* and *Pondage*, leaft Marchants farming Marchants, & fo goe free themfelues, prefume to be like Kings or Princes fellowes ; to whom alone fuch Rights are due, and therefore to none other, as b eing the onely knots to tye *Maieftie* and *Loyaltie* fo faft and fure together. Now, who ftriues to out-runne the Lawes, makes haft but to confufion. But fuch it feemes are thefe, by the courfe of their proceedings. And therfore no maruell, if turning all our freedoms into their bondage, and all our birth-rights into their Farme or purchafe : from all the *Goodnes Trafficke* hath, and all the *Loue* our Marchants beare to our *Patrons* happie being ; they gaine a maffe of priuate wealth, by doing a world of harme.

If *Exchange* of *Goodnes* by Gold & Siluer, the 𝕭𝖔𝖉𝖞 & 𝕭𝖑𝖔𝖔𝖉 of *Kings* and *Kingdoms* (reprefented to vs in 𝖈𝖚𝖗𝖗𝖆𝖓𝖙 𝕮𝖔𝖞𝖓𝖊,) be the Spirit of *Trafficke*, and myfticall Cyment that glewes fo faft together the mutuall coniunction betweene *Soueraignes* & *Subiects*, by *Loue* and *Grace*, as religious Iuftice hath taught vs to beleeue. Then drawe thefe *Vndertakers* their Methods all from R o m e, where firft was taught the doctrine that enchaunts and tranfubftantiates our *Eucharifticke Sacraments*, (reprefenting to vs the 𝕭𝖔𝖉𝖞 and 𝕭𝖑𝖔𝖔𝖉 of C h r i s t, by 𝕭𝖗𝖊𝖆𝖉 and 𝖂𝖎𝖓𝖊,) to *Idolatrous Maffes*, and our Chriftian *Exchange* into Iewifh *Vfury*.

Laftly, if the K i n g be our Honour, the P r i n c e our Sun, *Trafficke* the Chariot, and *Shypping* the wheeles that beare our *glorious Lights* : Thefe beeing but the Horfes, that fo proudly fet forward to vndertake our *Goodnes*, and drawe vs all in tryumph : Forefeeing as I did, (my ftanding made mee fee, & my feeing mooud my Confcience not to hold my peace,) both the loofenes of their raynes ; their byt within theyr teeth, and danders of their courfe ouer Hills and Dales, bawkes and many bywayes, and all without a *Coach-man* or *Guyde* that I would fpy. (They commaunding all, and controleable by none for hindering of their Farme) I could not (my good Lords) out of Dutie and zeale to our *Patrons* fafety, and all your happy beeings, but

　　　　　　　　　　　　　　　　　　　　　　　　　　giue

**Marginal notes:**

2 What men they are:

14 R: 2. No Marchants that deale with fraights of Shyppes, or haue Shyps of theyr owne, or keepe any Wharfes, &c. fhall haue to do with the receipt of Cuftomes, &c. *Item* 20 H: 6. Cap: 5.

3: Whence theyr Doctrine comes.

*Vfury* firft practifed in *Rome*, by the Bancks of *Iewes* there, and in other Chriftian Countries, to draw home the Popes *Peter-pens*, and other exactions vpon the Nations & kingdoms that obeyd their Religion.

4: Whereto their Doctrine tendes.

# Alphabet *and* Primer.

giue Caution heere-to-fore of the fiercenes of their Courage, and desperate Carreere; that such as stood so nigh them, might be warnd at least to looke but to their heeles. But sith like sleeping *Minotaures* they nowe possesse the * *Center* of all our great Abuses, and inextricable *Errors*, and threatning all our Trades with daily, monthly, and yeerely Tributes, make *Trafficke* offer sacrifice to 1. **Kemphan**, & to 2. **Rymmon.** Let The- seus now take heede, and Ariadne looke about her; and with a smyle at least, at last reuiue the Spirits of their despised *Schollers*, whose wits haue no wills, and Endeuours no Ends, but how to spell, and learne to read theyr Countries *weale*, the pub- lique *Good*, and Soueraignes speciall *Honour*, that *Honestum* and *Utile* might still hold hands together. A smyle (I meane) of fa- uour to th' *Out-Ports* of this Land, aswell as that of *London*: be- cause, though *Iustice* haue a quickning power, and may protect our beeings; yet *Grace* it is relieues vs all, and *Mercy* makes vs liue.

* London.

1 *Extortion.*
2 *Usury.*

Preheminence.
Prerogative.

By this which hath been speld, your *Wisdoms* now may read, to what distresse and misery your *Publicans* are brought. That beeing Men as docible in Religion, as capable of Reason; Free men by their birthes, and of best education, Men euerie vvay made happy, saue in their names and callings: and in nothing yet more wretched then the Places of their Functions, (for I meane the *Out-Ports* onely, let *London* cleere it selfe,) are not- withstanding in worse case, (if worse may be) then were those *Brickmakers* that sometimes wrought in *Egypt*, who vvanting meanes to do their taske, had notwithstanding their idle Task- Maisters, whose credits had no beeing but in their disgrace, cō- maunded euen by those that should attend vppon vs, yea *Sear- chers* and *Sinners.*

But as the case now stands, sith all make loue to Tributes, & catch our Functions from vs, High and low, Rich and poore, both Noble and ignoble, because our Lessons spell pure Siluer and fine Gold: and yet our Names they scorne. Let *Iealousie* be called for, and let *Impudency* smell, what *Ignorance* hath added, and *Extremity* reformed in the abuses of our *Schooles*, by spelling well the Letters, but mistaking the purpose of a graue and wit- tie Counsellor, that sometimes gaue aduise in this very case of ours.

All catch & hunt for Customes, but shun the Name of Customers.

Sir *Tho: Moores* Epigram, *De fa- toribus abolendis.*

    " " *Sectile ne tetros porrum tibi spiret odores*
    " " *Protinus à porro fac mihi cepe vores. &c.*
" " Leaft eating 1 *leekes* (saith he) should cause thy breth to smell;
" " Take 2 *Onyons* strong, that sent will soone allay;
" " And if thereby the fauour seeme t'excell,
           L.        " " 3 Gar-

1 *Customer.*
2 *Controller.*

## The CVSTVMERS

" " 3 *Garlicke* be ſure will driue them both away :
" " But if the ſtincking breath of *Garlicke* ſtay,
" " What helpes vs then ? 4 *Tabacco* ? no, but at a word I thinke,
" " There is a thing can 5 *Vndertake* to make a viler ſtinke.

And let Experience now ſhow, and Truth be bold to ſpeak, and tell them to their faces, that ſtriue to raiſe thēſelues by ſee-king our diſgraces : That God did put and place as much Pro-fit and Pleaſure, (I ſay Profit as Pleaſure,) harts-eaſe , and ho-nour, in the quiet endeuours of *Cuſtomers* (ſo long as they were truſted,) through *Mercy, Loyaltie* and *Loue* ; as the deuill is able apt and wont, to mingle care and comber , loſſe and ſhame in the turbulent vndertakings of Extremitie , by Extortion and Shyfts.

---

And thus at laſt, the world may ſee and all men vnderſtand, in our Diſgrace, the K I N G S great loſſe, and *Kingdoms* greater wrong. For beſides that both our *Cuſtomes* with our *Staples*, are gone or conuaid out of ſight, (the ground of all our woes, that wee can no wayes mend,) our *Coyne* and our *Exchange* , beeing turnd into *Vſury*, by Subiects like to Kings, or like to Princes fellowes : our *Marchants* by *Societies* call all men *Enterlopers* that are not of their Sects, or linckt with them together. Our *Arts* engroſt by men of diuers *Trades*. Our *Trades* doe meete in *Companies*, our *Companies* at *Halls*, and our *Halls* become *Mono-polies* of Freedome, tyde to *London* : where all our *Crafts* & *My-ſteries* are ſo layd vp together, that outrunning all the prudence & wiſedom of the Land, men liue by Trades they neuer learnd, nor ſeeke to vnderſtand. By meanes whereof, all our Creekes ſeeke to one Riuer, all our Riuers run to one Port, all our Ports ioyne to one Towne, all our Townes make but one Citty, and all our Citties but Suburbes to one vaſt , vnweldy , and diſor-derlie *Babell* of buildings, which the worlde calls *London :* and *London* likewiſe cōtracted in it ſelfe, is made a Forreſt of ſhyfts, and Wildernes of ſinne. Where *Trafficke* liues confind, and be-

ing poſſeſt by Rats and Mice, and ſpirits of the Ayre, of whom as of Harpies may truly now be ſaid :

" " *Triſtius haud iſtis Monſtrum, nec ſeuior vlla*
" " *Peſtis et ira Deûm ſtygiis ſeſe extulit vndis.*

" " No monſters like to theſe may hap, nor curſe frō God befall,
" " Nor from the pit of hell ariſe, to plague the Realme withall:
Is ſo by fits tormented, both by water and by Land,
That how to heipe her now, we doe not vnderſtand.
But though fayth be frayle, and all our credit gone , yet dooth our vowes, compell vs ſtill by faſting and by prayer to doe our beſt Endeuours.

For,

# ALPHABET *and* PRIMER.

For, faultes there are no doubt, euer were, and euer will be many ; PERFECTION knowes no refidence but *Heauen*. And if we fay we haue no finne, there is no Truth within vs. Wherfore we wifh, and pray all thofe that reade this ALPHABET & PRIMER, to ioyne with our Deuotions, and with pure harts and humble voyce, to the Throne of GOD and his heauenly Grace, to pray but in this manner, faying after mee.

Almighty and moſt mercifull Father, wee haue erred and ſtrayed from thy wayes like loſt ſheepe, we haue followed too much the deuices and deſires of our owne harts , wee haue offended againſt thy holy Lawes, wee haue left vndoone the things we ſhould do, and we haue done the things we ought not to doe, and there is no health in vs. But thou O Lord haue mercie vpon vs miſerable offenders, ſpare thou vs, O Lorde, which confeſſe our faultes, and reſtore them that are penitent, according to thy promiſes, declared vnto mankind in Chriſt Jeſu our Lord: and graunt O moſt mercifull Father for his ſake, that wee may hereafter liue a godly , a righteous, and a ſober life, to the glory of thy holy Name.

> Cuſtomers generall Confeſſion.

¶ A Prayer for the Kings Maieſtie.

O Lord our heauenly Father, high and mightie , King of Kings, Lord of Lords, the onely Ruler of Princes, which doſt from thy Throne behold all the dwellers vpon Earth, wee humbly befeech thee with fauour to behold our moſt gracious and Soueraigne Lord King IAMES, and ſo repleniſh him with the grace of thy holy Spirit, that hee may alwaies encline to thy will, and walke in thy way. Endue him plentifully with heauenly gyfts, graunt him in health and wealth long to liue, that finally after this life, he may attaine to euerlaſting ioy and felicitie, through Jeſus Chriſt our Lord.

> Cuſtomers daily and Chriſtian Prayers.
>
> & per ſe.

¶ A Prayer for the Queene and Prince, and other the King and Queenes Children.

Almighty God, which haſt promiſed to be a Father of thine Elect and of their ſeede, wee humbly befeech thee to bleſſe and preferue our gracious Queene ANNE, Prince HENRIE, and all the King and Queenes royall Progenie. Endue them with thy holy Spirit, enrich them with thy heauenly Grace, profper them with all happines, and bring them to thine euerlaſting kingdome, through Jeſus Chriſt our Lord and onely Sauiour.

L 2.                                                    A

## *The* CVSTVMERS &c.

A Prayer for the Clergie, Lords of the Counsaile, all Magistrates, all Nations, and the Common-
People.

Con, per se.

ALmighty & euerlasting God, we most humbly beseech thee
to illuminat all Bishops, Pastors, & Ministers of ÿ Church,
with the true knowledge and vnderstanding of thy Word, and
that both by their preaching and liuing , they may set it foorth,
and shew it accordingly. To endue the Lords of his Maiesties
most honorable PREVY-COVNSELL, & all the Nobility, with
grace, wisedome, and vnderstanding. To blesse and keepe our
Magistrates, giuing them grace to execute Iustice, and maine-
taine Truth. To giue all Nations Vnitie, Peace and Concord,
And finally, to giue vs an hart to loue and dread thee , and dili-
gently to liue after thy Commandements. Grant this, O Lord,
for the honour of our Aduocate, & onely Mediator Christ Iesus.

THe *Customers* of the *Out-Ports* prostrate Petition to the KING our *Soueraigne*, for his Sonne
the PRINCES sake, to be made but as able as they
are euery way willing to do their Duties; that eating
the Bread of good Conscience daily , and freed from
temptations of Obloquy and shyfts , his Kingdome
beeing come, may still continue; and his Will performed in all Places alike; Forgiuing all as they would
be forgiuen: Conclude this their PRIMER with the
sanctified words; and enclude their Petition within
the compasse of that effectuall Prayer which our Lord
& Sauiour (the Sonne of GOD) hath comaunded,
and taught, saying;

Tittle, tittle, tittle,
Est
Amen.

OUr Father which art in heauen, hallowed be thy Name,
thy Kingdome come, thy will be done in Earth, as it is in
Heauen: Giue vs this day our daily Bread: and forgiue vs our
Trespasses, as we forgiue them that trespasse against vs: Let
vs not be led into temptation, but deliuer vs from euill: For
thine is the KINGDOME, the POVVER, and the GLORIE: for
euer and euer. SO BE IT. Amen.

¶ The Publicans humble Confession and
priuate Prayer.

*Nil sum, nulla miser noui solatia,* Massam
*Humanam nisi quod tu quoq,* CHRISTE *geris:*
*Tu me sustenta, fragilem tu* CHRISTE *guberna,*
*Fac vt sim Masse surculus* Ipse *tua.*

Magna, Magnus perficit
DEVS.

# HENRY ROBINSON

Henry Robinson, *England's Safety, in Trades Encrease. Most Humbly Presented to the High Court of Parliament* (London: Nicholas Bourne, 1641). British Library, shelfmark E.167.(5.).

Henry Robinson, *Briefe Considerations, Concerning the Advancement of Trade and Navigation, Humbly Tendred unto all Ingenious Patriots* (London: Matthew Simmons, 1649). Bodleian Library, University of Oxford, shelfmark Pamph. C 91 (22).

Henry Robinson (*c.* 1605–73), merchant and law reformer in London, was born into a wealthy London merchant family. His great grandfather, George Robinson (1490–1542), was a member of the Mercer's Company and the Merchant Taylor's Company and a land speculator. Henry Robinson matriculated at St John College, Oxford, in 1621, but left without taking a degree to go into the family business. He joined the Mercer's Company in 1626 and spent the following decade abroad as a factor for the family firm in the Low Countries and Leghorn. Robinson joined the East India Company in 1641 and almost immediately became its Secretary. He seems mainly to have traded in coral and saltpetre. In the turbulent years after 1640 Robinson was enmeshed in a lengthy fight to become Post-Master General, a very lucrative office at the time. Although he failed to gain this position he was offered the post of Auditor of the Excise in the mid 1640s. In 1649 he was appointed by the Commonwealth government as a member of a committee whose aim was to bolster foreign trade. The reason for this was most probably the publication of his most famous treatise, *Brief Considerations, Concerning the Advancement of Trade and Navigation*, reprinted here.

In the 1650s Henry Robinson's career as a state bureaucrat rocketed. He was appointed by the Council of the State to restore the coinage and to find means to strengthen the exchange rate, which was believed to have fallen sharply. In 1650 he was named Comptroller of Accounts for the sale of Crown fee-farm rents and Secretary to the Committee for the Preservation of Customs. According to his biographer Robert Zaller, 'as a merchant, projector and bureaucratic pluralist ... [Robinson] occupies a solid niche in the ranks of the London elite that supported the Parliamentary course in the civil war and staffed the offices of the Commonwealth'.[1] As a consequence of this, the Restoration meant that his public career was over.

Henry Robinson was a passionate advocate of religious freedom and toleration, and he promoted social, educational and legal change. For example he proposed that the Westminster courts should be abolished and replaced by a system of decentralized courts in each county, city, corporation and shire. He also suggested a national system of workhouses that would provide not only employment but also education to the poor. He was a radical, rationalist and reformer of extraordinary abilities and on occasions his views were far ahead of his own times. According to one writer, 'his conception of wealth was in advance of his age'.[2] Most certainly Robinson did not share the prejudice that often is connected with seventeenth-century 'mercantilist' writers that wealth was identical with gold and silver.

The first tract reproduced here was no doubt written in an attempt to gain a public job, although Robinson seems to have been unsuccessful in this, as he joined the East India Company shortly afterwards.

1   See Zaller's entry on Robinson in *Oxford Dictionary of National Biography* (Oxford: Oxford University Press, 2004).

2   *Palgrave's Dictionary of Political Economy*, ed. H. Higgs, 3 vols (London and New York: Macmillan, 1894), vol. 3, p. 315.

# ENGLANDS
# SAFETY,
## IN
# TRADES
## ENCREASE·

Most humbly Presented to the *High* Court
of *P* A R L I A M E N T.

*Mercatura si tenuis, sordida; si magna, splendida.*

——*Quærenda pecunia primum.*

**B Y**

*H*ENRY R*O*BINSON, *Gent.*

LONDON,
Printed by *E. P.* for *Nicholas Bourne,* at the South Entrance
of the Royall Exchange. 1641.

### To the Courteous Reader.

**M**Y firſt aime and pretence of penning this diſcourſe, as you will finde peruſing it, was, chiefely through brevitie to allure ſome one to caſt an eye on't, who duly conſidering of what conſequence the ſubject is, might in his owne ripe judgment digeſt fully, and prevaile for the home proſecution of it, in this Honorable Court of Parliament; but perceiving it doe's extend it ſelfe both beyond my expectation and the leiſure moſt men have at preſent from each dayes weightie employment, it feares mee, I may neede ſome *Proſpective*, or ſpecious prologue to invite my Readers, and therefore to whet thy appetite I will be bould to promiſe, no more than I'le performe, that *Nunc tua res agitur*, if wealth or ſecurity of the State concerne thee, and reading of this out thou may'ſt not onely finde made good the Title, that Englands trade is Englands ſafety, but meanes ſuddenly to encſeaſe the Kingdomes ſtock as much againe, for what concernes trafficking therewith, beſides the ſaving of his Majeſtie and ſubjects in their ſeverall affaires no ſmall ſummes yearly, and ſome other advantages not a little conſiderable; the Platforme of all which if thou ſee not herein delineated, the Author will bee bound to ſhow it thee, or make amends in reading twice as much of thine to as little purpoſe. Farewell.

## A Table of all the chiefe heades and paſſages.

### A

ASſignation or turning over bills of debt encreaſes the Kingdomes ſtocke ſo much as all ſuch bills amount to.  Pag. 37.

### B

Banke or Grand Caſhe encreaſes the Kingdomes ſtocke ſo much as the Capitall conſiſts of.  Pag. 34. 35 36.
Banke or Mount of charity to lend poore people upon pawnes.  Pag. 43. 44.

### C

Cabels, and Cordage to be made, and Hempe ſeede to be ſowed in England, 'c. 10.
Charity miſled to give to beggers able to worke, P. 13. 43. Publik Houſes as Bridewell in London to let poore people a worke,  Pag 14. 43.
Companies and Corporatiuns of Marchants, the benefit thereof. Pag 45. 46.
Cuſtomes with what conſideration and choiſe to be impoſed. P. 9. 10. 11. 20 21.

### D

Divines deſired to conſider the lawfulneſſe of intereſt or uſury.  Pag. 41. 42.

### E

Englands advantage over other Nations for encreaſe of trade. P. 2. 3. 8. 11. 21.
Exchanges with Forraigne Parts : Marchandizing Exchange : Faires and money Marts.  Pag. 38. 39. 40. 41. 42. 52. 54 55. 56. 57. &c.

### F

Fiſhing Imployment, the conſequence of it, maintayning the Soveraignetie of the Sea, and keeping us predominant over other Nations. P. 13. 14 15 16. 17.
England able to proſecute better than other Nations, keeping Lent and two fiſh dayes a weeke would exceedingly promote it.  P. 16.
Forces by Sea of greateſt power and advantages  P. 2. 16.

### G

Grand Duke of Florence moſt abſolute Prince in Chriſtendome,  P. 35. 36.

### H

Hollanders their ſtrength in Sea-forces. P. 1. 2. Their cruelties towards our Marchants at Amboina.  P. 22.
Husbandrie little improved in England in reſpect of other Countries as barren.  Pag. 44. 45.

### I

Inſurance differences to be decided by the Law-Marchant,  Pag. 33. 34.
Law-

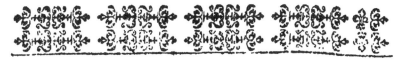

# ENGLANDS
## SAFETY IN TRADES ENCREASE.

He principall advantage wee have over all the world befides is thought to be our fhipping, which with our owne materialls as yet we build at home: but if Timber continue ftill to decreafe, we muft not onely bee beholding to others for it, but have no more fhips than they will give us leave; And yet the Hollanders who have no Timber at their owne growth, doe farre furpaffe us in number of fhips, fo that were it not for the courage of our Nation, under God, and our expertnes in Sea-fights, other Nations perhaps upon triall might at leaft bee troublefome to us, and that the Hollanders have fome hopes thereof, may bee well conjectur'd by the great difficultie wee finde in prevailing with them upon all occafions of their profit; as particularly in the fifhing bufineffe, the Eaft India trade, and daily diminifhing the Marchant Adventurers ancient priviledges in their jurifdiction to the great prejudice of this State: And if the Hollanders even in our memory thus fprung up not without our affiftance and welwifhes, and the French of late fo ftrong, both in the Ocean and Mediterranean Sea, as that wee can fcarce let out fuch Fleetes as either, how much more dangerous will their puiffance bee to our pofteritie? certainly it is confiderable for both of them, efpecially the Hollander is more likely, and hath better meanes ftill to advance himfelf continually more and more hereafter, than he had at firft to get to what he is at prefent: for it is not the large territories in the Low Countreyes, but their trafficke which doth enrich them, the firft ground of all their ftrength and greatneffe; and yet their trade confifts onely in fifhing on our Coaft, manufactures and trafficking forraine commodities to and fro, which fo much the more is by them ftill purfued, as they daily encreafe in fhipping and riches.

Thus doth it too too well appeare how other States and Princes will daily grow more and more rich and powerfull, and confequently after the fame rate in a fhort time of foure fufficient to give Chackmate unto us: The onely meanes I finde able to prevent this fhame and miferie are two.

B

One

**2** *Trades encrease*

One by endeavouring what is possible that our trade may bee enlarged wherein we have advantage over all the world, as I will show hereafter, and particularly by setting our selves close to the fishimployment.

The other, in procuring that other States and Princes rest contented to keep only such a number of men of warre as may not make us with just cause suspect their strength and force; neither is this course dissonant to reason, or without President or present practise, for if the levying an Armie of men by a neighbouring Prince give just jealousies, how much more may a Fleet of ships which cannot bee without men enough to make an Armie of at pleasure besides the capacity of conducing an other where they please? And even in this matter of shipping & maritime forces, the States of Italie are so precise and strict, as that the Pope himselfe, Kingdomes of Naples and Sicilie, Grand Duke, State of Genua and Grand Master of Malta keeps onely so many Gallies as are limited to each by generall consent amongst themselves.

But in regard the Hollanders may alledge it necessary for them to have continuall Fleetes at Sea to defend themselves against the Spaniards, it may be as necessarie for us to importune the King of Spaine to make an honourable peace with them, or, if he refuse, to joyne with the Hollanders and share with them in the bootie, for if we sit still, and they goe on conquering as is like enough, the more they get, the lesse able (if they please) shall we be to keep our selves from being conquer'd too at last, and living at others mercie, would at best bee but dishonourable, when if wee fare well, wee must conne them thanks and not our selves: Let us not then runne a farther hazard subjecting our selves to remaine betrai'd in the end by our owne flatterie: did wee but consider the ods wee had of other States in Sea-forces but halfe an age agoe; and now reflect upon the great Fleetes they make both in the Ocean and Mediterranean Sea, we may finde their power such at Present, as may render them justly to bee suspected of us hereafter, and unlesse wee show our selves sole Soveraigne of the Sea, and with our Trident Scepter give lawes (whilst we may) to all Nations there, wee must receive them from others, when wee cannot helpe it: Forraine Nations teach us the truth hereof alreadie by fishing in our Seas whether wee will or no, and the French in disturbing our trade the last yeare in the Mediterranean Sea, and enacting lawes prejudiciall both to it and our Navigation, which of themselves are able to beat us out of trade in time, and so much more, when Christendome shall be at peace, by which means the trade of Spaine will be free for other Nations which at present as it were we Monopolize to our selves,

and

### *Englands safetie.*    3

and our Clothiers and other Manufactors in swarmes flocking over into Holland to enjoy their liberties, (which God knowes how justly) but whether it bee true and due libertie, or only so suggested, it is equally dammageable to this State, since it causes their departure, and the ill consequences ensuing thereupon; it concernes us thertore(and that suddenly)to prevent others by good usage, get those backe againe that are gone, or hinder the progresse of their art and manufacture, which else both may, and justly too, bee counter-mined.

And whereas it may bee inferred by what I said before, that the enlarging of our trade would keep us still predominant over all other States and Princes, I will set downe some few indigested Notions towards the producing and continuing a flourishing State of commerce, which if wee doe not seriously apply our selves unto, other States will questionlesse bee too hard for us, and whatsoever trade they beate us out of and engrosse into their owne hands, will feede us with a bit and a blow, making us pay for it what they please, which will not only impoverish us, but ruine our Navigation, and subject us to become a prey at pleasure.

Briefly then the trafficke of England may be divided into Inland, and Maritime.

Inland is that which is practised from one towne or place unto an other within the Countrey, and by

Maritime I meane such as is used from any part of England beyond the Seas, which later is chiefely to be enlarged three manner of wayes, by Exportation, Importation, and Transportation.

1. By Exportation and venting our Native Commodities, as Lead, Tin, Waxe, or such others, as have little or no workemanship, but chiefely those that require and set a worke our Manufactures, as died and dressed Cloth, Perpetuana's, Sayes, Serges, and the like.

2. By importation of forraine commodities which wee any wise stand in need of, as Wines, Sugars, linnens, wrought silkes, but especially such as imploy the poore in manufactures, as Cotton Wools, raw Silke, and all such sundry materialls as advance our Navigation, Provisions of all sorts, and Ammunition.

3. By Transporting forraine commodities, either directly from one forraine Countrey to another, or bringing them first for any part of England, and afterwards carrying them out againe for such Countreyes, and at such times as occasion shall require.

In all which respects England may have advantage of all the World besides, by reason of her situation surrounded by the Sea, her Inhabi-

tants

4

### *Trades encrease*

tants populous for Manufactures, skilfull in Navigation, and unparalleld for safeties, her superfluitie of sundry commodities to furnish most Nations that stand in need of them, and lastly her Fishing, than which nothing is so peculiar to her, a treasure equall to that of both Indies in the richnesse, consequence and circumstances of it, in so much that if wee bee but sure to practise this, all other trades will follow, as I may say, of their owne accord, one, as it were, begetting another; for our Fish, Cloth, and other Woollen goods, Tin, Lead, Calfe-skins, Waxe, &c. doe not onely furnish us with such forraine commodities as wee our selves want, but besides large returnes in money, may store us with quantities of all sorts to supply other Nations; And though as I said, if our fishing and Cloathing bee but lookt to, our trading both Inland and Maritime will continually encrease, yet it may likely bee much furnished, and brought sooner to perfection, if all these seventeene particulars bee observed.

1. By granting priviledges to sundry Townes and places, especially Sea-Townes most commodiously situated for fishing Traffike and Navigation.

2. By bringing interest downe to 6. *per* 100. at most.

3. By lighting of the customes especially of goods exported.

4. By cherishing and furthering our severall Plantations in Virginia, Bermudus, Saint Lawrence, Saint Christophers and elsewhere, especially perswading to inhabit and fortifie, so farre as may bee requisite, the Banke of New-found Land where we catch that fish.

5. By using all possible meanes for prosecuting and advancing the Fishing imployment in generall.

6. By setling stricter orders for overseeing and sealing cloth, and all sorts of Woollen goods.

7. By encouraging new manufactures with immunities and priviledges.

8. By free exporting of forraine commodities with little or no Custome, which will make England the Emporium of all other Countreyes:

9. By his Majesties protecting the East India Companie, whereby ther may regaine that trade, and settle another in Persia if possible.

10. By constituting a Court of Marchants, where all Marchants, an: Marchantlike causes and differences may be summarily dispeeded without appeale unlesse by his Majesties especiall grace in case of palpable injustice.

11. By erecting of a Banke where payments may bee made by assignation.

12. That

*Englands safety.*                                                          5

12. That a courſe be taken for ſecure turning over bills of debts from one man to another.

13. That a Faire or money Mart be ſetled like that of Placentia in Italy or Lyons in France, where moneyes are drawne as by exchange and returned back againe every three moneths.

14. That Inland trade and Navigation which is carriage of goods and Marchandize within the Countrey bee facilitated and promoted.

15. That all Marchants trading for one place and Province be contracted into a Corporation.

16. That there be Commiſſioners as a peculiar and ſelect Magiſtrate of ſo many as ſhall be thought fitting to ſit weekely adviſing and conſulting for the advancement of trade and Commerce.

17. And laſtly that all Marchants have certaine immunities from being called to inferiour offices and ſervices where they live, and either priviledges of due reſpect, whereby they may bee encouraged to continue, and others to betake themſelves to ſo honourable a calling.

1. To the firſt then, which is the granting privilidges to ſundry Towns and places, eſpeciall Sea Towns moſt commodiouſly ſituated for Fiſhing, trafficke and Navigation, ſince London is not onely populous enough, but likely ſtil to be much more even till its owne greatneſſe prove a burden to it, for wee ſee both houſe rent, proviſions for victualing of all ſorts, firing and other grow continually exceſſive deere, the conſumption whereof being ſo great, in ſo little a circuit, cauſes them to be fetched ſo farre off, as the very portage of ſome of them exceeds the firſt coſt, whereas if ſuch others as are likely ſtill to flocke to London if not prevented, were wonne to ſettle themſelves about Marchandizing in ſome other place or Port, theſe proviſions would be neere hand to them, and conſequently better cheape: Beſides it is no policie for a Prince or Kingdome to have ſo great a multitude, or proportion of their wealth and ſtrength in one place, how ſtrong ſoever, becauſe if peſtilence come amongſt them they infect one another; if dearth or ſcarcitie of any thing neceſſarie, they are apt to mutiny; if warres they may bee beſieged, and then ſo farre from helping, as they helpe onely to ſterve one another, and what is no leſſe conſiderable, their overballancing number and riches, were it not ſecured by the untainted loyaltie of thoſe Cittizens, and as well ordered by their good government (whereof wee have often ſeene experience) might be a temptation of ill conſequence; Wherefore to prevent this, as alſo not to venture all wee have, or ſo great a

B 3                                                          part

**6** *Trades encreaſe*

part of it at one ſtoke, and diſperſe and multiply trade throughout the whole Kingdome, it may be requiſite to endow ſome Sea Townes, eſpecially with ſundry priviledges, and immunities; but firſt they muſt be ſituate where they may have all proviſions cheape, and advance ſomewhat thereby of what they would have ſpent in London; then they ſhould bee ſuch as have ſecure Ports and Roades capable to receive and harbour ſhips of all burthens; next it is neceſſary they bee torun'd with ſtrong walls and ditches, if a Caſtle bee not thought ſittiſie t to protect the Inhabitants, and people of all ſorts encouraged to dwell there by ſuch meanes as may beſt prevaile with th m : as firſt by a free trade to pay little or no cuſtome, eſpecially for goods outward, or ſuch inward as are to bee againe exported; then if need require they may be furniſhed with houſe-rent free for ſome yeares, and hopefull men of good report, who living there ſo far off, will perhaps finde no credit, with moneyed men in London ſhould be accommodated with competent ſummes at a low intereſt of about 4. per 100. for where men have moneys, they will continually be plodding how to imploy them beſt, and ſo make new diſcoveries in trade to the future inriching of Prince and Countrey together with themſelves. And whereas at preſent all England, at leaſt Scotland and Ireland for the moſt part are furniſhed with forraine commodities brought firſt to London, then wil theſe ſundry new Townes and Staples of trade as they encreaſe, not only bee able to provide themſelves, but the Country alſo that lies neere them with the ſame at better rates, and yet prejudice London very little, becauſe, as I conceive, the greateſt part of that Countrey, and ſuch as come to inhabit there, made ſhift before to live without them, moſt whereof were more ſuperfluous than neceſſary; and were it onely to make theſe new Townes of Staple Magazines and Warehouſes of Corne, Wine, Salt, Fiſh, Flaxe, Cotton Wooll, Tobacco and other forraine commodities, to furniſh our Northerly neighbouring Nations, we may compaſſe it with the ſame advantage which others doe and better, if wee uſe but the ſame policie, following our fiſhing, and providing for our ſhipping.

2. The ſecond way to enlarge trade is by bringing downe intereſt to 6. per 100. at leaſt. for Intereſt is the rule by which wee buy, ſell, and governe our ſelves when wee are to imploy our moneys both in building, planting, trading, &c. as thus : A Marchant buying a commoditie to ſend abroad or bring for England, calculates what it coſts, and what it is likely afterwards to ſell for, & finding it may produce 8. or 10 per 100. concludes this is more profitable than intereſt,

and

### Englands safetie.

and therfore refolves not to put out his money at ufe, but imploy it in trade, & having no money of his own, is contented to borrow, becaufe he perceives he may likely advance by this imployment to pay the ufe, and referve a convenient profit for his paines, which certainly would not fucc. ed fo often if Intereft ran higher, for if that bee a more profitable and fecure way of thriving, fuch as have moneys will decline trade, and put it out to ufe, and thofe that have none, either quite forbeare to borrow, or undoe themfelves with intereft at fo high a rate: Neither can any thing materially bee objected againft this bringing downe of intereft, fave that ftrangers will not fend their moneys hither to be put out at fo low a rate and fo abridge the trade, but to this may well be anfwered, it were good they brought none at all, being better to have a little trade with a greater profit to bee divided amongft our felves, than a larger trade with leffe benefit on it, and that chiefely to goe to ftrangers.

But for our owne ufurers, whereas it is ordinarily alledg'd how this courfe would make them call in their moneys and buy lands, it is as eafily anfwered, how all the land in England is bought already, and if any one that hath bought refolve to fell againe, furely it is not with intention to keepe the money by him in a cheft without fructifying, fo that let whofe will buy or fell land, be the intereft brought downe to what rate foever, our money'd men will not long be fullen, but fo much money as is in England will bee traded with by thofe that owe it, or put out at intereft at five or fix *per* too. when men muft give no more for it, fince *dulcis odor lucri*, fomething hath fome favour.

But true it is that land will bee the dearer for it, and perhaps at firft Corne, Wools and all kinde of victualing and manufactures the like, which if it bee granted, I hope wee fhould in conclufion finde no worfe effect than that Husbandmen would hereby be brought to a frugall dyet, or ftirr'd up to become more induftrious fetting their wits and hands a worke for improving of the foile, wherein queftionleffe they come fhort of other Nations, and might thereby well advance in the great encreafe of yearely fruits whenfoever their Farmes come to bee enhanc'd; And yet me thinks in faying if landes be improv'd to thirty yeares purchafe, Corne, Wools, &c. will rife accordingly, there is a fallacie which captivates many mens underftanding, for furely hee cannot be juftly faid to buy land at thirty yeares purchafe, who racking the rent of what it was before fqueefes his Farmers after the rate of twenty yeares, which if the Land-lord do not, the Tenant will have no caufe to demand deerer for his Corne,

Wooll

**8** *Trades encrease*

Wooll &c, and impossible it is that Land should rise unlesse interest money fall; for whereas it may bee objected the scarcitie or store of money will raise or bring downe Land, it is by no other meanes than raysing, or bringing downe interest first: and besides the Farmers upon all occasion are likelier to discharge a rackrent by multiplying the fruits thereof through industry, than raising of the price, for that would onely teach us to be furnish'd from abroad, which if wee cannot doe as well as other Nations it were pitty but wee wanted; Spaine, Portingall and Holland, have very little Corne of their owne sowing, and yet eate as much bread as we doe; the Hollander hath no Sheepe to sheare, and yet makes cloath as good cheape as England, so that if wee cannot enjoy the advantages we have above them, let us at least be contented to far as they doe, and bring downe interest to the same termes, whereby trade may florish as it doth with them. And if trade bee but encouraged by giving priviledges to our decay'd fishing Townes, and practising what is proposed here following, I suppose it may appeare there will not only bee suddenly found money enough to drive the present trade, but that wee are farther capable to become the wealthiest Nation in all the World. And whereas I made transportation, which is the furnishing of other Nations with forraine commodities, the third meanes of enlarging maritime trade, unlesse we can have moneys here at interest as cheape as forraigne Nations, or else advance some other way what wee pay more than they doe for use money, they will keepe us from that trade and the benefit of it, for if they can undersell us three or foure per 100 which is a competent gaine for a halfe yeares imployment, wee may bee sure not to thrive amongst them, but desert a project so advantagious as the Hollanders have not such another to live upon; and to conclude this point, since the lawfulnesse of putting money out at interest is so much controverted, it might be no small motive to us at least to put the use of it at a lower rate.

3. The third consideration was lightning of our Customes, in imposing whereof heretofore perhaps the chiefe aime and intention sometimes was to increase his Majesties revenues, but speciall care ought to be had therein by lightning our native commodities which will cause a greater exportation of them, and charging it on the forraine which will hinder their importation, and yet they too selectively not all alike; and here it is worth remembrance that a great part of forraine commodities brought for England are taken in barter of ours, and we should not have vented ours in so great quantity without taking theirs, for wee must not expect to bring away all
their

## Englands safetie.

their moneys, and our commodities not much more necessary to them than theirs to us: but Cotton woolls, Grogralne yarne, Gold and Silver-thrid or Wire, raw Silke and such others which with us are imployed in sundry Fabrickes and Manufactures setting our poore people a worke should bee lightly charged, especially for such a quantity of those manufactures as are againe exported: But Sattins, Taffeties, Velvets and such others as have their full workemanship abroad should bee well charged, which hindring them to be brought in in such abundance, would imploy our owne people in making the same sorts at home, but this must bee done with caution, and by degrees insensibly, least it become countermined: And though this may seeme, or doe lessen the Kings Customes for the present, it will after be recover'd againe infallibly encreasing trade, and a little Custome upon a great trade is equivalent to a great custome on a little trade, and the people employed and multiply'd to boote which are both the strength and riches of a Kingdome, and yet other meanes (if need be) may be thought upon to countervaile this lessening the Kings revenues in the interim. Provisions of victualls, especially corne, Butter, Cheese, which are the poore mans food, who hardly advances more than will cloath and feed him at ordinary rates, should be free of all such charges; Wine perhaps may deservedly pay good custome, since wee may bee without it, at least the abuse is great in so great consumption of it, and a heavie custome may hinder the importation thereof in part, but the Subject will still be the more deceived in it, unlesse it bee severely prohibited for Vintners or others to mingle and sophisticate it, or sell one sort for another, by which meanes notwithstanding the greater customes, they may put a lower price on it to intice their Customers.

To charge Jewells as Diamonds, Pearles, Rubies and such like superfluous ornaments with great customes, would scarce hinder the importation, for since the custome may be stollen with so much ease, many would be tempted thereunto, desiring to advance no more than the stolne custome, and to search mens pockets and their breeches exactly (for otherwise as good no search at all) may perhaps bee thought against the liberties of this Nation, I am sure much contrary to their humour. Besides Jewells are wealth and riches in a Kingdome and consequently good credit to it, which though, if they were so much money, might be imploy'd better and improved, yet certainly they are a treasure, and in case of necessity may sted a Kingdome, and will only abound after that a Kingdome aboundeth with wealth

C

and

and money, the fuperfluitie whereof is onely converted into Jewells, and fuch other riotous expences.

And whereas fundry Statutes have formerly beene alledged for rating both native and forraigne commodities , now that wee are in time of Parliament which hath power to make new or repeale the old, mee thinks we need not fo much oblige our felves to what paffed heretofore in this behalfe , as to examine whether there bee the fame reafon for rating this or that commoditie, and encreafe or pull down: the cuftomes accordingly : wherein two things may well bee aymed at; firft the raifing a revenue to the King , and fecondly to produce a flouliihing ftate of traffike to the Kingdome, and as the former muft not bee forgot , fo may the latter bee found of fuch neceffitie as that without it both King and Kingdome ere long will come far fhort of the revenues and abundance which hitherto they enjoyed; wherefore our drift muft primarily be to enlarge trade.

Since then two Nations carrying cloth or any other wares unto a market, the beft cheape will out of doubt fell fooneft and thereby eate the other out of trade; and in regard a neceffitie lyes upon us to finde out vent and iffue for our feverall manufactures and commodities whereby the poore people may continually be kept a worke, if this be not to be compaffed by felling cheaper than hitherto we have done, & that Marchants cannot poffibly fell cheaper unleffe they be eafed in the cuftomes, certainely there may arife not onely a conveniencie, but a peremptorie neceffitie that it bee fo for preventing greater mifchiefe.

Wherefore when fetling the booke of rates be ferioufly confidered of and weighed , it may in all likelihood appeare that fome native commodities and manufactures will juftly require the freedome of all cuftomes and fuch like charges , and others efpecially forraigne for as good reafon to be charged double, whereof if one ballance the other, the revenue will bee the fame as formerly, befides the encreafe in generall which will undoubtedly attend a well ordered State and Goverment of trade ; but if by this meanes the wonted revenue fhould for the prefent be impayred, that may be raifed by multiplicitie of other, meanes, each wherof would be leffe burthenfome or dammageable to the Body Politike., than any courfe how plaufible foever, which proves an obftacle to trades enlargement : wherefore I muft crave leave to preffe this farther, and fay I fuppofe there will be found upon due enquirie, neceffitie of freeing broad cloath and fome other Woollen manufactures from all or the greateft part of cuftomes unleffe

we

## *Englands safety.* 31

wee can keepe other Nations from making the same forts, or be contented the vent of ours should continually decrease, untill we be quite beaten out of it by forraigne Nations, who could not thrive so well therein, unlesse they had been able to undersell us, I wish therefore it may be throughly thought on and in due time prevented.

Yet for the decay of our Woollen Staple in some Countreyes wee cannot remedie it by withdrawing our customes and other charges, unlesse we prevaile with those states that they not only not impose new duties, but pull off such as are of latter times imposed contrarie to our ancient priviledges in their jurisdiction, and the Royall treaties and capitulations on Our States behalfe with Theirs respectively, wherein if I should particularize, it would appeare very notorious how in some Countreyes our cloath and other commodities have exceedingly beene burthened, purposely to keepe us from bringing them thither, and encreasing the manufacture thereof amongst themselves, which succeedes so well with them, as if wee bee but a little longer contented with it, for what concernes redresse, we may for ever after hold our peace.

Yet if such advantages may be layde holde of betweene States and Princes in amitie and alliance, and wee as ready to practise them as they, perhaps others might be glad to beginne a *Palinodia.*

Would the Hollanders take it kindly that wee forbid them fishing on our Coast and drying their netts on our shoare? would those of Brabant, Flanders, &c. to whom reciprocall trade and intercourse is of greater consequence like well it were withdrawne? can France drinke all the wine she makes, or heare willingly a bill of banishment against her babies and such like toyes for exporting no little summes of golde and silver yearely? If wee prohibite the importation of Currance but a yeare onely which costs us 70 m. pounds Starling ready money, would not the State of Venice see wee can better live without them, than their subjects of Zante and Zafalonia without bread, or eate currance in lieu of bread? and yet, poore people! they have no other shift; surely then if wee knew our own strength, they might well bee induced to let us have them upon moderate conditions without multiplying the custome and other duties in such prodigious manner as now they come to exceed the very cost and principall it selfe: We have not five thousand pounds worth of trade with them in a yeare besides these currance so dammageable to our selves, and for our friendship, however they regard it, it is of good consequence to them, in that the greatest part of their woolls from Spaine, and the rest from

C 2         Constan-

Conftantinople is moft commonly brought in Englifh. fhipping, which if they come fhort of, our own cloth may find fo much more vent in Barbarie and Turkie ; I purpofely forbeare to enter upon others, thefe few will evidently demonftrate our abilities to play with other Nations at their owne weapons, if wee bee provoked thereto.

But fome commodities there are which fhould not be reported neither with, nor without Cuftomes faving upon mature deliberation, as Ammunition of all forts, Timber, cordage, Pitch, and all other materialls of fhipping and Navigation, which may in time offend our felves ; yet when wee have advance, and it is probable our Neighbours, (nay very enemies) will have them from other parts, then had wee beft ferve them, and get the benefit thereof, whereas otherwife they will through neceffity feeke out and bee able to provide themfelves elfewhere, wee loofing what wee might fecurely have advanced, and perhaps be farther prejudiced in the confequences thereof : As in the tranfportation of Iron Ordnance whereof wee might have furnifhed all the world, but holding them at fo high a rate taught the Germans, Danes, and Swedes, to finde meanes and make them better cheape at home to this Kingdomes dammage above 20 m. l' *per annum* befides the imployment of fo many people. And certainly there are Offices which in Chriftianity wee owe to our very enemies, much more our Chriftian neighbours, and Proteftants moft of all (which makes mee wifh even with zeale and fervencie the Hollanders proceedings and carriage towards us were fuch as might not make them jealous of us in this or any other refpect) the omiffion whereof in us God Almighty knowes how to punifh even with *Lex talionis* if hee pleafe; yet I thinke we are not the only finners in this kinde conceaving that Nation ufes their utmoft art againft us and all the world befides in this refpect, the French having likewife of late yeares much encroach'd herein : And it is remarkeable how our Tin not long fince being raifed from Duckets 16. to Duckets 26. in Legorne, and other forraine parts proportionably, a mine of Tin is lately found in Barbarie from, whence quantity being brought for Italy hath pull'd the price of ours back-againe to about Duckets 16. as it was heretofore, and may perhaps finde the way to France, Turkie, and other Countreyes too, hereafter.

And in furnifhing our enemies with provifions and ammunition defenfive or offenfive me-thinks there is a policie not a little confiderable, in that they being fitted from time to time by us at a moderate

rate

## *Englands safetie.* 13

rate price makes them live securely and seeke no farther, expecting to have it brought unto them according to their custome, in which case if for our advantage at any time wee have just cause to denie it them, it is very likely we may supprize them, on a sudden before others not being used thereto can bring it them, or they perhaps bee able to provide themselves elsewhere.

4 The fourth meanes is by increasing and improving our new Plantations in the Westerne Ilands and encouraging to others; this is a matter of exceeding great moment enlarging both our Dominions and our Traffike; if people of good report and ranke could be prevailed upon by immunities and priviledges to bee the first Inhabitants in any new discoverie, certainly the businesse through their orderly and good government might succeede more prosperously, but for want of such it were farre better there were power and authority given to take up all beggars both men and women throughout these Kingdomes and send them for some of the new Plantations, all delinquents for matters which deserve not hanging, might bee served so too without sparing one of them, and all such persons in the meane time bee kept in houses for the same purpose, and forced to worke or starve, untill the time of the yeare and ships were ready to carry them away; and as these might likely doe better there, betaking themselves to get a living, so should wee not onely free the streetes and countrey of such rascals and vagrant people that swarme up and downe at present; but prevent many others, some whereof are successively borne and bred so, the rest brought to the same begging lasie life by their ill example, and a great summe of money saved, which uses yearely to bee given to such vagabonds to no purpose but to make them worse through the encouragement they have to continue so by our misled charity and daily almes.

But of all other Plantations that of Newfound Land may deserve to be furthered, not only in regard of the fertilitie of the Iland reported to bee great, but also for the more secure and commodious prosecution of our fishing trade on those banks, in which imployment a dozen of men only in a few moneths time are able to improve their labour to farre greater advantage, than by a whole yeares toile in tilling of the ground or any handicrafts mysterie whatsoever: and this leades me to

5. The Fishing trade upon our owne Coasts the fifth meanes of enlarging commerce, and of such great importance as that upon due consideration, it may chance, bee found not onely the Grand, but sole

meanes

meanes of our future commerce and propriety : for however of late ages, and even at prefent, we are of confiderable ftrength and credit to all the world for cloathing fo many of them with our Wollen commodities, yet if we confider ferioufly thereof, and fee wee cannot at prefent vent in Germanie and the Low Countreyes, one third part of what wee ufed in former times, being beaten out of it by their fubtilty and induftrie in making the fame themfelves, wee may perhaps deferved̄ly have caufe to feare that our Woollen Staple, and Manufacture efpecially, will by degrees wheele away from us in that viciffitude whereto wee finde all other fublunarie States and things obnoxious : And though as it were to recompence thofe loffes and encourage our farther endeavours, Divine Providence hath difcovered us how to utter a confiderable quantity of cloth(though not anfwerable to the decay in Germanie and the Low Countreyes ) for Turkie and Mufcovia, yet for the latter wee are fcarce likely to enjoy it long, the Hollanders ferving the fame market with our owne Cloth carried thither from Ham-rough upon bettertermes than wee can, which might perhaps be prevented by putting a greater charge and cuftome on fuch forts of Cloth fent for thofe parts, which are not fpent there, but carried for Mufcovia or Barbarie, were it not that hereafter they will likely be able to make the Cloth themfelves, and fo debarre us totally ; But for Turkie, whereas fome few latter yeares wee have fent above 2 om. Clothes died and dreffed, it is certaine we cannot continue the trade in the future with any profit for above halfe that quantity, efpecially fince wee muft likely forbeare thofe Countrey Cotton-Woolls which ufed to furnifh us for returnes, being now ferved with better cheape of our owne plantation in the Wefterne Ilands.

But for my part, I fhall not thinke our felves fecure of any trade or ought wee have, which the craft or power of Neighbouring Nations fhall any wayes bee able to beguile us of, and therefore moft earneftly doe wifh, wee may, whil'ft that we may, endeavour to eftablifh our fecurity and trade upon our owne foundation, and that muft bee our fifh imployment, able to beget and draw after it all trade befides, being the Schoole and Nurferie of Marriners and Navigation, and briefely a Treafure more rich, and in fundry refpects to be preferred before the Spaniards in the Weft Indies, whofe ftore with Gods bleffing will continually encreafe as often as the Moone, whofe influence fo much predominats thofe Creatures, and though another Kingdome of fifh fhould bee difcovered, fuch Nations as are fituated neere us, will bee neceffitated to feed on ours : What pittie is it then that fo

many

*Englands safety.* 15

many fishing Townes alongst our Coaft fhould bee decay'd, nay what ignominie and bad goverment to pay and maintaine Strangers for taking of our owne fifh? Certainely if ever wilfulneffe or negligence of not improving a Talent in this World bee punifhed hereafter, ours will bee inexcufable; My purpofe is not to enlarge fince others are better able, and I cannot fo much as think ferioufly thereof without a profound difturbance and vexation to my felfe, whil'ft I revolve in my mind the greateft carelefneffe that ever men committed, faving that fome of our Predeceffours did the like, and our fucceffours will doe no leffe, for all that I can doe; and therefore had beft defift to torment my felfe in rayling fpirits, unleffe I could againe alay them.

Wherefore I will only fay, if wee doe not get into our owne managing the greateft proportion of the fifhing trade, our trafficke will not onely decline, becaufe it cannot otherwife bee the greateft, and that (as the greater fifh the leffer) hath capacity to eate out and devoure the reft, but the very finues and ftrength of the whole Kingdome, the onely ground worke whereof is trade and commerce, will bee fhaken and quite ruined in the end, at leaft whatfoever State elfe fhall enjoy it, will keep us at their mercie; and therefore if wee either want moneys, men, knowledge to catch and cure the fifh, or ought elfe to eftablifh this only Pillar of our future wealth and fafetie, let us either prevaile with other Nations by waiges and faire meanes for their affiftants, or not fuffer any of them to fifh on our Coaft, fave fuch as will come and inhabite in our Sea-Townes with their wives and families, making themfelves free Denizens and depofiting fuch a portion of each voyages profit in a fecure Banke for that purpofe which fhall punctually pay them and their children if neede bee the intereft, and reftore the Principall unto their Grand-Children, who may then bee thought quite naturalized and not likely to depart the Kingdome, or elfe fuch Boates whofe men unwilling to dwell amongft us may bee permitted to fifh, fo they take halfe Englifh marriners and Adventurers in the voyage of whofe returne for England we are alfo to be fecured.

And fince our Soveraingrty on the Seas is fo evident, and the pollicie of State for our fecurity permits us not longer to neglect it, mee thinks our neighbouring States and Princes fhould not interpret amiffe, if they refufing thefe or the like offers (without which hereafter we fhall not poffibly be able to continue and maintaine our jurifdiction) we doe with utmoft rigour totally forbid them fifhing; for even in this extremitie it will moft evidently appeare unto an equall Judge, that what wee doe is only to fecure our felves and Kingdomes;

For

For as upon the Continent the Armie that commands the Field roves where it pleases forcing the wholeCountrey to contributions; so doth a Fleet at Sea and Seacoast much more speedily & powerfully offending and commanding those Kingdomes by Sea In one moneth , which the most puissant Armie is not able to march through in a whole yeare: & that the fishing trade(since it encreases shipping marriners & brings home in returne to them that follow it , money and all sort of wares for a greater valley than al the trade of England does besides) wil eltate whotoever followes it in this Prerogative, is undeniable amongst such as know the wealth and consequents of it : Besides although both French and Hollanders so long as they are countenanced by us , may in likelyhood prevaile against the Spaniard, his forces being so much disperfed amongst his other enemies , yet what they get is so much advantage as may bee used against our selves in time , and if the latter chance but to loose an Armie and we either unprepared or unwilling to assist them, then is their whole Countrey endangered, which being narrow will bee runne over and plundered whilst they stand a-maz'd at their Armies overthrow , and their multitude of people encreasing onely so much more one anothers distraction , will but further their owne confusion, which in their shipping will afterwards bee brought home to us , unlesse wee doe prevent it by enabling our selves to contrall with all the world besides at Sea, in which sove-raignty the fishing of Herrings King of (men as well as) fish; is onely powerfull to maintaine us.

And yet before I leave this point I will be bold to adde there is no course so easily to bee taken without offending of our Neighbours that will infallibly in some proportion secure us of the fishing as by exactly requiring (not by halves as hitherto) the strict keeping Lent and two fish dayes a week at least throughout all three Kingdomes, and besides increase our Cattell no little policie, especially at present to bee practised, for multiplying (Fishermen I would willingly) as the case stands, receive this pennance from Popery , and thinke to merit more of the whole state , than by all their works of supererogation.

And for such as object the unwholesomnesse of a fish dyet, if this were the greatest disorder they committed, I believe they would have more health and Physicians fewer fees , there being ( although more delicacie yet)lesse gluttonie and surfetting in fish than flesh, and I hope it will not be found injustice in the State upon occasion of such consequence to regulate our appetites , which wee our selves neglect to the prejudice of our health in particular, and endammaging the common-wealth in generall.

The

*Englands safetie.*  17

The decay of trade is in every bodyes mouth from the Sheepe-sheater to the Marchant, and even a weak Statist, without *Gallikoes* prospective glasse, may see both our wealth and safetie therewith declining, and if this greatest mischiefe no lesse than the ruine of a Kingdome may as easily be prevented, shall wee with *Naaman* over-slip the benefit because the meanes are facil.? And not regard one crying out to Englang, *Fish and be rich and powerfull*, because fishing is so frequent a recreation? I know full well this fishing imployment hath sundry times beene attempted not without great losse, and yet am altogether as confident the ill successe succeeded from the managing and bad goverment thereof to bee made appeare upon due enquirie: First, because our men are as good Marriners, altogether as well able to brooke the Sea, endure the toile, fare as hardly, and capeable of attaining to the knowledge as any Nation whatsoever: Secondly, We may have boates and all sorts of vessells, Nets and other instruments as cheape and fit for the purpose as any can bee made: Thirdly, our Sea-townes are situated more commodious and neere unto the places where the fish is taken, so that whereas other Nations spend time and charge to goe towards the frie, that may bee said to come to us; for all which respects, or some of them wee may infallibly bee enabled after a while to take and sell fish better cheape than other Nations, and if all wayes else doe faile to prosecute this designe, I shall be ready (when commanded) to propound one that will not.

6.  The sixt is the restoring of our Woollen Staple, and this must bee by seeking to export the greatest quantity wee can of Woollen goods dyed and dressed in their full manufacture, as also by setling such a course as the Officers who are only to seale the cloath if it hold in length, breadth, good spinning &c. may not passe it over so carelesly more regarding their fees than the care belonging to their Office.

For the first, I know the enterprize was made many yeares since in seeking to send nothing but dyed and dressed Cloth into Germany and the Low-Countreyes, and how prejudiciall it proved to us in teaching them to make cloth of their owne, rather than bee so stinted by us, and since chiefely in Holland by imposing dayly new taxes and customes upon all our Cloth spent there both white and cullour'd, but if at that time in a quiet way wee had onely taken the Custome and charge off from the Cullour'd and by degrees put it upon the white still rayfing it infenfibly, it might in all probability have done the feate, the cheape collour'd beating the deere white Cloth quite

2 Kin.5.
11, 12,
13.

D  out

out of ſervice, and for preſent wee can onely make this uſe of it, that unleſſe wee give out Cloth both white and colour'd at cheaper rates than they make theirs of the ſame goodneſſe, wee muſt looke quite to looſe the trade.

But for the ſearchers of the Cloath that it bee compleat in all the perquiſites, mee thinks it might well be compaſſed; and it is of great conſequence, for the Marchants here in England who deale for great ſummes and quantities cannot looke ſo preciſely on every Cloth, examining of it end for end, and when it comes beyond ſea hee that buyes it can only ſee the muſter and the outſide, receiving the great-eſt part of it upon truſt and publique faith which Marchants deale more in than for readie money, and afterwards perhaps it may bee ſent hundreds of miles farther before it bee opened, or the defects knowne untill it come to bee meaſur'd out; Wherefore this charge and care of ſearching and ſealing all Woollen goods may very well bee intruſted to the next towne where the cloth is made, and they imploying whome they pleaſe to receive the benefit, for their behoofe, may bee obliged to utmoſt dammages and penalties upon every over-ſight therein committed.

And for Fullers-earth, Woolls or any other materialls which con-duce to cloathing wee muſt not onely forbeare to carry them our ſelves, but hinder others what we can from doing ſo.

7. The ſeventh is the encouragement of all manufactures at pre-ſent practiſed in England, and bringing in of new, which is of wonderfull conſequence and benefit eſpecially to a populous com-monwealth, in regard it ſets multitudes of poore people a worke, who thereby maintaine their wives and families in good order, which otherwiſe might bee burdenſome, and perhaps ſtarve. Theſe manufactures are one maine cauſe hath made the Hollanders ſo nu-merous and brought them to this greatneſſe, wherefore in imitation of them wee ought to cheriſh all thoſe that are already ſetled, as Weavers of Woollen and Silke ſtuffes, Weavers and Knitters of Silke and Woollen ſtockins, with which latter a pretty trade hath former-ly beene driven but almoſt quite declined ſince our laſt warre with Spaine, during which time through want of ours, they began to make them in the Countrey improving it ever ſince and thereby with the great cuſtomes upon ours at home bereaved us of that trade; ſo as when wee looſe one, if wee bee not ingenious to get another in-ſteed thereof, wee ſhall bee ſtript of all at laſt: The very varying and new fangling of manufactures is conſiderable, cauſing them to finde

vent

vent both at home & abroad as they happen to pleafe the fancie of thofe Nations to which wee fend them ; and if fuch as fet their wits a work herein were taken notice of, and rewarded by fuch a commiffion or peculiar ftanding Magiftrate who fhould have the fuperintendencie over all trade and trafficke many would likely be encouraged by the credit of it, but gaine would provoke all ; And the fame Magiftrate to punifh all abufes in manufactures of what fort foever either in perfonall or penall mulcts ⅓ whereof to go unto the King. ⅓ unto the Magiftrate and ⅓ to the Informer, who it he fo defire, is to be concealed.

Weavers then of all forts of linnen both fine and courfe are to bee invited out of France, and the Low-Countreyes, and Walloones and other French, both for making of lighter and finer forts of Wollen ftuffes, and are generally farre more ingenious for inventing of Laces, Buttons, and what elfe is deem'd requifite to the accomplifh't apparelling ( fo thought at prefent ) *à la mode*, wherein all Europe fpeake true French though not the fame Dialect, for where all ufe not the felfe fame fafhion, yet they varie theirs as much as French : but thefe Laces and Buttons may perhaps onely helpe to encreafe our owne expences at home, and are fcarce likely to grow exportable into forraine Countreyes, where our Woollen commodities are chiefely requefted becaufe good cheape.

The multiplying of falt, but chiefely making it with falt water deferves likewife particularly to bee continued and cherifhed, not fo much for imploying many people, but that wee cannot well paffe without it, being as neceffary to us in a manner as is our meate ; Our fifh imployment cannot fubfift without it, and the preferving both of fifh and flefh the chief e fuftenance of our long voyages and Navigation, fo that if poffibly it may bee compaffed, and made in England to bee afforded hereafter when brought to full perfection at the fame or fomewhat a higher price, than wee ufed to bee ferved at from abroad, queftionleffe it will bee good pollicie rather than expect it from others who will denie it us in greateft neede, and wee found both unskilfull and unprovided of moft of the materialls to furnifh us therewith ; yet fomewhat wee may pay more for this, fince as it is faid the flefh and fifh cured with this falt eates more pleafant, and befides making it our felves wee fhall not onely have it at a conftant price which before did much varie, rifing and falling exorbitantly as more or leffe ftore came

**20**          *Trades encreaſe*

from abroad, which was ſo much the more hazardous, in regard many ſhips brought it only when they could get no other imployment, thereby telling us there was no gaine in it, and wee cannot expect men will bring it us to loſſe : But the importation thereof being continually prohibited , and freedome for all to make it in the Kingdome , where and when it may bee moſt for their advantage , I conceive they may have Ware-houſes and Magazins up and downe the Countrey , to conſerve it in , and afford it all yeare long at ſuch a rate as may be for our common good and benefit. And ſurely it may ſerve us for a Maxime of direction in all ſuch like caſes, that whatſoever is neceſſary or ſo uſefull, as probably wee cannot bee well without it, wee ſhould by all meanes poſſible ſeeke to ſecure our ſelves of it within our owne juriſdiction without being ſubject to the mercie and reliefe of others in our greateſt miſerie and diſtreſſe & thus ſtanding upon our owne foundation what ere befall other parts or Countreyes of the world, we may not onely ſtill remaine the ſame amongſt our ſelves, but be Arbitrators of their welfare alſo.

The making of Cabells and all manner of cordage is likewiſe conſiderable , for which cauſe the groweth of Hempe in our Kingdomes might bee encouraged and may well hereafter bee more practized becauſe it ſets many a woike , and being ſo inſeparable to navigation with many others , which are all to be furthered by priviledges and immunities to the workemen , eſpecially the new Inventors and Promotors , and the materialls which are thus imployed in manufactures to be imported with little charge and cuſtome, to the end the Marchants and Manufactors may finde a competent gaine and make a trade of it.

By this meanes the Hollanders who have little of their owne growth to feed upon, cloath, or promote Navigation ſave butter and cheeſe, have yet ſuch ſtore and proviſion of corne, wine, fiſh, ſhipping , ammunition, and all other things neceſſary and delicious, as their owne naturall wants are not onely aboundantly ſupplyed , but ſeverall other Provinces of larger circuit than their owne repleniſhed with their ſtore to the great wonder of the world , in that they having no materialls conduceable to ſhipping can build, ſell ſhips, and let them out to fraight, cheeper than any other Nation.

8.  The eight is making England the *Emporium* or Warehouſe from whence other Nations may bee furniſhed with forraine commodities of all ſorts, and this may likely have effect, if ſuch

                                            forraine

### Englands safetie.　　　21

forraine wares bee not onely exported free of charge, but most of the duties which were pay'd at their importation bee restored againe, efpecially if a Denizen brought them in, and carries them out againe, wherein the chiefe rule to governe our felves mult be ny ordering it in fuch manner as that we may furnifh other Nations with them full as cheape as they can have them eliewhere, for this is a maine engine wherewith fome people advance themfelves and hinder others.

This tranfportation and ferving other Nations with forraine commodities is of greater benefit and conf. quence to fome States than the exportation of their owne, and yet in this wee are equally with them capable of the fame imployment by reafon of our fituation, nay fome of our Sea-Townes where thefe Magazines may be rayfed, and Marchants invited to inhabit, lie more neere feverall Neighbouring Provinces than they, and whereas fome Countreyes during the Winter feafon have their fhips often kept in by ice fome moneths together, we may from hence put out all windes and weather,and a fhip at Sea feldome but advances fomewhat towards her Port: Befides the Hollanders having no native commodities to follow the Turkie trade, and by reafon of the Algier Pyrates fo much infefting, and the Spaniards no little awing them at entring in and out the ftraights, they are quite driven out of it, fo that were it well ordered we might fervethem, and the French too (bought out ofthe turkie trade by us in cheape felling of our cloth to our owne loffe) with all manner of Turkie commodities, Cotton-Wools and fuch others as come from our Wefterne Plantations, and upon dearth of Corne, or fcarcity of any other thing, wee providing to furnifh other Nations, and keeping their Warehoufes as I may fay in our Kingdome, fhall not onely not want our felves,but bee furnifhed far better cheape than they and neceffitate them to have continuall dependency upon us.

9. The ninth is the promoting of the Eaft India Trade, which however hitherto dammageable to thofe that followed it in particular, yet upon due fearch and eftimation will bee found wounderfully confiderable, the rather becaufe thofe Territories being fo vaft, farther difcoveries of new trades might be expected dayly,as well for venting of our owne commodities as importing others at cheaper rates,if that fociety were better countenanced at home and not fo grievoufly difturbed abroad, the Hollanders in policie of State have reafon to defire nothing

**2 2**                              *Trades encreafe*

fo much as to weary out and conftraine them to abandon it,
which unlefse it bee prevented, wee may juftly feare will take effect, being to be obferved and collected by the proceeding of the
*Amboina* bufineffe that nothing will bee left unattempted,for full
accomplifhing whatfoever may farther advance their ftrength
and profit.

And although at prefent the Flemmings carry little of their
fpices into the Straights, becaufe they fell them better neerer
hand, as alfo in regard the Pyrates of Algier doe oftentimes
make prey of them,& fo much raife the infurance as they thrive
not in the trade, yet if wee fuffer them to beate us quite out of
the Eaft Indies, we muft not only loofe the trade wee drive in o-
ther parts with the advance of India Commodities, and pay
deere for what wee fpend our felves, but when ere this come to
paffe, being then ftored with fpices, Callicoes, and other Eaft
India wares, enough to ferve all Italie, Turkie, and Barbarie,
which fo foone as they begin to practife, the reft of our trade in
the Mediterranean Sea will then as faft decline, the Hollanders
cheape fraight beingable of it felfe to eate us out in time without any other Stratagem or plot.

Wherefore there is no longer time for dallying, wee muft
whileft wee are able make our owne lawes and conditions, ftill
keeping our felves fo much more ftronger, as no Nation may
ever have power or ability to fpurne againft us: and for to warrant and encourage us in executing of it, we have not onely
the maine ground and pollicie of the State to keep Neighbouring Nationsfrom growing over powerfull, efpecially fuch as
above others are more fubtill and forward to offend us, when
craftily and fecurely to bee compaffed; but too too juft caufe
of revenge have wee againft the Hollanders for their unheard of
cruelties and injuries done us in the Indies, whereof we have required juftice and reftitution in fo milde a manner, as taught
them hitherto onely to fleight and put us off,by which proceedings though the Eaft india Companie being wearied out for
want of the States protection and affiftance fhould bee prevailed
upon to receive an inconfiderable defpicable allowance holding
no proportion with their wrongs, becaufe they can get no more
at prefent,yet I hope his Majeftie will never paffe it over in fuch
manner,as may enbolden them to attempt the like againe: None
admires their induftrie more then may felfe, or defires their
good fucceffe,but with the fame charity reflecting on our felves

at

## *Englands fafety.* 23

at fome , defire withall wee may rather bee alwayes able and willing
to aide them , than ever neede, or have neceffity to be aided by them.

But vaine it is for us to thinke or ftudy the enlarging trade , unleffe we profecute the Eaft Indian with all might and maine ; for if
trade muft chiefely bee advanced by Exportation , Importation , and
Tranfportion as I faid at firft ; That of Importation we generally ex-
claime againft our felves,and juftly too for being fo great and overballancing our Exportation as is objected,that brings us fo farre in debt,
as nothing but our moneys the blood of traffike will fatisfie; and of
Exportation what can wee farther hope from it hereafter ? hath not
all the Cloth we vented from North to Eaft of late yeares beene fould
to loffe ? Certainly our Marchants will make it plainely appeare they
cannot live by the trade at prefent, nor yet hope to fell at better
rates in the future, unleffe we fend out leffe ; fo that both Exportation
and Importation muft bee leffened that trade may bee inlarged , although it feeme a Paradox : This you'le fay is a deplorable Eftate and
yet it is ours , and we muft make the beft of it , or fare the worfe our
felves.

We muft not only bee contented but really leffen our Importation
and confumption of forraine goods at home , nor reft there neither ,
but refolve to doe the like for Exportation fending out leffe Cloth
hereafter, and this is not all neither, but wee muft lade it as little as
may be with cuftomes and other charges,elfe all other Nations almoft
who have already begun to make Cloth , will be able to underfell and
beate us quite out, fo that a Mafter-piece it would bee, if poffible, to
give them fo good cheape abroad , as others might not make to live
by it,and then both our Wollen-Weavers and other manufactors that
fo unkindly left us,may happily returne againe,and fuch as have been
taught by them doe the like , through difcontinuance become unapt,
or at leaft in time both one and other fpin out their owne thrid too ;
when,and not fooner,may we expect to fell more quantities of cloth at
better prices, which then,and not till then,may fafely be inhanc'd,nor
without due pollicie and difcretion to prevent the like feverall difa-
fters into which through our inconfiderate proceedings we finde our
felves plunged at prefent : But if I ( like a hard-hearted Chirurgion
that unmercifully torments a Patient in fearching and lancing of his
wound , and afterwards uncharitably leaves him without applying a
foveraigne balfome for to cure it ) doe here conclude , I fhould not
only faile of my intention and pretention in this foregoing difcourfe,
which was both to demonftrate a Poffibilitie and meanes of trades in-
largement , but be juftly cenfurable for anticipating our miferies , re-

prefenting

presenting them all at once to the publicke view in their most dire-
full and maligne aspect, whereas their naturall motion will onely o-
vertake us by degrees.

Since therefore the exportation of Cloth our most staple commodity, and importation and consumption of forraine wares must be diminished, to make good what I intended towards the enlarging our
trafficke notwithstanding, the remainder of our Stocke, People, and
Labours, which of late heve beene imployed in making more Cloth,
and bringing in more superfluities than wee could well digest, must
necessarily bee set a worke some other way, and this may not onely
have eff.ct by practising new manufactures, Fabrickes, and the fishing
imployment, but also by transportation to our farre greater benefit
and advantage: Now nothing can bee imagined so much to further
transportation as the prosperitie of the East India trade, wherefore as
it is not safe for us to part with any Countrey trade how small soever,
because the wealth and welfare of this Kingdom may justly be measu-
red by the Kingdomes traffick, so least of all may we forgoe this of the
East Indies, which though at present in vents not our native commodities in such quantities as Germanie and Turkie, yet the money we
save by furnishing our selves with Spices, Callicoes and other India
wares at moderate rates in great abundance, and yet send larger store
out againe to other Nations, and the good hopes and likelihood wee
have to multiply this trade in all dimensions, may render it so considerable, as that if Marchants by their former ill successe, through the
Hollanders unbrotherly proceedings, should not be found to prosecute it, his Majestie and whole State have just cause to keepe it up
though it were to losse at first, and if all meanes else faile, moneyes
levied for maintayning it, cannot bee so grievous and prejudiciall to
these Kingdomes, as the losse of it would likely bring poverty and
ruine on them in the end.

For though the pres.nt Companie being dissolved, it is like enough
that many particular Marchants will adventure by themselves, for
what will they not adventure? yet if the Hollanders can counterminde
a whole society, that had so great a stocke, so well setled, so well governed abroad, & still likely to be countenanced at home, what may then
be expected from ordinarie private Marchants who have no succession, perishing one by one in their Individuals? but that the Hollanders will have so much more advantage over them, and they not being
otherwise able to make a voyage, at length turne Pyrates and prey upon one another: A Corporation it must be and a powerfull one too,
that followes this trade, able to plant Colonies by degrees and make
                                                        head

*Englands safetie.* 15

head in the Indies if need be against the Hollanders incroaching &
proving there too weake may here be righted by his Majestie than
which, nothing certainly will more keepe the Hollanders from at-
tepting their utter extirpation;they must have factories established
up and downe where their ships may be sure of victuals and reliefe
in their distresse; they must bee such as have stocke enough to contract and deale with States and Princes for great matters as well
as small, which though a private man doe undertake for, yet shall
bee not be credited: These few amongst infinite other reasons may
necessarily inferre that none can manage this waightie busines to
the just improvement save a joynt and well governed stocke and
Companie which will yet afford another notable advantage, that
now presents it selfe to my memory, for the future benefit and safetie of this State, in that (which yet will bee much more when they
begin to flourish as is expected ) being accustomed to have sundry
Warehouses and Magazins full of Bisket,Fish,Flesh,Butter,Cheese,
Wine and Vineger to make beverage of, Caske, Anchores, Sals, all
provisions of Navigation bought by them at times and seasons to
most advantage,&Mariners that tarrie at home expecting their imployment,when ere the King or State should have occasion of a sudden expedition, this provident Societie without dammage to their
peculiar affaires, might lend or sell them of all sorts to the great
advancement of the interprize ,which sometimes not onely delay
makes hazardous, but utterly disapoints, as at present , is thought,
about a Fleet of twenty ships onely to be sent against the Pyrates of
Algier at Sea, and cannot bee got soone enough in readinesse for
want of Marriners and provisions.

    10. The tenth is the erecting of a new Court, or Magistrate
consisting of Marchants where all March nts and Marchantlike
causes and differences should bee summarily decided without appeale, saving through his Majesties speciall grace in case of palpable injustice, and this Court to condemne in Principall, Interest,
charges, dammages , and fines too , if the cause in their judgements
might have seemed plaine to most men of ordinary apprehension,
to the end that knaves and litigious persons may bee deterred from
moving suites without good ground, or withholding any thing
that belongs unto another.

    These Courts are set'ed in Italy, France , and many other
Countreyes with good successe, being grounded upon reason, and
practise of Marchants dispersed throughout the world, for most
part , without respect to the Municipall lawes and priviledges

[E]          of

of any particular place or Kingdome, for if it should not bee-
one and the same, but varie according to severall Dominions
and Jurisdiction, a Marchant adventuring himselfe, or his
Estate abroad, in a case of one and the same nature might bee:
cast both wayes in severall Countreyes without a possibility of reliefe.

This Court then ought for very good reason to consist of Marchants, in regard a Marchant of good naturall endowments bread
at least a competent Grammer Scholler, having lived abroad,
experienced in customes and affaires of sundry Countreyes, may
questionlesse be a generally more knowing man than any other of
what profession soever, and so better qualified for decyphring the
intricace and various difficulties ( which seeme to many as darke
obscure Hi roglyphicks ) arising from this profession: For, as the
Mysterie of Marchants is more subtill and active suddenly multiplying contracts infinitely beyond all others; so doe spring from
thence more knottie and abstruse differences and disputes, far better understood, and consequently to be judged and ended by understanding Marchants, yet happily the assistance of a skilfull Civilian
with name of Chancellour or such like, I conceive, may not doe
amiss to bee subordinate to the Marchants, for otherwise he may
likely too much sway, and with his more volubil tongue overtalke
the Marchants and run away with the cause according to his singular opinion: yet must he not be meale mouthed neither, for then
will he be overaw'd much more by the Marchants who have such
odds in number.

But a speciall care this Court must have to dispatch each cause
with all possible expedition, for these of all other can worst admit
demurers; because either the commodities which Marchants strive
about are perishable, or ships must goe on their voyages, Marriners may not tarry behind and loose their service, and the very
time eates out eight in the hundred from him that suffers on whatsoever summes in controversie; and though (as I conceive) next to
unhealthines, law suites may justly bee thought the greatest misery
in this world to all in generall, yet Marchants of all others are lesse
able to attend them; for law suites, as the case stood, were growne
as haz rdous as playing at dice, and reckoning the butlers boxe too
boote, the Lawyers fees and charges have much the odds, onely in
this the Gamster has advantage, that though hee loose, each cast
still puts him out of paine: whereas sometimes a mans suite at
Law outlives himselfe, and perhaps the cause lost afterwards
                                                        becaue

## Englands *safetie.*

becaufe, he could live no longer to defend it; and yet if hee had not dyed, fhould never have beene ended: but my meaning is this, that whofoever goes to Law, muft *hoc agere*; and a Merchants affaires require *totum virum*; now fince a Merchant ought onely, and can be all but in one of thefe, this Court will bee the more bound in equitie and juftice to free him from the other.

And fince this Law is fo troublefome, and chargeable to all forts of people and conditions, if in a particular office fo appoynted, all judgements, morgages, contracts, and bargaines, and incumbrances whatfoever, of Lands, Houfes, Offices, &c. ( the juft Title whereof wee cannot, by looking in his face, know to whom belongs ) were neceffarily to be regiftred, and the partie that owes them in a booke compendioufly to be made Creditor and Debtor when he fells them, his title onely being to be preferred in cafe of controverfie, who had his contract regiftred in this Office, and Credit in the faid Book, unleffe omitted through defau't of the faid Office, which in fuch cafe muft appeare by Coppie of the Contract under-writ by this Officer, remaining with the true proprietor of thofe Lands, houfes, &c. it would certainly prevent the greateft part of Law-fuits in *England*, fince going to that office, a man intending to make a purchafe, and paying a fmal matter for the fearch, as he may fee (and have Copie of it if he pleafe) to whom the goods belong'd, were morgaged, or interiourly ingaged, and fo bee fure the Title's good.

The fame Court of Merchants, if thought requifite, may likewife end all differences about infurance, obliging the infurer to runne all hazzard imaginable or not imaginable, or that may, and do happen to fall out of all kindes and natures, and to pay whatfoever loffe that happens on goods affured in fuch words: for the intention of the infured being to fecure themfelves from all cafualties that poffibly could happen in this world, ought therefore to have each finifter, though difficult accident interpreted in their favour: In cafe of loffe, the Infurers fhould bee conftrained to pay without the leaft abatement, and be paid the *Premium* when they fubfcribe the policies, whereby the infured would have better opportunitie to pick and chofe the rareft men to under-write his policie, and the Infurer to be freed from all loffes: the newes whereof was heard before the *Premum* was paid, which muft appeare in writing by a particular receipt, befides that of the policie, where they fay to have received it at that inftant of fubfcribing; and fometimes cannot get it notwithftanding in many yeares after: the Infured likewife

E   might

**34**                    *Trades encreaſe,*

might be bound to runne adventure of $\frac{1}{4}$ part himſelfe on every ſhip, which will not onely hinder much deceit, that might bee practiſed, but cauſe him to endeavour the ſafetie of all the reſt: much more may likely appeare juſtly to be reform'd in due place and ſeaſon.

The tenth is the erecting of a Banke or Grand Caſh on ſuch foundation and ſecuritie, as all men may thinke their monies more ſure there, than in their houſes, whereby they may bee induc'd to bring them in, and receive a certaine moderate intereſt of about 5. *per* 100. or keep them there, till they ſhall have occaſion to diſpoſe of them, or pay them to another: and theſe payments, when the Bank hath once got credit, may be done by aſſignation, or turning them over from one man to another, without any reall aſſuring of monies: which beſides ſaving trouble to tell ſo much money, becomes exceeding beneficiall to a Common-wealth, increaſing the trade and traffick ſo much more as all the monies this Bank hath gained credit for doth import: as for example thus:

Suppoſe I be caſh-keeper to ten wealthy men, that amongſt them al for the moſt part have 10000 *li.* ſtil lying dead, expecting a good opportunity and advantage to purchaſe Land, or otherwiſe: I that am Caſh-keeper, knowing there can be no occaſion of theſe ten thouſand pounds till ſuch a time; or if there ſhould be ſooner, know where to have as much to put i'th place of it, and withall having the owners conſent, doe put theſe ten thouſand pounds out at intereſt, or imploy it in one commodity or other for my owne account and benefit, to the encreaſe of Trade, which is equally done as well with credit as ready money.

Thus a Banke is no more than a Grand Caſh-keeper of this whole Kingdome, or ſo many as doe bring in their monies, whereof few or none will make any ſcruple, when due ſecuritie be given, and this ſecuritie at preſent perhaps will bee deſired, no leſſe than the High Court of Parliament; which, if they pleaſe out of their deep wiſedomes to reſolve upon, and the monies which ſhall lie idle to be made uſe of, for their benefit and behoofe, to take account thereof in their Trienniall Parliament, and diſpoſe it to the good of the Common-wealth, with their gracious permittance, I ſhould in all humilitie be bold to ſay, there never paſſed Act of Parliament ſo capable to advance the trade and welfare of this Kingdome, with ſuch facilitie and ſpeed as this, as I doubt not but to make better apparent when e're I be commanded.

And whereas it may be thought, that few will bring their monies into

## Englands *safety.*

into this Banke, conceiving it not so safe for them to lye thus depo-
sited in a Monarchie, as if it were a free state, especially since the
monies in the Tower were so lately seized upon without regard of
violating the publick faith, which in States and Princes affaires
ought to be kept so much more sacred, as Princes are exalted above
Subjects and termed Gods. I will crave leave to present unto their
consideration the state of *Tuscanie*, well knowne to have continually flourished in peace and plentie, ever since the politique and
sage family of *Medici* had rule and government there. f, and it
may justly have beene observed unto this day, that no Prince makes
use of a larger prerogative, and proceeds in some cases more arbi-
trarilythan these who yet end and sentence according to the Lawes
in full force of equitie and justice.

This Prince in what part of his state so ever hee bee, gives audi-
ence twice a weeke to all that come, though very beggers. ( O that
our gracious Soveraignes more large affaires could but permit him
to grant his loving and loyall Subjects the like but once a month,
whereby we might not onely have beene sooner eased of many just
grievances, but his Majestie perhaps both truer and speedier in-
formd of the causes, & so better enabled through his profound judgment to prevent these great distractions, which have and doe still at
present so much perplexe these Kingdoms) and no man delivereth a
Petition, but within three dayes at farthest, shall be certaine of a
reference, so that his prerogative and arbitrarie proceedingss are
so farre from being injust, as they serve onely in casualties, which
the Lawes have not provided for, certaine conjunctions which
may not expect, or thcu regard, the Ceremonial. Rites, and slow or
over-hasty foot-steps of a Court of Justice ( may it upon this occasion be so termed without offence ) and to prevent the *summum
jus*, which even by Proverb wee have learnd to terme but *Summa
injuria:* In this state I say, whose Prince is so absolute and Soveraigne as none in Christendome so much ( notwithstanding the
Popes supremacy, which in his owne understanding is of unlimited
extent ) there is such course took for due administratiou of justice,
distinguishing betwixt *meum* and *tunm*, and preserving each mans
propriety in his goods, as not onely those Natives, but others, strangers, think not their estates securer, then depositing them in the *Florentine* Banke, which is by them called *Monte di Pieta*, where they
have five *per* 100. interest *per annum*, and may receive out the
principall at pleasure : In the same Banke are infinite summes left
by particulars for the like interest, entail'd upon their posteritie,

which

which cannot be remov'd, or al enated : And that you may gheffe how vaft a Capitall this Mount or Banke confifts of, it lends like-wife upon Pawnes at 5¼ *per* 100, and to a landed man upon fecuritie of fuch another, which is equall to a Morgage, becaufe their Lands being regiftred in an office for that purpofe, the true title thereof is feene in an inftant, and as his Majeftie here in *England*, fo the Banke there is to bee firft fatisfied in cafe of Bankrupt, and what is thus lent, by the beft infor-mation I could get, was thought to bee above a million fterling. Befides, there is another kind of Bank in *Florence*, which is called *il giro*; as thus, Every three moneths the Merchants of *Florence* chufe one amongft themfelves of beft credit, who is to be (as it were) the generall Cafh-keeper of all moneyes de-livered, or taken by exchange, for that prefent Faire; the manner whereof you will finde explaned at large hereafter, fo that what moneyes bee delivered, or drawne by any man during this Faire, the fayd generall Cafh-keeper makes him Debtour or Creditour, turning the flyd fummes over from one to the other, provided hee be fuch a man as hath money in his Cafh, and at three moneths end hee makes up his Cafh, payes everie man his owne, and the Merchants choofe another for the next Faire, or three moneths following.

Now if the benefit and convenie cie of thefe Banks are thus enjoyed in *Tufcany*, where the Prince is fo abfolute; but with-all, his Treafurer and other Minifters fo punctuall in payments and other dealings for the Princes peculiar fervice, as no Merchant can be more; for which caufe Merchants hold it more fecure, and feek rather to deale with them, than with the beft meere Merchants like themfelves: Why may not we, under fo pious and gracious a Soveraigne, in a Kingdome founded and eftablifhed upon fuch wholefome Lawes, expect the like good fucceffe from a Banke in *England*? For being fo exceedingly beneficiall both to King and Countrey, as would daily ftill more and more appeare, wee may eafily beleeve it fhould bee furthered and cherifhed by both; the rather fince it may bee fetled and credited by Act of Parliament, with command that neither principall nor profit fhall bee ftirred or employed, fave for their account, according to expreffe order & direction of the Trienniall Parliament, whereto onely fuch as over-fee and manage it, may be made accountable, if fo thought fitting.

*And as it may be obferved amongft Merchants and prodigall Spend-thrifts, that fuch as are bad Pay-mafters, or of little credit, can neither buy,*

## Englands *safetie.*

buy, sell, or bee entrusted to such advantage as others are : So is it doubtlesse with Princes and their Ministers that are not punctuall in their dealings ; for in delaying payments, the verie time unto a Merchant eats out eight per centum in a yeare, besides the inconveniencies which may befall him by being disappoynted, and this verie justly too, is so fearefull unto most Merchants, that those few as are more adventurous, will not deale with such Ministers of Princes as are bad Pay-masters, but upon such odds as must needs bee an excessive dammage to the affaires of those Princes ; and yet this cannot well be remedied, untill the cause be first removed ; for since gaine is that which all, especially Merchants, doe chiefly aime at, it might be justly thought indiscretion for any one in buying, selling, or any businesse of like nature, to refuse the more punctuall Pay-master, and take the lesse at the same price: and how much his Majesties affaires have suffered in this kind, such as were employed in them doe best know. But for my part, I may be bold to wish they be managed hereafter with such credit and punctualitie, that which formerly was lost for want thereof, may be hereby regained: more may, though not well so publikely, be sayd on this subject, and the consequence of it, both for the private benefit and publike welfare of his Majestie and Kingdomes ; and part thereof will be obvious to such as have the managing of it, as will infallibly appeare when it once comes to be put in practice.

The twelfth is the secure turning over bils of debt from one to another, against moneyes or wares, as thus : A Merchant sels an hundred pounds worth of silks unto a Mercer, to pay at 12 moneths, and desirous to buy an hundred pounds worth of *Perpetuana's* ; but having neither ready money to disburse for the present, nor credit to be trusted at time, gives this Mercers bond of an hundred pounds unto whom he sold his silks, in payment of the *Perpetuana's*, and so is still doing something, whereas otherwise having no other estate but this hundred pounds, hee could not have traded againe, untill those twelve moneths were expired, and the Mercer payd him his 100 pounds : but if this course be once made secure and currant; it will in the same manner as the Bank before spoken of, add livelyhood unto Trade, and encrease the stock of the Kingdome; for what concernes traffiquing with it, so much as these Bils turned over amount to: when a man that hath neither money, nor credit to be trusted at time, may yet follow trading with the debts that others owe him: In this case a bill of debt (which likewise may be in print) must be made by every one that buyes commodities paiable to such a one, or his Assignes, or Bearer therof, & so often as bils happen to be

turned over

over unto others; to prevent differences it may not bee amiffe to
have fome notice taken of them, and regiftred, the parties being
prefent before the Chancellour in the fore-mentioned Court of
Merchants, paying a fmall confideration for the officers, making
record of them in a publick Book for fuch purpofe; and thefe Bills
being once due, to carry prefent execution with them.

The thirteenth, that fome courfe be agreed upon in the nature
of a Faire, or money Mart practized much in *France*, as that of
*Lions*, and *Placentia* in *Italy*; by which meanes a man of credit
may be furnifhe'd with what fummes of money he pleafes at an inftant, and pay them in againe the weeke following, or when hee
will; which accommodation cofts fuch as make ufe of it in thofe
parts where 'tis ordinarie fomewhat more than downe-right intereft.

The originall of thefe Faires, as alfo the unnaturall ufe of Exchanges grew thus: Divines in former times continually exclaiming a-
gainft Vfurie, which thofe of the *Roman* Church doe ftill to this
day, voting it a mortall finne, to take whatfoever the leaft benefit
or encreafe, by expreffe agreement for the ufe of money, preffing it
unceffantly upon the confciences of their Penitentiaries, fuch as
having ftore of monies, though they found no more beneficiall,
certaine, and eafie way of imploying them than downe-right intereft, which they could not get abfolution for from their Ghoftly
Fathers, were forc'd to fet their heads a work, and fo invented,
or rather adulterated the true and moft laudable ufe of Royall Exchanges in two refpects: one was, that Vfurers obferving how in all
Exchanges, as namely betwixt *London* and *Venice*, & *vice versâ*, he
that was the deliver had moft commonly the advantage, which
was caufed in regard, that ( as in all things elfe fo ) a fumme of prefent money ( may juftly be, and ) is thought fomething better worth
than the like fumme or quantity being abfent, and not to be received till after a terme expir'd, be it more or leffe; in which interim the taker may make ufe of the faid fumme of money,
imploying it in Merchandize or otherwife, as he pleafe to his beft
advantage: whereupon the Vfurers of *Venice*, although they had
no occafion or juft neede to have their eftates in *London*, on
which was firft grounded the truely genuine and legitimate ufe of
money-Exchanges, to prevent the inconvenience, trouble, change,
and cumbrance of tranfporting monies in *fpecie* from one Country
to another, underftanding of Merchants, that defired to take up
monies in *Venice*, and pay the value of them in *London*, told them
                                                            they

## Englands *fafety.*

they had occafion to deliver monies in *Venice*, and fo agreed with them; as for example: *A. B.* a Vfurer delivers in *Venice* a Ducat to *C. D.* a Merchant, taking his Bill of *Exchange* upon *E. F.* to pay unto *A. B.* or his affignes, fifty pence a piece fterling in *London*, three moneths after Date. *A. B.* makes the fame partie *E. F.* Affignes, to get acceptance of the Bill, and payment of the fifty pence in due time, and having received it to returne it him backe againe by Exchange to his moft advantage. At three months end, *E. F.* delivers in *London* this fiftie pence unto *G, H,* and takes his Bill of Exchange upon *L. M.* to pay unto *A. B.* the Vfurer in *Venice*, or his Affignes, the value of it three moneths after Date, which is by them agreed to be after the rate of foure pence fterling for a Ducat: So that *A. B.* the Vfurer for delivering a Ducat by Exchange in *Venice*, after fixe moneths is poffeffed of his Ducat returned backe againe, with the value of three pence fterling more, which after the fame rate is 12. *per* 100. on whatfoever fum or fums he had thus deliverd by Exchange.

The fecond way which the Vfurers found out, not fo much to falve their tender Confciences, as to benefit themfelves more by than down right Intereft, was, by framing an imaginarie Exchange betweene two places, as *Florens* and *Placentia* in *Italy*, betwixt w there is no juft caufe of correfpondence, Exchanging, Traffique, or fending monies from either place unto the other, and agreed amongft themfelves in *Florens*, that whofoever (to be underftood of good credit and repute) would take monies by Exchange, for *Placentia* might doe it in this minner: that is, whofoever will take up money from the beginning of *June* at fuch rates as fhall be agreed on, may, but that unleffe he give order for the payment of it in the meane time in *Placentia*, by a correfpondent of his owne, or another with this Vfurer, will helpe him to (who drawes provifion of $\frac{1}{3}$ *per* 100. on all fummes charg'd upon him, or return'd by him) it muft bee recharg'd and neceffarily fatisfied in *Florens* the beginning of *September* following, and this is by them cald *La fiera di fan Gio. Baptifta.* The fecond, (for they have foure of thefe faires, or Money-Marts in a yeare) is called *La fiera di fan Carlo*, from the beginning of *September* to the beginning of *December*. The third, *La fiera di Purificatione*, from the beginning of *December* to the beginning of March. The fourth, *La fiera di fan Marco*, from the beginning of *March* to the beginning of *June*: in all which three laft, what monies are drawne in the beginning muft be extinguifhed in *Placentia* in the Interim, or will

returne

4 *Trades encrease,*

returne necessarily to be satisfied in *Florence*, at end of the third moneth currant following, as in the first Faire is declared : And this is the state of their Money-Faires, or Marts before mentioned ; whereby, although it be *usura palliata,* those indulgent and overcha-ritable Romanists suffer themselves to be led blind-fold, for saving both soules and purses of their Clients : For though they put a dif-ference betwixt it and plaine Interest, or Usury, because in the for-mer there is not only no certaine gaine agreed on, but a possibility of losse, yet the losse to him that makes use of money thus by ex-change, is so far certaine, as he had better be content to pay eight *per centum,* sure all yeare long, than run the hazard of this uncer-tainty : But that which undeniably concludes this course to be al-together as bad as usury is, that these Usurers deliver moneyes in *Florence* by exchange, to receive the value in *Placentia,* and having received the value of it in *Placentia,* have no use for it there, nor know what to doe with it, but returne it back againe for *Florence,* which no man in his perfect senses would trouble himselfe about, and run the hazard of bad debts, were it not for great hopes and probability of gaine to countervaile the whole. Whereas the com-mand or precept at last was, *Luke 6.35. Date mutuum, nihil inde spe-rantes* ; So that these money-Faires, and taking up moneyes by ex-change, to enjoy the time and use of money only, is just the same with taking up at interest or usury, neither better nor worse, and how lawfull usury is I will not take upon mee to determine, the rather, because that onely Protestant and Papists Doctors, Divines and Lawyers, doe disagree about the definition of Usury ; but both one and other have furnished us with sundry definitions of it, much varying amongst themselves ; but that on both sides neerest agreed on is this, *Usura est lucrum receptum à Creditore pro usu rei mutuò datæ:* and yet this only reaches to actuall usury, and not mutuall also and intentionall, which rests equally condemned *in foro con-scientiæ:* neither does this hold in every actuall receit of profit, benefit, or advantage, in consideration of what is lent ; for wee may take for lending of an house, and then it is house-rent ; for len-ding of an Horse, and then is hire ; for lending a Slave, or an Ap-prentice to work for others, and then it is wages ; with sundry o-thers which might be alleaged, and neither of them thought unlaw-full, or fœneratitious : But if in stead of *rei* there were put *pecuniæ* into the definition, as thus, *Usura est lucrum receptum à Creditore pro usu rei mutuò datæ:* And this agreed upon to be the true defini-tion : for my part, I should think the taking of one, or ten, *per cent,*

were

## Englands *fafetie.*

were both equally ufurie, and not in our power to qualifie one more than the other, and of this opinion are all Roman Divines and Lawyers.

But certainly, if it be but free to argue it, the precept or command of *Date mutuum nihil inde fperantes*, being interpreted according to the aforefaid definition might not onely feeme fomewhat repugnant unto reafon, but unto Scripture it felfe *Deut*. 23.20. (*extraneo ifti dabis in ufuram, fratri autem tuo ne*; for if Vfurie were abfolutely unlawful, as murther, adulterie, &c. God would not have permitted it to Wards, Aliens, or Strangers, then in regard there may be an occafion of borrowing, as in a rich man that cannot be faid to doe it for need: for which caufe I am not bound to lend him, but becaufe he fees certaintie of profit, and rather than I will bee his hindrance of fuch a profit, me thinks I find my felfe in a manner oblig'd to lend him what I could, and intended otherwife to imploy my felfe not without good hopes of benefit: and may not I in this cafe of certaine profit to my neighbour in borrowing, and certain dammage, (for the imploying it is alwayes valued at fomewhat) to my felfe by lending, take intereft for my money, and fo he get more by borrowing, and I by lending? (fuch a certainty, which though leffe I was contented with, than to run hazard of a greater) which if it be granted, I onely inferre, that we know not the precife *adaquate* definition of ufurie, and fo believe the rather, in that the moft common received one cuts not off all lending, onely even upon hopes of profit, if for miffing of our hopes we doe forbeare to lend, but would be found to vitiate moft contracts, bargaines, and fales, fo commonly practifed by all nations to the multiplying of trade, and reliefe of whole Kingdomes, and can ot bee reformed without the ruine of $\frac{3}{4}$ of all commerce throughout the Vniverfe.

But, as I faid, prefumption 'twould be in me to determine a matter of fuch great controverfie, yet I am fo tender of it, as that I doe moft earneftly defire and pray it were by our Divines taken into ferious confideration, and by them declared how farre our intereft money, and fundry fo much practis'd contracts were obnoxious to it: the rather in regard, though I never met with Author that did pofitively declare, the taking 8, or 10. *per* 100. not to be ufurie, or lawfull, yet whole Countries practice it with little or no fcruple; fo fweetly and powerfully doth gaine and lucre benumbe the confcience, which many notwithftanding have

F   fought

sought to awake by writing and loud preaching, terming it to be flat usurie, forbid throughout the Scripture, and utterly sinfull and unlawfull ; but at this studie and consultation of our Divines I crave leave to be bold, and entreat them not to disdaine that light which expert Merchants might give them in th's poynt, or otherwise conceive I shall alwayes bee able to furnish them with new cases, which they before never thought on, and acknowledge to need new decisions : But if lending money at a moderate interest bee as lawfull as politickly usefull to the Common-weale, then is it likewise much more commodious to take up monies by Exchange to trade withall, and most of all in the manner of a money Mart, or Faire, as above declared, (provided it may be ordered in such sort, as the interest or usance import no more than what is allowed by statute in downeright interest ) because in this faire a Merchant may take up money at an instant to furnish his occasions more speedily, and if hee please extinguish or pay it the weeke following ; By this meanes may men bee punctuall in their payments, and having no monies in Cash, supply themselves by this faire for payment of their debts, untill their owne come in, and this punctualitie will bee so much more requisite and necessarie, when turning over of Bills comes in request, and those Bills have present execution, all which will adde incredible activitie and livelihood unto our trade which otherwise might languish.

The fourteenth is that inland Trad and Navigation, which is the carriage of goods within the Land bee facilitated and promoted, and th s done by making Rivers Navigable, cutting artificiall ditches of such depth as that the water may stand still in a levell, or be kept in by sluces or flud-gates, and boats laden with all commodities drawne by man or beast : High-wayes should likewise be kept cleane of Robers, in good order and reparation ; and if conveniently, be gravel'd, which would render them more passable. So great care hereof is had in *Germanie*, *Italie*, and some other Christian Countries, nay by those Barbarous people of the great Turks Dominions, as most part of their goods are carried to and fro twentie or fortie dayes journey out right, and at present besides many others, the chiefe Trade betwixt *Venice* and *Constantinople* is drove by Land ; I meane from *Spalato* to *Constantinople* ; and many not over-fine, but bulkie goods, as *Venetian* Cloth, Turkie Grograines, Moha'res, Cordovans, Waxe and others are thus conducted at easier rates. 'Tis likewise much conducing

## Englands *safetie.*

ducing to encrease of trade , to have posts setled in such other parts of *England* where they are wanting , and the portage of inland Letters to be lessened about one halfe : for the Inland trade being yet but yeurg in the infancie, cannot well bee at so great a charge for Letter carrying, which in *Italy, France, Germanie, Holland,* and oth.r Countries stands not in halfe of what wee pay : and although 'tis certaine . that Merchants and others omitting to write weekly Letters unto their correspodents , doth much prejudice their businelle , and consequently the generall trade and benefit : yet I verily believe, and not altogether without experience, that many a man 'oth run the hazard of his businelle, rather than write, and pay sixe pence to read his Letter : 'tis true that the Schoole-malters of *England,* being paid their standing and extraordinarie wages cut of this office doe cause postage of Letters to be so high : but farre better would it bee , that they were satisfied some other way lelle hurtfull unto trade, whose hindrance brings the greateft hurt of all.

And whereas before I have given my consent for all vagabonds, Beggers , and delinquents, not bad enough for hanging, to bee fert for the new Plantations , yet if that be not approve I , or belides that courfe, it may be very requilite that publike houses were built , where luch as are will'ng to take paines, but finde no imployment , may bee let a worke to beat hemp , or other toyle learn'd at firft fight for a moderate hire , untill they have earn't somewhat towards imploying them in their owne callings ; and the same heules to keep at work thofe other v. grant and idle people , untill it be thought fitter to thip them quite away ; The building and flocking of thele houfes, efpecially in *London* , and other great Cities, would be a matter of no great charge , but certainly of wonderfull charitie, and a meanes to reclaime many ill difpofed wretches, and make them, *will they nil they,* in fome fort become ferviceable to the Common-weale.

There is alfo another work of chariti , which I am very zealous to make mention of, in hopes this Citie fo famous for deeds of mercie , or fome well difpofed perfon will foone put in practice, which is the erecting of a Mount of charitie , and lending it fuch monies, (no great fumme 'twould be ) as might furnifh all commers as farre as fortie fhillings a piece , at ten *per cent.* upon pawnes worth $\frac{1}{4}$ or $\frac{1}{3}$ more than is borrowed for twelve months ; which beeing expired, the pawne unredeem'd to bee fold at out crie:

This

## 44 *Trades encreafe,*

This may well feeme a fecure and gainfome bufineffe to be embraced by a particular rich man for profits fake, and like enough to prove fo : but fure I am, it would bee an exceeding great reliefe to many hundred poore people about the City of *London* onely, that are glad to pay, becaufe they can hav't no cheaper above thirty *per centum*, nay after the rate of double the Money for a yeares intereft, and leave a pawne to boot fometimes.

Did I not conceive thefe workes of darkneffe to be kept from eares and eyes of thefe whofe authority might hinder fuch extortions in punifhing them, or their purfe and almes prevent them by erecting a Mount of Charitie to prevent them, I fhould bee fearefull they had much to anfwer for : Believe me there are thoufands in this City whofe faces are thus grinded, yet live, whofe fuccour would bee of fo much greater confequence to the whole maffe of Inland commerce, being ftirring people, whom need hath made induftrious, and taught to turne their peny as you heare, or elfe could never live under fuch extortion, which notwithftanding at laft muft grinde them quite to powder before their time, for fcarce being able in their youth, by reafon of thefe blood-fuckers, heavie burthens to fave fo much for hemfelves as will keep life and foule together, age comming on though few of them doe live fo long, when they cannot trudge up and downe fo faft, fhift fo well for themfelves, nor fare fo hardly, muft quickly break both back and heart : wherefore if private bountie provide not for their redemption, the publick cannot be better imployd.

The improvement of our Lands and hufbandrie my juftly here bee thought upon, the rather becaufe I feare mee wee come fhort herein of moft *Chriftian Nations* : for in what Countrie fo populous lyes there fo much ground waft ? or being manur'd to produce fo fmall a crop ? Tis certaine, that both in hot and cold *Countries, more marfhie Lands, more drie, more fandie, more clayie are till'd and improv'd to far greater advantage, and yet have not fuch a ftore of Dung, Chalke, Marle, and others to qualifie their great defects, fo that it may appeare, our lazineffe and want of induftrie to be the onely caufe of barrenneffe.*

But I have knowne a policie practifed elfewhere amongft people over-flothfull, that would not worke above halfe the weeke, if they could get money enough to feed them for the whole, and that was by clapping excifes and taxes upon what they eat and

drank,

## England's *safetie.*

drank, fo that a weeks labour with this fawce, whet their ftomacks, as they were well able to eat out what they earned afterwards in a whole week by Sunday night, A very fit falve for fu ·h a fore,for cure whereof all experiments are few enough to put in practice ; yet I wifh wee may begin with more mild at firft, and confider what meane:, and encouraging the Husbandman to be more induftrious, might prefent themfelves ; for certainly hee is too dull and carelefi of his owne profit in particular, which is a parcell of the generall, in that it may be obferved, how many of them have not fo much as a fruit-tree, or pot-herb about their houfes or cottages : the barrennefse of the foyle cannot excufe this totally, there being none found fo curfed by nature ; but if the time they beake in the Sun, and liquor themfelves at Ale-houfe in the fhade, were fpent about improving it, would by degrees compell it to produce fome fort of roots, herbs, and fruit, as are both profitable, pleafant, and wholefome for their nourifhment, far more fometimes, than folid maffie food of flefh, cheefe, and pudding, by reafon of their practice, being where ere they come, or what ere they eat, to cram themfelves to the throat, which fince they will, is yet lefse dangerous in diet of light digeltion than the other, that nothing but a whole dayes plowing or delving can put over, and cleare their braines ·from fumes.

The fourteenth is, that all Merchants trading into one place and Province be contracted into a Corporation, the want whereof, or the non-obfervance of their Charters and Priviledges, both at home and abroad, hath no little prejudiced the trade of all parts in generall ; for by this meanes they could not agree, nor keep themfelves from under-felling one another in our native commodities, nor over-valuing of the forraine, both which we have juft caufe to complaine of, could we as eafily find a remedy to redreffe them.

Befides, if they were fo many Corporations ; they would bee better refpected and regarded by Princes and States, where it concernes them to refide, and might better, and with more credit and advantage, capitulate with them for divers priviledges and immunities.

I know there are many that cry out, to have merchandizing left open and free for any one to trade, where, when, and how he will ; which I may confeffe would much encreafe it for the prefent, not without advantage perhaps of fome particular men, and this, may bee, might laft fome yeares too, this Kingdome being fo populous, and altogether as adventurous, though one halfe were undone, the rest, too greedy of gaine, would scarce beleeve them, but make triall also, and so run on headlong unto our utter ruine, which must needs be the conclusion of all affaires managed by such as observe no good order, nor understand well what they goe about.

For preventing whereof, the first and best step may bee by this Honourable Parliaments confirmation of their severall Charters, or if need be, by granting new, with larger priviledges and power, in force whereof such severall Societies understanding their owne mysteries best, may have full authoritie to order and governe them accordingly. What was before sayd concerning the necessitie of a Corporation, for the better managing of the *East India* trade, though in that especially most necessarie, yet it is in all others of exceeding great importance for the verie selfe same respects, though not in so large a manner ; for where no government is, disorders must needs spring up, and no possibilitie of a redresse, but from experience of such as brought them in, which they only measure and attaine to by their owne ruine : yet one *Item*, and that no slight one, I will give more, which is, that of all other Nations, the *English* have most need of this superintendencie and government, because no Merchants so young as they, neither at home nor abroad, are entrusted by others, nor deale for themselves in such great summes of money as *English* doe.

The sixteenth, that there be a Commission, or a peculiar and select Magistrate of so many as shall ee thought fitting, to sit weekly, advising and consulting all advantages of commerce, amongst which some understanding Merchants will be necessarie, and the same Merchants to be as often, and as much as possible, of the Court of Merchants before mentioned, where hearing the state and decision of all differences betwixt Merchants, would be much for their owne information, and instructing their Associates of this other Magistrate which now I speake of, and not onely enable them with some course to remedy and prevent them for the future, but thereby also to advance traffique.

The seventeenth and last meanes is, that Merchants have certaine immunities from being called to inferiour offices and services where they live, and other priviledges of due respect and repute given them, whereby they may bee encouraged to continue, and others to betake themselves to so worthy and honourable a calling.

# Englands *safetie.*

Of Merchants breeding, abilities, and advantage they have above all others, if they but employ it well, and that Merchandise is the grand colu une and foundation of this Kingdomes wealth and safetie, I have given a touch before, knowing withall full well the saying of, *Faber quisque fortunæ suæ:* And that a man, what ere hee be by inward worth and value, shall only bee to others what hee can make himselfe knowne to bee; yet something everie Merchant should fare the better, in being so necessarie an Instrument of the Weales welfare; and although it may chance bee truly observed, how such Merchants for the most part thrive best, that regard not the superficiall complement and ceremonies of Gentilitie, more attending their businesse at Exchange than Court; yet it might bee no ill policie to cherish and respect them, bearing with such of them as doe lesse regard the quainter and more courtly proceedings of the times, the rather in that slighting and despising them, as some great Courtiers have beene thought to doe, was but a means to thrust them into a sinister conceit of Court, teaching them to avoyd and shun all kinds of appearance, negotiation and treatie, (even when it concerned themselves and publ que good sometimes) with such as perhaps in Merchant-like affaires are well neere, not seldome as far from understanding them, as to bee understood by them in others. And whereas I have heard it objected by some of good rank too, that it was not so necessarie such great respect were given to Merchants, in regard they sought onely their owne benefit and profit, and that if one were discouraged from trading, another would be encouraged to follow it; with their leave I should be bold to answer, that this argument holds not, for that all encouragement is little enough, because the more the better for the State in generall, and one Merchant to be valued as hundreds of ordinarie men, because many hundreds of men are employed and maintained by one Merchant. And if some of their weaknesses were not taken notice of with such *Emphasis,* and they (which in all other Mysteries and Sciences is approved requisite) were but patiently permitted to speake, using their owne language and termes of Art, (wherein his Majesties superabounding graciousnesse towards them on all occasions was President sufficient) they would be found well able to expresse themselves, and justifie their proceedings, and King and Court keeping touch in contracts and agreements, not only be willing to deale with them for their owne just gaines sake, but as they might likely, learne somewhat a more courtly manner and

43                              *Trades encrease,*

and behaviour (leſſe neceſſarie in them) from Courtiers; ſo could Merchants adviſe them much more for the good government and husbanding their eſtates, a thing not diſhonourable for any to bee well vers'd in his owne buſineſſe, which cauſed the Italian proverb, *Mai s' imbratta le mani con far i fatti ſua,* A man never fouleṣ his hands with doing his owne buſineſſe ; and everie one, wh.theṛ he will or no, is a Merchant for what he buyes or ſels, be it lands houſes, or whatſoever elſe, and more gentile it is to ſell Cloth, Silk, Sattins, Jewels, &c. as meere Merchants doe, than Cattell, Hay, Hides, Wooll, Butter, Cheeſe, as Cuntrey Gentlemen, and others of beſt note and worth.

*And beſides it may be obſerved, that Merchants for moſt part are of the ſame ſtock and Familie for Gentry, though the younger branch, and many perhaps wantiĝg means to blazon it in due equipage and colors to the world became in a ſhort time very unable to give any account of it at all, which diſaſters many younger brothers of England have been ſubject to, till advancing by Merchandizing their eſtate and fortunes above the elder brothers the Heralds made them beholding to them for their own birthright, & if as in Italy eſpecially the States of Florence, Sienna, Piſa, Genua, and Lucca, where they continue Merchants from one generation to another, we ſhould do the like in England, the greateſt part of the whole Kingdome and riches would quickly belong to Merchants; and although by this courſe the ſeate of Merchandizing would queſtionleſſe be much improved by long experimented obſervations conveyd unto poſterity from Father to Son ſucceſſively, which would not onely enable them to deale and better countermine the craft and ſubtilties of forraign Nations, but hinder in a great part ſuch often failings and bankrupts; yet ſince as I conceive the greateſt cauſe which makes many noble families in Italy ſo to continue Merchants, is, that countries being ſo populous abounding with monies & little land to purchaſe, neere one halfe of the whole Territory belonging to Monaſteries, Covents, and other Eccleſiaſticall Fraternities, which may in no wiſe be alienated; ſo I conceive it more laudable and agreeing to make a flouriſhing Kingdome and Commor-wealth, for a Merchant being bleſſed with a competent eſtate to retire himſelfe from the cares and troubles of the world (which certainely a Merchant of great dealings is of all others moſt ſubject to) the better to ſpend the remainder of his dayes in thankfulneſſe to that God who even then had an eye over him, when perhaps little thought on, undoubtedly not ſo much as ſhould have bin, as alſo that young Merchants, I meane younger brothers or ſuch as*
                                                                        *have*

have little or no meanes may come forward, which cannot poſſibly be, if the whole trade bee engroſſed onely by men of wealth and their poſteritie.

And now having run over theſe particulars, which prove more then I expected, and ſomewhat further proſecuted then I at first intended, though not well to bee omitted, in regard they may for this cauſe oppreſſe the memorie, give me leave to adde theſe few words as it were for burthen of the whole.

That unleſſe the fiſhing imployment and Eaſt India traffique be followed and enlarged, other Nations will gaine upon us, our trade infallibly decline daily, and the whole State with the ſame ſpeede and paces poſt on to poverty and utter ruine.

Thus then though I knew well, ſundry had writ more largely and worthily of this ſubject, yet was I moved to give a touch in briefe, as you have ſeene, perſwading my ſelfe though there were nothing newe herein (w'ich yet cannot be juſtly ſayd by what I ever met with either in manuſcript or Print,) ſome ſew might turne it over beeing ſhort, that could, nor would not bee troubled with a volume, and hereby be prevailed upon to move this High Aſſembly for imploying ſome due proportion of their grave wiſedome in conſultation, eſtabliſhing, and enlarging trade, which next to the buſineſſe of Religion and our Lawes well hoped to be by them both religiouſly & legally provided for, may perhaps juſtly claime the third place, whereby not onely the Kings revenues will bee encreaſed, but in time his Maieſtie come to need no other revenues, nor the Kingdome other ſecuritie or Bulwarke.

Here I would have put a period, but perceiving there are many well acquainted with theſe affaires who attribute the decay of trade to the overballancing of it, and the Merchandizing exchange, give me leave to paſſe a word thereon.

By overballancing of trade is meant, that wee bring into, and

conſume

50 *Trades encreafe,*

confume in England forraigne commodities for a greater valew, then we fend and fell of our Native Commodities abroad, by which means we come indebted to forrain Nations, and have no other way to pay or extinguifh it, but by transporting of our moneys, which will utterly ruine a trade and Kırgdome in the end;

For anſwere whereunto it may bee faid, that though greater quantities of forrain wares ſue be brought in, then we fend out of Native, yet it doth not follow neceſſarily that our gold and filver muſt goe to pay for them, in regard that Italian, Spaniſd, French, and Dutch doe many times fraight Engliſh ſhips, whereby good ſoms of money are yearely raiſed by our Nation abroad, and may ſerve to pay for the advance of forrain commodities that we bring in, at leaſt for ſuch a proportion as this freight money imʒo ts, which is to a conſiderable vallew.

But for my part, though in this point I have not declared my ſelfe throughout this ſhort diſcourſe, my opinion is, that our trade of Native commodities is not overballanced by the forraigne, nor gold and filver conveyed out, (unleſſe firſt b ought in,) in ſo large manner as is ſuppoſed, for there being no Mines in England that produce any ſtore, and wee having likely at preſent though conceald as much ready money as ever, at leſt before our inteſtine broyles diſperſ'd th m, and never more rickes in plate, if any coyne, either gold or filver hath beene carried out, as queſtionleſſe there hath, being to be ſeene apparantly both in France and the Low Countries, yet that filver and gold was firſt brought into England, for it growes not here, and then though ſome proportion be exported: yet if a greater bee firſt imported (which hath certainly beene ſo, for otherwiſe we ſhould have none at all left by this time) the riches of the Common-wealth will not decline, though they might flouriſh more if the exportation could totally bee hindred; and howſoever this will be found a taske moſt difficult, yet it is the courſe which we are likelieſt to prevaile with.

For ſince the Chaos and whole body of trade is not managed joyntly, but by the particular Merchants and members of it, one whereof fends out native Commodities, and brings his returnes home in Bullion, or by Exchange; another brings in forraine commodities, making over monies by Exchange to pay for them; and a third exports native commodities, and imports forraine too; if when there ſhould be a ballance made hereof, and our importation

# Englands *safetie.* 51

tion of wares found to exceed our exportation, which in such case must needs bee paid for, one way or other, and so invite our monies over, what remedy can bee taken without disturbance of the whole trade ? If flatly you prohibite the bringing in of forraine goods, forraine Nations will doe the like with ours, and at last both bee reduced to receive from one another such onely as are necessarie, or most usefull : wherefore a better course to moderate this ballance, would be with dexterity to lighten or lade either scale in the custome and other charges, which may insensibly make one deare, and the other cheap, as is afore declared, with sundry such other meanes, all tending to enlarge traffique. And although other Princes might likewise doe the same in their dominions ; yet many of them are so necessitous at present as will perhaps rather suffer some inconvenience, and runne the hazard of a greater, but absent, and future dammage, than lessen their revenues.

For if the trade were ballanc'd, we are lesse able to reduce that first, and therein prevent the exportation of monies, then first by hindring monies through strictest diligence, and severe penalties, from being exported, and so in consequence secure the over-ballancing of trade ; for to use this diligence rests in our selves, and being independant we may practise it without exceptions to other Nations ; and if once effected, though no more Bullion should be brought in, which yet will alwayes come more or lesse, nothing could prejudice us, or breed scarcitie hereafter.

But before the exportation of monies can be prevented throughly, 'tis necessarie wee know who are those that may likely transport them, and the causes that move, and enable them so to doe.

Such then as transport monies are either Merchants or Travellers, and both moved thereunto, either because there is more to be gotten by transporting them in *specie*, than delivering by Exchange, or else because they have no experience or acquaintance with Merchants here or abroad, or desire not to trust them, but thinke it securest to adventure their monies with their persons, which in such case they have alwayes ready about them where ere they goe ; but delivering by Exchange cannot many times receive the value where they will, if they resolve to goe any other way, but where their Merchants hath credit, and promised to pay them : and these later are chiefely either such as goe away to enjoy the li-

G 2　　　　　　　　　　　　　　bertie

　　　　*Trades encreafe,*

bertie of *Amſterdam*; and for moſt part they goe privately, and will not be knowne by delivering their monies by Exchange; and therefore carrie them in *ſpecie*, or elſe are Ambaſſadors, or private Gentlemen that goe abroad to travell, but in ſuch number, and each carrying with him for the moſt part fiftie or one hundred pound: nay many times double as much, which at yeares end draines the Kingdome of a very conſiderable ſumme; and therefore perhaps it might not be found amiſſe, that a Banker or Exchanger were eſtabliſhed at *Dover*, *Rie*, or ſome other Port (where all Travellers eſpecially ſhould be obliged to imbanke) that of himſelfe were enabled with credit, and obliged to give Bills of Exchange, and Letters of credit for moſt places of *France*, *Holland*, *Italy*, *Germanie*, and *Spaine*, unto all Travellers, they delivering him firſt ſuch monies as they had there preſent to carry along with them, or afterwards to deliver other Bills for other monies, brought and delivered them in like manner, and all at the true and juſt value of the Exchange; for herein *Travellers* to my knowledge have ſuffered much; which being prevented by ſetling the courſe aforeſaid, every *Paſſenger*, *Mariner*, or other of what ſort ſoever may well bee prohibited upon ſtricteſt penalties of life and goods, to carrie aboard either Boat or Ship above twenty ſhillings ſterling at the moſt.

And for Merchants, (unleſſe ſome pedling French Merchants) they commonly underſtand themſelves, and ſeeking their owne advantage, may either deliver their monies by Exchange, or ſend or carrie them over in *ſpecie*, according as one or other ſeems moſt beneficiall to them

Now it may not be amiſſe to take notice, that it hath never or very ſeldome beene obſerved, more advantagious to carry monies over in *ſpecie* for what forraine parts ſoever, than deliver them by Exchange, and therefore probable that Merchants who underſtand their profit, and ſo much aime at it, have delivered their monies by Exchange from time to time, and not ſent them over in *ſpecie*, as is ſuppoſed: yet I muſt tell you, there was perhaps a time (which I well believe) and may too often bee ſo againe hereafter, that ſtrangers ſhall have ſo great quantities of monies by them; all which if they ſhould reſolve to deliver by Exchange, the Exchange would fall ſo low in their owne diſadvantage, (for more or leſſe deliverers or takers raiſe or bring downe the

## Englands *safetie.* 53

the Exchange, which will more plainly appeare hereafter ) as it might cause the transportation *in specie* to bee more beneficiall than the Exchange, and certainly wee had neede provide for such a time ; for if Merchants have exceeding great summes to deliver, and finde no Takers save at extravagant low rates, nor Wares to imploy them in, to profit, they will run the hazard of conveying them away privately *in specie*, to prevent a greater dammage and losse of time, by keeping them dead in *England.*

*And these Merchants questionlesse for most part are strangers; and furnished with these monies three manner of wayes.*

First, by great sums of monies made over to them by Exchange from forraine parts, in regard the Exchange of *London* hath used to bee so advantagious to the deliverer abroad, through the under-valuing of our monies in respect of other Countries, occasioned, because there are, or would bee, more deliverers of them than takers.

Secondly, by sale, and proceed of goods that strangers bring in, which they doe in great quantitie, because they pay but little customes, onely 2½ *per cent.* more than *Dennizens*, and export none of our Native commodities, because they pay greater customes, on some I think as much againe as wee doe ; and that which is the greatest shame, the Herring, and other sorts of fish taken by them in our Seas, nay verie Ports, and sold to us for a verie round summe yearely ; a great part whereof received in the Port Towns where wee buy the fish, cannot easily be prevented without stricter diligence, and execution is carryed away, never to returns againe.

Thirdly, by their infallible halfe yeares incomes, and Revenewes of such vast summes of money as they keep continually at interest in *London*; and if you demand the *summa totalis,* which all these make, I can onely answer you. *Pauperis est numerare pecus :* but howsoever indefinite, that it is immense, will hereby appeare.

Consider the great quantities of goods of all sorts wee export hence for forraine parts, the greatest part whereof is sold for money, and many hundred thousand pounds sterling thereof made over hither by Exchange ; and yet strangers have more monies to send out of *England*, than we have to bring into *England,* which is most evident in that the Exchange from forraine parts

G 3                                    (according

54                     *Trades encrease,*

(according to the intrinsecall value of the severall *species* respective'y ) to *England* is more advantagious, than to *England* from
forraine parts ; for even as the scarcity of any commoditie makes
it to be more valued , and held at a dearer price ; so there being
few deliverers abroad of monies for *London* which are *English,*
in respect of the Takers, which are strangers, and many Deliverers in *London,* which are strangers in comparison of the *Takers*
which are *English* , the few *English 'Deliverers* abroad, and *Ta-*
kers at home stand upon their termes, bringing the Exchange in
their favour, and this is called the *Merchandizing Ex hange* , because quite opposite to the nature of Exchange, which was found
out to prevent carriage of monies up and downe : this invites the
exportation of them in *specie,* and therefore a table of Rates is propounded which should stint the Exchanging our severall Coyns
with those of other Nations , according to the paritie and puri-
tie both in weight and goodnesse of allay, and so settle the price of
Exchanges for all Countries, which Merchants might not exceed in
delivering or taking monies by Exchange.

For *answer hereto , I con eive it may be granted , that in delivering monies by Exchange in England for forraine parts we receive not
the true value or* par *according to the intrinsecall goodnesse of the
Coyne ; but this is our advantage, and onely dammageable to strangers , because they ( and not* English *) are the Deliverers in England ; neither will this Merchandizing Exchange likely carrie away
our monies , so long as the Exchange produces as good profit , as the
money it selfe, if it were transported, would yeeld in specie , which for
the most part may hitherto have beene observed; but hereon , as also about the said Table of Rates , I hope it may give a little
light to enlarge somewhat more , though not altogether so Metho-
dically.*

*Granted it is then ( by me at least ) that our monies are underva-
lued by Exchange with strangers , and that though we may commonly
make as much of them by Exchange, as carrying them in* Specie, *to
spend in ordinarie payments , yet the Mint in forraine Countries
may give more for them, ( otherwise they are not undervalued ) and
this profit from the Mint may doubtlesse intice them over : but whether a Table of Rates can prevent this or no ; or if it could , whether
such a Table might not prove more prejudiciall in another respect, will
be the question.*

For

## Englands *safetie.*

For though our moneyes be under-valued, it is our advantage, in regard we *English* doe buy our owne moneyes thus under-valued, so often as wee take moneyes by exchange in *England*, or deliver them by Exchange abroad, and strangers are they that sell us our owne moneys thus cheap, or under-valued, so that this is but buying and selling good cheap, whilst strangers sell good cheap, and we buy it: and this profit wee have questionlesse upon all our moneys delivered for *England*, out of the proceed and sale of our goods abroad. Neither is this all, for since we advance in delivering our moneyes abroad by exchange for *England*, we are enabled to sell our cloth and other commodities the cheaper; for if for 35 shillings I leinish delivered abroad, I can have 20 shillings sterling in *England*, I may sell my cloth for one eighth part lesse in Flemmish money, than if I were to give 40 shillings Flemmish to have 20 shillings sterling in *England*, being all one to a Merchant that sels for money, and delivers it afterwards by exchange, to sell his wares at a bad price, and have a good exchange for his moneyes, or sell his wares at a good price, and have a bad exchange for his moneyes.

This stinting then, as it will bring the Exc'ange in favour of the English coyne, and consequently beat downe the price of what commodities Forrainers sell in *England*, thereby encreasing the vent of them; so will it raise the price of our commodities sold abroad, and diminish their vent, which being well considered, may perhaps prove a dammage to us, at least for such a portion as is sold for money to be made over hither by exchange, for though we seem to get so much the more as we sell our commodities the dearer, yet when we remit the provenue by exchange, by reason of this stint, we lose by exchange a part of what we advanced on our commodities; and what we lose by exchange, onely a few Merchants strangers make benefit of; and what wee get more in the price of our cloth, comes out of all their purses that weare our cloth, which proving deare to them, will make them leave wearing it, and hinder so large a vent as formerly.

And I beleeve it will bee thought more beneficiall for a Commonwealth to vent store of their native commodities, at such lower, but moderate rates, as both Manufactors and Merchants may live thereby, though with lesse profit, than to sell a lesse quantitie at greater rates, the profit of the greater parcell in the whole exceeding

ding that or the lesser, especially so many men more being set a
work untill we have other employment for them ; and the rather
it concernes us to sell good cheap, in that all other Nations now
almost make cloth of their owne, or other cloathing. which may
serve mere as well : So though it be granted that our moneyes being under-valued by exchange hinders importation and invites exportation, which notwithstanding through severitie may be in part
prevented ; yet since under-valuing our coyne, wee get in making
our moneyes home by exchange, and by that meanes can afford our
cloth the cheaper, and so vent greater quantitie, the most beneficiall state is to be wished for, which perhaps upon due scrutinie, may
appeare to be this low exchange, in respect of the intrinsecall value of our moneyes, the rather for that though they were raised but
to the pretended just paritie and par tie ; yet that would likely
bring in verie little Bullion more, which besides the losse of time
in expecting a ship to bring it hither, carries the charge of Insu-
rance with it, and when it is here, I can have but the just value at the
Mint, and so much I should have had for it by exchange, accordi g
to the table of rates, besides usance which is use or interest from the
date of the bill of exchange, till it be paid in *England*; so then the
benefit which I might have made by exchange, being taken from
me through this table of rates, and no profit to be got by Bullion,
the money which would otherwise have beene made hither by exchange, will likely be employed in forraine commodities, whereof
there comes to a great quantitie already.

Besides stinting the Exchange may seeme lesse needfull through
this following consideration, which is, that as there was anciently
no exchange at all by bils, so may we presuppose the like case at present, & find that an English Merchant abroad may buy forrain commodities for money, or take them in barter agai st English commodities, without so much as a thought or consideration of the exchange ; as thus :

An English Merchant carries abroad with him an hundreed peeces of yard-broad *Perpetuana's*, which cost with all charges fortie
shillings *per* peece, is 200 pound starling : At *Ligorne* hee sells these
hundred peeces of *Perpetuana's* at dollers 11 Spanish Reals of ⅘ *per*
peece, which make dollers 1100 in all, and knowing that *Florence*
black Sattins are a vendible commoditie in *England*, and may likely yeeld him about 11 shillings *per* yard, buyes of a Florentine Merchant

## Englands *safetie.* 57

chants 183. *li.* ⅓ of *Florence* black Satins ( for plaine Sattins are
fold in *Florence per* pound ) at Dollers 6. of ⅜ *per* pound, which
amounts to Dollers 1100. the full provenue of his 100 peeces Perpetuanaes, and the 183 *li.* ⅓ containe about braces 5¼ *per* pound,
which is braces 100 8¼, whereof braces 4. make yeards 2½ are
in all year s 630. which fold at 11—*s. per* yard, as was fuppofed,
yeelds 346. *li.*—10 *s.*—0 sterling ; out of which he knew likewife the custome and charges of the Sattins were to be deducted:
And in like manner he might have put off his 100. peeces of yard
broad Perpetuanaes at Dollers 11. *per* piece in Barter or Truck
to be paid in *Florence* black Sattins at Dollers 6. *per* pound, which
will produce the fame reckoning about 300. *li.* for his 200. *li.*
carried out in Perpetuanaes, fo that it appeares a Merchant may
buy or fell, and bartar for forraine commodities to this benefit,
and bee altogether ignorant of the Exchange ; which ignorance
'tis true might have prejudic'd him , as also his not knowing the
intrinfecall value of thofe Dollers 1100 of ⅜, and fo have brought
them for *England* in *specie* in cafe of gaine, or that the Exchange
would have produced better profit than the Satins : But thus much
I conceive may follow hereupon, that we need not stand fo perem-
ptorily upon rating or stinting the Exchange, for what concerns
all forraine commodities to be bought or bartered for by us a-
broad , and for what monies wee make home from thence hither
by Exchange, 'tis our advantage that the Exchange bee low, and
the Kingdome advances more upon the whole proportion of monies made home now , the Exchange being low , than it would
get by a part of it, being brought home in Bullion or *specie*, if the
Exchange were higher : And wee cannot expect that all should
come home in Bullion : for that ( prefuppofing the poffibilitie)
would utterly impoverifh other countries, and caufe thofe Princes,
to prohibit the exportation of it , and the verie fcarcitie it felfe,
through our exporting it , would make it in a fhort time fo hard
to come by , and our commodities for the fame caufe fo much beaten downe in price, as the trade without doubt would bee quite
abandoned at laft ; for it is our benefit that monies bee plentifull
alfo in fuch Countries where we carrie our commodities to fell;
and fhall otherwife have little encouragement to continue it, fo
that a moderation is to be defired, and muft be obferved in all proceedings, left we fare as *Alexander* the great, who having neare

H                                                    conquered

conquered the whole world, wept bee ufe there was no more left for him to conquer.

And yet I will farther adde in favour of this Table of rates for ftinting the Exchange, that fince the ftatute permitsus not to take above eight *per cent,* for ufe or intereft money, which is hoped (for the further quieting of Confciences and publick good) may yet be brought to 6 *per* 100. in regard as we fell our commodities cheaper or dearer, according to the long or fhort time wee give with them, or the partie to whom we fell, being of great or leffe credit and efteeme, and many defiring to put their money out at intereft, fomewhat under the ftatute, to a furer man, than at a higher rate, to one whofe credit or eftate is not thought fo good; evenn fo is it in Exchanges, and I know not well how it can be helped, yet as the rate of interelt is ftinted to all alike, in fuch manner as none may take above the ftatute; fo were it to be wifhed, that for ufance fingle, double, or treble, they fhould not require of any above the rate of ftatute intereft, which the Bankers or Exchangers will yet be able to counterminde by putting the price of the Exchange fo much more in their favour, unleffe that bee ftinted too: And this might feeme veric facile, if there were nothing in it fave the prevention of transportating monies to and fro, and juft as many Takers as Deliverers; for then he that defires nothing but his monies in another place, if he can have as is likely, the juft value according to the intrinfecall worth by Exchange receives a great accommudation, and the price being once fetled to remaine conftant, needs onely look after the fureft men to Exchange withall; and a Merchant may likewife for fame reafon know fooner what he gets or lofes by fale of his commodities; whereas now he cannot untill his monie be likewife made over through the uncertaintie of the Exchhange, which falling or rifing ftill varies fomewhat. But put the cafe I had urgent occafion to ufe 100 *l.* in *Paris,* and find no body that will take it by Exchange, if it be free for one to export it, or prohibited, but the danger or penaltie not anfwerable to my expected profit, no doubt I may likely be moved to export it in *fpecie:* but if there be another who has the value of 100 *l.* in *Paris,* and equally defires his 100 *l.* pound here as I do mine in *Paris,* both of us alike underftanding the true intrinfecall value of the feverall *fpecies,* it is probable wee two fhall quickly agree to exchange with one another, according to the reall.

## Englands *safetie.*          59

all *par* : But if there be sundrie Takers and Deliverers, though equall on both sides, some whereof being over-hasty either in deliveting or taking, out of feare their turnes would not otherwise be served ; this may cause the Exchange to rise or fall above or beneath the *par* on one side or other. But if there be more Deliverers than Takers ; that is, more monies to be delivered by Exchange from *London*, then returned by Exchange to *London*, and that all yeare long, and for many yeares together, as hath beene most certaine in respect of *England*, with forraine parts, doubtlesse the few Takers will have more opportunitye to stand upon their termes, in bringing the Exchange downe in their advantage by so much undervalueng of our monies : And though this be very obvious to any mans apprehention, yet it may be made further appeare so ; thus :

'Tis then first presuppos'd upon good ground as you have heard, that the undervalving of our monies by Exchange is prejudiciall to such as are deliverers of money by Exchange in *London*, and takes by Exchange abroad.

Secondly, that these Takers abroad, and Deliverers here at home are strangers, is likewise presum'd ; and

Thirdly, that out of the sale and provenue of our goods exported there are great summes of mocey returned hither weekly from abroad will as easily be granted.

Now since this undervaluuing our moneyes by Exchange is onely dammagable to the Deliverers at home, and Takers abroad, and both these are strangers, why doe strangers deliver here in *England*, and take abroad by exchange thus to their losse ? certainly nothing but necessity can force them to contiuue losers all yeare long for sundry years together : nor can there be any necessitie, had they not such store of monies, which they must necessarily deliver here, and that in far greater quantitie than wee have return'd us from abroad by sale of our goods exported.

So then if it be granted, as well it may, that strangers have more monies to send away, than we have to bring into the Kingdome, though a Table of Rates were established as is propounded, yet strangers would have the same or greater encouragement some times to export monies in *specie* ; for whereas at present the Exchange being favourable to the Takers at home, and Deliverers abroad which are English, the English are moved through

gaine

gain to take a good proportion of thofe monies which the ftrangers muft neceffarily make over by Exchange, or fend away in *fpecie*, for they have occafion to ufe them in other Countries : But this Table being fetled in dammage and prejudice of the Takers at home, and Deliverers abroad being Englifh, the Englifh will forbeare to take at home, or deliuer by Exchange abroad, fo that whereas ftrangers di form rly export onely a part of their monies, they will now be conftrained to convey away the whole : wherefore I will onely adde, that though this Table be fetled for Exchanging, yet fince there may, and that likely enough, as great neceffity befall ftrang rs to export monies notwithftanding, it will be altogether as requifite to practice exacteft diligence alongft the Coaft, and ftricteft penalties for preventing exportation of them ; and if it prove by this meanes to be fecured, then may this ftinting Table be verie well forborne, in that the fting lies in the exportation of our monies, and the undervaluing them is the benefit of the Englifh, who are the Takers at home, and Deliverers abroad, and by the low Exchange at home, and high Exchange abroad enabled to fell their Cloth fo much better cheap, and confequently, venting the greater quantitie, at laft win the whole trade from other Nations.

Since then as the fcarcitie of every commodity makes it more to be efteemed, and yet money through want or plentie raifes or deminifhes the price of all things ; in fame manner doth it predominate the Exchange ; for as the Takers and Deliverers of money by Exchange doe over-ballance one another, fo doth the Exchange rife or fall accordingly, as is demonftrated by daily experience ; and ftrangers being found thus replenifhed with monies to caufe the undervaluing of our *fpecies* by Exchange, if to ripe judgements and underftandings it appeare fo prejudiciall to the State os is alledged, which for my part I doe not as yet apprehend, (though I confeffe it invite the exporthtion of our monies, fince diligence may reclaime it in the greateft part) certainly the onely remedy muft be to take away the caufe, which furnifhes them with fuch ftore of monies, and that is by preventing the great Revenues they make of intereft monies in *England*, which continually they draw from hence to furnifh their occafions, no otherwife than everie man doth for receiving of his Rents in one Countrie which hee intendeth to fpend in another : and fecondly, by raifing the
cuftomes

cuſtomes of ſtrangers goods, eſpecially inwards , both *Spaniards,* *Germanes,* *Italians,* and thoſe of the Low Countries, all ſo much as may keep them from buinging in ſuch qnantities as formerly.

Others are of opinion, the exportation of our moneys might be hindred by raiſing them in *Denomination,* or embaſing the allay ; but if other Princes doe the like, wee are ſtill where wee were : beſides, this would encourage many private Mint-Maſters in *England,* and Strangers to bring it from abroad, though not altogether ſo much as braſſe money, yet povertie and ruine would be the end of it ; but had this latter motion taken effect, and greater *Species* beene once made currant, what through counterfeiting at home, and importing from abroad, it would in probabilitie ſo exorbitantly have encreaſed, untill braſſe kettles had beene more worth than braſſe money, by how much the workmanſhip of kettles is more coſtly.

Then would a full period have beene put to trading, and no dealing or exchanging heard of, ſave barely to ſuffice nature, and ſo remained untill the braſſe money had ceene called in againe, which then muſt needs be grnwne ſo common, as not eſteemed or accounted a reward worth working for.

But if this over-ballancing of trade were granted, and merchandiz ng exchange found to bee ſo dammageable to the Commonwealth as is alleaged , ſince certainly they cannot be well prevented otherwiſe, it will ſerve exceeding appoſitely to enforce the burden of this diſcourſe, which is :

*That unleſſe the fiſhing imployment and* Eaſt India *traffique be followed and enlarged, other Nations will gaine upon us, our trade infallibly decline daily, and the whole State with the ſame ſpeede and paces poſt on to poverty and utter ruine.*

What greater encouragement can poſſibly bee expected ? The treaſure of the fiſh employment is knowne to yeeld millions yeerly

62 *Trades encrease,*

ly (by our permiſſion) unto others; and from the *Eaſt Indies,* beſides the venting of our owne commodities, bringing in their Spices and others hither, and the trading up and downe in the Countrey, to exceeding great benefit, wee may in time hope for all ſilver and gold that ever came out of the Weſt, or any other parts; for into *Turkie* we have ſeene it carried daily, thence for *Perſia,* and other Eaſterne Quarters, but never returne back againe. And for my part, however they are ſayd to eſteeme theſe of *Europe* one eyed, and all other Nations elſe quite blind, in compariſon of themſelves, I cannot think them ſo beatified in this world, but that wee might through induſtrie find out ſomewhat which they want, and ſo be able to furniſh them; or that they be only covetous, and ſo reprobately admirers of the God *Mammon,* as they might not in time be prevailed upon to exchange him for the only Deitie.

All theſe particulars, ſome wherof deſerve large tracts & volumes of *Encomiums* & encouragements, I have only pointed at, though longer than I intended, to the end this ſupreme Aſſembly might reflect thereon, and enforming themſelves more at large, from ſuch as can exactly give directions, in due time provide for all, to the honour of his Majeſtie, wealth and ſafetie of theſe Kingdomes, and perpetuall renowne of their deep wiſdomes, to which Poſteritie will attribute ſo flouriſhing an eſtate, next unto God Almightie, whoſe infinite goodneſſe I ſhall continually implore for their proſperous proceedings, untill He pleaſe to bleſſe them with a thrice happie concluſion to King and State, and Both in One, *Amen.*

# FINIS.

# *Errata.*

PAg. 1. line but two, for *foure*, read *force*. for *Chackmate*, read *Checkmate*. p. 4. l. 2. f. *safeties*, r. *sea-fights*. p 4. l. 14 f. *furnished*, r. *furthered*. p 10. l. 21. f. *compassed by selling*, r. *compassed but by selling*. p. 12. l. 7. f. *reported*, r. *exported*. p 14. l. 1. f. *proprietie*, r. *prosperitie*. p. 16. l 8. f. *valley*, r. *vallew*. p. 19. l 15. f. *whac*, r. *what*. p. 22. l. 23. f. *mucst*, r. *much*. l. 26. f. *of the state*, r. *of state*. p. 24. l. 8. f. *heve*, r. *have*. p. 33. *l.* 36 f. *rarest*, r. *surest*. p. 34. l. 13. f. *assuring*, r. *issuing*. p. 35. l. 27. f. *thou*, r. *then*. p. 36. l. 18. f. *slid*, r. *said*. p. 37. l. 17. f. *which*, r. *what*. p. 39. l. 4. f. *pence a peece*, r. *pence*. p ib. l. 12. f. *foure*, r. *fortie seven*. p. ib. l. 30. f. *with*, r. *which*. p. 20. l. 25. f. *that only*, r. *that not only*. p. ib. l. 40. f. *rei*, r. *pecuuie*. p 41. l. 10. f. *to Wards*, r. *towards*. p. ib. l. 17. f. *care*, r. *case*. p. ib. l. 29. f. *than*, r. *rather than*. p. 43. l. 12. f. *read*, r. *send*. p. ib. l. 13. f. *Schoole-masters*, r. *Post-masters*. p. 44. l. 12. f. *prevent*, r. *redeeme*. p. 50. l 9. f. *that*, r. *the*. p. 51. l. 17. f. *ballanc'd*, r. *over-ballanc'd*.

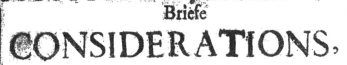

Briefe

# CONSIDERATIONS,

Concerning the advancement of

# T R A D E

## A N D

# NAVIGATION,

Humbly tendred unto all ingenious PATRIOTS;

Purpofely to incite them to endeavour the felicitie of this Nation, by con
tributing their Affiftance towards the En-
largement of TRADE, and NAVIGATION;
as the moft fure foundation.

By *Henry Robinfon*.

*London*, printed by *Matthew Simmons* next doore
to the Golden Lyon in *Alderfgate ftreet*, 1649.

# To the Courteous Reader,

Hese latter dayes ha*ve* been spent in vindicating both our Civill, and Church liberties; during which controversies, I ha*ve* not hid or kept my talent idle, though a small one; but, as occasion presented, ha*ve* endeavoured to improve the same for the common good; especially concerning the point of persecution, Church-discipline, and maintenance, oft'ner than any one I know, though namelesse to publique view; not so much for safety of my person, which yet could not escape, as for not prejudicating such arguments as I then brought, which the greatest part of People, who in those times of Tyranny, that begets ignorance, were apt to look upon the very best with an over-biasea understanding, which were produced by any body, not authorized by a Call; much like that esteemed Parochiall, Prelaticall or even Papall, from whence it will be found to accrue its pedigree, its originall.     A 2                 But

## To the Reader.

*But having contrasted above a seven yeares Ap-*
*prentishipp against persecution for conscience sake,*
*I presume we have not only cleared it up, but gained*
*that liberty, never hereafter to be indangered; and*
*conceive it is now high time, to thinke upon securing*
*of the Nation, as touching civill immunities, both to*
*the present and future generation, with all things cor-*
*ducing to the plenty and happinesse thereof; to root up*
*and reforme the rotten constitution of our lawes and*
*customes; to anathematize the endlesse vexatious*
*proceedings therof, with their unmerciful expensivenes;*
*to invite the importation of* Bullion; *regulate the*
*marchandizing* Exchange, *and prevent the exporta-*
*tion of the little remainder of our moneyes, to esta-*
*blish a flourishing Trade both* Inland *and* Forreign,
*whereby the* Navigation *may be continued, and ad-*
*vanced, and a ready way found out,* how all manner of people may get a livelyhood both with
cheerfulnes and a good Conscience.

*That my thoughts have not been unimployed here-*
*in, may appeare, by a small Treatise Entituled* Englands safety in Trades increase; *dedicated unto*
*this Parliament, some few monethes after the first be-*
*ginning; which if it had been token into due conside-*
*ration, and made use of, might have somewhat con-*
*duced to the better settling and securing both of our*
peace

## To the Reader.

*peace, and plenty, though it appeare not to every vulgar eye, as well amongst our selves, as in relation to our Neighbours; I would be loath to be thought to boast thereof, or to thinke the better of it, because it was mine owne; but, to omit the sundry weaknesses and errours, both of penning and printing, through over hastinesse, if I should say, that the subject matter thereof is of greater concernment, than is imagined, and such as hath not publiquely been propounded unto any Nation, since the discovery of the* West-Indies; *it is only to provoke all ingenious men, and such especially as are in authority to make this Nation happy by prosecuting of it to the height, wherein I should be very glad and ready to have occasion of continuing my best assistance for bringing of it into speedier practise and perfection.*

*And because most men are best prepared to receive advertisements at such time, and in such particulars as they are sufferers; it may perhaps be now more seasonable to make repetition of a passage out of the said Treatise, of* Englands safety in Trades increase, *where I thought it my duty at that time to give the Parliament this seasonable information, concerning the danger of the* French Nation, *their then endeavouring, and even beginning to be powerfull at Sea, in these words, viz. page* 1. If the French of late so strong, both in the Ocean, and Mediterranean Sea, as that we can scarce set out such Fleets as they, how much more dangerous will their puissance be to our posterity.

And secondly, did we but confider the odds wee had of other States in Sea-Forces but halfe an age agoe, and now reflect upon the great Fleets they make both in the Ocean, and Mediterranean Sea; we may finde their power such at present, as may render them juftly to be suspected of us hereafter, and unlesse we show our selves sole Soveraigne of the Sea, and

## To the Reader.

and with our Trident Scepter give Lawes, whielſt we may to all Nations there, we muſt receive them from others when we cannot help it : Forraigne Nations teach us the truth hereof, by fiſhing in our Seas whither we will or no; and the French in diſturbing our Trade the laſt yeare [1640] in the Mediterranean Sea, and enacting lawes prejudicial both to it and our Navigation, which of themſelves are able to beat us out of our Trade in time : *And how farre forth this hath been verified, ſuch particular Marchants, as have loſt their Ships and Goods to great values, have felt already, and the whole Nation will be ſenſible of too late, if not ſpeedily prevented : I held it my duty by a ſecond edition, to become a Remembrancer of my Countryes ſufferings in this particular, and have now diſcharged my Conſcience; humbly leaving them to be redreſſed, by ſuch as are in authority, who I hope will ſhortly, not only finde leaſure, but ſtrength and reſolution, to reſcue us both from our open enemies, and ſuch as more ſlighly undermine and threaten our deſtruction ;*

## FAREWELL:

Briefe

( 1 )

# Briefe Confiderations

### Concerning the advancement
### of Trade and Navigation.

Conceive it will appeare upon inquiry,

1. That in whatfoever Country the greateft ftock of money and credit fhall be raifed ; there will the greateft Trade of the world be. eftablifhed.

2. That the greateft Trade of one Countrey, hath a capacity of undermining, and eating out the leffer Trades of any other Countryes.

3. That the greateft Trade will be able to make the greateft number of fhipping. And,

4. That what Nation foever can attaine to and continue the greateft Trade, and number of fhipping, will get and keepe the Soveraignty of the Seas, and confequently, the greateft Dominion of the World. — If

( 2 )

If this be true, it will a little conceerne, especially all well-willers to the Common-wealth of *England*, whom all Neighbouring States looke upon with an envious malignant aspect, timely to confider, in what posture and condition, our Trade is, as well within our felves, as in relation to other Countryes.

Tis well knowne, that even till within thefe ten yeares, our Trade was famous amongft all knowne Nations, and at the fame time, our Ships at Sea, as dreadfull to whomfoever became our Enemies; but as neither our Trade, nor confequently our fhipping were improved, to one quarter of what they might have been; even fo, fome other Nations had then advantage, and did get ground upon us, in fuch manner; that if but for fome few yeares longer they continue proportionably to gaine upon us, in Trade, Riches, Martiners and Shipping, it will be impoffible we fhould defend our felves from their puiffance; and fo much the rather, in that our Trade at prefent, as touching exportation, is not one fourth part of what it was ten yeares agoe, as will appeare by the receipt of Cuftome.

If then we defire to be long free from the Yoake of Forraigne Dominion, and to enjoy that liberty, which we have fo dearely purchafed, it concerns us ferioufly, to inquire into all the wayes and meanes, whereby Trade and Navigation may be increafed and multiplyed unto the utmoft.

The Trade of *England*, may briefly be divided into Inland and Maritim.

Inland Trade, is that which is driven in every Citie, or from one Towne or place unto another, within the Land, according to the increafe whereof, both

exceedingly

( 3 )

the whole Nation, in their refpective ftations and callings, is not only accommodated, and enriched, either by what they deale in, or with what they ftand in need of, but the Maritim Trade, is likewife therby advanced, by ekportation of the o-verplus of al fuch commodities as the Inland trade hath pro-duced more then are fufficient for fervice of the Nation.

This Inland Trade, is chiefly to be improved by encrea-fing, and continually imploying all manner of Artificers, and efpecially of Manufactors, not only of our old and new *Draperies*, the product of our *Native Staple*, the *woll* of *Eng-land*, but even of forraign unwrought materialls, as *raw filk*, *cotton wooll grograin*, *yarne*, *Hemp*, *Flax*, *&c*. which by pollitick ordering, might be fo mannaged, as that though the materials come from abroad, yet fo much cordage, filks, linnins, or o-ther ftuffs, as are required & brought in from abroad, for the ufe of *England*, might be made amongft us, to the fetting a worke many thoufands more of poore people.

In order whereunto, it is neceffary, either that thofe un-wrought Materialls be carryed to and fro, upon the cheapeft termes, where thefe People live, that muft worke them up, into their full manufacture; or elfe that the Peo-ple fet up their habitations in fuch places, where thefe un-wrought materialls are to be had cheapeft; For,

That which makes any commodity dearer in one place then another, is chiefly the carriage, according to the neer-neffe, or diftance from one place where it is made, or grows, unto another where it is to be fpent; particularly of *wooll*, it may be obferved, that great ftore thereof is brought to *London* to be fold, and the fame *wooll* carryed againe into the Countrey to and fro, perhaps to different places, to be *carded*, *fpun*, and *weaved* into *Stuffes*, and thefe *Stuffes* brought up againe to *London* to be fold, through fo often ca_riage by land muft needs come to coft fo much dearer; the redreffing whereof, and

To make all things alike plentifull with all People
B

through-

( 4 )

throughout the Land, it is neceffary to reduce, as much as may be, all ftragling Tenements, Villages and Townes, together into fo many *Cities*, neerer to one another, that there may be People enough of each Trade, Calling and Occupation, for fupplying one anothers occafions within themfelves, with whatfoever fhall be commodious and neceffary both for their own fuftentation, and in order to advancing the Inland Trade of the Nation.

And in regard all parts of the Earth, doe not produce all fruits alike, neither in plentifullnes, nor goodneffe, it is neceffary thefe Cities fhould be fcituated, neere unto Navigable Rivers, or where artificiall ditches may be made, for conveying all things to and fro by water, from one Citie to another : though this be a great worke and of great charge, fince it is feafeable, it muft be done, otherwife, fuch Nations, who in this refpect either have got the ftart of us already, or fhall begin to practife it before us, will have fuch advantage of us, as that weee muft neceffarily become fubfervient to them, and continue at their mercy.

Another way for increafing Inland Trade, is to make all materialls, not only *Sheeps wooll*, but *filke, hempe, flax, Goates-haire, Cotten-wooll* and the like, free from Excife, Cuftomes, and all manner of Taxes, whereby the People of this Land may be enabled, to worke them up into their full Manufactures, and vent them abroad as cheape as other Nations.

And becaufe Neighbouring Nations have not only through our want of fore-fight, bereft us of our peculiar prerogative, of furnifhing all Forraigne parts with *Iron Ordnance*, gained the grand fifhing imployment from us, made new difcoveries of *Tin* and *Lead* Mines, in prejudice of ours; but for thefe twenty yeares together have been ftealing away our wollen Manufacture, which through continuance of this warre, and rot of Sheepe, are reduced to a-

bout

( 5 )

bout ¼ of what they were, it is more then neceſſary.

Firſt, That there ſhould be a ſevere prohibition againſt killing ſheepe for ſome few yeares, that may in ſome meaſure recover our ſtock of wooll againe. And

Secondly, there is as great a neceſſity of engroſſing, all or the greateſt part of the wools of *Ireland*, *Scotland*, and *Spaine*, into our owne hands, for ſome few yeares together, before theſe Nations be aware thereof, as the only courſe for getting our native workmen home againe, and hindering the progreſſe, and eſtabliſhing theſe manufactures in other Countryes; and if moneyes ſhall be wanting to compaſſe ſo great a work, the Propounder hereof, will undertake to diſcover how it may be furniſhed.

The other branch of Trade called *Maritim*, conſiſts in exportation of our native commodities, importation, and tranſportation of Forraign.

The advantage to be made of *Maritim* Trade, is to procure the exporting of as great a quantity of native commodities as poſſible, whereby ſo many more of our People may be ſet a worke, and finde money for their Wares : And as this will be very much furthered, by ordering matters in ſuch manner, as that they may be furniſhed with materialls in all parts of the Land, upon the eaſieſt termes; ſo likewiſe by ſuffering our native Commodities in their full manufacture, and artifice, to be exported with little or no Cuſtoomes or other charges.

As touching *Importation*, that ought to be managed in ſuch manner, as that all Forraigne neceſſary Commodities, as Victualls of all ſorts, *Ammunition*, *Pitch*, *Tar*, *Timber*, *ſheeps wooll*, *Goates haire*, *raw ſilke*, *Hempe*, *Flax*, and other unwrought materialls, might be encouraged to be brought in, in greater abundance, and ſuperfluities; as wrought *ſilkes*, *Wines*, *Fruits*, and *Sugars*, (which three laſt we may ſhortly be ſufficiently furniſhed with, from ſome of our owne

B 2          Plan-

( 6 )

Plantations) by taking off the greateſt part of Cuſtomes from the former, and charging it on the latter.

And Tranſportation, I terme the bringing in of forraign Commodities, into any part of *England*, to be carryed out again into any other Country; and this doubtles would be muchinlarged if al or moſt part of the out-Ports, were made free Ports; that is, that whatſoever Forraign commodities were brought into any of the ſaid out-Ports, & the Cuſtoms paid; whenſoever they were again extraƈed, the ſaid cuſtoms ſhould be forthwith returned to him that extraƈed the ſaid goods.

By this courſe, *England* would become a *Ware-houſe* or *Store-houſe* of all manner of Forraigne Commodities, from whence, not only *Ireland* and *Scotland,* but even *France,* the *Low Countryes,* and nether parts of *Germany, Muſcovia, Norway, Denmarke, Swedeland,* and *Dantzick,* with all thoſe parts adjoyning ( beſides *Italy* and *Spaine* ) might moſt commodiouſly be furniſhed, not without large imployment to our ſhipping, and great benefit to our Marchants.

This is that Trade whereby our Neighbours, the *Hollanders,* and *Zealanders,* ſo much increaſe both their Navigation and their wealth, their owne *Territories* are ſo ſtraight and barren, as would neither feed nor ſet the twentieth man a worke, in which reſpeƈ, they are neceſſitated to be induſtrious, and get themſelves a living, by becomming Purveyors to other Nations.

Whereby they have this advantage into the bargaine; that ſuch Nations as are thus provided for, by them, of all neceſſaries, muſt continually live at their mercy, be contented to be fed with a bit and a knock, and alwayes be forced to ſtand in awe of them, leaſt they ſhould picke a qnarrrell, and ſet the Dice on them, or ſtarve them out-right, before they could be relieved from other hands.

And unto the People of our owne Nation, would redownd

( 7 )

downd another advantage of no fmall concernment, in that, when all the out-Ports were thus ftored, with all manner of Forraigne Commodities, the Countryes which lye neere thofe out Ports, would firft furnifh themfelves therewith, at far eafier rates, than now they can from *London*, in regard of the charge of bringing them from *London*, to fuch refpective Ports, befides the loffe of time, for which, Intereft is likewife reckoned, and charged upon Account thereof.

But if it be objected that this courfe will leffen the prefent Cuftomes, and Revenue of the Common-wealth, it is anfwered, that a little Cuftome on a great Trade, is equivalent to a great Cuftome on a little Trade, befides the multiplying of fhipping, *Marriners, Manufactors,* and *Artificers* of all forts, and fetling the publique Revenue and Trade upon a fure foundation.

Another way of advancing both our importation, and tranfportation, is by requiring reftitution of fuch Plantations, as the *Hollanders* moft fubtilly bereft us of, both at, and fince the exercifing their cruelties upon our Marchants at *Amboyna*, by which ftratagem of theirs, they have almoft worried us out of the *Eaft India* Trade, which if we apply our felves to againe, as alfo in the *weft Indies, Perfia, China, Guiney,* we may not only be enabled to furnifh our felves, and other Forraigne Nations with all forts of their Commodities, which wee ftand in need of, but even plant Colonies there, and imploy as many of our Ships, and *Marriners* as we can make ; (an unknown Trade, and therefore gainfome) by tranfportation of their Commodities, from one Port unto another within thofe Countryes, whereby we hall not only advance great fummes of moneyes yearely or fraight thereof, but make difcovery both of their weakneffes and neceffities, as well as of their ftrength and riches, to bee much more improved upon all occafions unto our great advantage.                              And

( 8 )

And laſt of all, or moſt of all, the grand fiſhing-imploy-
ment, that which is predominant over all others, as having
in it ſelfe, a capacity of drawing all other Trades after it,
not only ſerving as a Nurſerie for breeding *Marriners*,
and compleatly Victualling us for three dayes a weeke, but
alſo ſupplying us, with ſuch ſtore of all ſorts of fiſh, to be
tranſported to other Nations, as may bring us home in returnes, Commodities of all ſorts, more then were needfull, both for our owne occaſions, and ſupplying of our
Neighbours.

This fiſhing imployment, is of greater concernment
and benefit unto the *Hollanders* and *Zealanders* at preſent,
than all the Trade of *England* ever was to us, in its moſt
flouriſhing condition, which if they ſtill goe on enjoying
to themſelves, they will dayly get ſo much more advantage
over us ; for this fiſh, which coſts them nothing but a little
toyle, except Nets to catch them with ; beſides all things
elſe, they purchaſe *Maſts*, *Timber*, *Pitch*, *Tar*, *Cordage*, and
all other materialls, although they have none of them of
their owne growth, they can build ſhipping cheaper, and in
greater quantity, than we can doe, which is worth the taking notice of in time.

By reaſon of our ſcituation, we have the advantage of them
for ſetting upon this fiſhing worke ; we have the Frye
come home to our very doores in ſhoales, even all along
the Northerne and Weſterne Coaſts, whereas others muſt
make a journey to ſeeke them out, which imports expence
of time and Charges.

And if formerly the plenty of fleſh-meate made us neglect ſuch opportunities, the ſcarcity and deareneſſe thereof at preſent, ſhould ſo much the more move us to em-
brace

( 5 )

brace it, and the Parliament out of pure neceſſity engage us
to it, by enjoyning us to forbeare all manner of fleſh-meats
three dayes a weeke.

Now as Government and Order is neceſſary in all Affaires ; ſo that there might be good order and rule obſerved in trading, it hath been thought requiſite by our Anceſtors, to reduce almoſt all Traders into ſo many ſeverall
Companyes, according to the reſpective places they traded to; but whereas this courſe was intended for multiplying and advancing Trade, for inhauncing the price of our
native Commodities, and bringing downe that of Fortaign,
it is now become the great obſtruction, through the private
intereſts and over ſwaying of particular men ; I wiſh therefore that both the ſettting open and at liberty all Trade free
aliket o all men, and the incloſing of it by Charters and Corporations, may be ſeriouſly debated and agreed on, that it
may neither be quite ruined, for want of good Government, nor yet obſtructed, no leſſe then if monopolized, by
colour of a Corporation.

And for Concluſion to what I have ſaid, I will only add
this, that unleſſe an Act be ſpeedily paſſed againſt cutting
downe Timber or wood, whether for firing or building of
Ships or Houſes, ſave in ſuch places as Sea-Coales cannot
be had for firing ; and withall for putting all former Statutes in execution, for ſecuring us unto all generations,
with continual ſupplies of Timber for ſhipping, and that in
the meane time, whileſt they are to be had, we may be forced upon fetching all Maſts and Timber from abroad, free
of all Cuſtome, and all manner of charges, as the *Hollanders*
have done continually ; our Navigation firſt or laſt muſt
neceſſarily be endangered through the exceſſive deareneſſe
and

( 10 )

and decay of Shipping, and whatſoever courſe be taken for
advancing ↄ ↄde, it will never ſucceed currantly, and with
equall ſucceſſe to other Countryes; unleſſe bills of Debt
may moſt compendiouſly and ſecurely be aſſigned over
from one man unto another, by authority of *Parliament*,
and that there be a particular Court of Marchants, and o-
thers well verſed in Marchandizing, erected, for ſpeedy
determining all differences about trade and Navigation,
concerning other matters incident hereunto. I ſhall deſire
the Reader to be referred to a more large diſcourſe intitu-
leed, ENGLANDS SAFETY IN TRADES IN-
CREASE, printed by Mr. *Nicholas Berne*, at the South-
entrance of the *Royall Exchange* 1641.

# FINIS.

# DECAY OF TRADE

*Decay of Trade. A Treatise against the Abating of Interest. Or, Reasons Shewing the Inconveniencies which will Insue, by the Bringing Downe of Interest Money to Six or Five in the Hundred, and Raising the Price of Land in this Kingdome* (London: John Sweeting, 1641). Cambridge University Library, shelfmark Pryme d.308.

It was a common view in the middle of the seventeenth century that a favourable balance of trade with foreign countries would lead to an inflow of money, which in turn would cause prices to rise and interest rates to fall. Moreover, this would boost trade and industry as well as increasing the price of land. It was often argued that the Dutch miracle was due to very low interest rates, which made it profitable to invest in, for example, trade, which gained comparatively lower profits in Holland than it did in England.[1] However, not all agreed upon this. In this anonymous pamphlet the author interestingly enough uses the opposite argument and seeks to show the danger of lowering the interest rate. It will lead to money flowing another way, the author argues. Instead of being invested in England, foreign money will be invested in Italy and elsewhere, which will lead to less trading among English merchants. If land prices rise this will also lead to high prices of export wares such as wool which, our author argues, will lead to a decay of trade and bring unemployment among the poor. The pamphlet ends with a discussion of poor relief; a theme which we will return to in Volume 4 of this collection.

---

1    See the headnote to Josiah Child, Charles Davenant and William Wood, *Select Dissertations on Colonies and Plantations*, in Volume 3 of this edition, pp. 253–4.

# Decay of Trade?
## A
# TREATISE
## Againſt the abating of
### INTEREST.
### Oʀ

Reaſons ſhewing the inconveniencies which will inſue, by the bringing
downe of Intereſt money to ſix or five
in the Hundred, and raiſing the
price of Land in this
Kingdome.

By a well wiſher of the Common-wealth?

Printed at London for *John Sweeting.* 16 4 1.

S.I

# Reasons Against
## the Abating the Rate
### OF
# INTEREST.

*Wherein first is shewed how that it is not necessary to the raising of the price of Lands, for that (beside the too much assistance of accidentall causes) Forraigne Trade may by a more beneficiall way effect the same.*

He Purchase and price of Lands in this Kingdome, doth rise and fall by no other *a* wayes and meanes ( for the common benefit ) then by the profit or losse which is made by the over or under balance

*a* The price of our Land may be raised also by a great increase of our people & strangers, which would cause the more consumption of forraign wares, & a lesse Exportation of our own, wherby the Kingdome would be soone impoverished.

A 3                    lance

**2** *Reasons against the abating*

lance of our *b* Forraigne Trade, that is to fay,
when we bring in and confume yearely a leffe
value in Forraigne wares, than we export in
our owne Commodities, we may reft affured
that the difference is brought in and doth remaine to us in fo much Treafure. And contrariwife, if wee confume a greater value in
forraigne wares than we doe export of our
owne Commodities, Then is our Treafure
exhaufted to ballance the account with ftrangers:

Daily experience doth alfo teach us, that
in thofe Countries where monies are fcarce,
there the Lands and native wares are *c* cheape,
*Ireland, Muf-* fo likewife where money doth abound, there
*covia, Poland,* the lands and wares are *d* deare; And thus it
*the East Indies,* appeareth that although this Kingdome may
*and many other*
*places:* be rich in it felfe, yet it cannot be inriched
*d Spaine, Italy,* but by *e* Trade onely, by adding Treafure to
*the Low Coun-* our wares, which Treafure being the price and
*tryes, &c.* meafure of all our other meanes both perfon-
*e.* Our wares
make us rich, all and reall, it doth thereby enable many, and
our Treafure multiply the number of Purchafers, which
doth inrich us. confequently doth caufe the fellers of Lands
to raife the price; But if Lands be too much
raifed, then the proprieties of monies (or
many of them) will indeavour to deliver it
for more profit at Intereft, to fupply the occafions of thofe who will imploy it in forraigne Trade or otherwife; which doth increafe.

## the Rate of Interest.

creafe his Majefties Cuftomes and Subjects Imployments.

And if the Rate of the Intereft be abated thereby to inforce the monyed men to turne all their meanes into Lands, then many loffes will prefently follow both to the King and his Subjects ;

The ill confe-quences of the Abatement of Intereft.

Firft, if we take the bufineffe as it now ftandeth in this Kingdome, There are many men who have great fummes of ready money, although they have neither Skill nor *f* Will to manage it in Trade of Merchandize, except they fhould doe it to the ruine of themfelves and others alfo, who have more knowledge and experience; yet their money is ftill taken up at Intereft and imployed by able Merchants to the benefit of the King and his kingdome ;

*f* Much money is put to Intereft by the Gentry, Widdowes, and Orphans.

Againe, if the Rate of Intereft be abated, it will prefently decline the quantity of our Trade; for monyed men will find meanes to make it over into the *g* Bankes of *Italy*, and other places, where it may yeeld them greater profit.

*g* The Banks of *Italy* do manage the monies of their Gentry Widdows, Orphans, or whofoever.

The proofe of this Truth is feene in the practice of divers Nations, efpecially, I will inftance the *Dutch*, whofe Lands are *h* little and very deare, becaufe their people are many, and although the Intereft ufually given in their Country, doth yeeld them at leaft double

*h* The *Hollanders* wealth & foundation for forraign Trade proceeds not from their Native wares, but from their fifhing in the Englifh Seas, & other induftries which here I omit.

ble

## 4

## *Reasons against the abating*

ble the profit of their Lands, yet they convey a great part of their monies into other
Countries where they finde moſt gaine. And
it is very probable that at leaſt one third part
of all the monies which are delivered in *London* at Intereſt, appertaineth to the *Dutch*, who
manage it here by their Factors.

And if it be objected that it is our prejudice to ſuffer Strangers to carry away the
profit of Intereſt from his Majeſties Subjects, The anſwer is, that (beſide their freedome of Commerce) this loſſe by Intereſt is
repaid with great advantage to his Majeſtie
in his Cuſtomes and Impoſts (outward and
inward) by the increaſe of trade, which ad-
deth alſo unto the Subjects imployment in
ſhipping and diverſe other kinds. The Merchant alſo who disburſteth the Intereſt to the
Stranger, doth thereby reape a greater benefit to himſelfe in his trade; which cauſeth
him to take up the money at Intereſt : All
which gaines may import about 40 *per Cent.*
yearely.

Now if the Intereſt here were brought to
a lower Rate, then our Trade would certainely decline, and the afore written profits to his
Majeſtie and his Subjects would be loſt;
and lands would fall in price. For there is no
doubt that not onely Strangers, but alſo the
Engliſh would convey their monies and their
plate

## the Rate of Interest.

plate also (if it be coyn'd into money) into
those Countries where they can finde greater profit: Nor can any strict law prevent this
evill if gaine may be obtained.

*i Baby, Turkie, Spaine, the East Indies, Ireland. &c.*

And if it bee yet further objected that a
low Interest will give the Merchant greater
encouragement to take up money to inlarge
his trade.

The answer is already given, that when the
Interest is low, the Merchant shall finde little
or no mony to take up, which would disacco-
modate and perplexe others also who are no
Traders, and force them daily to sell Lands
at *k* low rates to supply their occasions, unto
which I adde only, that 2 or 3 *per Cent.* abated
in Interest, is farre lesse considerable in the
Merchants gaine than it would prove in the
monied mans losse.

*k Where mony failes there land must fall.*

I might produce some other reasons to
proove that the abating of Interest will carry our money out of this Kingdome, decline
our Trade, and bring downe the price of our
Lands, &c. but I omit them for brevity.

**B**                           **The**

**6**

# The Intereſt which is
## given in ſeverall Countries.

$$\left.\begin{matrix}12 \\ 15 \\ 18 \\ 20 \\ 25 \\ 30\end{matrix}\right\} \textit{per Cent} \text{.yearely.}$$

The Exchanges for *Italy*, upon the Faires of *Piacenza* and other places, give 8, 9, 10. 11, 12, *per Cent.* more or leſſe according to the times of plenty or ſcarcity of money in thoſe Countries.

Reaſons

# Reasons against raising the Price of our

# LANDS.

F the price of Lands should
be improved to thirty yeares
purchase as is desired, shall
not the fruites thereof, the
Labourers hire, the Cattell,
and all mens expences bee
raised in proportion? Shall not the Native
Commodities of this Kingdome, which serve
for forraigne trade, as Corne, Wooll, and the
like together with their manufactures be proportionably raised?

*Italy* is a rich Country, and very populous,
which makes their Land worth neere thirty
yeares purchase, whereby also their Corne
Victuals, Cloath, &c. are sold at farre greater
prices than we pay here in *England*, where

B 2      Land

Land is much cheaper, and the people nothing neere so many in proportion, each
Countries bigneffe duly confidered.

When our wares are thus made deare, whether fhall we carry them ? in what Country
fhall we vent them ? when at the prices they
are already raifed of late yeares, we finde that
the Merchants gaine is fo little that many are
difcouraged to follow their Trade as formerly they did; Is not the ufe of our Wares in
Forraigne parts much declined, Mines of
Lead and Tynn e being lately found out in o-
ther Countries.

The Company of Merchant Adventurers
did heretofore vent fourefcore thoufand
Cloathes yearely in the Nether-lands. And
now (fince the difturbance by the Project of
Dying and dreffing of our Cloathes here,
which had a faire fhew, but a bad effect) they
vent not above thirty thoufand Cloathes
yearely, which it feemeth alfo they performe
to very little profit; for the Netherlanders
of late yeares doe make Cloathes as well, and
as good cheape as we can doe, with Woolls
from *Spaine*, which are of our *Engl fh* race
granted them in the Raigne of King *Henry*
the feventh, and Queene *Mary*. Now, confider I pray you, how, and where we fhall vent
our Native Wares, if we raife their price to a
higher rate than other Nations can and do afford them.                                    The

## *the Price of our Lands.* 9.

The Exportation of our Corne which formerly returned us much money is now totally loft by its *a* dearenefle here, And if our exportations thus decreafe daily, how fhall we performe our Importations without exhaufting our treafure.

I muft confeffe that within the time of my remembrance the vent of our Cloth in *Turky* is increafed about ten thoufand Cloathes yearely, but the reafon why, is worth our obfervation. The *Venetians* for a long time did ferve *Conftantinople* and divers places in *Turkie* with broad Cloath, untill the *Englifh* about 50 yeares paft, entring into the Trade in thofe parts, and being able to affoord their Cloth better cheape than the *Venetians*, they did in few yeares drive them totally from that trade of Cloth in *Turky*.

*a* The multitude of ftrangers which are now in this kingdome do much increafe our confump. tion of forrain wares & decreafe the Exportation of our nativecommodities, which is a direct way to impoverifh this kingdome. They alfo begger our poore people by depriving them of their manufactures & raifing the price of corne, victuals, rents, & the like,

And thus we fee by plaine proofe that cheape wares doe increafe trade, and deare wares do not only caufe their leffe confumption, but alfo decline the Merchants trade, impoverifh the Kingdome of Treafure, leffen his Majefties Cuftomes and Impofts, and abate the Manufactures and Imployments of the poore in Shipping, Cloathing, and the like, which are matters very confiderable to be well and duely ordered for the good of the Common-wealth.

*FINIS.*

# THOMAS VIOLET, AN HUMBLE DECLARATION

Thomas Violet, *An Humble Declaration to the Right Honourable the Lords and Commons in Parliament Assembled, Touching the Transportation of Gold and Silver, and other Abuses Practised upon the Coynes and Bullion of this Realm: Presented the 12th day of April, 1643* (London: R. H., 1643), extract, pp. 1–24. British Library, shelf-mark 104.f.25.(2.).

Thomas Violet (d. 1662) was a goldsmith and alderman of London. He appears in the records in the middle of the 1630s when he was imprisoned on diverse charges, among which the export of gold and silver led to twenty weeks in prison and he only obtained his pardon after paying a fine of £2,000. After 1640 he took the side of Charles I and plotted against the republican government, for which he was sent to the Tower of London for four years. As a consequence of this he changed his political sympathies and in 1652–3 he served on behalf of the Commonwealth government in court suits against the owners of the ships *Samson*, *Salvador* and *George* for exporting silver out of the country. During the 1650s and early 1660s he wrote several petitions appearing in the state papers forcibly condemning the transportation of money from England.

The tract included here was undoubtedly written in order for Violet to make up for his earlier crime of exporting money, for which he was sent to jail, and it seems to have been written just after he had been imprisoned in the Tower. It is one of the most vitriolic in its critique against the export of money from such a late date.

An Humble

# DECLARATION

## To the Right Honourable the

### Lords and Commons in Parliament

Affembled, touching the tranfportation of
Gold and Silver, and other abufes practifed upon the Coynes and Bullion of
this Realm : prefented the 12ᵗʰ
day of *April*, 1643.

Wherein is Declared the great mifcheifes
that have befallen the Common-wealth,
by the above-faid mifdemeanours.

By
THOMAS VIOLET of *London* Gold-fmith.

¶ LONDON, Printed by *R.H.* 1643.

( 1 )

AY it pleafe this Honourable Aſſembly, to take into their conſideration , the great miſchiefes and inconveniences that have hapned unto this Kingdome , and moſt eſpecially ſince the firſt yeer of his Majeſties Reigne , by the exporting of Gold and Silver into Forreigne parts , to the ineſtimable damage of the Common-wealth,by the great abuſes of many Gold-Smiths and others, in culling and ſorting the heavie current Coines of this Kingdome , to the end to tranſport or melt down the ſame ; and in buying and ſelling Gold and Silver above the price of the Mint ; by which meanes they fore-ſtall the Mint, and with the Gold and

B                              Sil-

## ( 2 )

Silver thus bought, for the most part furnish
Merchants and others to transport the same,
being either the species and peeces of For-
reinge Gold and Silver, or the current Coins
of Gold and Silver of this Kingdome.

Which Offences being of a high and transcendent nature, and such as by the Judge-
ment of Parliament, 5 *Richard* 2. *chap.* 2.
tend to the ruine and destruction of the
Common-wealth; for which causes all former ages have been very carefull to prevent
these mischiefes.

And neverthelesse the covetousnesse of
many men hath been such, that notwithstanding all these Laws and severall proceedings, and Sentences had and given against
them in an extraordinary way in the Court
of *Star-chamber*; They have of late yeeres
transported so much Gold out of the Kingdome, that as it is credibly conceived by
those that pay and receive great summes of
money, there is not the tenth part of the
Gold

## (3)

Gold left, that was in the Stock of this Kingdome in the beginning of his now Majesties Reigne, so that our new and old Gold is ten times more plentifull in *France* and in *Flanders* than it is with us in *England*, to the unspeakable losse of this Kingdome.

That in the Ninth, Tenth and Eleventh yeer of his now Majesties Reigne, His Majestie being informed, and taking notice of the plenty of *English* Gold and Coines current in *France*, and of the abuses and disorders above mentioned, befalling the Coyne and Bullion of the Kingdome, and taking the same into serious consideration, by the advice of His Privie Councell directed, that the transporters of Gold or Silver, the melters down of the current Silver Coynes of this Kingdome, the buyers and sellers of Gold and Silver at above the price of the Mint, their Agents Instruments and Assistants, should with all diligence be found and severely punished, ac-

B 2

cor-

## ( 4 )

cording to the Laws: which care of His (and those that endevored therein ) neverthelesse for some time tooke no effect: and notwithstanding it was generally conceived and understood ( as the truth was ) that great quantities of Gold were weekly carried into *France* ; yet were the Instruments used therein so few and secret, and the wayes and means for the transporting the same so cunningly and closely contrived, that the same could not either by the intercepting of Letters, or by the Merchants or Factors Books of accompts, or the Books of the Gold-Smiths ( as formerly it had been in the case of the *Dutchmen*, about the yeer 1618. ) be found out or discerned, for the Letters were for the most part written in Cyphers and Characters, and subscribed and signed by strange and unknown names, and yet well known to the Factors and Correspondents; and for the contents of the Letters, they made mention of *Needles, Blades, Gloves,*

Rib-

## ( 5 )

*Ribbon*, roles of *Tobacco*, and such like things to be sent over, and meant by those names: and for the accompts, the same was entred in the accompts kept of Exchangers, so that no man upon perusall of such Books, could finde any other thing mentioned but Bills of Exchange : others kept double accompts; and such as had been lesse warie and close, presently upon the first report of the first that was questioned touching transportation, cancelled and defaced all such Books as could any wayes manifest their dealings in the same ; and though divers Merchants Books of accompts were seized on, by order from the Lords of the Privie-Councell, and under Examination in the Hands of S<sup>r</sup>. *John Bankes* His Majesties then Attorney Generall, M<sup>r</sup>. *Diconson* and M<sup>r</sup>. *Trumball* then Clerkes of his Majesties Councell, and divers others, yet nothing could be proved by their Bookes.

Now His Majestie and the Lords finding

B 3         that

## ( 6 )

that the abuses and offences above mentioned, were acted by, and paffed through fo
many hands, and grown to fuch a height that
the fame could not be reformed without ex-
emplarie punifhment, and confidering the
difcovery and profecution of all offences of
this nature fo fecretly and cunningly contrived as aforefaid, would very hardly ( if at
all ) be difcovered and found out with any
diligence of fuch as were not acquainted
with the faid contrivances:

Hereupon this Declarant, being by fome
detected before the Lords of His Majefties
Privie Councell, to be a tranfporter of Gold
and Silver, and therefore fuffered a long imprifonment ( with perill of his life,and loffe
of much of his eftate, abroade and here ) was
by His Majeftie and divers Lords of the faid
Councell commanded and enjoyned to attend and profecute in this bufineffe of tranfportation of Gold,for the fervice of His Majeftie and the Common-wealth, for which

he

## (7)

he was to receive his enlargement, with promise of his Pardon.

And further, to more encourage him
therein, a promise in his Majesties name was
declared by the then Lord Keeper *Coven-
try*, M<sup>r</sup>. Secretary *Cooke*, and other officers of
State, that this Declarant, besides his enlargement and pardon, should afwell have satisfaction of fuch money as he should expend in
the difcovery and profecution of Delinquents for the forefaid offences, asalfo to receive a reward for his time taken and fpent
in this fervice, out of the Fines of fuch Delinquents as should by other teftimonies then
of this Declarant be proved to be offenders :
Upon which Commands and Promifes of the
Kings Majefty, and to preferve and keep himfelfe from the evills then depending on him,
he underteoke this fervice, as S<sup>r</sup>. *John Banks*
now chiefe Juftice of his Majefties Court of
*Common Pleas*, S<sup>r</sup>. *John Cooke*, befides divers
others of honour and quality, very well
know.                                          And

## ( 8 )

And thereupon this Declarant attending his Majefties faid Attorney afwell with fuch names as this Declarant had prefented touching the premifes, as with fuch as fome others had named for tranfporters; foon after, his Majefties faid Attorney, 22 *June* 11°.*Car.* filed a Bill in the *Star-chamber* againft divers perfons that had offended touching the premifes and after, the 30<sup>th</sup> of the faid *June*, another Information was exhibited againft other offenders in the *Star-chamber.*

That both thefe Informations were profecuted in the *Star-chamber*, and brought to fentence by the great care and diligence of his Majefties faid Attorney, as this Remonftrant humbly conceiveth ; but fo as all the endeavours and labours of making the difcovery, and finding out the witneffes, and bringing them from *France* and other places, and the charges thereof, refted wholly upon this Declarant, and all other neceffary Fees for Counfell and other attendances was disburfed

## (9)

fed by this Remonſtrant, for no other perſon disburſed one penny in or about the ſaid
ſervice; in the proſecution of which ſervice,
and to bring fourteene offenders to be cenſured in the *Star-chamber*, beſides three
which were Pardoned by His Majeſty; it
coſt the Declarant above 2000ˡ. above ſix
yeers ſince disburſed, there having been ex-
amined in Court above one hundred Witneſſes, found and brought up at this Declarants proper coſt and charges as aforeſaid,
and about three yeers time ſpent in the daily attendance of that ſervice.

Both theſe Informations, by the continuall
attendance charge and induſtry of this Declarant, and the great and due care of his
Majeſties then Attorney, were (notwithſtanding many difficulties, in reſpect of
ſome witneſſes to bee found and brought
out of *France*,) made fit and brought to
hearing in the *Star-chamber*, within the ſpace
of about a yeere and a halfe, *viz.* in *Hillary*
                    C                           Terme

( 10 )

Terme in the twelfth yeere of His now Majesties Reigne; and there were found guilty, and cenfured by the Lords, fuch perfons and fuch Fines fet upon them as follow, *viz.*

| 25 *Jan.* 12 *Car. In the firſt Cauſe.* | | 17 *February* 12 *Car. In the ſecond Cauſe.* | |
|---|---|---|---|
| *Charles Franke* | 4000$^l$ | *Peter Herne* | 2000$^l$ |
| *Robert Ellis* | 4000$^l$ | *Jo. Terry* | 2000$^l$ |
| *Iſaac Romeere* | 3000$^l$ | *Timothy Eman* | 2000$^l$ |
| *Jacob Delew* | 1000$^l$ | *Iſaac Brames* | 1000$^l$ |
| *Roger Fletcher* | 1000$^l$ | *Henry Futter* | 500$^l$ |
| *Rich. Cockram* | 1000$^l$ | *Henry Sweeting* | 500$^l$ |
| *John Parrat* | 2000$^l$ | *John Perrin* | 100$^l$ |

*The totall of the ſaid Fines amount to the ſumme of* 24100$^l$.

S$^r$. *John Wollaſton* Knight, and *William Gibs* Eſquire, both Aldermen of the City of *London*, being informed againſt in this Information,

( 11 )

formation, by his Majesties then Attorney Generall; procured his Majesties gracious Pardon, and so were discharged.

Many others there were that were Delinquents, and charged by the said Bill, besides those who were sentenced, some whereof were taken off by order of the Lords, as charged only with selling Silver above the price of the Mint, and *Peter Fountame* who was informed against for transporting of Gold, procured his pardon upon payment of 1100$^l$.

After all these proceedings at this Declarants cost and expences, the Delinquents being fined at 24100$^l$. this Declarant being informed that there was way made by the Merchants to some of the Lords to have these Fines mitigated, and them installed in a manner to nothing, ( divers Merchants and others informing the Lords, that it was no prejudice to the Common-wealth to transport Gold and Silver ) hereupon this

C 2　　　　De-

# ( 12 )

Declarant attended the Lord Keeper *Coventry* and M^r. Secretary *Coke*, and they acquainted His Majeſtie therewith, and told His Majeſty, that if the Fines were mitigated, it would but in effect give licenſe to tranſport Gold and Silver, and deſired His Majeſty to ſignifie His pleaſure to the Lords, that the offenders ſhould be cōmitted to the *Fleet* if they would not pay their Fines, and not goe at liberty as they did. Whereupon His Majeſty was pleaſed to ſend a Meſſage to the Lords in *Star-chamber* by the Earle of *Holland,* that His Majeſties pleaſure was, that the tranſporters of Gold ſhould pay their Fines impoſed on them by the Lords in *Star-chamber*, or elſe the Warden of the *Fleet* to take them into cuſtodie; and that there ſhould be no mitigation of their Fines, for that would but encourage the tranſportations of Gold and Silver, by which means no treaſure would be left in the Kingdome : notwithſtanding which expreſſe Command

from

( 13 )

---

from His Majeſtie, (though this mitigation was forborne for a while ) yet ſhortly after the ſaid offenders managed their buſineſſe in that manner, that they got themſelves off the 2410ol. for 1720l. and 1100l. more Mr. *Fountaine* paid; in all 2820l. onely *John Parrat* his Fine, who was a chiefe Inſtrument in the diſcovery of theſe offenders, remained on him ſtill without mitigation at all.

By which the tranſporting of Gold and Silver hath rather been ſleighted and licenſed then hindred , it having coſt this Declarant more in the proſecution than was payd in by the ſaid mitigation ; the effect of which mitigation in manner aforeſaid, hath been, that many of thoſe who tranſported Gold before the filing of theſe two Bills , have ſince followed it more than ever, as this Declarant beleeveth, knowing they can get more in a moneth by tranſporting of Gold into *France* and *Flanders*, than they ſhall pay according

C 3         to

( 14 )

to like mitigation to get off, were it proved againſt them.

In the time of this imployment ( by His
Majeſties Command ) the Declarant did receive divers interruptions in the proſecution
of the tranſporting of Gold and Silver, and
was impriſoned and detained cloſe priſoner
for many dayes, by one *Meſy* and *Stockdale*
Meſſengers, by warrant ſigned under Mr.
Secretary *Windebanks* hand, onely for proceeding againſt tranſporters of Gold and
Silver.

And ſome others, in doing their duties in
ſeizing Gold and Silver water-borne, according to ſeverall Statutes, have been ſued and
impriſoned to their great oppreſſions, contrary to the Lawes of this Kingdome.

That ſoon after theſe two Bills already
cenſured in the *Star-chamber*, at this Declarants coſt, his Majeſties then Attorney Sr.
*John Bankes* filed a third Bill againſt tranſporters of Gold and Silver, and for melting
downe

( 15 )

---

downe the heavy current filver Coynes of this Kingdome ; but by reafon of the great charge and disburfments to bring the two former Bills to fentence, the Declarant was unable to proceede any further till he could receive fatisfaction from his Majefty, according to His promife to this Declarant, for the moneys he had disburfed in that fervice, which this Declarant did from time to time fue for.

Firft expecting the fame out of the faid Fines according to the faid Declaration, untill fuch time as the fame was reduced to the fmall mitigation, as aforefaid, and that all difpofed to his Majefties fervice : whereupon this Declarant was inforced to Petition his Majefty for fatisfaction according to His Promife formerly made to this Declarant, as aforefaid ; which Petition HisMajefty 10ᵗʰ *March* 1638. referred to the now Bifhop of *London* then Lord Treafurer, the Lord *Cottington*, and Sʳ. *John Coke*, principall

Se-

( 16 )

Secretary, who calling unto them S¹. *John Banks* his Majesties then Attorney Generall, were to confider thereof, and make report to His Majefty in their opinions what fatisfaction they thought fit to be allowed for his fervice ; but their Lordfhips, though often therein attended by this Declarant and moved therein by S⁺. *John Coke* (who had principall charge from His Majefty touching this fervice ) to take the faid Petition into their confiderations ; yet nothing was therein done by their Lordfhips, to his great damage and difcouragement to proceede further in this fervice, that fo much concerned the Common-wealth, and all trade ; and thereupon the Declarant being difabled thus , all proceedings upon the third Bill ceafed.

That befides the fourteene offenders fentenced in *Star-chamber* & pardoned, as aforefaid, there are many other Merchants, Goldfmiths and others, that have tranfported Gold and Silver out of the Kingdome , that
have

( 17 )

have fold Gold and Silver at above the price of the Mint, that have furnifhed much light gold, Englifh and Forraigne, and great quantities of Gold and Silver to Merchants and others to tranfport, that have culled and melted downe the weightieft current Silver Coines, as fhillings, fixpences and half crowns, all which offences are againft the common Lawes of the Kingdome, and feverall Proclamations, as may appeare by what fhall be hereafter declared : which Laws for the difcovery and profecution appoint, that fuch as profecute and bring to difcovery any of the aforefaid offences, are to have a moyitie of what they can prove to be tranfported, as what they feize, and to be water-borne to tranfport : And the wifedome and policie of State hath, upon free and generall Pardons at Parliaments, exempted it out of the free pardon, thereby the more to terrifie and reftraine men from venturing in that kind, to tranfport gold or filver, or to melt

D                           down

## ( 18 )

down the current filver coynes of the Kingdome.

That divers Gold-fmiths of *London* are
become Exchangers of Bullion of gold and
filver, and buy it of Merchants and others,
pretending to carry it to the Mint ; but indeed they are the greateft inftruments for
tranfporting that are; and, in a manner, they
are only thofe who furnifh tranfporters with
Fnglifh and forreigne gold, Spanifh money,
Rix-dollers, Piftollets, Cardacues; culling
and melting down the current filver coynes
of this Realme for plate and filver thread :
and no doubt, when a true reprefentation of
the abufes of fuch Gold-fmiths, Finers, and
Wyre-drawers, as hath been formerly, and is
daily practifed by many of them, fhall be
made appeare; this Declarant doubteth not
but this high Court will think fit to take the
fame into confideration, and provide fome
meanes to reftraine them from doing the
Common-wealth that damage as formerly
hath been done.                          That

## ( 19 )

That fome of the Gold-fmiths make it
their ufe and practice to buy light Englifh
gold of fhop-keepers and others, which by
the Laws of this Kingdome, wanting beyond
remedy, ought to be bought as Bullion, and
upon the fale, ought to be defaced, and new-
coyned in the Mint : But they take another
way ; for they fell all this gold to tranfport,
though it want 4. 5. or 6 graines above the
allowance, and that a 20ˢ. peece will not
make 19ˢ. to be coyned in the Mint ; yet the
Gold-fmiths will not abate above 2ᵈ. or 3ᵈ.
and fometimes but 1ᵈ. in the peece, let the
gold want what it will ; by which meanes
they out-give the Mint : And the gold which
the Gold-fmiths buy of the Subjects, thinking it is to carry to the Mint to be new-
coyned to paffe in current payment, they
put it into a dead Sea, never to be made ufe
of in our Common-wealth : For weekly
*French* and *Englifh* have bought up this gold,
let it be as light as it will, at 19ˢ, 9ᵈ. 19ˢ, 10ᵈ.

D 2                    and

( 20 )

and 19$^f$, 11$^d$. and ſo after that rate for all
other gold, to the value of many hundred
thouſand pounds; for by the Gold-ſmiths
rule, the Mint is alwayes laſt ſerved, as being
the worſt Chapman, and giving leaſt for it;
for after all hands are full, both for tranſporters, Plate-workers, Finers, and Wyre-drawers; then that, which they cannot vent otherwiſe, commeth into the Mint; which the
Officers of the Mint know very well : and
if gold and ſilver never came into the Gold-
ſmiths hands, (which Merchants ſell to them,
beleeving they carry it all to be coyned) far
more gold and ſilver would come into the
Mint, than now doth.

For, many thouſand of dollers and *Spa-*
*niſh* money they furniſh yearely Merchants
with, that trade for *Norway* and *Denmarke*
and other parts, to tranſport ſilver for thoſe
parts, to the great weakning of the ſtock of
this Kingdome, and hindrance of the ſale of
our wollen commodities, which (before that
per-

( 21 )

pernitious way was found out) thofe Countries vented much of. Befides the hindrance
of the fale of our commodities, the King is
hindred of his Cuftome; for the Merchants
drive a trade inward and outward, and fo pay
the King no cuftome: For inftance; *Hambrough*-Merchants bring great quantities of
Rix-dollers from *Hambrough* and other parts
of *Germany*, and pay no Cuftome, becaufe
the State hath ever made gold and filver free
to be imported without Cuftome, which the
Merchants ufually fell to the Gold-fmiths,
and the Gold-fmiths for the moft part fell
to the Merchants that trade in *Norway* and
*Denmarke*: which dollers are clofely packed
in fome part of the fhip, and fo no Cuftome
paid, either for bringing in the filver, or fending it out; and no commodities, in a manner, other than filver, are tranfported into
thofe parts by the faid Merchants, confidering the quantity of their returne; For
what they want in goods exported from
D 3                        hence,

( 22 )

hence, they muſt make up in money: If great returnes of commodities from *Norway* and *Denmarke*, and few commodities exported from hence, the Ballance muſt be made up with ſilver; for no Nation will give us commodities; but there muſt be a ballance for goods imported, by goods exported, or by treaſure.

That from the yeare 1621. many Goldſmiths and Caſheers of *London* culled the weighty ſhillings and ſix-pences, to make into plate, ſilver-wyre, and to other manufactures: for moſt of that time, we having warres with *Spaine*, little or no ſilver came from thence; ſo likewiſe hath little or no ſilver from *France* in that time: and no ſilver could be brought out of *Holland*, by reaſon it went ſo high by Plachart; for Starling-ſilver paſſed in *Holland* for $4^{d}$ *per* ounce higher than it made in our Mint, ſterling being in *Holland* at $5^{s}.4^{d}$. *per* ounce; ſo that no ſilver could be imported from *Holland* to ſupply our mint:
which

## ( 23 )

which the Gold-fmiths and others perceiving, prefently fell a culling the filver moneyes current : and the money being coyned in the mint at 5ˢ. 2ᵈ. the Goldfmiths,
Finers and Wyre-drawers did raife it up to
5ˢ. 3ᵈ. *per* ounce, and melted down all the
weighty fhillings and fixpences and left none
to pafle betwixt man and man, but light moneies and clipped ; and did exceed the rate
of the mint, by giving for Starling 5ˢ.3ᵈ. *per*
ounce, and 5ˢ. 3ᵈ.⸴. *per* ounce,and fometimes
more : by which meanes there was no filver
brought into the mint for ten yeais,to fpeak
of, ( but the filver which came from *Wales* )
to the great damage of the Subject, and benefit of themfelves : this will appeare by the
mint-books. And if fome ftricter Lawes be
not made than are yet in force, if filver
fhould not come from *Spaine*, the Gold-
fmiths and Cafheers would prefently fall to
their old way of culling of the current filver-
moneys againe. All thefe feverall offences
                                        are

( 24 )

are humbly prefented to this high Court to take into their juft confiderations , that the faid offenders may be found out , and fome ftrict Law made to deterre others from practifing the like for the future.

And this Remonftrant humbly fheweth, that in the profecution of this fervice, which fo much concerneth the Common wealth,he hath expended 2000ˡ. as before he hath declared.

His humble prayer is, that if this honourable Houfe fhall command him to proceede in this fervice for the Common-wealth, that out of the Fines of the Delinquents , which fhall be proved to be offenders , he may be reimburfed the faid feverall fummes he hath formerly laid out , and damage for his forbearance for his fervice formerly done about the tranfporters,and fuch other fummes as he fhall expend in the profecution of this fervice to bring up witneffes and other neceffary expences, out of the Fines of fuch as he fhall

bring

## ( 25 )

bring and prove to bee Delinquents.

In projects, as the Wine, Salt, Soape, Tobacco, and many of the like nature , where
private men cozen the Common-wealth; yet
all these offences this Declarant humbly conceiveth, put together, are not of so prejudiciall consequence to the Common-wealth as
the transporting of Gold and Silver, the culling and melting downe the current Silver
money of this Kingdome, the selling of Silver
and Gold above the price of the Mint : for
in Projects one man cozeneth another , but
the stock remaineth in the Kingdome; but
for a man to act any of these foresaid offences,
tendeth to the destruction of trade, robbing
the Kingdome of the treasure : And to keep
the Mint from coyning, is as to let the water
out of the Cysterne, and yet to let none in ,
and then the same will quickly be drawne
dry.

It is to be feared, that the industry of many ages cannot replenish the Kingdome with

E                                          so

## ( 26 )

fo much Gold as hath been tranfported out
of it fince the firft yeere of His Majefties
Reigne ; for it is an infallible rule , that
where Gold and filver is over-valued,thither
will it be tranfported by merchants and o-
thers , for it continually reforts where it is
moft made of ; and if you feeke to raife it
here, the remedy is worfe than the difeafe,
for then you take from the Gentry, and all
fetled Revenuers,as much of their meanes as
you raife the current money ; for if Gold
fhould be raifed in *England,* for example,the
20ˢ. to 26ˢ. as it is in *France*; either higher or
lower ; you fhould buy no more at your
market for 26ˢ. than you could before for
your 20. and contrariwife, if your 20ˢ.were
but 14ˢ. you fhould buy as much for your
fourteene fhillings, as when it paffed at 20.
fo that whenfoever money is raifed, theloffe
falleth moft upon the Nobility and Gentry
and certain Revenuers,who lofe fo much out
of their inheritance,which they have let out
in leafe, as mony raifed.　　　　　**The**

( 27 )

The Declarant humbly conceiveth, the easiest way to fill the Kingdome with Gold, which it wanteth, is, according to the patterne of the Statutes of 14 *Ed*. 3. *cap*. 21. in case of transporting of woolls, To enjoyne the Merchants-Adventurers, Turkey-merchants, and exporters of Corne, Fish, or any manner of amunition, or the like; and Merchants that deale in other commodities of the Kingdome with other Countries, to bring into this Realme a proportion of gold upon the returne of the Merchandize : by which meanes the Common-wealth in time may recover this great mischief under which it suffers; and if not speedily stopped, there will not be left Coyne to maintaine Trade.

All merchants that trade for *Spain*, know, that when the West-India fleete commeth not into *Spaine*, the trade for that yeere is lost; and no money, no trade. If this be an infallible rule for *Spaine*, which suffers so much for the forbearance of bringing in of

E 2          treasure

## ( 28 )

treafure for one yeare, and is fupplied the
next out of the Indies, and till their Fleet
come home, no dealing with Merchants;
This Declarant doth humbly prefent, how
much more it doth concerne this Kingdome,
which hath no *Weft-Indies* to fupply the
Treafure tranfported, to provide and carefully keepe in the Kingdomes ftock, which
once tranfported, cannot be drawne back,
but upon unreafonable tearmes; which will
impoverifh all the Gentry to an ineftimable
value; and as long as it remaineth out of the
Kingdome, all trading and commerce de-
cayeth, the fubjects are unable to pay Subfidies and other duties, and it is one of the
greateft mifchiefes that can befall the Common-wealth.

And at this prefent in *France*, the native
Merchants there match us with fuch a point
of policy, that it would be hard for our merchants to be mafter of; for fince the raifing
of our 20ˢ peece to 26ˢ there, this Declarant
hum-

( 29 )

humbly defireth it may be taken into confideration,how they have advanced the price
of their commodities according to their advanced moneys,to the full fumme of 6ˢ in the
pound more then they were before : and as
for Wines of the growth of *France*, they are
fo deare, that they coſt the Merchants there
above 30 in the hundred, more then they
did before Gold was raiſed;and yet our cloth
and other commodities are little raiſed
there : by which means moſt of the Wines,
and Linnen,both cut-work and black bone-
lace, and other fuch like commodities in
*France*,are imported into this Kingdome,on-
ly in returne of Gold tranſported for *France:*
The like thoſe of *Flanders* have filled *England* with Thred, cut-works and *Flanders-*
laces, both Silke and Thred, and many o-
ther unneceſſary commodities,which for the
moſt part are ſtollen in without paying of
cuſtome, and draines the Kingdome of its
money both in City and County, moſt of

E 3                    the

the said commodities being bought in *France*
and *Flanders*, with the Gold tranſported out
of this Kingdome, to the value of many
hundred thouſand pounds; moſt of the commodities which have been returned from
*France* and *Flanders* for our Gold, being
utterly uſeles in a thriving Common-wealth.
And to give a ſtop to theſe miſchiefs, will require great & ſound deliberation, for coyne
is the treaſure of the Kingdome and publique meaſure of all commerce, and the vitall
ſpirits of all trade in the Kingdome, and
therefore ought tenderly to be preſerved.

It is recorded, that one of the greateſt
workes Queene *Elizabeth* did for this Kingdome, was the reducing of the moneys, when
they were embaſed, to Sterling : and doubt-
leſſe it is as great a benefit to ſettle a Law for
the bringing in of gold for exportation of
ſome commodities, to repleniſh that loſſe
which the Common-wealth hath received by
exportation thereof.

All

## ( 31 )

All men know that no great defigne can be done without money, in Common-wealth or Kingdome: which made the French King lately, when the warres were between *Spaine* and them, to fet fuch a rate upon Gold, that they drained all Chriftendome of gold; and it is beleeved, they doe efteeme (having moft of the gold of Chriftendome in their Kingdome) the poffeffion of it to be as good a ftrength as any amunition they can have; for it makes them capable of any great action. All Merchants, and others, that have been at *Paris*, know, what great fummes are taken up there, and in other places of *France*, by the King, of Bankers and others, for his warres; which is raifed with that expedition and eafe as is incredible, but to thofe that know it; and moft of the payments paid in gold, which is a great benefit faving convoy, one waggon of Gold being as much in value as fifteen in Silver, which, as that Kingdomes- bufineffe ftands, faves much in the portage;

and

## ( 32 )

and if they had not drawn in our gold, they could not have done thofe great bufineffes as they have done; and they found it to be true, that it was one great point of putting the Kingdome into a pofture of defence, by filling it full of treafure : the confideration of it, this Remonftrant humbly leaves to this Houfe.

Now that generall Lawes and Statutes from time to time have provided againft tranfporting of gold, or melting down the current coyne, and buying filver and gold at above the price of the Mint, appeareth by Statutes 9 *Ed.* 3. both forbidding the tranf-porting of the gold of the Kingdome, and the melting down the current filver coynes, by Gold-fmiths or others, into plate.

*Stat.* 14. *Rich.* 2. *cap.* 12. Commiffions made through the Realme, for to enquire of fuch as had conveyed the money of *England* out of the Kingdome, to the prejudice and damage of the King and Realme.

*Stat.*

(33)

*Stat.* 17. *Ric.* 2. *cap.* 1. There fhall be no melting of the current money to make any thing, by Gold-fmiths or others, upon paine of forfeiture.

2 *Hen.* 4. *cap.* 4. No perfon to tranfport gold or filver, either in coyne or bullion, upon paine of forfeiting as much as they might.

4 *Hen.* 4. *cap.* 10. No Gold-fmith or other perfon to melt downe the current filver coynes of the Kingdome, upon paine of forfeiting foure times the value.

9 *Hen.* 5. *cap.* 1. All Statutes heretofore made touching the good and lawfull government of Gold and Silver, and not repealed, to be in force.

2 *Hen.* 6. *cap.* 6. Upon a grievous complaint made in Parliament, that great fummes of Gold and Silver were tranfported into *Flanders* and *Burdeaux* out of this Kingdome, it was ordered and enacted, that no Gold or Silver fhould bee tranfported out of the Realm.      F      And

( 34 )

And becaufe it is fuppofed, that the money of Gold is tranfported by Merchants-aliens, It is ordained, that the Merchants-aliens fhall finde fecuritie with fureties in the *Chancery*, that they fhall not tranfport gold or moneys out of the Kingdome, upon paine of forfeiting the fum or the value; and if any doe contrary, and that duly proved, and he fo doing be gone over Sea, then his pledges fhall pay the King his faid forfeiture; whereof he that the fame efpied, and thereof gave notice to the Treafurer or the Kings Councell, fhall have the fourth part.

2 *Hen.*6. *cap.*12. To the intent that more mony be brought into the Mint, It is ordained, that neither the Mafter of the Mint, nor Changer for the time being, neither fell nor caufe to be fold, nor alien to no other ufe, but apply the fame wholly to coyne, according to the tenure of the Indenture made betwixt the King, and Mafter of the Mint.

4 *Hen.*

( 35 )

4 *Hen.7.cap.*13. Item, Where in a Parliament begun and holden at *Weftminfter* the 16 of January, the 17 of *Ed.* 4. No perfon to carry Gold or Silver either in Bullion or coyn, nor Jewels of gold, but fuch perfons as be difpenfed with by the Statute of *Hen.*4. upon paine of felonie, to be heard and determined as other felonie is; the which Statute to endure from the feaft of Eafter the 18 of *Ed.* 4. unto the end of feven yeares next enfuing : Since the which 7 yeares expired, the Gold and Silver coyne of this Realme hath and daily is conveyed into *Flanders, Normandy, Britany, Ireland,* and other parts beyond the Seas, as well by Merchants-ftrangers as by Denifons, to the great impoverifhing of the Realme, and greater is like to be, without remedy thereof haftily provided. The King our Soveraigne Lord, the premifes confidered, by the advice of his Lords Spirituall and Temporall, and the prayers of the Commons in the faid Parliament affem-

F 2                                    bled

## ( 36 )

bled, and by the authority of rhe fame, have ordained and enacted and eftablifhed, That the faid Statute made in the 16 yeare of *Ed. 4.* be and ftand a Statute good and effectuall, with all the premifes in the fame obferved and kept and put in due execution, from the feaft of the Purification of our Lady, which fhall be in the yeare of our Lord 1489. to endure to the end of 20 years next enfuing.

1 *Hen.8.cap.*13. An Act made, that whofoever fhall carry any gold or filver or jewels out of the Realme, fhall forfeit double the value, the one halfe to him that fhall feize it, or therefore fue by action of debt at the Common Law. This Act to endure to the next Parliament.

5 and 6 *Ed* 6. *cap.* 19. An act touching the exchange of gold and filver, that whofoever gives more for gold and filver then it is or fhall be declared by the Kings Proclamation, fhall fuffer imprifonment by the fpace

of

## ( 37 )

of one yeer, and make fine at the Kings pleafure, the one moity to His Majefty, the o-
ther moity to be to the party that feizeth
the fame, or will fue for it by Bill, Plaint, or
Information or otherwife.

1. A Proclamation againft giving for
light Gold more then is current, 21° *July*,
17° *Jac*[i].

2. A Proclamation againft melting Englifh money, 18° *Maii.* 9° *Jac*[i].

3. A Proclamation againft buying and
felling Gold and Silver, at higher prices then
the Mint, 14° *Maii.* 10° *Jac*[i].

4. A Proclamation againft tranfporting
of Gold, 23° *Maii.* 10° *Jac*[i].

5. A Proclamation againft profit for
Gold and Silver, and melting Englifh money
for Plate; Wafte in Gold and Silver, 4° *Feb*[i].
19° *Jac*[i].

6. A Proclamation againft tranfporting
Gold and Silver, and melting down the current coynes of the kingdom, 25° *Maii.* 3° *Car*[i].

E 3                    From

( 38 )

From all which Statutes and provisions it may be gathered, that the current money and Bullion of the kingdome, is the Subjects, only to use between man and man, but not to abuse: for no man by the Law can buy or sell them by way of Merchandize at higher rates than they are Proclamed; if he do, he is finable by the Law : he that washeth, clippeth or lesseneth the current coins, commits treason: He that exports the treasure of the kingdom, either in Bull on or current Coyn, being taken, loseth them : he that melts downe the current Gold or Silver of the kingdom for plate or other manufactures, commits a forfeiture; and transporting of Treasure hath formerly been made felony, as by the severall Statutes and Lawes to this purpose appeareth.

By these and divers other Lawes and Statutes , His Majesties predecessors have endevoured the retention and preservation of the Coine and Treasures within this Kingdome, but could hitherto never effect it.

And

( 39 )

And of late, the eafie efcape of Delinquents for thefe offences, which have been
taken, hath given the boldneffe to offenders
to goe on : and Time, the trueft Schoole-
mafter, hath taught all ages to know, that little penalties could yet never interpofe betwixt the Merchant and his profit.

*FINIS.*

# [JOHN HOUGHTON], ENGLAND'S GREAT HAPPINESS

[John Houghton], *England's Great Happiness: or, A Dialouge between Content and Complaint. Wherein is Demonstrated that a Great Part of our Complaints are Causeless* (London: Edward Croft, 1677). British Library, shelfmark 1471.df.2.

John Houghton (1645–1705) was a pharmacist and author born in Waltham Cross, Herefordshire. He was a member of the Society of Apothecaries from 1672, and became apothecary and master of the pest house in Finsbury Fields. After his marriage in 1687 he moved to London city, where he kept an apothecary's shop but also dealt in the selling of exotic overseas products, such as coffee, chocolate and spices. In London he moved in mercantile circles and his brother Henry was a merchant trading to Virginia.

Houghton's 1677 pamphlet included here was his first publication and led to his election as a member of the Royal Society in 1680. However, his best-known work is probably a monthly publication entitled *A Collection of Letters for the Improvement of Husbandry and Trade*, which appeared from 1681 to 1683. Included were articles and notices on agriculture and land improvement written by husbandmen farmers as well as by members of the Royal Society. In 1691 he started a second series of letters published weekly which would run up to 1703. It contained commercial information of different kinds, including a register of the price of Bank of England stock as well as other stocks, including those of the East India, Hudson Bay and African companies.[1]

The text reprinted here follows Houghton's dialogue style, this time between a 'Content' and a 'Complaint' arguing between themselves over the economic situation in England in 1677. The Complaint puts forward the popular argument of the dire threat of France and 'our underballance' of trade with that country, while the Content disagrees and argues that the situation is not at all so

---

1  For further information, see the entry on Houghton by Anita McConnel in *Oxford Dictionary of National Biography* (Oxford: Oxford University Press, 2004), and see also *Palgrave's Dictionary of Political Economy*, ed. H. Higgs, 3 vols (London and New York: Macmillan, 1894), vol. 1, p. 333.

bad. Without doubt is the author on the side of the Content, arguing that the country has more wealth now than it had one or two decades earlier.

# ENGLAND'S
# Great Happiness.

## OR, A

# DIALOGUE

### BETWEEN

## CONTENT *and* COMPLAINT.

### WHEREIN

Is demonſtrated that a great part of our
Complaints are cauſeleſs.

And we have more Wealth now, than
ever we had at any time before the Re-
ſtauration of his ſacred Majeſtie.

---

By a real and hearty Lover of his King
and Countrey.

---

*Say not thou, What is the cauſe that the former daies were
better than theſe? for thou doſt not enquire wiſely concerning this.* Eccl. 7. 10.

---

*LONDON,*
Printed by *J. M* for *Edward Croft,* and
are to be ſold at the *Printing-Preſs*
in *Cornhill.* 1677.

# THE
# CONTENTS
## OF THIS
# DIALOGUE.

A

# The Contents.

The

# The Author to his Book.

MY *little Book, when you do look*
    *In:o the World that's curious;*
*You must take care, you don't ill fare*
    *From those men that are furious*

*Against all things that reason brings*
    *To contradict their humours;*
*And scarce are pleas'd, unless they're eas'd*
    *By spreading forth false rumours.*

*But if that they ought 'gainst thee say,*
    *And make it truth appear;*
*Then I'l submit and think it fit,*
    *That you the blame should bear.*

*But if they will be murm'ring still,*
    *Partic'larizing men, that idly spend,*
*Or fates do lend a hand to Ruine: then*
    *'Twill be but meet* Poor Robin *see't,*
*And answer them with glee, because such fools*
    *Are the fit tools T'employ such men as he·*

# ENGLAND'S
# Great Happiness;

## OR A

# DIALOGUE

### BETWEEN

*Content* and *Complaint*.

*Content.* HOw do you, Mr. *Complaint* ?
 *Complaint.* Your Servant Sir,
 I'm glad to fee you well : What
 News?

*Cont.* Why, all the talk is of the *Blazing Star*,
and Whale that's come to *Colchester*.

*Compl.* God grant they forbode no ill News, I'm
afraid on't. The French King they say is at *Callice.*

*Cont.* Well, what then, I hope he knows the
way back to *Paris.*

*Compl.* Nay he need not come hither, here
     B      are

## 2  England's *great* Happiness.

are enough already to eat us up, I profess there's no trade, I don't know what we shall do, there is not a penny stirring, and men break like mad, if these times hold we shall be all undone.

*Cont.* You Complainants are a sort of the worst condition'd people in the World, I won't say 'tis impossible for God to please you, but I'm sure his B'essings of Peace and Plenty won't.

*Compl.* Plenty say you! yes, here's plenty enough of broken Merchants and Citizens.

*Cont.* True, one of them of a sort is too much, but yet I dare say there is more wealth in *England* at this time, than ever was at any before his Majesties Happy Restauration.

*Compl.* What then makes the Complaint?

*Cont.* Because such as you are hardly ever well when you are doing otherwise.

*Compl.* You talk strangely.

*Cont.* Well, I think 'tis so easie to make out, that while we are drinking a glass of Wine, I may convince, or put you to a non-plus.

*Compl.* Say'st thou so? Well I'le try, but instead of Wine let's drink a dish of Coffee; for I profess whatsoe're you think, I find them hard times.

*Cont.* Well, a match, but I suppose you go thither because 'tis the Complaining School, and you may be entertain'd with false jealousies an hour for a penny. Come Boy give me a dish of Tee, for I'm for something that heats and wets, and by its sweet taste give some reason to be contented.

*Compl.* For all this give me some Coffee.

             *Cont.*

## England's *great Happiness.*

*Cont.* Well, now let's hear your Complaints, and we'l confider them one by one.

*Compl.* There are a great many at prefent, I'le only mention five, *viz.*

1. Carrying the Money out of the Nation.

2. People's over-high living.

3. The too many Foreigners.

4. The Enclofure of Commons.

5. The multitude of people that run into trade, and fell fo cheap that one can't live by another.

*Cont.* Are thefe your great Complaints? I can hardly forbear laughing, for thefe rightly confidered are fome of our main temporal advantages. A great encreafe whereof would make us fo rich as to be the envy of the whole world.

*Compl.* I fhould be glad if 'twere fo, I pray let's hear what you can fay for the exportation of money. There s law againft it, and a great many wife men complain of the *Eaft-India Company* for that reafon.

*Cont.* I muft not gainfay Law; there was once a law to ftint the making of Malt; but fome of our Gentlemen are now of other minds, witnefs the Act for exportation of Beer, Ale, and Mum. The complaints againft the *Eaft-India* Company, if they were for the Nation's happinefs, would they were encouraged, and let it go as our Parliament fhall in their wifdom think fit, but fome wife men think it beft as 'tis, however 'tis our great advantage to export Money: For the aforefaid Company brings in a great ma-

*Our great advantage to export money.*

B 2                                        ny

**4** England's *great Happiness.*

ny more goods than we confume, the over-plus whereof is exported: By which part I fuppofe none will difpute a profit. Wherefore whatfoever they bring in more, muft be all exported, (we being already over-ftockt) which undoubtedly will enrich us according to its proportion. But this they cannot do without money. For I fuppofe them men that very well underftand their own intereft (by which I am apt to judge all) and do think that if they could fell that cloth in *India* for two and twenty Shillings, which cofts them here twenty, and fell enough, they would never carry out one penny: for they pay no freight out, and two and twenty Shillings if it be really two and twenty Shillings, will buy more goods than twenty Shillings will do. But if the *Indians* will not buy our goods, they muft have our money, or we muft knock off that Trade which the *Dutch* will heartily thank you for, and give you a golden god to boot.

*Comp.* Ah but we confume abundance of their Commodities here.

It is more profitable for us to confume *Callico*, than other foreign linnen.

*Cont.* Beft of all, for the more *Callico* we ufe, the lefs other linnen, and that faves abundance of wealth by being to us (at firft hand efpecially) much cheaper; and alfo pulling down the price of forreign linnen, I have heard fome fay almoft half. But about this *India* trade you may fee more at large by ingenious Mr. *Mun*; and a Letter call'd The *Eaft-India* trade a moft profitable trade to the Kingdom, printed 1677.

*Comp.* This is fomething, but what think you

of

## England's *great Happiness.* 5

of the *Norway* trade that takes away so many of our Crown pieces?

*Norway* trade a profitable trade.

*Cont.* I think well of that too, for that kind of timber we cannot be without, and I suppose our land can be better imploy'd than in great groves of such like. It also employs a great shipping, and makes us build Houses, Ships, and Cases for Merchandise, at cheap rates, and if we might have a thousand Saw-Mills, for ought I know they might do us as much kindness as Engine Looms, and for all the talk of the short sighted Rabble, employ twice the people too.

*Compl.* You speak plain, but what think you of the *French* trade? which draws away our money by whole-sale. Mr. *Fortrey* whom I have heard you speak well of, gives an account that they get sixteen hundred thousand pounds a year from us.

*Cont.* 'Tis a great sum, but perhaps were it put to vote in a wise Council, whether for that reason the trade should be left off, 'twould go in the negative. For Paper, Wine, Linnen, Castle-Sope, Brandy, Olives, Capers, Prunes, Kidskins, Taffaties, and such like we cannot be without; and for the rest which you are pleas'd to stile *Apes* and *Peacocks* (although wise *Solomon* rankt them with Gold and Ivory) they set us all a-gog, and have encrea'd among us many considerable trades: witness, the vast multitudes of Broad and Narrow silk Weavers, Makers of Points, and white and black Laces, Hats, Fanns, Looking-Glasses, and other glasses as I'm told the best in the world, Paper, Fringes, and gilded
Leather,

The *French* Trade a profitable Trade.

**6**       England'*s great Happiness.*

Leather, which in a short time is like to be made as cheap here, as in *Holland* or any other place. Wine of several fruits, Sider, Saffron, Honey, Spirits, and such like: and some cause improvements by farther Manufacture, others we export with great profit, and have a great variety to *Variety of* satisfie all sorts of Markets, causing their Neigh-*Wares for all* bours that sell the like, as Salt, Wine, Linnen, *&c.* *markets a great* to sell us much cheaper with abundance other ad-*advantage.* vantages. I must confess I had rather they'd use our goods than money, but if not, I would not lose the getting of ten pound, because I can't get a hundred; and I don't question but when the *French* gets more foreign trade, they'l give more liberty to the bringing in foreign goods. And I think you'l be asham'd to deny the Canary's a little when *Spain* yields you so vast quantities. I'l suppose *John a Nokes* to be a *Butcher,* *Dick a Styles* an *Exchange-man*, your self a *Law-yer*, will you buy no Meat or Ribbands, or your wife a fine *Indian* Gown or Fann, because they will not truck with you for Indentures, which they have no need of? I suppose no, but if you get money enough of others, you care not though you give it away *in specie* for these things: I think 'tis the same case.

*Compl.* 'Tis well if it be as you say, but what think you of your next proposal? Our High Living.

*A general* *Cont.* He that spends more than he is able to *High Living a* pay for, is either fool or knave, or in great ne-*great improve-* cessity; but I suppose not this to be the Nati-*ment to arts.* ons case; for if it were, we must owe more to other

## England's great Happiness. 7

other Nations than they to us, though we gave
them all we have to boot, which if you think,
moft of the Merchants that have foreign Factories in the *Eaft* or *Weft Indies*, *Africk Streights*,
*Spain*, *Portugal*, *Baltick*, *Eaft Countrys*, *Hanfe-
Towns*, *Scotland*, *Ireland*, with *France* and *Holland* too, will condemn you. But our height
puts us all upon an induftry, makes every one
ftrive to excel his fellow, and by their ignorance
of one anothers quantities, make more than our
markets will prefently take off; which puts
them to a new induftry to find a foreign Vent,
and then they muft make more for that market;
but ftill having fome over-plus they ftretch their
wits farther, and are never fatisfied till they in-
grofs the trade of the Univerfe. And fomething
is return'd in lieu of our exportations, which
makes a further employment and emprovement.

If it won't do this, why do you complain of
*France* getting our money for their trifles? if
it will, why fhould we not encreafe it as high
as ever it is poffible ? If we make fix confiderable Laces and export but one, I fuppofe for it
we may bring in more money than the firft coft
of them all; which is far better than to import one and let our people fit idle for want of
imployment.

The *Venetian*, *Spaniard*, *Portugeeze*, *Dutch*, The former
and *Englifh* have drove the great trade of the great traders.
world, and fetcht the gold and filver : but when
they had done, they eagerly carried it to *France*
to buy their guegawes, and thereby made them
always confiderable : and I had rather get a thoufand

## 8 England's *great Happiness*

fand pound by lace and fringes, than nine hun
dred by the beft broad cloth that ever I yet
faw.

That honeft way that finds moft employmen,
and gets moft money, is fure the beft for any Nation, and this fine manufacture joyn d to our
fhipping will perhaps make us the moft potent
the Sun fhines on.

Take away all our fuperneceffary trades, and
we fhall have no more than Tankard-Bearers,
and Plow-men; and our City of *London* will
in fhort time be like an *Irifh* Hut, or perhaps
*Carthage* mentioned in *Virgil Travefte.*

If you have reafon, here's enough to fatisfie:
but if not, fhould I bring ten thoufand undeniable arguments you'd ftill complain.

*Compl.* I meet but with very few of your mind:
but I pray let's hear your thoughts of the next
propofal? which is, That 'tis our happinefs to
have abundance of Foreigners, for I'm fure the
general cry is that they eat the bread out of our
mouths, they fell their goods when we can't,
they work cheaper than we, live in holes, pay
neither fcot nor lot; and if we fhould have many
more of them, fure we fhould have nothing to
do.

Invitation
of Foreigners
a great advan-
tage.

*Cont.* You are never well full or fafting; you
cry up the *Dutch* to be a brave people, rich, and
full of Cities, that they fwarm with people as
Bee-hives with Bees; if a plague come, they are
fill'd up prefently and fuch like; yet they do all
this by inviting all the World to come and live
among them. You complain of *Spain* becaufe
their

## England's great Happiness.    9

their Inquisition is so high, they'l let no body live among them, and that's a main cause of their weakness and poverty. You find fault because some of our people go to *Ireland*, and the Plantations, and say we want people at home to fill our Cities and Countrie-towns, and yet you'l allow none to come and fill up their rooms. Will not a multitude of people strengthen us as well as the want of them weaken *Spain?* sure it will. Would you not be glad if the Duke of *Lorrain* should destroy as many Villages in *France* as are destroy'd in *Alsatia*, and thereby destroy 100000 people? I dare say the most part of you would. I pray then would it not do as well if an hundred thousand *French* would run away leaving their houses to drop, and fight against the *French* King, or at least work for money to pay taxes to them that will? I think you won't gainsay it. In Sr. *Walter Raleigh*'s observations concerning the causes of the magnificency and opulency of Cities, 'twas the best policy that old *Rome* had, and by it they were brought to their height. *Tamerlan* the great was of the same mind, and *Constantinople* owes its greatness to the same contrivance. Would not Foreigners living here consume our corn, cattle, cloth, coals, and all kind of things we use? and would not that cause our lands to be better till'd, and our trades increas'd? would they not bring several new trades with them, or help to encrease those we have? witness the Flemmings in the time of *Edward* the third, the Colonies of *Colchester*, *Canterbury*, and *Norwich*,

*The advantages of Multitudes.*

*Examples of profit by Foreigners.*

C                    the

## England's *great Happiness.*

**10**

the Silk-trade in *Spittle-Fields*, the Tapiſtrey-makers in *Hatton Garden*, *Clarkenwel*, and elſewhere, M<sup>r</sup> *Todin* the rare Pewterer in St. *Martins Lane*, the Husbandmen in the *Fenns*, and divers others, and doth not every Trades-man among them employ two or three *Engliſh* to attend them either in making tools, winding ſilk, or ſuch like, beſides buying all their materials here? Do you think the firſt rough materials of a piece of ſilk of ſix pound a yard coſts twenty Shillings? is not the other five pound better earnt and ſpent here, than to give the whole ſix pound to *France* for't? No man in *England* loves it better than I, and I love no Nation more than another, but for their vertues, or as they relate to the welfare of *England*: but ſome of our great complainers will ſpend a groat when they are not worth two pence, and work but two or three days in the week, therefore others out-do them.

Strangers pay neither ſcot nor lot, 'tis true, but 'tis becauſe they are diſturb'd, and are hardly ſuffer'd (or at leaſt encourag'd) to take houſes, but otherwiſe they'd quickly be like us, and the next generation would not be known from Engliſh.

You ſeldom hear of any diſturbance they make in the State, for they are not all of one mind, and cannot agree if they would, they come for ſafety, quietneſs, and livelyhoods, for which and other good reaſons, if the Paliament think *A hearty Wiſh.* fit, I could wiſh there would twenty thouſand come in next year.

*Compl.*

## England's *great* Happiness.　　　**1 1**

*Compl.* At this rate all the World would be invited hither.

*Cont.* Amen, fay I ; for then our King would be universal Monarch, and I'd never fear a prejudice either to Church or State if all were to be hang'd that should teach them caufelefs complaining principles.

*Compl.* Enough of this, but if you are for Enclofures the poor will complain of you, and curfe you to the pit of Hell: and a great many of the rich will give you but little thanks.

*Cont.* All this fignifies nothing ; one good reafon prevails more with me than all their cries and curfes, if they were ten fold: and I'm fure that God is a God of reafon. As for the Gentry I refpect them highly, but a great many are more rul'd by a vulgar error, and falfe maxims, than the dictates of their own reafon. But if I thought it would not be much for the advantage both of Gentry and Commonalty I would not fay a word more on't. But I pray confider that inclos'd ground will fometimes yield treble to what common will, but if fow'd with Clover, Sant-foin or fuch like, fometimes fix, eight, or tenfold, when Corn bears a good price, and 'tis for the Land's advantage 'tis plow'd too, and after the Crop is off fow'd with Turnips or fuch like, and this with the help of good tillage and dung, (which our good Husbandmen know now pretty well how to procure) done every year, when the other muft lye waft one in three.

A great deal will be turn'd into Orchards and

*Enclofure and*

*Its advantage.*

*Horticulture a great advantage.*

C 2

and Gardens, four or five acres of which sometimes maintains a family better, and employs
more labourers than fifty acres of other shall
do. Hops, Saffron, Liquorish, Onions, Pota-
toes, Madder, Artichocks, Aniseeds and Cole-
seeds will thrive but ill in Common Fields, and
I suppose none will deme an Acre of these to
yield more money than so much Wheat: Whither goes it then? why, surely into the owners
purse or labourers pockets.

For the cry that the poor will be starv'd,
it is not worth a rush, for few of them make
the benefit for lack of stock, and perhaps they
spend as much time in looking after their titts,
runts, and tupps, as would gain them by an indifferent Handy-craft, twice the profit.

And how that parish that traded but for ten
thousand pounds a year, and now for twenty
thousand, should be more likely to famish, and
twice or thrice the employment for the poor
starve them, I confess is to me a paradox. E-
ver since old *Tusser's* time, it has been observed
that where there's most common, there's least
good building and most poor.

Enclosure must needs encrease more great and
small cattle, and an encrease of Hydes, Tallow,
and Wool, with finer manufactures of them
than formerly, can never either depopulate or
impoverish.

*Compl.* I must confess that most men yield it
to be most profitable. But is it lawful to take
away that we have enjoy'd time out of mind?
and we must not do evil that good may come on't.

*Cont.*

## England's great. Happiness.     13

*Cont.* I muſt confeſs this is your main argument; and I being neither Divine nor Lawyer
perhaps may not give to it ſo good an anſwer
as ten thouſand wiſer men can do. But 'tis
well that I have prov'd it profitable: But I ſuppoſe this Iſland before it was inhabited to be
all Common; which was ſomething altered by
the firſt Occupants, and encreas'd according to
the good husbandry, populacy, and needs of the
people, and why this preſcription ſhould not
prevail as much as yours, I know not. It doth
in *America*, and I believe all the World over.
In *China* I hear there is not an Acre of Common
Land.

    *Whether it be lawful to encloſe.*

I muſt confeſs I know no Statute that gives
full power to encloſe all the Common-Fields,
in the Kingdom; but in my weak judgment
there are ſeveral that do much encourage it.
Eſpecially when it is for the advantage of the
whole; witneſs the two firſt Acts for encloſing
the Fenns, and the 4 *Jac.* 1 r. for part of *He-
refordſhire*, caus'd by the good husbandry of
ſome of the inhabitants. And I think the 3
*Edw.* 6. & 3. will go a great way. And the
inducement and ground of the Act call'd Trade
encouraged 15 *Car.* 2. 7. runs thus *verbatim.*

*Foraſmuch as the encouraging of Tillage
ought to be in an eſpecial manner regarded and
endeavoured, and the ſureſt and effectualleſt
means of promoting and advancing any trade,
occupation or myſtery, being by rendring it profitable to the uſers thereof, and great quantities*

    *The reaſons for the Act call'd Trade encouraged.*

*of*

**#4** ## England's *great Happiness.*

*of Land within this Kingdom for the present ly-*
*ing in a manner waste, and yielding little, which*
*might thereby be improv'd to considerable profit*
*and advantage (if sufficient encouragement were*
*given for the laying out of cost and labour on the*
*same) and thereby much more Corn produced,*
*greater numbers of People, Horses, and Cattle*
*employed, and other Land also rendred more va-*
*luable.*

How far the inducements and grounds of
Acts of Parliament run, I know not, but they
shew their designs; and how this can be done
better than by Enclosure, my ignorance won't
reach to; but I have prov'd it most advantage-
ous to the owner, and I think wealth and a
treble labour, will quickly encrease People, Horses, and other Cattle, the plenty whereof, of
necessity must quickly make other Land more
valuable.

If leave were given, all the barren land in
*England* I suppose would soon be improv'd.

I believe you'l be asham'd to urge the 25. of
*Hen.* 8. and 13. because the cheapness of our
Corn, Cattle, Wool, Pigs, Geese, Hens, Chick-
ens, and Eggs, are in a great part the ground
of your complaint.

I chiefly aim at that we call Common Field-
Land, where men claim a propriety, and can
say, Thus many acres are mine; but for the o-
ther that lye always open if the Lord of the
Manour gets all in his own hand, or the Pa-
rishioners can agree, I wish 'twere all so serv'd,
and

England's great Happiness. 15

and I think there's few with good reason can be against it.

As for the Kings Forests and Chaces, if they were imparkt, and kept to himself, I believe timber would thrive ne'r the worse, or the neighbouring corn, nor perhaps would there be a less breed of good Horses; But arguments are endless. Boy give met'other dish of Tee.

*Compl.* I pray do nothing rashly, but drink first. Well suppose I grant that you have law and reason enough on your side: what will you do against the beggarly multitude, that will pull down your Fences, turn Cattel in, and spoil your Corn, or what other improvements you shall make in your new Enclosure? if you sue them you know the old Proverb, *Sue a Beggar*, &c. and they have nothing to lose, their punishment will ne'r make you satisfaction, and except you have a large purse, and courage too you may chance be tired.

*Cont.* 'Tis true, this is a great impediment to the good work, but a great many have conquer'd it, and I believe had the former ages went the same way to work, which an ingenious Justice, and another of my good friends (whom you well know) have done, we should long e'r this have had more Milk and Honey. For instead of narrow Ditches and high banks, which might quickly be thrown down and fill'd with ease, they have made their Ditches, seven, eight, or ten foot wide, six foot deep, and carried away all that should make a hurtful bank, planted quick, and with Damms, stop water to

ful

*A way to inclose in spite of the Rabble.*

fill up as high as they can or think neceſſary. By this means the Rabble want materials to re-fill, unleſs they'l bring it with them, or dig one ditch to fill another. But as what relates to Ryots, Treſpaſſes, and other law tricks, the Countrey-Men I believe are wiſe enough.

*Compl.* This is a way indeed, ſurely this will do or nothing, but let them incloſe or do in the fields what they will, what can you ſay for the multitude of Trades-men?

Multitude of traders a great advantage.

*Cont.* Say for them! I have ſaid enough in what I ſaid juſt now of Foreigners: But how-ever ſomething more.

That man that gets moſt money over and a-bove his expences, ſurely will be richeſt; ſo likewiſe will that trade: but ſuppoſe there were formerly twenty Linnen-Drapers (or any o-ther Traders) and they clear'd each five hun-dred pounds a year, it will amount to ten thou-ſand pounds; but now there are forty Drapers and by under-ſelling each other they clear each but four hundred pounds a year, this will make ſixteen thouſand pounds. I ſuppoſe this Company do plainly thrive: But ſhould eigh-ty get but three hundred pounds each, it would amount to four and twenty thouſand pounds beſides the employment of four times the Ships and Labourers, with the like encreaſe of his Majeſties Cuſtoms, and this is the caſe of moſt of our old trades, only beſides the quantity of men, the particulars have moſt of them ſo much in-creas'd their quantities, that with leſs profit
they

## England's great Happiness.

they every year spend more, and give their Children better portions.

Moreover there are a multitude of new Trades; and that variety of Arts should undo a Nation, I believe was never known in this world or in *Utopia*.

When you keep Bees, you are loth to suffer Drones among them. Good Bees are the seventeen Provinces, and you cry them up to the skies, and say that two or three years peace will make amends for all the Calamities they have endured this War: But the like Industry in *England*, added to a prodigious Plenty, will quite spoil us.

Do not some of our Trades-men spend one or two hundred pounds a year, whose parents never saw forty Shillings together of their own in their lives? Doth it not make the Capons and Custards go off at a good rate? Doth it not mightily encrease his Majesties revenue, by Customs, Excise, and Chimney-Money? Doth it not make a tax light, by having many Shoulders to bear the burden? And were it not for this, his Majestie must like *Spain* and *Denmark*, when he hath occasion hire ships, from perhaps his ill-humour'd Neighbours. But God be thanked things are in a better case, and if I should live forty years longer, I hope to see *London* as big again, and all the Towns in *England* strive to imitate it. *The advantages of many Traders.*

*Compl.* Well, I'l trouble you no more at present, and confess that what you say seems to have

D                              a great

18                         England's *great Happiness.*

a great deal of truth in't; but I don't know, people do complain.

A diſſwaſive from murmuring. *Cont.* And ever will; but I prithee leave off this humour of murmuring, either diſprove what I have ſaid, or for ſhame bluſh to complain. Remember that you are a rational creature, don't make your own and others lives uncomfortable by refuſing to enjoy thoſe Bleſſings Providence hath heap'd upon you: St. *Paul* with far leſs liv'd a happier life. What Comfort can his Majeſtie have, when for all his good Government, Care, and Protection, you reward him with a meſs of Complaints? Don't Judaize and complain more when you are fed with Manna and Quails, than when you fed on Leeks and Garlick. Murmur not like *Corah* and his Crew when your King is *a Moſes.* You know that of 6cccco. that came from *Ægypt,* there went but two into the *Land of Canaan.* Moſt of the reſt periſhed for this crime. When *Moſes* beg'd any great Matter of God, he commemorated his former loving kindneſſes, and O God of *Abraham, Iſaac,* and *Jacob* was of great concern in a Jews petition. 'Tis the remembrance of the *French* King's Victories makes him go on with courage: And would we but The word *impoſſible* a great diſcourager of Arts. conſider the great things we have done, it would perhaps make us believe nothing to be impoſſible either in Arms or Arts. Let's bleſs God for all his mercies, and particularly for our good King, whoſe greateſt Care hath been to keep us in peace, and procure us plenty, which I think will prove better arguments to

gain

## England's *great* Happinefs. 19

gain any needful thing, than the irkfom and caufelefs complaints of a thoufand generations. The fum of all is this; If we have great Ma- Signs of Wealth. gazines for War, and multitudes of brave Ships; If we have a Mint employ'd with more Gold and Silver than in a confiderable time they can well coin; If it be an affront to caufe one to drink in any worfe mettle than Silver, if great part of our utenfils be of the fame; if our Trade be ftretcht as far as any trade is known; if we have fix times the Traders and moft of their Shops and Ware-houfes better furnifht than in the laft Age; if we have abundance of more good debts abroad than credit from thence; if many of our poor Cotagers children be turn'd Merchants and fubftantial Traders; if our good Lands be made much better, and our bad have a fix-fold improvement; if our houfes be built like Palaces, over what they were in the laft Age, and abound with plenty of coftly furniture; and rich Jewels be very common; and our Servants excel in finery the Great ones of fome Neighbour-Nations; if we have moft part of the trade of the World, and our Cities are perhaps the greateft Magazines thereof; if after a deftructive plague and confuming fire, we appear much more glorious; if we have an u-niverfal Peace, and our King in fuch renown that he is courted by all his Neighbours, and thefe only the marks of poverty, then I have been under a great miftake: But if it doth otherwife appear, as certainly it doth to all ra-

D 2 tional

tional men. Then I may ftill go on with my maxime and fay,

*We have more Wealth now, than ever we had at any time before the Reftauration of his Sacred Majeftie.*

A Comparifon.

The Jews were never well fetled till the time of *Saul,* and then Wealth flow'd in like water fpilt upon the ground: you might fee it coming, and it being a ftranger they ftood gazing and cry'd ahah! witnefs, *David's* lamentation over

2 Sam. 1. 24.

*Saul, He clothed them in Scarlet, and put ornaments of Gold upon their apparel.* But in *David's* own time it grew to a pretty handfom brook; but in *Solomon's* time to a profound River. But then the cuftom of their Wealth

Our now complaints.

took away the fenfe of it, they cry'd that times were hard, there was nothing to be got, they were the old ones that got eftates, he that would get one then, muft have tug'd hard for't; and that fuch like talk they had, is witnefs *Solomon's* reproof, *Say not thou, the former times were better than thefe, for thou doft not enquire wifely concerning this.*

Juft thus it hath been with *England,* Queen *Elizabeth's* time was like *Saul's,* when by taking a few *Spanifh* Ships, and almoft beginning a Navigation, made us cry ahah! In the time of King *James* and *Charles,* for want of Silver the Gold made a pretty handfom gliftering, but now Gold doth much abound, and Silver is hardany thing efteemed of. It flows in fo often like a deep river, there is hardly any notice taken of it.

*Compl.*

## England's *great Happiness.* 21

*Compl.* I muſt confeſs I can't anſwer you, but ſurely that which every body ſaith, muſt needs be true.

*Cont.* Well if you are ſo wilful as not to be convinc'd, I'm ſorry, but however this advantage to my ſelf I'l reap, I'l give God thanks for his great Bleſſings, and enjoy them while you ſit murmuring and repining for what you don't want, and like *Midas* ſtarve in a monſtrous plenty. A good reſolution.

However conſider what follows.

*Neither murmur ye as ſome of them alſo murmured, and were deſtroyed of the deſtroyer.* 1 Cor. 10. 10.

*Wo unto them, for they have periſhed in the gainſaying of* Core. Jude 11.

*Theſe are ſpots in your Feaſts of Charity.* 12.

*And are murmurers and complainers, walking after their own luſts.* 16.

*Tour murmurings are not againſt us, but againſt the Lord.* Exod. 16. 18.

*Do all things without murmurings.* Phil. 2. 14.

*And the people ſpake againſt God, and againſt* Moſes, *wherefore have you brought us up out of* Ægypt, *to die in the Wilderneſs? For there is no Bread, neither is there any water, and our ſoul loatheth this light bread.* Numb. 21. 5.

*And the Lord ſent Fiery Serpents among the people, and they bit the people, and much people of Iſrael dyed.* 6.

*Many when a thing was lent them reckoned it to be found, and put them to trouble that helped them.* Eccluſ. 29. 4.

*Till he hath received he will kiſs a mans hand, and for his Neighbours money he will ſpeak ſubmiſly:* 5.

**England'***s great* **Happine***ss***.**

*mi**ss**g*: *but when he should repay, he will prolong the time and return words of grief, and C O M-*
P L A I N   O F   T H E   T I M E S.

Rev. 22. 11,

He *that is filthy, let him be filthy still.*
Come Boy take money.
However dear Friend, farewel.

---

*F I N I S.*

---

# WILLIAM CARTER, AN ALARUM TO ENGLAND

William Carter, *An Alarum to England to Prevent its Destruction by the Loss of Trade and Navigation; which at this Day is in Great Danger* (London: Mary Fabian, 1700). British Library, shelfmark 1029.e.62.

Nothing is known of William Carter. According to Robert Watt his name was either William or Wooll.[1] He also published *An Abstract of the Proceedings of W. Carter, being a Plea to some Objections Urged Against Him* (London: for the author, 1694).

The pamphlet reprinted here, as so many during this period do, argues that England is at a loss in its trade with France, which is the main cause for the current 'underbalance' of trade – with dire consequences for England, for example in land prices. Moreover, in this tract the standard critique against the East India Company appears with the usual argument that it 'carries away our money'. More than anything else this is a patriotic piece, with the message that England must be more aware of the French threat to its wealth and security. In a sense, trade is merely another weapon in the national struggle between the two rival countries.

---

1    R. Watt, *Bibliotheca Britannica: or, A General Index to British and Foreign Literature*, 4 vols (Edinburgh and London: A. Constable and Company, 1824), vol. 1, p. 197r.

# A N

# ALARUM

## T O

# ENGLAND,

## To prevent its Deſtruction

### By the Loſs of

# *Trade* and *Navigation*;

#### Which at this Day is in great Danger.

##### *Submitted to Conſideration in time.*

---

# By *W.* *C.*

---

*L·O N D O N,*
Printed by *K. Aſtwood,*for *Mary Fabian,*
at *Mercers Chappel* in *Cheapſide,* 1700.

i

## TO THE
# KING's
### MOST
## Excellent Majeſty.

*May it pleaſe Your Majeſty,*

AS the Multitude of your Subjects is an Honour to Your Majeſty, ſo the Employment of them, is both Your Safety and Riches.

### *Great Sir,*

Theſe few Lines do therefore, Humbly crave Your Majeſties Peruſal, becauſe they

A 2　　　make

ii　　*The Epiſtle Dedicatory.*

make it appear, That the Trade and Manufacture of this Nation, ſupports the Government, and conſequently the Revenue of the Crown in each Branch thereof; which is Humbly ſubmitted to Your Princely Conſideration by

*Your Majeſty's*

Moſt Obedient

and Dutiful

Subject and Servant,

*W. C.*

THE

# THE

# PREFACE.

T IS certain that Trade in General is a Great Benefit to, and a Main Support of any Nation; and the Wollen Manufacture of this in particular : Therefore 'tis of Great Concernment, to endeavour by all means possible, to preserve and increase it. But to our Sorrow, we have our Ears fill'd with daily Complaints of the great Decay of it; and the most effectual means to find out a Remedy, is to enquire into the Cause. I did in the Year, 1669. express my Fears to King Charles II. of a great Decay of our Wollen Manufacture; by what I Observ'd then, and by woful Experience we have found it come to pass.

*I*

# iv The Preface.

I have in the following Papers endeavoured to represent the Causes of it. And
the General Cause I have obferv'd to be,
the Trading into those Parts, whither but
little of our own Manufacture is exported,
and the Returns of Forreign Commodities to us, are made by purchase with our
Money. The Particulars of which, I have
inftanc'd in our Trade with France ;
which during the Two Laft Reigns, gave
them the Advantage of near Four Millions per Annum of our Money ; while
but little of our Manufactures was ex
chang'd for theirs. The like is inftanc'd
in the Eaft-India Trade, which is mainly
carried on by our Money, and the Callicoes, &c. which are imported from
thence ; not only hinder our own Manufactures at Home, but lay a Foundation of
the Lofs of our Trade in the Wollen Manufacture, both with Flanders and Germany. This Mr. T. Smith has hinted
in a Sheet he wrote the laft Year, concerning the Eaft-India Trade ; fhewing how
pre·

# The Preface. v

*prejudicial it was to our Silk and Wollen Manufactures, which at prefent are well fetled among us. It tends to our Impoverifhment, by taking away the Employment of our Poor ; depopulates the Nation, leffens the Value of Lands and Horfes ; and expofes us thereby to the Contempt of our Neighbours.*

A N

[ 1 ]

# An ALARUM, &c.

IN the Preface of a Difcourfe, Intituled, *Awake Sampfon:* Printed in the Year, 1696. I hinted that that was intended to be a Preparatory for a General Alarum.

Since we were told in the Year, 1678. that there was then a Defign to fubvert the Frame of our *Englifh* Government, the Deftruction of the Proteftaut Religion, and to adulterate the Coin, and had we took that caution given us timely, we had prevented many of thofe Evils, which we have fo fenfibly fince felt.

And fince the Defigns of our Enemies have been varioufly exercifed, ( *viz.* ) to deftroy Trade, to invade Property, to alter ou Religion, and to adulterate the Coin of the Nation, which hath coft us fo much lately to retrieve ; let it be a caution to us in other cafes for the Future.

It may feem to fome to be needlefs now, to talk of an Alarum feeing we are at Peace ; yet the following Difcourfe will evidence that in the Subject I infift upon, we have more need to be call'd upon now, then in a Time of War : The Reafons are many, but in General, we know in War Watches are fet, and People do never fleep fecure from Noife ; but in a Time of Peace Perfons are apt to be too fecure : I prefume, there is no juft Occafion to make an Apology, for waking a Perfon in danger of a Fire, tho' he is forc'd to it againft his Natural Difpofition ; and that fuch a-Perfon would

B                                          not

[ 2 ]

not be offended, if pull'd out of his Bed when the Flames are about him ; tho' he do not fee it his Eyes being fhut, and he in a found fleep : It is the Condition of *England* at this time. We have been oft in Danger, and the Fire as oft quench'd, and tho' (generally fpeaking) we have had very many and great awakening Providences founded in our Ears, *Yet we have been like the deaf Adder that ftoppeth her Ears, and will not hearken to the Voice of Charmers, tho' charming never fo wifely*; and do not confider a Secret Train is laid to blow us up, and tho' we have hitherto been preferv'd almoft to a Miracle, yet whether we have any grounds to expect it always, I cannot tell; my Faith is weak : But on the contrary, tho' we in this Age do not pretend to Prophetick Infpiration, nor do I as little to Prognoftication, yet by Common Obfervations any Man may predict, what Conclufions neceffarily follow fuch and fuch Premiffes ; or in a more familiar way of fpeaking, we know if we keep a certain Road on Shore, or fteer our Courfe at Sea, whither at length it will bring us.

' How we have taken our Courfe thefe Forty Years is too Notorious, and for which the Land mourns ; ( I would be glad to be deceiv'd if my Fears are groundlefs ) that it may vomit out many of its Inhabitants, at leaft fome of us fall fhort of our Expectations.

' And had I not made fome Obfervations, of the wonderful Goodnefs of God to this Nation ; as before hinted : I fhould have defpair'd of any hopes of being faved from an utter Deftruction, for the Dangers we are now in

are

[ 3 ]

are fo great, that tho' we are at prefent ( Bleffed be God ) at peace, yet when I confider, the many thoufands that have lived comfortably in the Trade of our Wollen Manufacture, and which have contributed to the Support of the Government, and Maintenance of the Poor; are now ( and like to be more ) reduced to want themfelves, having no Employment; by reafon that many of thofe Countries that we have formerly fupplied with thofe Goods, do make not only for their own Ufe with out Wool, but fupply other Forreign Countries alfo; and not only fo, but that we have cut off as it were, and difobliged both *Ireland* and *Scotland* in fome late Acts; I am not without my Fears what the Effects may be, befides our Domeftick Confumption of Forreign Manufacturies, and hindring our own, &c.

But If it be faid by fome, ( as it is ) that if we loofe our Woollen Manufacture, we may employ our poor in a Linnen Manufacture, &c. I muft anfwer as I did on a like Occafion, about the Year 1669. in a Tract, Entituled, *England's Intereft by the Benefit of the Woollen Manufacture:* ( viz. ) " I am the more " large in the Demonftration of this Affair, " not only becaufe this hath coft me many " Years Labour and Study to confult all forts " of concern'd Perfons, befides my own Ex- " perience about it; but alfo becaufe it is fo " hard to convince People of the meaneft Ca- " pacity, and fome of the wifer fort, how to " cure this difmal Malady which fome defpair- " ing of, have rather thought of fetting up " fome other Manufacture in lieu of endeavour-

B 2 ing

## [ 4 ]

" ing to prevent the Exportation of Wool, and
" manufacturing that at Home, as that of Lin-
" nen, &c. which is in my Judgment a great
" Miftake, for other Countries have the Ad-
" vantage of *England* in that, but not in this
" of Cloathing ; and it will be found that all
" or moft Trades in *England*, wholly diftinct from
" this of Cloathing, bring not the Tythe of Ad-
" vantage that this doth.

And to confirm my Sentiments herein tho' fo
long ago writ, I crave leave to add the Opinion of a late Author, who fays,

*Divine Providence that appoints to every Na-*
*tion and Country a particular Portion, feems to*
*allot to England which was the firft Acceptable*
*Sacrifice to his Omnipotence, that of the Flock the*
*Produce of which, is the moft Univerfal Covering*
*of all Civilized Countries of the World.*

*Our Wollen Manufacture is a Talent, which no*
*Nation hath to that perfection as we have ; this*
*hath been for many Ages the Support of the Nation,*
*imploying the Poore at home, and our Men and*
*Ships at Sea. Now to decline this, and fet up*
*another Manufactory, looks like an Extravagant*
*Mechanick, who by his Improvidence hath loft his*
*own Art, and thinks to retrieve his Misfortune by*
*taking up that of another Mans : This is condemn'd*
*in particular Perfons, and therefore much more to be*
*fo in a Community.*

*But it will be faid, There is not Imployment for*
*the Hands of the Nation in the Wollen Manufactory ;*
*and fince, Linnen carries away fo much of our Money,*
*it feems the Intereft of the Nation to imploy idle Hands,*
*in that which will keep Money in the Kingdom.*

*Now tho' both thefe Affertions have too much*
*Truth*

[ 5 ]

*Truth in them, yet neither of them have weight e-nough to enforce the Conclusion, That the Linnen Manufactory is the only Remedy. If we search into the Bottom of our Distemper we shall find another cause of our Disease.*

*It is not because there is less Wollen Manufactory used in the World than formerly, that our Trade declines, nor yet because we make more than formerly ; Nor is it altogether to be assigned to the late War : For that our Trade decay'd in the latter part of King* Charles *the Second, and all the Reign of the Late* King. *The Reasons then for our Decay in the Wollen Manufactory seem to be these,*

**1.** *The Growth of Course Wollen Manufactory in,* Germany, *with which the* Venetians *Trade to* Turkey.

**2.** *The Prohibition of our Wollen Manufactory in* France.

**3.** *The Increase of the Wollen Manufactory by our Neighbours with the help of our Wool, so that in some things they out-do us in the Price they can sell at.*

**4.** *By the great Wearing of* East-India *and other Silks, and the Use of* Calicoes, *which was formerly supply'd by our* Tammies *and* Says.

**5.** *The Want of the Consumption of* Ireland, *&c.*

*Now if there be any thing in all I have said, it seems reasonable to consider well ; before the Nation gives up its Staple and long-continued Trade for a Shadow, as I take the Linnen Manufactory to be : For although I believe it can never come to effect, yet so far it may go, as to injure that of the Wollen, by diverting some that are now in it, and so raise the*

B 3                                        *price*

## [ 6 ]

price of Spinning; than which nothing can be more prejudicial; for as I mention'd before, nothing can retrieve our lost Trade abroad, but underselling our Competitors: So then we must labour to make ours as Cheap as we can, and not set up another Manufactory. To bid who gives most for Spinners, is a ready way to ruin the Cloathing Trade of England, but not to set up the Linnen.

Let us consider, besides what hath been said before of injuring the Woilen Manufactory: How it will affect the Kingdom in the two Pillars that support it, That of the Rents of Land, and the Imploying our Ships and Men at Sea; which are thought the Walls of the Nation.

For the Rents of the Land they must certainly fall, for that one Acre of Flax will employ as many Hands the Year round, as the Wool of Sheep that graze twenty Acres of Ground. The Linnen Manufactory imploys few Men, the Wollen most, Weaving, Combing, Dressing, Shearing, Dying, &c. These eat and drink more than Women and Children, and so as the Land that the sheep graze on raiseth the Rent, so will the Arable and Pasture that bears Corn, and breeds Cattel for their Subsistance.

Then for the Employment of our Shipping, It will never be pretended that we can arrive to Exportation of Linnen; there are others and too many before us in that: And the Truth is, he that cannot thrive at his own Trade, will hardly do it in that of anothers. If we are beat out of our Inheritance the Wollen Manufactory by Forreigners, over whom we have such Advantages in our Wool, Fullers-Earth, and long Continuance in the Trade; it can be nothing less than a Miracle, for us to take from them their Linnen Manufactory, in which they have so much the Ascendant over us.

## [ 7 ]

*I shall end this part of my Discourse with the*
*Answer of a West Country Man to his Neighbour,*
*that ask'd, what Voyage he had made in a Fishing*
*at* New-found-land, *that proved not good?* I have
made (*said he*) a brave Voyage, as you may
guess, for I have sold my Bible, and bought a
Tobacco-Box: *Would it not be so to this Nation,*
*if we should change the Noblest Manufactory in*
*the World, for the poorest and most despicable : So*
*are those People in all parts of the World, that are im-*
*ployed in the Linnen Manufactory, which only*
*thrives where the Country is crowded with Poor, and*
*Bread not to be had, at the Charge of the Parish,*
*where the Tenant is but a Vassal to his Lord, and*
*there is no power in any to relieve, but in the Lord*
*who is strange to the Practice. It is a Mistake in*
*them that believe the Linnen Manufactory in* Holland, *to be the Product of their own Country : It is*
*only the easier part, that of Weaving and Whiting,*
*most of the Thread comes from* Saxony.

Thus much for this Author, from whence
we may Conclude, That if the Riches and
Strength of *England,* were first of all begun
from our Wollen Manufacture by King *Ed. 3d.*
and brought to a greater Perfection in the Reign
of Queen *Elizabeth;* we also ought to take the
same care in its preservation : Otherwise we
may be reduced to that mean Condition *Eng-*
*land* was in, when Land and other Commodities
was of no Value, till about the Time of that
Famous Princess Queen *Elizabeth,* whose Long
and Prosperous Reign had raised this Nation
to that Riches and Strength, as elsewhere is
enlarged ; and Sir *Walter Raleigh,* as a Wise
Statef-

## [ 8 ]

Statef-man, and Lover of his Country, ( as many, if not moſt of that Queen's Council were ) had began well to promote *Englands* Intereſt, but was in the Reign of King *James* the Firſt undermined by the Intereſt of *Spain*, which was then ſo prevailing that that unfortunate Knight was taken away.   But in the latter End of that Reign, and the whole of the three Laſt Kings, inſtead of the *Spaniſh* the *French* Intereſt has ſo much prevailed amongſt us, that we are now under the ſad Effects thereof, and that King about the Year 1661. upon a De-ſign he had to have forbidden the Trade be-tween *France* and *England*, ſuppoſing the Va-lue of *Engliſh* Commodities ſent into *France*, did ſurmont the Value of thoſe that were tranſported hither :  The following Particulars were laid before that King. ( *viz.* )

|  | *l.* |
|---|---|
| 1. There were then tranſported out of *France* into *England*, in Velvets, Sattins, Cloath of Gold and Silver, yearly to the Value of | 150000 |
| 2. In Silks, Taffaties, Ribbons, *&c.* to the Value of | 300000 |
| 3. In Silks Ribbonds, Galloons, Laces, Buttons to the Value of | 150000 |
| 4. In Serges, *&c.* to the Value of | 150000 |
| 5. Beavors, Demy-Caſtors and Felt-Hatts, | 120000 |
| 6. In Feathers, Belts, Girdles, Hatbands, Fans, Hoods, Masks, Gilt and Wrought Looking-Glaſſes, Ca-binets, Watches, Pictures, Caſes, Medals, Tabulets, Bracelets, | 150000 |

7. In

[ 9 ]

| | *l.* |
|---|---|
| 7. In Pins, Needles, Box, Combs, Tortoife-fhell Combs, | 020000 |
| 8. In Perfum'd and Trim'd Gloves, | 010000 |
| 9. In Paper, | 100000 |
| 10. Iron-monger Ware, | 040000 |
| 11. In Linnen Cloth, | 400000 |
| 12. In Houfhold-ftuffs, Beds and Hangings, | 100000 |
| 13. In Aqua-Vitæ, Syder, Vinegar, Vergis, | 100000 |
| 14. In Wines, | 600000 |
| 15. In Saffron, Caftle-foap, Honey, Almonds, Olives, Capers and Prunes, | 150000 |
| Befides Five or Six Hundred Veffels of Salt, yearly amounting unto all about | 2600000 |
| And all the Commodies exported hence at that time amounted but to | 1000000 |
| So that by this Act the Ballace on the *French* came to | 1600000 |

Upon which the *French* King foon laid afide his Defign of Prohibition, and inftead thereof increafed the Duties laid upon all our Wollen Manufacture imported into his Dominions, of what was imported in the Year 1654. and 1660. (about which time we exported more Goods, efpecially of our Wollen Manufactures to *France*, then was imported from *France* into *England* in thofe Years. ) But the great Increafe of *French* Commodities imported into *England*, was after the Arrival of King *Charles* the Second. And we may rationally conclude, that the Duties paid to the *French* King when the aforefaid Goods, valu'd at 2600000 *l.* were

ex-

⌈ 10 ⌉

exported, together with the Freight, and what
was paid for Cuftom when imported, as alfo
the Profit to the Merchant and Retailer, and
by the Advance of Price by our Fancies, the
faid Summ of 2600000 *l.* may be rationally
increas'd to 3000000 *l.* fo that the Confumers
of the *French* Commodities advanced the
*French* Intereft and impoverifhed our felves ;
but then after this time in 1662. the
*French* having got vaft Quantities of our
Wool to encourage that Manufacture, greater Duties were impofed on our *Englifh*
Commodities in the Year 1664. and further
increafed in the Year 1667. not only on our
Wollens but on all our *Englifh* Commodities,
even great Duties upon our Shipping, that I
my felf having occafion to go to *Lille* in *Flanders*, could not land at *Dunkirk*, tho' I had no
Commodities in the Veffel without paying Tun-
nage ; but this was not all, but the *French* King
reftrain'd and confin'd the Importation of our
Wollen Manufactures to his Ports of *Callice*
and *Diep*, and other Goods to fome other in-
convenient Ports : By which means, and by
the Encouragement of the Confumption of the
Cloths, Stuffs, *&c.* made by his own People ; it
amounted to a Prohibition of our Commodities in many cafes.

And by the way, it hath been examin'd
that in the Year 1674. or thereabouts ; there
was imported from *France* Silks to the Value
of 300000 *l.* and in Linnen Cloth 500000 *l.*
and Wine and Brandy, 217000 *l.* where
we may alfo Note, that if fuch a Quantity
was legally enter'd, there was fome of all
those

[ 11 ]

thofe Commodities run, as it's called (*viz.*)
Stolen and paid no Duties ; befides all forts
of Lace, when in that Year our Exports to
*France* amounted but to 171020 *l.* and it was
further Obferved, that in the Year 1675.
the Importation of Wine and Brandy was almoft doubl'd of what it was before, and at
the latter End of the Reign of King *James*
it was much more increafed, ( *viz.* ) the Importation of *French* Wine and Brandy.

The great Lofs of the Trade we formerly
had with *France* of near 1500000 *l.* per *Annum*,
which we exported of our Wollen Manufacture
to that Kingdom ; occafion'd that Famous and
Worthy Sir *Matthew Hale*, late Lord Chief
Juftice to fay that our Populoufnefs, which is
the greateft Blefling a Kingdom can enjoy ;
is become the Burthen of our Nation : The
uneafinefs of this Burthen upon us thefe late
Years, hath occafion'd many unufual Remedies
and Attempts, many New Acts of Parliament
in the Reign of King *Charles* the Second, being once mifled, our Uneafinefs made way for
a further Defign upon us, as a Man being out
of his way will be ready to liften believingly
unto almoft any Direction. In the 15th. *Caroli* 2.
there was an Act made for the Encouragement of Trade in its Title, whilft the Body
of the Act was no more, than to encourage
the Exportation of Corn ; ( the low Price thereof being as before, occafion'd by fo many
thoufands want of Employ, and could not
have Money to buy Corn ) and to give Liberty
to carry away our Bullion, which help'd one
ftep forward. In the next Place followed
the

## [ 12 ]

the Act againſt importing Cattle from *Ireland*, which was a Cure like the reſt that led to farther Inconveniencies, this was in the 17th. *Caroli* 2. After which a free Liberty was given to Export Leather, which was in the 20th. of that King's Reign, directly contrary to former Statutes ſucceſſively. And to compleat the whole Deſign, in the 25th. *Caroli* 2. there was an Act made, to take off Aliens Duties upon all Commodities of the Growth, Product and Manufacture of our Nation, except Coals; which fully anſwer'd their End. All the Priviledges of *England* were given away by wholeſale, whilſt all thoſe Acts proved but turnings in a Feavor, which gave ground to the Diſtemper upon us, no way affecting the true cauſe, and this not matter of choice; if any other way propoſed, the Countrey Air was ſoon thought beſt, (*viz.*) the Parliament ſent home, ſuch was our Caſe in thoſe Reigns; &c.

Of which Acts I ſhall by and by more enlarge upon, but to ſpeak more of the Trade of *France* and the Conſequence thereof; for as we loſt the great Advantage that formerly we had by the prohibiting of our Wollen Manufacture in that Kingdom, during moſt of the two laſt Reigns; ſo the unequal Duties laid upon the *German* and *Flanders* Linnens, the Product of our Wollen Manufacture, and by the ſmall Duties laid upon the *French* Linnen, and *Eaſt-India* Calicoes, and Muſlings purchaſed with our Money. This in my Judgment being impartial (*viz.*) (not concern'd in Intereſt) muſt in reaſon be the main Occaſion;

[ 13 ]

fion; at leaft a Foundation for *Germany* and *Flanders*, to encourage the Wollen Manufactury in thofe parts: And it's well Obferv'd by the Author of a little Tract, Intituled, *The Intereft of* England *confider'd*; Printed in the Year 1694. (*viz.*)

*The fine Linnens of* Flanders *and* Germany, *have come in competition thefe many Years with the Calicoes and Muflings of the* Eaft-Indies; *and the fine Dowlace and Gaufes of* France, *one the Effect of our Manufactory, the other of our Bullion, and yet you will find upon the Book of Rates, if I miftake not, all the Linnen of* Flanders *charged with about three pence an Ell Cuftome, and the fine Dowlace of* France *not at one half penny; and the Callicoes of the* Eaft-Indies *but at two pence a piece.*

Now as that unequal Trade was carried on, all the time almoft of the two Late Reigns, fo the Neceffity in the late War in doubling the Duties upon *Flanders* Linnen, which is almoft half the Value of much of their faid Linnen, and the unfeafonable timing of the Lace Act, which did (as was lately affirm'd in a Committee, &c.) occafion a *Flanders* Merchant then in *London*, dealing much in Lace, to go over to *Flanders*, and put the States upon the prohibiting our Wollen Manufacture.

And tho' this occafion'd the faid Prohibition, yet confidering the little Quantity of Lace, at leaft vifibly brought into *England*, in comparifon of the Linnen imported formerly from *Flanders*; cannot be the Original, tho' it may be the Inftrumental Caufe as before hinted.

Hereby it may appear how we have loft our
Trade,

[ 14 ]

Trade, and how infenfibly our Treafure was exhaufted, and our Nation beggar'd, whilft we neglected our own Intereft, and Strangers (fuch as proved our great Enemies) were diligent to make their Advantage by us, but moft of thofe Evils might have been prevented, had we really affum'd our Anceftors regard to our Wealth and Grandeur.

But leaving Particulars let us be more general, for tho' we are agreed, that Trade is the main Spring from whence Riches flow, yet we do as much differ in the Method of acquiring thereof, and there is certainly as much need of Regulation in Trade, as of Laws to fecure one Man's Right from being invaded by another, for it's now become as neceffary to preferve Government, as it is ufeful to make Men rich.

And notwithftanding the great Influence, that Trade now hath in the Support and Welfare of States and Kingdoms, yet there is nothing more unknown, or at leaft that Men differ more in their Sentiments; than about the true Caufes that raife and promote Trade.

The Merchant and other Traders, who fhould underftand the true Intereft of Trade, do either not underftand it, or elfe left it might hinder their private Gain, will not difcover it.

Some Writers about Trade, do in their Treatifes better fet forth the Rule to make an Accomplifh'd Merchant, than how it may be moft profitable to the Nation. And thofe Arguments every day met with from the Traders, feem byaffed with private Intereft, and run
contrary

[ 15 ]

contrary to one anothers, as their Intereſt are oppoſite.

And how fair and convinciug ſoever their Premiſes may appear, for the Enlarging and Advancement of Trade.; the Concluſions of their Arguments, are directly oppoſite.

The Reaſons why many Men have not a true Idea of Trade is, Becauſe they apply their Thoughts to particular Parts of Trade, where-in they are chiefly concern'd in Intereſt; and having found out the beſt Rules and Laws or forming that particular Part, they govern their Thoughts by the ſame Notions in forming the great Body of Trade, and not reflecting tn the different Proportion betwixt the Body ond Parts, have a very diſagreeable Conception; and like thoſe, who having learnt to draw well an Eye, Ear, Hand, and other Parts of the Body, ( being unſkilful in the Laws of Symmetry ) when they join them together make a very deformed Body.

Therefore whoever will make a true Repre-ſentation of Trade, muſt draw a rough Soetch of the Body and Parts together, which though it will not' entertain with ſo much Pleaſure as a well finiſh'd Peice; yet the agreablenesſ of the Parts may be as well diſcern'd, and thereby ſuch Meaſures taken, as may beſt ſuit the Shape of the Body.

The Reaſon why I uſe this ſimilitude, is from the Experience we have of the miſerable Effects we now, and may more hereafter feel of this ſeparate Trades that have been carried on in this Kingdom, (*viz.*) that ſome few Per-ſons gain great Eſtates, when the Nation in general

## [ 16 ]

general decays, as in many Particulars may be
inſtanc'd, (*viz.*) the *French* Trade all the Time
of the two late Kings, that ſuch Merchants
who imported vaſt Quantities ( and ſome that
run their Goods and paid no Cuſtoms ) of
ſuch Commodities that were purchaſed with
Money, and tended to debauch the Nation,
then the *Eaſt-India*, by both thoſe Countries
this Nation hath leſſen'd the Employment of
near Five Hundred Thouſand Perſons, for by
ſuch a Number of Perſons out of Employ, or
double that Number but half Work ; it's all
one the Nation muſt be greatly impoveriſhed
thereby : For before that time when People
were fully imployed, ſome Families could earn
in the Cloathing Trade by ſpinning and weaving Twenty, and ſome Thirty Shillings *per
Week,* tho' ſome leſs, others more; which was
moſt ſpent by them, and laid out with the
Farmer and Graſier, who was thereby better
able to pay their Rents to the Nobility and
Gentry ; by which means the Value of Lands
were kept up, but when ſuch a Number of
Perſons beforementioned had no Employment,
it's not probable the Commodities can be
ſold, which neceſſarily ſunk the Rents of Lands,
and this was the Occaſion of the *Iriſh* Act,
( as that before of Corn ) to prohibit the Importation of Cattle, ſuppoſing that would be
a means to ſupport the Value of Lands in
*England :* But the Miſtake is now ſo manifeſt,
that we have by it loſt a great part of our
Trade, and laid a Foundation to looſe all,
and it was well Obſerved by Mr. *Tho. Manly,*
a Juſtice of Peace in *Kent,* ſhortly after that
A&

[ 17 ]

Act past upon another Occasion about the Exportation of Wool; ( *viz.* ) *If the* Irish *Wool enables the Forreigners to carry on that Manufacture hurtful to us, we have small reason to assist them further, least we imitate those good Men, who break the Pot, because their Wives break the Pitcher, and ruin our selves because* Ireland *hurts us.*

For if it be true, as is by some affirm'd, ( and by Demonstrations made good ) that *England* gain'd by the Trade with *Ireland* before, and in the beginning of the Reign of King *Charles* the Second, Two Millions *per Annum:* It is plain, that Act laid the Foundation of our ruin, for before that Act was in force, the *Irish* contented themselves with Trading only with *England,* by which Trade we received so great an Advantage, but since the *Irish* have been necessitated to seek for a Trade elsewhere, which they have found to be our Loss. And tho' the late Act about the Wollen Manufacture in *Ireland,* was well intended to encourage our own; yet as things now stand, I am not without my Fears that it will not be so advantagious as was expected, and as it might have been done another way : I would be glad if I am deceiv'd in my Fears.

Before I pass *Ireland,* I would crave leave to insert a part of a Discourse writ by Mr. *Andrew Marvyl,* and printed in the Year, 1677. ( *viz.* )

*The fall of Rents, and cheapness of Wool, and decay of Manufacture in* England, *being suggested to be principally occasion'd by* Ireland, *the* Irish *Cattle were the exportation prohibited by an Act of Parliament, and declared to be a publick Nusance.*

C                                           *Ad-*

# [ 18 ]

*Admitting that some of those Counties might* be *be prejudiced by the Importation of* Irish *Cattle, yet whatsoever Profit accrued to others by it, did upon the mutual Necessities of all, settle into* the *Common Stock of the Nation.*

*And it seems but reasonable, that whatsoever private Obligation a Parliament Man hath to the Place where he is Elected; yet when once he comes to sit, his Trust and his Mind is enlarg'd; and he does no more consider himself as the Politician of a Shire, or the Patron of a Burrough, but as a Representer of the Universality: Whereas otherwise, if any County, one or more chance to be more fertile than other in Members of Parliament, and they act by such narrow Measures, the decision would be by Multitude, not by Reason.*

*And notwithstanding if we were to tell Counties, those that are not advantaged and are really agrieved, make the greatest Plea; for if we account like Merchants by Profit and Loss, all the Profit that can be made ( and that very small ) by this Act, returns to such Counties which are proper for breeding, and that small profit is lost to them, if not much more by their Corn for want of Trade by it, and the whole Nation hath hereby lost in great measure, the vent of it's Home and Forreign Commodities to* Ireland, *and the increasing Product to* England *in General, by* Irish *Cattle* in *Specie.*

*But as to the Political Point, you did herein as much as in you then lay, to cut off all that strong a more natural Dependance of* Ireland *upon* England, *and to govern it rather by force of Authority, than by the influential Benignity of Interest. But and I am no Politician, dare say in General, that it concerns you to use us kindly, and to indulge us*

*is*

[ 19 ]

2 all things that tend to *civilize, cultivate, and
people this Nation.*

*Memorandum*, This was written by Mr.
*Marvyl*, under the Notion of a younger Brother
in *Ireland* to an Elder Brother in *England*;
the reason was that it might not be thought
his Writing, because he was not willing to dif-
oblige the *North* Country Members, being his
Friends, they being for that Act.

The next Act was about Leather, the Effect
of which hath leſſen'd the Employment of many
Thouſands in that Manufacture; ſo that Act
hath given Advantage to Forreigners, contrary to the deſign of the ſaid Laws, and more particularly one lately made in the 12*th.* Year
of *Car.* 2. as by the Preamble of that Act may
appear; wherein 'tis Evident that the Deſign
thereof was for,

1. The ſetting on work the Inhabitants of
this Realm.

2. The Improving the Native Commodities of
this Country to it's beſt, fulleſt and utmoſt Uſe.

3. And that the Advantage accrewing hereby, might redound to the Subjects of this Kingdom, and not the Subjects of Forreign Realms.

Wherefore theſe three Deſigns were either
good, and ſufficient Motives for the Prohibition therein expreſt or not; if Good and Sin-
cere, then whatſoever is contrary muſt be to
the prejudice of *England.*

So that if thoſe Acts before-mentioned are contrary to the true Intereſt of *England*, and notwithſtanding have produced Effects contrary to Expectation, we ought to conſider whether it be proper that the ſaid Acts ſhould ſtill remain in force.

C 2 And

[ 20 ]

And then we added another Miftake, up<br>
a Suppofition that if Forreigners had a libert<br>
equal to our *Englifh* Merchants, it would un<br>
avoidably encourage and encreafe Trade; an<br>
therefore Aliens Duties were taken off; th<br>
Effect of which hath, inftead of that, laid :.<br>
Foundation to loofe the Freedom of the *Eng-<br>
lifh* Merchant, and let Strangers into the My-<br>
ftery and Advantage of our Manufacture, as well<br>
as ruin many of the Wollen Manufactures of this<br>
Kingdom, for when thofe Forreigners have got<br>
fome Credit, they have engroffed vaft Quantities<br>
of the faid Manufacture, and then leave the King-<br>
dom: So that all thofe Acts before-mentioned, in-<br>
ftead of promoting have tended to deftroy our<br>
Trade; and had not the late War fellout as it did,<br>
( which occafion'd the Confumption of fo much<br>
Flefh and Corn in the Fleet and Army ) it had<br>
been much worfe than now it is for the Far-<br>
mer and Grazier. Befides the General Decay<br>
of our Trade, which we fhould e're this time<br>
been more fenfible of. I fay again, had not<br>
the War came on at that time, we had not only<br>
loft our Trade, but the Liberty of Free-born<br>
*Englifh* Men.

And now we have Peace ( generally fpeak<br>
ing ) there is much caufe upon another Ac-<br>
count, to be afraid we fhall bring Deftruction<br>
upon our felves by the Methods ufed, now to<br>
promote a forreign Intereft, as we did *France*<br>
in the Two late Reigns; and tho' we are daily<br>
told of onr Danger, yet we will not credit<br>
thofe Cautions given us. Which brings to my<br>
Mind the Hiftory of the *Jews*, who tho' they<br>
were often told of their Deftruction that would

cer-

[ 21 ]

certainly come upon them, if they continu'd
to go on in those ways in which they were then
walking; and tho' this Warning was given
'em with the greatest Compassion that a Man
cou'd exprefs, and all imaginable pains taken to
convince them of the certainty of those Evils
that were coming upon them; yet they rejected all good Counfel, and flighted all the
Reproofs that were given them by their Prophets, until at laft Deftruction came upon
them to the uttermoft, and there was no Remedy.

I would alfo crave leave to inftance in the Cafe
of the *Grecian* Chriftians at *Conftantinople*;
that notwithftanding the many Warnings given
them of the Defigns of the *Turks* againft them;
yet how carelefs and infenfible they were, and
wou'd not make that provifion for their Defence which was required of them, and therefore, the Effects of that Carelefnefs was felt
by them, when the *Turks* came to poffefs that
great City : For at the taking of it by *Maho-
met* the Great, *At which time the Riches of the
Conquer'd was no better than Poverty, and Beauty
worfe than Deformity ; but to fpeak of the hidden
Treafure there found, paffeth credit ; the* Turks
*themfelves wondering thereat : Whereof if fome part
had in time been beftowed upon the Defence of the
City, the* Turkifh *King had not fo eafily taken
both it and the City. But every man ( as now
we here ) was careful how to encreafe his private
Wealth, few or none regarding the publick State ;
( it's ftill our cafe ) until in fine every Man with
his private Abundance, was wrapped together with
his needy Neighbour in the felf fame common Mifery,*

C 3                                            ( and

## [ 22 ]

*( and who knows what may fall out of the same kind*
*hereafter ) yet the security of the* Conſtantinopoli-
tans *was ſuch, that tho' they were always environ'd*
*with their mortal Enemies, yet had they no care*
*of fortifying ſo much as the Inner Wall of the City,*
*but ſuffer'd the Officers, ( which had the Charge of*
*it ) to convert the greateſt part of the Money into*
*their own Purſe.*

I dread to name my Fears, if *England,* which
( for many Generations ) hath been ſo Famous
to all the World, ſhould now be given up to
ruin, and be a prey to our Neighbours, and
thereby a Scorn and a By-word to the World,
by the Evil Practices of it's own Natives;
but were we unanimous and true to our real
*Engliſh* Intereſt, we need not fear all the World;
but on the contrary if we perſiſt in that de-
ſtructive Practice of private Intereſt, what Mi-
ſery may not juſtly be expected by us, when we
are ſo inſenſible of the Train that has been ſo
long laid to blow up thoſe good Foundations,
( which have been ſo many Ages agoe
eſtabliſhed by our Noble Anceſtors ) of all our
*Engliſh* Liberties and Properties : For I know
no Nation under Heaven, as at this Day enjoying thoſe Priviledges we do.

It's thirty Years agoe, there was a Tract
publiſhed, Entituled, *England's Glory :* ( as a
Caution to us againſt the Deſigns of its Enemies ) which I now fear is departing from us.
(I will not ſay as *Phineas's* Wife at the taking
of the Ark, *The Glory was departed from Iſrael* )
tho' I may ſay I fear it. I would not fore-
ſtale Providence, nor anticipate the evil Day,
yet if I could be any ways inſtrumental, to
awaken

**[ 23 ]**

awaken us out of that General Lethargy we are fallen into, I should greatly rejoyce; however, I shall endeavour to quiet an uneasie Mind, by discharging it this way, in giving some Account of that which hath occasion'd my Fears.

This Nation is hitherto own'd a Free People, but how long that Fredom may be enjoy'd no Mortal can conclude; for if we do ( as we ought ) seriously reflect on the condition of most Parts of the World, and more particularly many of our neighbouring Nations, how they have lost their Liberties and Priviledges they formerly enjoyed, and confider how we at prefent are upheld, and the Dangers we are in by our own Folly, and if we did but a little deny our felves, ( tho' fuppos'd ) prefent felf-denial, and really purfue our real and true *Englifh* Intereft ( *viz.* ) if I as a private Perfon or in Company carry on a Trade that may be advantagious to my felf and Company, which may not only be prejudicial to a greater Number, but tend to the deftruction of the whole Kingdom, and peradventure my felf at laft ; I therefore in fuch a cafe ought to deny my felf in my private and fuppos'd profit ; and by this happily preferve the reft from Deftruction : For if through the Lofs of our Manufacture fome Hundreds of Thoufands have no Employ, Hunger breaks through all Laws, we may not forget what happened not many Years fince of the *Weavers* in *Spittlefields*, and if that was fo dangerous in one branch of Trade then failing, and but part of this City of *London* ; what may we

C 4                                    not

## [ 24 ]

not fear, when it ſhall be the General Complaint of the whole Nation; which I fear,
we ſhall be more ſenſible of by feeling, than
by my writing: And tho' at preſent, thoſe
Perſons before-mentioned are ſome of them
remov'd, and others by turning their Hands
another way; which doth and will affect not
only the City of *Norwich*, but the Counties of
*Norfolk*, *Suffolk*, *Cambridge* and *Lincoln*, and
ſome other Counties; yet when it becomes a
General Complaint, I cannot ſee where we
can then have Relief.

I would not Omit the Collection of ſome
Things I obſerve in a ſmall Tract, printed
in the Year 1697. under the Notion of a
Letter to a *Parliament* Man; who ſays,

*I have hitherto given my Obſervations and
Thoughts in general, how all Nations have ac-
quir'd their proportions of Gold and Silver, and
that they have moſt, who depend leaſt on their
Native Product; Art and Labour are the only
Philoſophers Stone, that turns the Product of the
Earth into Gold.*

*You ſee, I have all along in this Diſcourſe ſhewn,
that it is by Labour and Manufacture Bullion
is brought into any Country.*

*Now if this be ſo, then we have that Foundation
left us, by which all the Treaſure of the World is
purchas'd. But if we loſe our Manufactures,
we at the ſame time deſtroy our Navigation, it
being our Manufactures which ſend our Ships
abroad, and they Likewiſe invite them home again
with Oyl and Dying Stuffs, &c.*

*If we make a right uſe of our preſent Exigences,*
*we*

[ 25 ]

we may turn them to the *Advantage* and *En-largement* of our *Manufacture.*

*Necessity* we fay is the *Mother of Invention,* and there feems reafon to believe it will be the *Father of our Riches* ; and if it had no other effect, but to abate our *Forreign Expence,* it might in a few Years fill this *Kingdom* with *Gold* and *Silver* ; it is not commonly confidered, how much faving multiplies *Treafure* : And fure this muft be of mighty *Advantage* to us, when we abate our *Forreign Expence* and encreafe our home, upon that which will bring us in *Bullion.*

*It is faid the Fair Sex are fhewing us the way how to fave and enrich thefe Nations, may they be the Happy Inftruments of doing fo great a Good:*

Vives *in his Book of a* Chriftian **Woman**, tells us, that he heard it reported when he was a *Boy,* that in a *City* of Spain the *Young Men* abounding in Wealth, gave themfelves up to *Excefs* and *Extravagancy,* which the *Ladies* obferving, and forfeeing that it would be the ruin of the *City* ; united in a *Refolution* that they would abate in their own, and defpife and turn their *Backs* on all *Men* that were *Extravagant* and *Gay* in their Cloaths

*The prefent Circumftances we are under, alters not my Opinion which I have given in another place, That the Parfimony of the Rich is the Ruin of the Poor* ; *and in Truth, in fome cafes Damage to themfelves* : But what I fay here of the *Expence* of our *Gentry,* relates to *Forreign Manufactures,* fuch as are more for *Curiofity* than *Ufe* ; and had it not been for our *Excefs* in them, the *Reign* of *King* Charles *the* Second had loaded this *King-*
*dom*

[ 26 ]

dom *with Coin and Bullion: Would it not then be
our greatest Wisdom, to retrieve that in this Reign
that we lost in that ; I mean our Senses
as well as Money; both which run a Tilt
while we exceed our Old Character of being Apes
of Imitation, and become Apes of Invention, our
Great Masters of Trade, sending Patterns for*
Indians *to work out the Money of the Nation from
the Rich, and the Bread out of the Mouths of the
Poor ; perhaps our present Necessities may make us
think : And if we did so, I believe we might yet
be the greatest People for Trade and Navigation
in the World ; and were rightly possest of that, we
need not fear the Power of all the World: Our
Element is the Sea, our Business is there, nor are
we Masters of our Possessions on the Land longer
than we command the Sea, and that is not to be
done only by Ships of War, it is our Fleets in
Trade, that are the Nursery of our Fleets in
War.*

*We are an Original in every thing and that I
take to be our Misfortune, as it might have been
our Happiness ; for certainly no Civilized People in
the World, would make so little of such Inestimable
Funds as we have to work upon; what would the*
Dutch ( *and to our shame, we may now bring in
the* French ) *do, if they had our Mines of Lead,
and Tin, our Fleeces of Wool,* &c. *And to compleat all, an Industrious and Ingenuous People to
manufacture and improve them. Can any one believe the Councils of* Holland *or* France *would
credit a few Merchants and Retailers that should
tell them, notwithstanding these mighty Advantages
you have above the World, you shall sell none of them,
if you will not wear the Livery of the* Indians, *and
that*

[ 27 ]

that you muſt purchaſe with your Money, not with
Commodities ; but them you muſt ſell to all Nations, and having turn'd them into Money ſend it
to the Eaſt-Indies : There muſt certainly be ſome
wonderful Charm in this matter, to make Men
fear that all the Nations in the World will com-
bine againſt us, if we wear not the Manufactures
of the Indies.

Money can no way be brought into the Kingdom, but by the Export of our Manufactures; ſo
that nothing but our ill Conduct can hinder us from
full Supplies of Gold and Silver. We account no
Man poor, that hath Flocks and Herds, tho' he
hath not Money; and the ſame Reaſon holds for
a Country that abounds with Natural and Artificial Commodities, that are as Neceſſary for Forreign Uſe as our Flocks and Herds at home; and
are not for Luxury and Luxurious Effeminate
Expences, but are Utenſils of Life and Society, which
a great part of the World are ſupplied with.

In the Year 1669. was laid before King
Charles the Second an Account, by what ways
the Trade and Riches of England was begun,
and alſo how it was undermin'd, and afterwards at ſeveral times Propoſals conducing to
our Preſervation, was alſo laid before that Prince,
&c.

And in the Year 1677. was publiſhed in
Print by divers Perſons, and more particularly
by Mr. Andrew Marvyl, what Evil Conſequence the Exportation of our Wool to France
was to England; and that there had been for
ſome Years near Twenty thouſand Packs annually imported into the Town of Callice,
                                                                and

## [ 28 ]

and much of it from *Kent* ; that before such
Quantities of Wool were exported, there was
a confiderable Trade of the Wollen Manufacture
in that County ; but it's now almoft loft, and
yet fome Perfons of that Country favouring
the Exportation of Wool, in their Prints feem
to be pleafed, that they have the lefs poor in
their Country thereby ; it's neceffary for fuch
to confider, what they would do with the Sheep
and Bullocks brought up to *London*, if all other
Countries now employed in Wollen Manufacture brought up thither ( which is the grand
Wheel that carries on Trade ) were as much
depopulated as *Kent*.

Give me leave to compare Profit and Lofs,
fuppofe *Kent* was the only County in *England*
which produced Wool, and that 6000 Packs
were yearly grown there, and put the Rate of
10 *l. per Pack*, which amounts to 60000 *l.* and
fo exported rough , but if that Wool was ma-
nufactur'd in *Kent*, and then exported, it would
amount to 720000. fo take out the 60000 *l.*
for the Wool, *Kent* would have gain'd 660000 *l.*
but now *France* hath got it ; and as they have
tafted the fweetnefs, and found the finues of our
Trade, fo they have not fpared any Coft to
gain it from us, by getting our Wool, either
by Craft or Force, for there was not more Art
and Skill ufed by King *Ed.* 3. in bringing home
the Wollen Manufacturers at firft to the Wool,
than hath been of late to export it to *France* ;
the Confequence of which is not only injuri-
ous to us, in the lofs of what we formerly exported of our Wollen Manufacture thither, but alfo by their fupplying Forreign Markets with the
Manu-

[ 29 ]

Manufacture made with our Wool much cheaper
han we, by reason of the cheap Workmanship
in *France*, the which is three or four times the
Value of the Wool ; which if the *French* had not
our Wool, they could not make any confiderable Quantity of the Wollen Manufacture
(*viz.*) Worsted, Stuffs and Stockings, which
is now a Confiderable Part of our Wollen
Manufacture.

But this is not all, but we have been impofed upon by the Confumption of the *French*
Manufactury in our own wearing, all the Reign
of the two late Kings, which was very great
before the late War ; but fince by the great
Encreafe of *Eaft-India* Commodities, the *French*
have been underfold : So that from the whole
matter, we have not only loft a great part of
the Export of our Wollen Manufacture and in
a way to lofe all, but much of the Confumption of our own wearing; the Evil Confequence
of which, I fear we fhall too fenfibly feel, and
to take Notice what is already paft ; as is very
well Obferved by Mr. *Tho. Smith*, in a Tract
printed the laft Year, which he hath alfo publifhed another ; Intituled, *Profit and Lofs*.

As to the Firft, The ruin of the *Tammy* and
*Green fay* Trade, fetled in *Suffolk* and *Norfolk*
for many years, the Ufe of thefe Commodies
was for our Home Confumption, which betwixt Twenty or Thirty Years agoe, the *Eaft-
India* Company brought over fuch Quantities
of *Callicoes* ftain'd, &c. which wholly turn'd
thofe of our Commodities out of doors, not
only the Wear here, but the Export of it to
*Ireland*, *Scotland*, and our Plantations, and the

People

## [ 30 ]

People employed forced to leave their Houses, which standing empty where Tradesmen inhabited, Landlords abating 20 *l. per Cent.* of their Rent, nay, offering large good Houses to any that would keep them in repair, which did also affect the Counties of *Lincoln, Leicester, Northampton,* and *Warwick* by the Fall of the price of Wool at that time.

The next Inftance is in *Spittle-fields,* there was firft the *Walloons,* and fince by the *Englifh* a very large Silk Manufacture fetled, till the *Eaft-India* Company fent Patterns and Workmen unto the *Indies,* and by that means beat the *Englifh* out of that Trade.

A third Inftance is, the *Glocefter-fhire* Cloth exported by the *Turkey* Merchants, which brings home Silk and Grogrin Yarn in return, which by the means of the *Eaft-India* Commodities, the faid Merchants Effects lye upon their Hands, and inftead of Exporting 30000 Cloaths in a Year, now 5000 ferve the turn.

The laft Inftance is, the miferable Condition of the Manufacturers of *Canterbury,* thefe People are Weavers of Silk, the Foundation of which Trade was laid in the time of Queen *Elizabeth,* when the Nobility and Gentry of *England* were in earneft to advance the Nation; when the Trades of *Norwich, Colchefter, London, Exon* and *Canterbury* had their Original, and greatly encouraged: And this of *Canterbury* I fhall particularly mention, what fell out betwixt the Years, 1697, and 1698.

The Traders in *Canterbury* upon fome profpect of Trade, provided Quantities of Goods
for

[ 31 ]

for the *Englifh* and *Weft-India* Markets, but the coming in of *Indian* Damask in the *Fleet Frigot*, the faid *Canterbury* Men were ruined, unlefs they could have metamorphofed their Fabbies, made of very rich *Italian* Silk, that came in Exchange for *Englifh* Serge, into *Indian* Silk; they muft leave Trading, or fell at 30 or 40. *per Cent.* lofs: By which means, half the Workmen of that Town of the weaving Trade, are now running up and down the Nation feeking Bread, and their Families left to the Parifhes to maintain, and the Trade by which that Town hath been upheld for an Hundred Years come to nothing : Thefe are fome of the paft Effects of the *Eaft-India* Trade, with refpect, to the *Englifh* Manufactury; and who fhall pay the Damage ?

The next Thing to be confider'd is, what further Mifchief this Trade may do to the other Manufactures of *England*, and this is to be Evidenced upon what they have begun and tryed upon; and partly upon this Suppofition, that whatever Commodity is made in *England* of Wool, may be imitated, and in many refpects exceeded in *Cotton* manufactured in *India*, and be afforded cheaper than our *Englifh* Tradefmen can afford theirs, and be New and Odd, and fo pleafing, that it will be the Intereft the *Indian* Traders to encourage fuch udes.

They have already brought over great Quantities of double Callicoes, ufed in the room of *Englifh* Flannels for Shifts and other Ufes; befides great Quantities of Cotton Stockings, which are both worn here, and exported to the *Weft-Indies*.                                        As

[ 32 ]

As for Stuffs, they have brought already great Quantities of Cotton Stuffs, dyed, stripped, plain, mixed Colour, in the directest opposition to Wollen Stuffs.

As for Silk and Cotton mixed, it were almost Endless to give an Account how many sorts of *Norwich* and *London* Stuffs, that are made of Silk and *English* Wool, they have imitated and outdone as to Price in Silk and Cotton, but we may Note, that the *New-Drapery* so called is much more than *Old*.

But suppose all those Manufactures should be ruin'd, sure they cannot hurt the Cloth Trade ; say the Agents of the *East-India* Company. In Answer, Why may not a Commodity made of Cotton put down Cloth. Cotton is as fine and soft as Wool, it may be spun as small or as large, it may be mill'd and dress'd dyed and stained, and when the *English* Merchant shall send over Cloth-weavers, &c. I question not but we shall have Cotton Cloth, and Knaves to make it a Fashion, and Fools enough to wear it ; and though those Calamities are upon us, and many more in view, though nothing but employing our People can preserve this Nation; yet that Trade must be free, tho' it brings the Nation in Bondage whereas formerly a Million at least were employed in the Wollen Manufacture, who were Instrumental in distributing near Four Millions *per Annum* for Bread and other Necessaries, which the Graziers and Farmers ( Tenants to the Nobility and Gentry ) received which Persons also did bear part of the Taxes which supported the Government, and there-

[ 33 ]

therefore in all reason one would think, de-
serves Confideration and the greateft Encouragement: Yet on the contrary, we find by
_ll Experience, that many are more fond of
the _Eaft-India_ Commodities than ever; fo that
that is encreafing, as may more evidently appear by a Printed _Lift_, which was this Year
given to the Parliament, of the Number of
Ships fent out and return'd in Two Years laft
paft, with feveral Remarks and Queries, and
Obfervations thereupon; an Abftract of which
I have here recited, and is as followeth.
(_viz._)

That there hath failed for the
Eaft-Indies _and_ China,  52 _Ships_
_fince the_ 10th. _of_ February, 1697.   } 1, 114,923.
_the Account of their Cargo of_ 26
_of their Ships amounts to_

   The Cargoes carried out by the
_Captains_, &c.                          } 111,993.

   Total of 26 _Ships amounts to_   } 1, 226,426.

   Note, By the _Rule of Proportion_,
52 _Ships muft_ carry out, _befides_
_what is taken in at_ Cadiz, _which_  } 2, 452, 852.
_is very confiderable._

Note, Of this great Sum not a 40th. part confifts of our Wollen Manufacture, and that they
find out does prevent a greater Quantity, which
would be fent out by the Turkey-Company; which
would return raw Silk to carry on that Manufacture in England.

            D                    Note,

## [ 34 ]

Note, *That according to the usual Accounts of the Sales by the Candle, the Goods amount to treble the first Cost ; if so, the whole Cargoes brought in will come to* } 7, 388, 55

*These sold by the whole-sale Buyer to the Retailers, allowing* 10 *per* Cent. *Profit to such Whole-sale Buyers comes to* } 738, 855.

*Total Value in the Retailers Hands.* 8, 127, 411.

*Memorandum,* When the Profit the Retailer makes of this great Sum, paid for by the Consumer, must of course encrease the said Sum; which is a Loss to the Nation.

Note, *That by a Computation of our Wollen Manufacture made in* England *in one Year, comes to but and the* East-India *Goods comes to near that Sum by the Rule of Proportion according to their present Trade.* } 4, 850, 558.

*Memorandum,* That in the *London-Gazette* of the 25th. of *January* last, that a Ship belonging to the *French-India* Company is arriv'd at *Diep* from *Surrat*; 'tis said her Cargo is worth near 200000 *Crowns,* and that great part of her Cargo consists in Gold and Silver, which she brought from the Isle of *Bourbon.*

Note,

## [ 35 ]

Note, *The Difference of this Ships Cargo, ours*
*ring over Wrought Goods to the Destruction of*
*our Manufactures, at the Expence of our Silver;*
the French *brings over Gold and Silver, to sup-*
*port their Government and Trade.*

Query, *Whether the Difference may not proceed*
*from the Discouragement, that the* French *put up-*
*on the* East-India *Manufacture some Years since,*
*as appears by the Decree which followeth.*

---

*A* Decree *of the* French *King's* Council
*of State, concerning* Callicoes *printed*
*in* East-India, *or printed in the King-*
*dom, and other* China *and* India *Silks,*
*Stuffs, and Flowered with Gold and Sil-*
*ver : Given the* 26th. *of* October,
1686.

**T**HE King being informed, That the
great Quantities of *Callicoes,* printed
in *East-India,* or painted in the Kingdom, and other *China* and *India* Silks, Stuffs,
and Stuffs flower'd with Gold and Silver,
have not only given Occasion of Transporting
many Millions, but also have diminished the
Manufactures of Old Established in *France,* for
making of *Silk, Wollen, Linen* and *Hemp stuffs,*
and at. the same time the Ruine and Destruction of the Working People, who, by want
of **Work,** having no Occupation, or Subsistence
for their Families, are gone out of the Kingdom ; the which, being needful to provide a
Re-

[ 36 ]

Remedy for, and for that Effect to hinder the
Trade and Sale in the Kingdom of the said
*Printed Callicoes,* and *India* and *China* Silks and
Stuffs, nevertheless granting to the Owners a
reasonable Time to sell them in. Having heard
the Report of Mounsieur *Pelletier,* Counseller
Ordinary of the King's Royal Council, and
Comptrollor General of the Finances; his Majesty, in his Council hath ordered, and doth
order, that from the beginning of the Day
of the Publication of the present Decree, all
the Manufactures established in the Kingdom,
for Painting of the White *Callicoes,* shall be
abolished; and the Moulds serving to the
Printing of them shall be broke and destroyed:
His Majesty doth forbid most expresly the re-
establishing thereof: Also to his Subjects the
Painting of the said *Callicoes,* and to the En-
gravers the making of any Moulds serving to
the said Impressions, under the Penalty of lo-
sing the said *Callicoes,* Moulds and other Uten-
sils, and Three Thousand Livres Fine, to be
paid without Diminution, one third part to
the Informer, the second part to the Hospitals
of the Place, the third to the Farmers of the
of the Revenue. And as concerning the Painted *Callicoes,* and other *China* and *India* Silks,
Stuffs, and Stuffs flower'd with Gold and Silver, his Majesty hath granted, and doth grant,
to the last of *December,* 1687. next, to the
Merchants and others, the permission of selling
them as they shall think fit: The same Time
being expired, his Majesty doth forbid all Persons, of what Quality and Condition whatsoever they are, the exposing and selling thereof;
and

[ 37 ]

and to particulars, the buying therof, doth order, That thofe found in all Ware-houfes and
Shops fhall be burnt, and the Proprietors condemn'd to the like Fine of Three Thoufand
Livres, paid as abovefaid.  His Majefty doth
permit, neverthelefs, the Entry, Sale and Re-
tail, of the faid White *Callicoes* in his Kingdom; paying for them the Taxes according to
the Decree of the Council the 30*th*. of *April*
laft, which fhall be Executed; and that of the
15*th*. of the prefent Month, to the laft of *December*, 1687. laft year.  His Majefty doth command the Lieutenant of the Policy of the City
of *Paris*, and the Intendents and Commiffaries
of the Provinces and Generalties of the Kingdom, to caufe the prefent Decree to be executed,
being publifhed and affixed in all Places
where need fhall be, that no Body fhould
be ignorant thereof.  *Done in the King's State-
Council held at* Fountainbleau. *Signed* Coquille.

*Note*, Several of the *French* Printers fince this
*Edict*, are come over hither, and fet up, and
follow the fame Employment.

*Query*, Whether the Printing of the Silks
and Callicoes in *England*, is not as prejudicial
to us as it was to the *French ?*

*Suitable to this may be well Obferved, fome* Obfervations *of that once Famous* Sir *Jofiah Child.* viz.

THat Wool is eminently the Foundation of
*English* Riches; and that the ways to equa-
lize, or over-ballance our Neighbours, in our
National Profit, by our Forreign Trade, are —
To prevent the Exportation of our Wool, and
en-

[ 38 ]

encourage our Wollen Manufactures : To en
courage thofe Forreign Trades moft, that vend
moft of our Manufactures, and that fupply us
with Materials further to be manufactured in
*England.* [ *Difcourfe of Trade,* p. 127, 156. ]

That its our Intereft, by Example, and other
Means, (not diftafteful) above all kind of Commodities, to prevent, as much as may be, the In-
portation of Forreign Manufactures. [*Pag.* 161.]
That it is multitudes of People, and fuch Laws
as caufe an Encreafe of People, which principally
enrich any Country. [ *Preface.* ] —— That Lands
( tho' excellent ) without hands proportionable,
will not enrich any Kingdom. That whatever
tends to the Depopulating any Kingdom, tends
to the Impoverifhment thereof. [ *Page* 165,
and 167. ]

That it is our Duty to *God* and *Nature,* to provide for and employ the Poor. That fuch as our
Employment is for the People, fo many will our
People be. [ *Page* 56. 174.] —— That it's the Intereft of a Kingdom the Poors Wages fhould be
high; for wherever Wages are high throughout
the whole World, it is an infallible Evidence of
the Riches of that Country ; and where-ever Wages for Labour runs low, its a Proof of the Poverty of that place —— That the Expence of *Forreign
Commodities,* efpecially *Forreign Manufactures,* is
the worft Expence a Nation can be inclinable to,
and ought to be prevented as much as poffible.

*To which may be added a Note of the Obfervation of
the Author of the* Effay *on* Ways *and* Means. *viz.*

T IS evident that our Wollen Goods are fold
in feveral Countries, namely, *Holland, Hamburgh;*

**[ 39 ]**

*burgb, Germany,* the *Hans* Towns, and all the *East* Countries; many of which Places will not be able to take off our Wollen Goods, unless we deal for their Linnens. And in Fact, and by Experience, it has been seen in the Case of the *East-India* Trade, since there has been imported from thence vast Quantities of Linnens, such as *Callicoes, Muslins, Romals* for Handkerchiefs, which answered the ends of *Lawns, Cambricks* and other Linnen Cloth, we have not exported that vast Quantity of Drapery to those *Northern* Parts, of which Sir *Walter Rawleigh* makes mention. As our Call for their Linnens had diminished, their Call for our Draperies has proportionably decreas'd; and not only so, but these People have been compelled by Necessity to fall upon making course Wollen Cloth, by which they supply themselves and other places, which we were wont to furnish.

Note, *That there has been exported to the East-Indies in about 2 Years, almost one third part as much silver as has been coined in* England, *since the Re-coining our Money.*

Query, *Whether it be not as reasonable to send our Money to the* East Countries, *to buy up Corn ( which is very cheap ) to feed us, as 'tis to send it to the* East-Indies, *for Garments to cloath us.*

Query, *Whether it be not as necessary to restrain the Trade in the* East-Indies, *as it was to put a stop to the Exportation of Wollen Manufacture from* Ireland.

Query, *Whether the* East-India *Traders (if not restrain'd) may not in a short time, bring over vast Quantities of Stuffs for Mens Wear, since they have lately imported fin* Cotton Druggets *very fit for that purpose, and sold at Cheap Rates.*

Query,

## [ 40 ]

Query, *Whether the sending above two* Mill. *to the* East-Indies *to make our wearing Apparel, while our own Poor starve for want of Employment, be not a Consideration of great weight and deserve some speedy Remedy.*

I shall therefore, from the whole Matter conclude, that if it be from our Manufacture that the Riches of this Nation come ; and if it be chiefy from thence that our Shipping is employed, and our Marriners bred; if it be from our Trading alone, and from the Riches which it brings, that his Majosties *Customs* are raised ; and that our Fleets have been hitherto built and maintained, and the Dominion of the Seas preserved ; then it is and must be from our Manufactures, that our Bullion has been brought in, and that our Trade hath been encreased, and by which the Rents of the Nobility and Gentry have been advanced.

And therefore, it may be easily granted, that there is no higher Temporal Interest in this Nation, than that which sustains the Nobilities and Gentries Rents ; that which preserveth the Revenues of the Crown, and encreases our Navy and Shipping.

Then in regard our Manufacture doth this, the Encouragement of it must necessarily be the greatest Interest of the Nation to preserve it ; and whoever pretends the contrary, tho' under never so fair Disguises ; do either greatly betray Ignorance of what is *England's* Interest, or plainly prove to be a Promoter of a Forraigners,

*F I N I S.*

# RICHARD WELTON, THE GREAT ADVANTAGES OF NAVIGATION

Richard Welton, *The Great Advantages of Navigation and Commerce to any Nation or People: Represented in a Sermon Preach'd at Deptford before the Right Honourable the Corporation of the Trinity-House, on Trinity-Monday, 1710* (London: S. Manship, 1710). British Library, shelfmark 694.e.9.(6.).

Richard Welton (1671/2–1726), a clergyman of the nonjurist Church of England, was born at Framlingsham, Suffolk. At the time he wrote the tract included here he was rector of St Mary's at Whitechapel in London, where he served from 1697 to 1715. As a supporter of the controversial London minister Henry Sacheverell, Welton in 1710 gave a sermon in which he root and branch attacked what he regarded as the prevailing conformism of the country and spoke in favour of an absolute monarchy. He was accused of holding Jacobite views and in a sermon of 1714 he spoke of the name Stuart as 'the glory of our country'. As a consequence he had to leave all his clerical positions, and moved to a nonjuring congregation at Whitehall, London. In 1717 one of his meetings, where 250 people were gathered, was raided by government agents. In 1724 Welton emigrated to America, where he was appointed rector of Christ Church in Philadelphia.

In his views Richard Welton was hardly a 'mercantilist writer' of the ordinary type (to the extent we can find any), nor was he a consultant administrator or merchant. He wrote extensively on religious matters, but also held definitive views on economic subjects.[1]

The message of this sermon is that trade and navigation can make a nation rich and powerful, and it combines religious language with a civic humanist message. However, trade can also be lost – just like in classical Tyrus – if it is carried out without virtue, that is to say without the common good as a general goal. Moreover, it can also be lost if we rebel against God and true religion in succumbing to pride and self-righteousness. We can also note the viewpoint put

---

1    For more information, see the entry on Welton in *Oxford Dictionary of National Biography* (Oxford: Oxford University Press, 2004), written by Richard D. Cornwall.

forward here of a 'natural' division of labour between different countries, without doubt laid out by God at creation.

*The Great Advantages of* Navigation *and* Commerce *to any Nation or People:*

Reprefented in a

# SERMON

Preach'd at

## *DEPTFORD,*

BEFORE

The Right Honourable

# The Corporation

OF THE

# TRINITY-HOUSE,

On *Trinity-Monday,* 1710.

---

Publifh'd at the Requeft of that Honourable Body.

---

By *R. WELTON,* D. D. Rector of *White-Chappel.*

---

*Quæ Regio in terris veftri non plena Laboris?*

---

*LONDON :* Printed for *S. Manfhip,* at the *Ship* againft the *Royal Exchange* in *Cornbill,* 1710.

## To the Right Honourable

# The Master, Wardens, Assistants, and Elder Brethren,

### O F  T H E

# *Trinity-House* of *Deptford-Strond,*

Right Honourable,

IN *Answer to Your Commands, I once more present You with the following Discourse: And indeed it is entirely with Submission thereto that I presume to do it ; being very sensible that it must needs fall short of what the Subject does require :* 'Tis not to be imagin'd that both Sea *and* Land *can be incompass'd within the narrow Limits of an Hour's Confinement.*

*However, if I have, in any Measure, answer'd the Great End ; that which ought to be the main Design of all Our Labours, viz. the Encouragement and Promotion of* Good *; If by setting, the Useful, the Glorious Works for which You are so Eminent, in a true and proper Light, I have represented to Your Country how happy they are through Your Service ; and therefore how much they ought to Bless that God that has Bless'd and Prosper'd You, I cannot but own that I readily Publish what I had the Honour to Preach before You.*

　　　　　　　　　　　　　　　'Tis

# The Dedication.

'Tis certain that, under God, You have been the Support, and Instrumental to the Glory of this Nation, which otherwise must have been long ere this time sunk under the severe Influences and Oppression of so tedious and devouring a War: 'Twas You that supply'd this Body Politick with new Strength and Vitals; and so constantly repair'd its Decays with fresh Blood and Life.

May You have the Blessing to be still Promoting the Honour and Interest of Your Country! May You never meet with any Discouragement of Your Merit! And may those who understand not, who have no Light into, what You have been Bred up to, the Misterious Traces of Your Noble Profession, may these never be set over You in Honour, become Remora's to Your Ships, and, indeed, Impediments to Your Enterprizes and Adventures.

And may Your more Private Services of the Publick, Your Well-disposed Necessary Hospitalities, prepare that Everlasting Entertainment for You, at that Heavenly Feast at the Resurrection of the Just. These are the Hearty Prayers of,

Right Honourable,

Your Devoted

Humble Servant,

R. Welton.

I

# E Z E K. xxvij. 33.

*When thy Wares went forth out of the Seas,*
*thou filledst many People ; thou didst enrich*
*the Kings of the Earth with the multitude*
*of thy Riches, and of thy Merchandise.*

IN the foregoing Chapter, we have the Prophet *Eze-kiel* beginning his terrible Denunciation against the Famous City of *Tyrus* : A City very Confiderable for the Commodioufnefs of her Havens, and the Multitude of her Ports; for the Riches of her Traffick, and Greatnefs of her Merchandife.

Her Scituation was upon a Rock in the *Mediterranean* Sea ; by the Convenience and Advantage of which fhe became the moft Eminent Mart and Empory of the then known World : Her Warehoufes were a Map of the Univerfe ; her Shops a Compendium of all Nations : So that within her Walls one might fee the Creation drawn in little, that is, the Growth and Product of all Lands that were then difcover'd.

Yet this Rich and Glorious City, for her Abominations, is threatned with Vengeance and Deftruction from Heaven ! God tells her that He would difmantle her Strength, and flain her Glory. *I am against thee, O Tyrus,* Chap.26. 3,4. *faith the Lord God, and will caufe many Nations to come against thee ; and they shall deftroy the Walls of Tyrus, and break down her Towers: I will fcrape her Duft from her, and make her like the top of a Rock : i. e.* I will leave no Momument nor Memorial of her ; not one Stone upon another that fhall not be thrown down ; fo that the Rock on which thou art built fhall be again as bare as it was before thy Foundation And that fhe might the better fee to what a low Condition fhe was to be reduced, the Prophet in the 27th Chapter fhews her from what a

B                                    Height

Height fhe was to fall : For, from the beginning of it to the 26th Verfe, he fets forth the Honour, Wealth, and Beauty, of her profperous Condition, that fo he might the more fully reprefent the Greatnefs of thofe Calamities that *Nebuchadnezzar* would bring upon her, which he doth from the 26th Verfe to the end : In the clofe of which he brings in the Seamen and Pilots taking up a Lamentation to bewail the Miferies and Downfall of this Potent City; of which Epicedium my Text is a part. And this is of the fame Nature and Argument with the defign of the whole Chapter : For here, the Mariners, that they might fet forth the Horrour of her Deftruction, do likewife make mention of the Happinefs fhe enjoy'd in the former Times of her Trade and Commerce. *When thy Wares,* fay they, *went forth out of the Seas thou filledft many People, thou didft enrich the Kings of the Earth with the multitude of thy Riches, and of thy Merchandife.*

Having already, in my laft Difcourfe before this Honourable Affembly, reprefented the Wonders of God upon the great Waters, and therein exprefs'd the particular Engagements which thofe of the Navigable Profeffion lay under, from the Inftances of the Divine Providence peculiar to themfelves ; it is but requifite that I fhould make ufe of this Occafion, to reprefent likewife in as juft a Meafure to the World, the great Obligations that lye upon them to God upon your Accounts ; which I had but juft time to mention, when I had laft the Honour to fpeak before you. And in order hereunto, nothing will be more proper, that I know of, than for me, in the Firft Place,

I. To Confider the Great Ufefulnefs of Merchandife and Traffick in General : My Text tells us, that *it fills many People, and doth enrich the Kings of the Earth.*

II. Confider we likewife the Great Profperity and Benefit that it brings to thofe *Cities* and *Kingdoms* that are Skill'd and Practic'd in it. 'Twas this made
*Tyrus,*

## of Navigation, &c.

*Tyrus*, fo Renown'd a City, that fhe is here faid to *Enrich the Earth with the Multitude of her Riches, and of Merchandife.*

III. And in the Laft Place, for all our Admonition, I will fhew the Reafon, what it was that provok'd God to bring Deftruction upon *Tyrus*, that we avoiding the Caufe, may not become fo fad an Example to others, as fhe was to us.

I. Then I will Confider the Great Ufefulnefs of Merchandifing and Traffick in its General Influence. *Tyrus* is faid to *fill many People with her Wares that fhe fent out to Sea* ; and to *Enrich the Kings of the Earth with the Multitude of her Riches and Merchandife.* She was not only a Wealthy Opulent City in her felf, but of general Profit and Advantage to all the Neighbouring Countries ; fhe is therefore ftiled in the 3d Verfe of this Chapter, the *Merchant of the People for many Ifles.*

It was to her *Jerufalem* ow'd the Beauty and Statelinefs of *Solomon's* Temple ; 'twas from *Tyrus* they had all their Chief Artificers ; and from *Hiram's* Navy their Gold and Almug-trees that made That Glorious Structure, *The* 1 Kings 10. *beauty of Holinefs, and the Praife of the whole Earth.* 11, 12.

Neither was this City of *Tyrus* only Ufeful, by her Traffick, to the *Jews,* * but to *Dedan,* and to *Raamah,* * *Olim pro tu* and *Sheba,* and *Chilmad,* and *Haran,* as we find from *clara bibliu* the 20th, 22d and 23d Verfes of this Chapter ; *i. e.* in *Genitus, &o.* their Modern Names to *Arabia Felix,* and *Armenia,* and *Plin.* *Media,* and *Mefopotamia,* and to almoft all Places that Traded either upon the *Mediterranean* or *Red Seas.* Indeed, It was to *Tyrus,* and fuch other Cities given to Trade and Commerce, that we owe the Ufeful Art of Navigation, that has been fo remarkably Improv'd by our *Englifh Drakes, Columbus's,* and more ftill by *YOU,* whom Chronicle muft never be fo *difhoneft* as to forget : *They* firft Invented, and left it to your Predeceffors to be Improv'd, but to be *perfected by Your Selves.*

Thus the *Tyrians,* and their Neighbours the *Sidonians,* are therefore faid to be the firft that ever fet out a Ship to

B 2 Sea,

**4** *The Great Advantages*

* *Prima Ratem Ventis credere dicta* Tyrus.
Tibullus.
Ταΰς ᾗ Σιδρίνς Τελχεστρ ναΰς χςτασχνάσρυς *Clem. Alex.*

Sea, according to * that Poetical Historian; to which Scripture it self seems to add some Confirmation: For even in the Days of *Solomon* we find them such Expert Mariners, that it is said *Hiram* sent in the Navy *his Servants, Ship-men that had Knowledge of the Sea, with the Servants of Solomon,* 1 Kings 9. 27.

And as they were the first Inventers of this Art, so they were Towns and Places given to Merchandise, that afterwards did very much Improve it.

Thus the *Grecians,* that lay so Commodiously upon four Seas, and had so many fair Ports and Havens, and Trading Towns, made many Additions to this Art: The *Bœotians,* we read, Invented the Oar; the Men of *Crete,* the Masts and Sails; the *Tuscans,* the Anchors; and the *Neapolitans* of *Malphi,* the Compass, which was afterwards perfected at *Antwerp.*

And as Traffick was the Parent of Navigation, so by the means of this the greatest Advantages of all sorts have succeeded to Mankind; and particularly these, *viz.* 1. The Supply of the Wants and Necessities of every Country. 2. The Advancement of Learning and Civility that have hereby been spread. And 3. The Propagation of *the most Holy Religion of Jesus Christ,* that hath hereby been diffus'd and made known through the whole World.

1. Then Merchandising is of Great Use, as it is the only way of supplying the Wants of all Places or Countries. Indeed there is no Nation so absolute of its self, but is capable of receiving an Advantage by Commerce; God having not laid up all the Treasures of his Providence in one Place, but has given to every Country its particular Blessings, that so there might be a Mutual Dependance of the several Parts and Kingdoms of the World upon one another.

Therefore we find by that Map of Commerce, set down in this Chapter, that *Tyrus* had one sort of Wares from one place, and another sort from another.

* Ver. 12.  From * *Tarshish* her Silver, Iron, Tin and Lead; from
† *Javan,*

† *Javan, Tubal,* and *Mesech,* her Vessels of Brass; from † Ver. 13.
* *Judah* and *Israel,* her Wheat of *Minnith,* her Honey, * Ver. 17.
Balm, and Oyl; and from † *Damascus,* the Wine of *Hel-* † Ver. 18.
*bon* and white Wooll. So that they had not one fort of
their Commodities from all, nor all of 'em from any one
of these Places.

So admirably indeed hath God difpenced the Bounty of
his Hand, that thofe Countries that have the leaft fhare of
the Sun's Rayes, have fomewhat yet Peculiar to them to
make 'em Ufeful, that they may not be forfaken, and left
Unaffifted by the Reft of the World : Upon which Account God has alfo left fome Imperfection even in the moft
Affluent and Fruitful Places, fo that they might want and
ftand in need of the Affiftance of the Produce, even of the
moft Naked, Barren, and Remote Places.

This was the Occafion and Foundation of Navigation
and Commerce; which is the great Band that ties all the
parts of the World together : This like the two Hemi-
fpheres unites all into one Globe, that we might all, as
Members of this great Body, take Care one of another.

So wonderfully indeed are all Parts of the Univerfe
fram'd and fet together, that we may well conclude this
Point, with that holy Admiration of the Pfalmift upon the
like Subject, *O Lord, how manifold are thy Works! In Wifdom haft thou made them all! The Earth is full of thy Riches!
So is the great and wide Sea alfo alfo, wherein are things in-
numerable—— There go the Ships,* &c.

2. To Commerce and Traffick in general we owe, in a
confiderable meafure, the Advancement of Learning and
Civility, hereby promoted : Learning and Civility do
ufually travel together ; and that Nation that receives the
one, cannot well exclude the other ; it being almoft as
impoffible for a Man to be a Scholar and a Salvage, as it is
to be a Vicious Perfon and a true Chriftian.

Learning therefore wherever it came, as it enlightened
Mens Underftandings, fo it polifhed their Manners ; bettering their Demeanour, as it enrich'd their Souls.

Thus we find the Account of *Mofes,* that as *he was
brought up in all the Learning of the Egyptians,* fo he was
one

one of the *Meekeft* and beft Temper'd Men upon the Earth.

Indeed, all the chiefeft and nobleft parts of Human Literature do tend to * the teaching of us the Government of our Appetites and Paffions, and the raifing of our Minds above low and contemptible things ; and this muft needs fmoothen and civilize any Temper.

* ————*Ingenuas didiciffe fideliter Artes Emollit Mores, nec finit effe feros.* Ovid.

Now for the Advancement of thefe two Things, fo great in themfelves and fo advantagious to Mankind, we are beholding to *Phænicia*, of which *Tyrus* was a City: That was the firft Kingdom in the World that was remarkable for Shipping, that invented Letters and propagated Learning : It was * *Cadmus* the *Phænician* that taught *Greece* her Alphabet; and found out that which *Galileo* ftiles † the choiceft of all Human Inventions.

Κάδμ⊙ ϛ ϣιντῆ ἐ ϑ ϑ γεϱμα μαιτικῆς Ἑλλμων Ἑυϱετᾶς. *Clem.* *Alex. Strom.* Lib. 1. p. 311.

† *Admirendarum omnium Inventionum Signaculum.*

Indeed it can hardly be exprefs'd how much Learning ow'd and was beholding to him, who firft taught us to draw the Sentiments of our Minds upon Paper, and to make a Thought vifible, and a wife Saying to laft to the World's end; to reduce all Voices to twenty-four Characters, and to exprefs all Sounds with the Draughts of a Pen.

Thefe two Miraculous Arts of Characters and Navigation were the Inventions of * that happy Nation; but without the latter, the former had been of little Ufe.

* *Ipfa Gens Phœnicum in Gloria Magna Literarum Inventionis & Siderum, Navalium, &c.* Plin. *Nat. Hift.* T. 1. l. 5. c. 12.

Thus we fee then, The Ships that put to Sea, like thofe Stars that direct 'em in their Voyage, work for a General Good; and like *them*, not only conduce to the Plenty, but alfo to the Enlightning and Adorning of a Kingdom.

Thus Learning, like the Church in the Ark, hath been both propagated and preferv'd by her Watry Pilgrimage, whilft the Light of our Knowledge, like *that of Nature*, hath feem'd to *arife from the Sea.*     It

It is then to our Navigation and Commerce we owe, that we do not like the Ancient *Picts* and *Britains*, the Original Natives of this Island, neither understand Learning nor Civility, being equally naked both in their Souls and Bodies : It is to this we owe, that we do not, like our Barbarous Ancestors, offer up Human Sacrifices, and *our Sons and Daughters unto Devils.* Or that we do not, like the Men of *Florida*, eat those Strangers that visit our Shores : It is to this we owe that we have Excellent Laws, a well Constituted Government, and such famous Nurseries of Learning in our Land ; and above all, *A way of Worship and Religion : A Church so Pure and Heavenly in its Institutions and most Sacred Ordinances,* that tho' indeed it has gone through many a bitter Storm of *Persecution*, yet God, at *the Expence of Miracles,* has still preserv'd it ; and if our own Lukewarmness and Hypocrisy do not provoke Him unto Judgment, we doubt not but He will still make your Ships as a Wall of Brass to secure and defend us.

These are the Noble, these the Glorious Advantages we owe to your Profession ! It was Navigation, Merchandising and Commerce, brought Learning from * *Phœnicia* to *Greece*, from thence to † *Rome*, and from thence by degrees to us.

How thankful then ought we to be to *the Father of Lights, the giver of every good and perfect Gift,* that through Your Means we live not still as Men *without God in the World ;* that we fall not at this present time under that sad Description of the *Gentiles* given by St. *Paul ;* that God hath not given us over *to a Reprobate Mind ;* that we are not without Understanding, without Natural Affections ; *i. e.* that the Light of the Gospel is not hid from us, but that we have been enlightned into the Knowledge of a Christ, and that the Promises of Salvation have been brought over and

revealed

Ἑλληνας ἢ καὶ Φοινίκων. *Clem. Alex.*

* Phœnices *primum Mercaturia & Mercibus suis magnificentiam & inexpl. biles cupiditates omnium rerum importaverunt in* Græciam. *Vid.* Chap. 4. Lib. 12.

† *Ad hunc modum dicatur Terra omnium Terrarum Alumna, qua Cælum ipsum clarius faceret, Ritusq; molliret, & tot Populorum discordes ferasq; Linguas Sermonis Commercio contraheret ad Colloquia & Humanitatem Homini daret.* Plin. Nat. Hist. T. 1. lib. 3. c. 5.

revealed to us; and we have been directed in the *Ways of Pleasantness and Everlasting Peace.* This brings me to consider :

3. The great Excellency and Usefulness of your Vocation, as it hath in its General Influence been highly Serviceable in the Propagation of the Gospel. The bringing to us this *Pearl of great Price* was worth all its other Advantages ; this was its greatest Honour, the transcending Glory of all that You have done : For *what is a Man profited if he shall gain the whole World, and lose his own Soul ? Or what can he give in exchange for his Soul?* Not all the Wealth of the *Indies* ; nor all that Glorious Prospect the Devil presented our Saviour with, *the Kingdoms of the Earth with all their Glories,* can make amends for that Loss, or counter-ballance that Exchange ! Had we all the Riches of the World flowing in upon us without *the Means of Grace,* we should be but the meanest Slaves, whilst *led Captive by the Devil at his Will.*

St. *Paul's* Ship therefore, in which he carried about the Gospel, carried a far Richer Cargo with it, than that celebrated one of *Jason,* that brought the Golden Fleece from *Colchis.*

Happy it was for this Isle, that *Joseph of Arimathea* found a *Bark* to Transport him hither for our first Conversion ! Happy was it that our Children were sold Slaves in the *Roman* Markets, and that there were Ships to bring over St. *Augustine* for our Second : Without this we had been without Christ ; *Aliens to the Commonwealth of Israel, and Strangers from the Covenant of Promise, having no hope* : But by this Means, what was transacted at *Palestine* becomes ours ; and though we are not the Keepers of the Holy Sepulchre, yet we are Partakers of the Resurrection !

The Voyages of the Apostles were far more beneficial to the World than the fam'd Discoveries of *Columbus, Cabot,* and the rest : For they discovered but Earth, but these *Heaven, Immortality,* and *Glory.* And if the *Royal Psalmist* so valued *Israel* upon the account of that weak glimmering Light that they enjoy'd during the Institutions

tions of *Moses*, faying, that *God had not dealt fo with any Nation, neither had the Heathen knowledge of his Laws*; how ought we to efteem *ours,* that have *Life and Immortality brought to light through the Gofpel ?*

Since the Sun of Righteoufnefs then, like the Natural Sun, hath taken his Courfe towards us from the Eaftern Countries, let us take heed, left by our Difobedience and Unfruitfulnefs under his kind Influences, we do not caufe him, *like that,* to *fet* upon the more Weftern Shore, and leave us, for the Abufe of our Light, in final Darknefs !

And that we may prevent fo direful a Prognoftick, let us take St. *Paul's* Advice, in the 4th to the *Ephefians, That ye walk not henceforth as other Gentiles walk, in the Vanity of their Mind ; having the Underftanding darkened, being alienated from the Life of God, through the Ignorance that is in them, becaufe of the Blindnefs of their Heart : But that ye put off the Old Man which is corrupt, according to deceitful Lufts ; and be renewed in the Spirit of your Minds ; and that ye put on the New Man, which after God is created in Righteoufnefs and true Holinefs.* But,

II. I proceed now to the Second Obfervation I propofed from my Text, *viz.* Of the great Benefit and Happinefs in particular, that Commerce and Navigation bring to thofe Cities and Places where it is induftrioufly follow'd and made ufe of.

It is a General Maxim among the *Jews*, That He that breeds not his Son up to fome Calling, teaches him to be a Thief : And well is the Suggeftion enforced, becaufe nothing but Beggary and Vice ufually follows upon Idlenefs, and want of Bufinefs.

'Tis Trade and Employment that hath Rais'd all the Great and Flourifhing Cities in the World : 'Tis this fets every one to Work, and then there is no Complaining in the Streets.

Hence it is that Trade and Commerce hath been fo much the Care of Princes, that they have cherifh'd it as their beft Friend, and ftrongeft Allie : And many have

C            follow'd

follow'd Merchandising themselves, growing more Great by that, than the Sovereignty of their Crowns.

Had not *Solomon* kept a Fleet at Sea, he had never been as Famous for his Riches as for his Wisdom ; neither had he ever had that Great Character of his Magnificence, 2 Chron. 9. mention'd of him in the Book of the *Chronicles, That his* 20. *Drinking Veffels were of Gold, none of Silver ; becaufe in the days of Solomon that was not any thing accounted of.*

But more especially, the Truth of this Obfervation will appear, if we confider, Firft, How much this contributes to the Enriching of that City or Kingdom where 'tis followed. Secondly, How confiderably it advanceth the Strength and Potency of a People. And Thirdly, How it promotes the Honour and Reputation of a Place.

1. The Happinefs and Profperity of every Place is advanced highly by Commerce, where it is follow'd ; by that Riches and Wealth that it brings in for the Good and Advantage of that Place where a Staple is fettled : Without Riches a State cannot fupport it felf, nor appear confiderable to others : Thefe are the Sinews of War ; and Antidotes againft murmuring in Times of Peace. Its Pay makes the Soldier daring ; and when Peace and Plenty go together, it keeps Men from finding Fault with the Government. Whereas the *Melancholly of Debentures caft a damp upon the Publick* ; and indeed the Happinefs or Mifery of a Nation have a great Dependance upon fuch Prognofticks.

Now how much Merchandife and Commerce tend to the Enriching of a City, may very well be feen by this City of *Tyrus* : For though she was * * Tyrus *quondam Infula pra-* Built, as we are told, upon a Barren *dto mari Septingentis paffibus di-* Rock in the Sea, about feventy paces *tifa.* Plin. *Nat. Hift.* T. 1. lib. from the main Land ; though she had 5. c. 19. nothing of her own Growth, but her Zech. 3. 9. Induftry ; yet the Prophet tells us, that *She heaped up Silver as the Duft, and fine Gold as the mire of the Streets.*

Indeed,

## of Navigation, &c.     11

Indeed, if we confider the Goftlinefs of her Ships, and the Sumptuoufnefs of her Naval Furniture, we may well conclude her to be what one * ftiles her, *Urbs omnibus* *Strab.* *ditiffima*, a City Enrich'd to a fuperlative degree, with all forts of Treafure and Abundance.

And of this we have an Inventory in the beginning of this fame 27th Chapter of *Ezekiel* ; * *Her Ship-boards* * Ver. 5. *were of the Fir-trees of Senir, her Mafts of the Cedars of Lebanon.* † *Her Benches,* which the *Septuagint* renders † Ver. 6. her * *Cabbins, were made of Ivory by the Afhurites,* the ̓Οικος ἐλ moft Curious and Skilfol Workmen. * *Her Sails were* * Ver. 7. *of the fine Linnen of Egypt ; Her Ship-cloath of blue and purple,* the moft coftly Silks that were then in ufe. And how much fhe abounded in Wealth, thefe Inftances may ferve for a fufficient Proof.

But befides all this, the very tendency of Commerce leads to Gain by fetting Men to work ; by encouraging of Manufactures ; by venting of Commodities, and bringing a Return of all Things neceffary ; by fharpening of Mens Inventions, rewarding their Diligence, and exciting of Labour ; all which Things are the Parent of Profperity, and the Means by which all Men compafs an Eftate.

And therefore we have this fet down as the ufual Method of obtaining Riches, in the Wife Man's Difcourfe of the Vertuous Woman : He tells us, that *her Candle* Prov. 31. *goeth not out by Night ; that fhe layeth her Hands to the* from the 10th *Spindle, and her Hands hold the Diftaff ; that fhe maketh* Verfe to the *fine Linnen and felleth it, and delivereth Girdles to the* end. *Merchants :* And what the Effects of this Induftry and Diligence is, he tells us in the fame Chapter. *Her Houfehold is cloathed with Scarlet ; fhe confiders a Field, and buyeth it.*

2. This will further appear, if we confider how much Commerce adds to the Strength and Power of thofe Cities and Countries where its followed

He that Commands the Seas will eafily be Mafter of any Kingdom. They are not vaft Tracts of Land that raife

Empires; but Scituation, accompany'd with Navigation and Commerce. It's this enables a People to give Laws unto the World, and to extend their Dominion to what part of it they please : It's by this all the Difficulties of Distance are overcome; and Men are brought up to endure Hardship, and to despise Danger.

*Carthage*, though she was but an inconsiderable City in respect of *Rome*, which was at that Time the Metropolis of the World ; yet upon the account of her Skill in Navigation and Commerce, she disputed for that Title so briskly with her, that she could not have kept it long, had not *Rome* likewise grown Confiderable at Sea, and so beat *Carthage* by her own Art and Strength.

What was it that made our Ancestors so much Fear'd Abroad, and so Secure at Home ? But our Ships, those Walls and Bulwarks of our Nation ; without which we are but Prisoners in our own Island, and a Prey to every bold Invader !

*Nebuchadnezzar*, that Mighty Prince, stiled in the 7th Verse of the foregoing Chapter, *A King of Kings*, with all his Vast and Numerous Army, was no less than Thirteen Years a taking of this City *Tyrus*; so Strong, so Powerful, had her Trading and Navigation made her.

Indeed if it were not so ; If it did not make Strong those Places it makes Rich, it would but the more eminently expose them ; But doing Both, It very highly conduces to the Happiness of *that* City or Kingdom where it is follow'd.

3. The Truth of my Obfervation is yet more evident, as Commerce raises the Dignity, and advances the Honour of any City or Kingdom.

In the 23d of *Ifaiah*, ver. 8. this very *Tyrus* is call'd *the Crowning City* ; Her Riches and Atchievments abroad ; Her planting of Colonies in *Greece* and *Africk* ; the extraordinary Wealth and Grandeur of her Citizens, made 'em to be Reverenc'd and Respected, *as it is this Day with the Respective Individuals of this Eminent, this Honourable Body before whom I am,* among all the potent
Trading

## *of Navigation,* &c.          **13**

Trading Nations, even from *the uttermost parts of the Sea unto the Worlds end.*

For as it is Vertue derives Efteem upon Perfons, fo it's Power, Ufefulnefs, and a Prudent Management of Affairs, that makes even a Kingdom to be regarded and accounted of ; which Advantages, whatever place enjoys, It chiefly owes them to Commerce and Navigation.

Indeed, without Honour and Reputation a Kingdom cannot be compleat : It's *this* enables them to all their beft and moft neceffary Undertakings : Without *this* their *Alliance* would not be efteemed, Men could not make Leagues, or fafely have any Intercourfe with them.

But by Commerce the *Jus Gentium,* the Law of Nations, that binds all Men under an Obligation of Honour and Truft, was chiefly invented and fpread through the World.

But befides this ; If the Pains of Learned Men can reflect Honour upon the Country where they were Born and Live ; If the Valour of the Soldier can plant a Crown of Laurel upon the Head of the Prince for whom he ventures his Life, and fo earneftly contends ; Why fhould not thofe who Traffick upon the mighty Waters, who take *greater Pains, run greater Rifques, fhew greater Refolution than any fort of Men whatever,* why not They confer greater Honour likewife upon their Country and themfelves!

For if Honour be a juft Due to all painful and dangerous Actions, undertaken for the Publick Good ; if Nobility hath ever had its Foundation from Courage and Valour, and bold Sallies in what they undertake ; then certainly, Thofe, Eminent, as You are, in a Profeffion the *moft Dangerous and Uncertain,* and that requires *almoft perpetual Miracles* in its Support, have a juft Right to lay as great a Claim to it as any : For You ftrive not only with Men, but fometimes with the whole Four Elements together, which is the ftrongeft Proof that can be, of the moft *Generous Courage and Invulnerable Refolution.*

Methinks

Methinks the *Pfalmift* very excellently deſcribes this : *They mount*, ſaith he, *up to Heaven*; *They go down again to the Depths*; *Their Soul is melted becauſe of Trouble* : They have nothing left them for their Help, but only their Prayers; *they cry unto God*, and then He, by the ſecret, unfathomable Operations of His Power, corrects the pride, and quells the angry uproar of the Storm, and conducts them ſafely where they deſire to be.

Theſe are ſome of the Inſtances that meritoriouſly challenge the grand Characteriſtick of *Honourable* a-mong You, and tempts thoſe, even of the *Worthieſt* and moſt. *Noble Extract*, to add to their own Quality by be-ing Incorporated into Yours : And certainly, a Body ſo eminently Compos'd, in whom there is ſo adapt a Mix-ture of Native and Acquired Honour, muſt needs an-ſwer, as You do, the Great Ends of Your Miniſtration, in the various Inſtances of the Publick Good, and eſpe-cially in the peculiar one of Your Noble Charity; which though You ſo induſtriouſly Conceal, as a Thing beneath You, to make Proclamations to the World, what Pub-lick Good You are continually engag'd in, as it is uſual among thoſe whoſe leſſer Services require ſuch particular Methods of being known; yet Your Monthly Disburſe-ments to ſuch a Number of the Poor, Your Continual Succour to thoſe of Decayed Fortunes, and, what I am in particular by my Profeſſion engag'd to mention, Your *Care of the Souls of thoſe whom You Feed and Cloath*, and by Your prudent and laudable Management, ſhelter ſo Decently and Comfortably from any future Storms, even of Neceſſity and Want ; I ſay, above all the numerous Inſtances of a ſweet and abounding Generoſity to the Needy, the Means You diſpenſe to them of *ſerving God in Publick-Devotions, in the moſt Pure and Excellent Form of our Church :* Theſe are Glorious Arguments from what Principle You act ; and cannot but derive a Bleſſing, a Brightneſs upon *This Honourable Brotherhood*, equal unto that Reputation and Credit You Your ſelves derive upon Your Country.

*And*

And thus have I endeavour'd to anſwer what I propoſed, and ſhew the Uſefulneſs of Navigation and Commerce in its General Influence, as it makes up the Wants
of each particular Country ; as it hath Civiliz'd and In-
ſtructed the whole World ; and as it hath brought the
Glorious Light of the Goſpel to thoſe, and even among
the Reſt our own ſelves, *who ſat in Darkneſs and in the
Shadow of Death.*

I have endeavour'd alſo to ſhew You the particular Advantages it brings to the particular Cities and Kingdoms
where it is followed, of Riches and Strength, ſubſtantial
Reputation and laſting Honour.

Let us therefore ; we who are ſo profited by You, as
we are a People, let us conſider what Returns we ought
to make to God for theſe great Bleſſings and the Happineſs
we receive through Your Means, that He may ſtill bleſs
Your Endeavours for our Good.

For where God beſtows much, He certainly requires
much alſo ; and He ever expects that our Acknowledg-
ments ſhould quadrate and bear ſome proportion to thoſe
Bleſſings that He hath confer'd upon us.

When He exalts a Nation, or makes a City to flouriſh,
He looks that the Piety of it ſhould greaten with its
Condition ; otherwiſe, as He can *make a fruitful Land
barren for the Wickedneſs of them that dwell therein* ; ſo
for the ſame Cauſe He can *turn fenced Cities into ruinous
heaps.*

That Deadneſs of Trade that is ſo viſible amongſt us,
and ſo complain'd of, and thoſe prodigious Loſſes that
have been ſuſtain'd at Sea, although they may both be
deemed the Reſult of a long and tedious War ; yet what
is War therefore, but one of the heavieſt Judgments of
God upon a ſinful Nation ? Which ſhews us plainly, that
though we enjoy the Bleſſings that we do enjoy, chiefly
through Your Publick Applications, yet if we ſtill go
on to be Unthankful, and to provoke Heaven by our
*Rebellion* and *Diſobedience,* we have Reaſon to expect
that God ſhould more and more render even your Endeavours

deavours ufelefs and abortive. I will now therefore beg
leave,

III. And in the laft place, to fhew you what it was
particularly that provok'd God to bring that heavy Deftruction upon *Tyrus*, that we avoiding thofe Sins, may
not become our felves fuch a terrible Example to others
as fhe is to us.

1. It was the Atheifm and Pride of *Tyrus* that brought
Ruin and Mifery upon that City. They are charged in
the following Chapter, *That they fat in the Seat of God,*
Ezek. 28. 2. *and for having their Heart lifted up within them* ; *i. e.*
They afcribed, as many among us are apt to do, their
Welfare to their own Wifdom ; their Riches to their
own Diligence, and their Power and Advancement to
their own Counfels.

Such a Spirit of Atheifm did then, *and God knows does
now poffefs the Minds of Men,* that they take off their
Eyes from God, and fix them upon Second and Inferiour
Caufes : If Men of Trade grow Rich, how ready are
they to impute it to the well-laying of a Defign, to the
timely fending out of a Ship, or the over-reaching of
another ? Whilft Providence and the Bleffing of God are
wholly forgotten ! Thus they burn Incenfe to themfelves
fetting themfelves up for Gods, paying Adorations to
their own Fancies, without confidering how Atheiftically
they act in thefe things, and how abfurdly they difown
any fuch Being as their Maker !

When, alas ! one Dafh upon a Rock, one fmall Leak
in a Veffel, or a Pyrate on the Seas, at once ruines and
undeceives the Man ! And how Righteous were it with
God, *thus* to convince us, when an Argument of his good
Providence will not ferve the turn!

For how provoking muft we needs think it is to God,
when after he hath given us Corn, and Wine, and Oyl,
and every other Thing that He has created for our Pleafure, as well as Neceffity ; and we deny him the Offering

ing of Praife, but prepare the Sacrifice, the Glory for our felves!

How provoking muft it needs be, when He hath given us Deliverance, and brought us to the Haven where we would be, and our Goods in Safety, we then invert the Acknowledgment, and erect Altars to our own Praife!

If we think it impoffible for the Magnificence of this Kingdom, or City, to be deftroy'd ; or for our felves to be undone ; then defpife God, and walk in the Sight of your own Eyes ; and fay with proud *Babylon, I am, and there is none befides me* : But in the mean time let me advife fuch, with the Prophet, in the 6th of *Amos,* ver. 2. *Pafs now to Calneh, and fee ; and from thence go ye to Hemath the great* : *then go down to Gath of the Philiftines : be they better than thefe Kingdoms, or their border greater than thefe Nations* ?

Neither are thefe bofom Atheifms, thefe Infidelities in Mafquerade all ; but how many are there who openly fay there is no God ; *i. e.* who impute all Afflictions to Fate and Chance, and fo make Repentance needlefs, and Amendment impoffible ; whofe Minds are therefore fet upon the World, who propofe all Things without feeking or dependance upon God.

But thefe I fhall only admonifh in the words of St. *James, Go to now ye that fay to day, or to morrow, we will* Jam. 4. 13,14. *go into fuch a City, and continue there a year, and buy and fell, and get gain* ; *whereas ye know not what fhall be on the morrow* : *For what is your Life* ? *It is even a Vapour that appeareth for a little time, and then vanifheth away.*

2. A fecond Sin that *Tyrus* was charg'd with, was a general Diffolutenefs and Corruption of Manners.  Hiftory tells us, That they and the *Sidonians* worfhip'd the Goddefs *Aftarte,* or *Venus* ; *i. e.* They ferv'd only their own Lufts : They were come to that height of Wickednefs, that they rais'd Temples to their Vices, and look'd on the moft Beftial Acts, as on Acts of Devotion.

D                     Befides

Befides, Their Intemperance and Luxury was very great, for which God threatens them in the 25th of *Je-remiah*, ver. 27. *Drink*, faith he, *and be drunken, and fpue and fall, and rife no more, becaufe of the Sword that I will fend among you.*

Now one would Rationally think that fuch Men as thefe fhould not be found in a Chriftian Country, much lefs among thofe that ufe the Sea, whofe very Employ-ment places them hourly fo near upon the Brink of Death, that the Ph'lofopher could not well tell whether to reckon them among the Dead, or the Living.

Of what an amazing Confideration is it to find thefe poor Souls generally without the Fear of God; without any Senfe of Religion.; to fee thefe Men imitating the Motion of their Ships, even upon Land, *Reeling to and fro, and ftaggering like drunken Men!* To hear of Chri-ftian Mariners Swearing and Curfing in a Storm, when even thofe Heathen ones in *Jonah* fo juftly upbraid them, *who call'd then every one upon his God!*

Whilft there are fuch Diforders aboard Your Veffels, how can You expect Your Voyages fhould be Profperous, or Your Undertakings Bleffed!

I'm fure our Mother, the Church of *England*, hath taken Care that it fhould be otherwife, and hath there-fore Compos'd a very Excellent and Ufeful Office for that purpofe. *It were well it were made more ufe of.*

But 'tis too juft a Remonftrance that we are now in fuch Circumftances, that thefe are not the only fort of Men upon whom thefe Crimes are to be charged: For what Frauds and Coufenage, what Riots and Drunken-nefs, what Whoredoms and Adulteries, what Oaths and Blafphemies, are there not practic'd by all Ranks, and Orders, and Conditions of Men amongft us! Infomuch that the Enquiry would be juft among the Generality of Mankind, what is become of that Serioufnefs and Mo-defty that was heretofore not only thought Effential to a Chriftian, but to the *Temper of an Englifh Man?* Surely God will vifit us for thefe Things, and *what fhall we do in the Day thereof!*  Is

## *of Navigation,* &c. 19

In this Cafe, it is our beft Courfe to take the Prophet *Ezekiel's* Advice, and *Repent and turn our felves from all* Chap. 18. 30. *our Tranfgreffions, and fo Iniquity fhall not be our Ruin.*

Then God will be Gracioufly Prefent with us in all our Adventures and Undertakings : He will *open the Windows of Heaven,* and pour down Bleffings upon us, Day after Day ; and after all, Crown the Mercies of this World, with the Unexpreffible Rewards and Glories of that which is to come. *Amen.*

*F I N I S.*

# ERASMUS PHILIPS

Erasmus Philips, *An Appeal to Common Sense: or, Some Considerations Offer'd to Restore Publick Credit* (London: T. Warner, 1720). British Library, shelfmark 1029. e.68.

Erasmus Philips, *The State of the Nation, in Respect to her Commerce, Debts and Money* (London: J. Woodman and D. Lyon, 1725), extract, pp. 1–14, 39–50. British Library, shelfmark 288.c.40.

Very little is known of Erasmus Philips (d. 1751). The first pamphlet reprinted here, *An Appeal to Common Sense*, was published in the aftermath of the collapse of the South Sea Company in 1720. His general view is that, although this collapse was a disaster, the effects will not last for too long. Philips's best-known work is *The State of the Nation*, an extract of which is also published here, in which he argued for greater commercial liberty. In the history of economic thought – following J. R. McCulloch – Philips is often mentioned as an outright free trader and as such a predecessor of Adam Smith. As a reading of the text will show, this is an exaggeration.[1]

Philips's great concern in *An Appeal to Common Sense* is that issuing state loans leads to private credit and loans being crowded out of the market. Hence the increase of the public debt implies increasing rents and a lack of cash credit for 'private' investment. The kind of critique provided here against too much public lending and spending has been common ever since the time Philips wrote this text. In the second part of this text our author makes a plea for more labourers to be put to work in useful manufactures – a standard argument. We may also note that in this second part he raises the banner of 'fair' trade – a concept which would haunt the discussion on trade in the late nineteenth century (and perhaps even today).

1    For further information on Philips, see the entry in *Oxford Dictionary of National Biography* (Oxford: Oxford University Press, 2004), written by W. A. S. Hewins and revised by Philip Carter; and *Palgrave's Dictionary of Political Economy*, ed. H. Higgs, 3 vols (London and New York: Macmillan, 1894), vol. 3, p. 102, where Philips's date of death is given as 1743.

*The State of the Nation*, the second text reprinted here, considers the general benefits of export trade, especially of manufactured goods. It is an intervention in the heated public debate on the Utrech peace treaty of 1713 and its consequences. Our author takes the Tory position and argues in favour of the treaty against the more protectionist Whig stance. It is interesting to note that he believes that 1688 was the best year ever for England in terms of wealth and trade. In the last part of the tract Philips has a lot of sensible things to say about money and price formation which shows that authors such as Philips were perhaps more 'modern' than is usually acknowledged. This extract covers pp. 1–14 and 39–50 of the original printed text. The material left out presents factual information regarding the costs of the French war before 1713 (chapter 2), a chapter on public debt (chapter 5) and a number of appendices of which the one on 'the Asiento' is perhaps the most interesting.

# A N

# APPEAL

## TO

# Common Senfe:

### OR, SOME

# Confiderations offer'd to Re-ftore Publick Credit.

By Mr. ERASMUS PHILIPS.

*LONDON:*
Printed for *T. Warner,* at the *Black-Boy* in
*Pater-Noster-Row,* 1720.

Price Six Pence.

( **1** )

# A N
# A P P E A L
## T O
# Common Senſe, &c.

### *The* INTRODUCTION.

Moſt Men when they appear to
the World in Print, affix to
their Works a Preface or a De-
dication; as to the firſt, I think
my ſelf under no Neceſſity to
make an Apology, my only de-

A          ſign

( 2 )

fign being to ferve my Country, and by a Method fo eafy, that had it not been obvious to Common Senfe, I fhould never have thought on't. As to the Second, I do not know how to ask the Patronage of the Great, having too great a Diffidence of my own Abilities, befides that in *England*, Greatnefs is fo Theatrical, and the Actors change fo often, that really I was at a lofs where to fix, I chofe rather to appeal to Common Senfe, a Quality every Man thinks he enjoys, and there I am fure to find as many Patrons, as there are Men that think as I do; perhaps that may be very few, yet I have this Satisfaction, to know I have

Mul-

## ( 3 )

Multitudes who are fo far of
my Opinion, that they have
always acted with a firm ad-
herence to the prefent Eſtabliſh-
ment, and will venture all to
maintain it.

T will hardly be credited
in future Ages, that
*England* Great as it muſt
be in Hiſtory, was brought almoſt
to the Brink of Ruin, in a few
days, without the Calamities either of a Foreign Invaſion, or an
Inteſtine War; when they ſhall
read how far our Arms have extended their Conqueſts, that we
held the Balance of Power of *Europe*, that our Credit was fo great,
that it reached the utmoſt Limits
of the World, when they ſhall

**A 2**          read

( 4 )

ſtad that *England*'s inviolable Faith, brought our Enemies at all times to ſupply us with Money to carry on the War againſt themſelves; how is it poſſible they will believe that a few days cou'd put a Period to this Greatneſs : They will certainly think they are impos'd upon, and the whole Hiſtory Romance and Fiction.

Nor will the Miſeries that fell on *France*, by a Scheme of the like nature, render the Story more Probable. *France* for many years, had not known what Credit was (except what was amongſt a few Merchants) for tho' the late King had made many attempts to reſtore it, yet the neceſſity his boundleſs Ambition brought him under, made him always ſtifle it in its

Birth,

( 5 )

Birth, it was not then to be wonder'd at, that a People whofe only
Security for their Money was their
Chefts, fhou'd unlock them to
taft the fweets of a great Intereft,
which they flatter'd themfelves
with from their Scheme, we faw
their Misfortunes, and did not wonder at it ; for when once a Nation
by precipitate Meafures make
their Capital exceed the Poffibility
of receiving a regular Intereft, there
is no doubt, but the Men of fore-
fight, will gather up as much
Money as they can in their Hands,
fo that the Innocent and unknow-
ing are fure to be the Sufferers.

'Tis indeed almoft Incredible,
to think, that a Nation as we
were, that had always acted upon
the Rule of an affured regular Intereft,

## ( 6 )

tereft, fhou'd plunge our Selves in
an Affair that was altogether Imaginary, whilft almoft every Man
at any Rate bought the Stock,
with no other Intention but to fell
out again, every Man confcious
that this fall wou'd be, and yet
flatter'd himfelf, that he fhould
fell out time enough to fave himfelf; 'tis certain, that when the
Stock was call'd a Thoufand, if
every Man had been in the mind
to fell out, if the whole Species
of *England* had been Collected in
one Heap, every Twenty fifth
Man cou'd not have had his whole
Money; but if Thirty or Foity
Cunning Men ( to fay no worfe )
had fhar'd four or five of thefe
Twenty fifth parts, it would naturally reduce it to one in a Hundred.                                    I

( 7 )

I think I have no Reaſon to con-
tradict the Belief of every Body,
that this was our Caſe the Conſequence is indeed deplorable, we
ſee Credit entirely loſt, no Faith,
between Man and Man, the Gold-
ſmiths and Societies of the beſt
Credit run out of their Caſh, by
Men that were reſolv'd to ſee as
much of their Eſtates as they
cou'd in ready Money, nay ſo pre-
valent was Fear, that take one
with another, every Man deſtroy'd
nine Parts of his Eſtate, to get the
tenth into his hands, this was
the Fact, the ſtopping the Circulation, neceſſarily bringing down
the Stock from a Thouſand to a
Hundred.

'Tis certain we had run up our
Credit beyond its proper ſphere,

and

( 8 )

and that unnatural Subfcription at a Thoufand finifh'd our Ruin ; it may be true, that when that Subfcription was taken in, the Price of the Stock might be Seven Hundred Seventy Five, and fo from the Credit of the Money to be paid in, it might bear fome proportion ; yet our Truftees, who fhould have known the nature of Credit better, fhould never have attempted at one blow to have deftroy'd it, by making a Capital fo large that no Intereft could poffibly be found for it, and I cannot help faying, That fourth Subfcription was the moft impudent attempt that ever was made by the worft of Men, a Subfcription was a Bait to catch even the moft Cautious, becaufe

of

( 9 )

of the great Premium upon the
three former, thus in a Morning
they drain'd us of two Millions
five Hundred Thoufand Pounds,
which had in great probability
come to Market, to have been lent
upon Stock, and had made up the
great differences there then was,
between Man and Man ; but 'tis
too plain, the whole defign of
that, was to be enabled ( by
robbing the People) to lend
Money to their Contractours to
pay them their Differences, while
the reft of the World were difabled to find Money any where,
upon Stock Security, to make
good their Contracts.    From this
Fatal Period the Stock declin'd
every day, great Quantities came
to Market, and People were

forc'd

( 10 )

forc'd to take what they cou'd
get.

I don't defign by this Declaration, to infinuate, that it was
ever poffible to keep up this
Scheme at a Thoufand; but
I am confident the unwarrantable
Practices of our Truftees, was the
occafion of our Credit finking fo
foon: I can't help obferving, that
even in its declination, upon a
bare Report, that the Bank was
come into meafures with them,
the Stock rife one Hundred and
ten *per Cent* in one day; its obvious enough the Spirits of the
People were well inclin'd to have
fupported it, provided they had
a probable Security, but as foon
as this Story was found an Artifice,
every day brought on fome new
Calamity.        I

( 11 )

I am very fenfible, that Mankind has not a greater Satisfaction,
than to hear an Invective againft
thofe People that have injured
them, and let the Writer be
what he will, he fhall be favoura-
bly read that expofes them.   But
this will avail very little to the
retrieving of what we have loft;
in this general diftrefs, we ought
to caft about, and fee by what
Methods we may fave our felves
from utter Ruin : Surely that
Man does not deferve pity, who
when his Ship is wreck'd, won't
endeavour to fave fomething; let
thefe Traytors (if they be fo) be
brought before that great Tribu-
nal, the Parliament, and if their
Treafon be prov'd, we need not
doubt but the Legiflature will do

B 2           Juftice,

( **12** )

Juſtice, in the mean time let us
ſee what we have left, and by
what means it may be improv'd
to our Advantage.

- The firſt I ſhall obſerve in
general, is, that Money is only
valuable according to the Proportion it bears againſt other Commodities; plenty of Money always occaſions the riſe of the
value of other Things, as ſcarcity of Money brings it down,
provided the Commodity is not
ſcarce too, and then, the demand
for that Commodity makes it riſe
in Proportion to the Neceſſity of
the Purchaſer. The next Thing
to be conſider'd is, that as Plenty
of Money reduces the Intereſt of
Money, ſo there can be no Intereſt ſo low, but People, will rather

( **13** )

ther choofe it than live upon their Principle; for many years paft, as the Ballance of Trade has made an increafe of our Money, Intereft has varied accordingly; at prefent the Intereft fettled by Act of Parliament is 5 *per Cent,* not but the Government has rais'd Money at four, which cou'd not have happen'd, if there had not been a greater plenty of Money than heretofore; upon this Suppofition 'tis experimentally true, that a certain regular Intereft for Money, with a probable Security for the Principle,-( for a real one was not to be found even when our Credit was greateft ) has been fufficient to 'Circulate the whole Credit of the Nation. I fhall not fpeak fpeculatively, but

( 14 )

but ſtate the matter of Fact: The Debt of the Nation was about Fourty ſix Millions, Six Hundred and Three Thouſand One Hundred Pounds, or there-abouts, for which an Intereſt was given of about Three Millions One Hundred and Eighteen Thouſand Pounds, I ſuppoſe no Body will affirm, that the People had any real Security for their Principle; for I believe one may ſafely ſay, that there is not Money in *Europe* ſufficient to pay off every Proprietor, yet the Intereſt being regularly paid, every Man was ſatisfied, and flatter'd himſelf he cou'd at any time receive his Principle; tho' were every Proprietor reſolv'd to put his Eſtate in ready Money, one with another

# ( 15 )

ther cou'd not receive four Shil‑
lings in the Pound : If Three
Millions or thereabouts then, were
fufficient to Circulate Fourty
Six Millions, at a pretty large
Intereft too, (and without doubt
with a very little addition it is
fufficient ) furely no Body will
fay, that we have not Money
enough in the Nation to fupport
the Stock at Four Hundred, or
Five Hundred, confidering if a
lefs Intereft would ferve, the lefs
Money is requir'd. This is very
obvious, if we confider the na‑
ture of Circulation ; for Inftance,
Four People, or Twenty, fell
each a Thoufand Pound Stock, no
body can fuppofe it is with a defign
to keep the Money by 'em, one
perhaps pays his Daughter's For‑
tune

## ( 16 )

tune to a Man whofe Eftate is
Mortgaged for the like Sum, the
Mortgagee Receives the Money,
Lends it again upon the like Security, the Borrower either pays
it away, and fo probably the
fame Money comes in a few days
to Market to buy Stock, as being
the ready Repofitory for Money
to lie at Intereft: Thus the fame
Money may ferve, by Circulation,
the Purpofes of Twenty People:
But it may be Objected, that this
Money may be broke in fmaller
Parcels, and fo from the fmall-
nefs of the Sums lie dead; 'tis
true, it may run fometimes in
fmall Streams, but it will at laft
meet in fuch a Bulk, as fhall
make People think it worth their
while to receive Intereft for it.
                                    But

( **17** )

But it will not be fufficient to fay there is Money enough in the Nation to make an Intereft for fo large a Capital, it muft be made demonftrative, that fuch an Intereft fhall arife out of the South-Sea Profits, as fhall convince Mankind, it will be to their Advantage to lay out their Money here.

There are two Things, which were they put in Execution, I believe wou'd contribute very much to it; the one is, the giving fuch an Encouragement to Trade, as fhall effectually bring the Ballance on our fide; the other, the giving the Chafes and Forrefts of *England*, to be Sold, or Improv'd to the Ufe of the Company.

C          As

( 18 )

As to the firſt, It is certain that the Riches of a Nation conſiſts of numbers of Induſtrious Inhabitants, who by their Labour and Application, furniſh their Neighbours with Materials either for Uſe or Pleaſure, and by this means become their Creditours, the Ballance of which Account, over and above the Goods imported, muſt be paid in Gold, or Silver.

The Feitility of our Soil, the Uſefulneſs of our Manufactures, the Ingenuity of our People, beſides the Conveniency of our Ports, makes us a Nation the moſt proper in the World for this Advantage, and hence it is, that notwithſtanding the prodigious Sums that we remitted abroad to

pay

( 19 )

pay great Armies for feveral Years,
yet our Country flow'd with
Money; nothing but the Benefits
of Trade cou'd have fav'd us,
and indeed nothing but Trade
can reftore us. 'Tis too melan-
choly a Confideration to think,
how much this has of late been
neglected ; The Merchant was
tempted to make ufe of his Money to buy Imaginary Treafures,
the Regular Courfe of Bufinefs
has been interrupted, and Ava-
rice took place of Induftry.

The Remedy I wou'd propofe
to this Evil, is to give the value
of One *per Cent.* Premium, upon
exported Commodities of the
Manufacture or Growth of *England*; this might be a Temptation
for 'em to gather up the Remains

C 2                          of

# ( 20 )

of their Subſtance, and ingage heartily in  their old Callings, to the Re-eſtabliſhment of Commerce, the only ſource of the Riches of this Country.

I ſuppoſe no Body can Object the Difficulty of finding ſuch a Sum to anſwer this Propoſal, ſince the Revenue of the Duty upon the Import will be ſo conſiderably augmented : And ſurely this may be given with that Caution, that no poſſible Fraud may elude the publick Benefit ; by this means Credit may be 'reſtor'd, and Money flow again in its ancient Channels. As it is abſolutely Neceſſary to have the Ballance of Trade on our ſide, to ſecure to us, not only the Money we are in Poſſeſſion of, but to obtain new Riches;

ſo

( 21 )

fo it will likewife be as neceffary
that the Fund for the Intereft of
the, South-Sea Stock be Regular
and Certain; if this be made
appear, there is no doubt but the
Money that is at prefent lock'd up,
will come out again, for the Neceffity is as great to the Monied Man
to have Intereft for his Money,
as to the Landed Man to have
Rent for his Eftate; a Principle
however large, muft decay when
you live upon it.

Let us look a little then into
the ftate of the South-Sea Stock,
and enquire which way they can
make a certain regular Intereft.
In a Pamphlet lately writ, call'd,
*The South-Sea Scheme Examin'd*,
the Author Pretends to demonftrate, that even upon the Bar-
gain

( 22 )

gain already made, the Stock is intrinfically worth Four Hundred, I will not pretend to enter into the Mathematical Calculation of this Propofition, nor is there one in fifty of the Purchafers that trouble themfelves with it, but are guided by an implicit Faith; but if it is really fo valuable, it wou'd be no fmall addition to it, if His Majefty, out of Compaf-fion to his ruin'd Subjects, wou'd be pleas'd to give the Chafes and Forrefts, to be Sold, or Improv'd for the ufe of this Company, the Nation certainly in general wou'd be benefited by this Conceffion; fince Numbers of People make the Riches of a Nation, thefe wafte Lands wou'd make Room for more Inhabitants, and confequently,

( 23 )

quently, not only enrich us, but ftrengthen us too; His Majefty's Revenues too wou'd be confiderably increas'd by the Quit Rent that wou'd be paid out of thefe Lands, as well as from the confumption of thofe Commodities they wou'd produce, and the Land Tax by Confequence made more confiderable. It may be objeɛted, that we cou'd not find Tenents for the Improvement of thefe Lands; in anfwer to that, I remember fome years ago an Aɛt of general Naturalization was thought Politically Good, I fhall not prefume to Reafon upon the Repealing of that Aɛt, but I believe I may affirm, that were that Aɛt reftored with proper Limitations, Foreigners of all Countries
wou'd

( 24 )

wou'd crowd to live under the be-
nign Influence of our Government,
and taft the fweets of a fruitful
Soil, a temperate Air, and above
all, the lafting charms of Liberty :
It may be true, that the amount of
the Sale of thefe Lands, will not
be very confiderable in fuch a large
Dividend; yet certainly it is fomething, and in its Confequences it
will be greater, as it will be a
means to encourage Foreigners to
bring their Money amongft us,
which muft of neceffity leffen the
Intereft of it, confidering that the
Strangers that do come, will generally be Trading People; if there
be any Inconveniencies in this, I
muft own my Ignorance, I don't
perceive them; but all I pretend
to is, a fincere Zeal to ferve my
Country,

( 25 )

Country, and wifh with all my
Soul fome effectual means be
found to fave us from the Calamities we lie under.

I have not yet been able to find
the means to look into the Survey
of the Forrefts and Chafes ; but
hope in a little time to give fuch
an Account of 'em, as fhall fatisfy
every Body of their intinfick
Worth.

*F I N I S.*

D

# OF THE

# STATE

## OF THE

# NATION, &c.

## CHAP I.

### *Of Trade in general, and particularly of the Trade of* England.

RADE is to the Body Poli-
tick as the Blood is to human Body, it diffues itself by
the minutest Canals into every part of a Nation, and gives
Life and Vigour to the whole   Without
this, no Country can be happy within herfelf, or fupport herfelf without againft the
Attacks of a powerful Neighbour

B

Trade

( 2 )

Trade it is that brings us all the Aids, the Conveniencies, the Luxury of Life, 'tis she that encourages all Arts and Sciences, gives Hopes to Invention, and Riches to Industry; Strength, Wisdom and Policy are in her Train; Plenty, Liberty, and Happiness are her perpetual Companions.

Even Money itself without Trade, like stagnated Water, is of little use to the Proprietor *Spain* is a living Instance of this Truth, the Mines of *Peru* and *Mexico* made that People think themselves above Industry, an Inundation of Gold and Silver swept away all useful Arts, and a total Neglect of Labour and Commerce has made them as it were the Receivers only for the rest of the World. On the contrary, *Holland* is the most remarkable instance of the Advantages of Trade. It would be needless to mention the Feebleness of her Origin, or the Smalness of her Territory, this Country, the stupendous Workmanship of Mens Hands, not able to support half her People from her native Product, is at present the Seat of Riches and Plenty; notwithstanding the continual Expence she is at to keep herself above Water, notwithstanding the several Attacks that have been made upon her by three powerful Monarchies, yet was she able to

expend

## ( 3 )

expend 22 Millions in the War with *France*, from the Year 88 to the Year 97, and in the laft War with *France* her Proportion of the Expence was 45 Millions, *viz.* for about 12 Years 120,000 Men every Year, which comes to (reckoning their pay one third lefs than ours) near 18,000,000 Sterling.

The Charge of their Fleet might be according to their own Account of their Number, which is thus.

| All Ships of the Line, befides a great many fmaller Veffels. | In | |
|---|---|---|
| | 1702 —— 55 | |
| | 1703 —— 50 | |
| | 1704 —— 56 | |
| | 1705 —— 56 | |
| | 1706 —— 54 | |
| | 1707 —— 49 | |
| | 1708 —— 53 | |
| | 1709 —— 50 | |
| | 1710 —— 43 | |
| | 1711 —— 40 | |
| | Total 506 | |

The Charge at the Rate of 30000 a Ship at an Average, including too their fmaller Veffels will come to } 15, 090, 000.

B2                    **Befides**

## ( 4 )

Befides their Subfidies of 40, 000 *Crowns per An.* to the Bifhop of *Munfter,* 100,000 *Crowns per An.* from 1704 to 1709 to the Duke of *Wirtemberg,* and 400,000 *Crowns* to the King of *Denmark,* which in all may come to — 250, 000. *Sterling.*

The Extraordinary of the War in the *Netherlands* — 65, 861, 821 *Livres.*

Which, according to their way of reckoning 11 *Guilders* to a Pound, may be about — 6, 000, 000.

Befides their Expence of Tranfports and Victualling, which might come in all to — 4, 000, 000.

And the Charge of about ten thoufand Men in *Spain* and *Portugal* from 1703, *communibus annis* to 1712, 1,825,000. allowing Twelve-pence *per Diem* to each Man. And this, at very low Computation, brings in their Expence to above 45,000,000 *Sterling.*

A very great Sum to be got in few Years time only by Induftry.

*England*

( 5 )

*England* too has had her Share in the Benefits of Trade, and her prefent Affluence is entirely owing to that Commerce fhe has had with the reft of the World; the many Millions fhe has expended fince the Year 88, have been replaced; and one would think fuch an Overplus in the Balance of the Account, by the Appearance of the Price of Commodities, that fhe is become richer than fhe was at that time.

Her native Commodities have been to her better than the Mines of *Peru* and *Mexico*. Wool, Lead, Tin, Leather, Butter, Cheefe, Corn, Tallow, &c. the annual Growth of her Soil, befides her feveral Manufactures, have been an inexhauftible Fund of Wealth . Yet it is probable that our Negotiations with the reft of the World for other things may bring us three parts in four more Profit than arifes from our own native Commodities.

Tobacco, Cotton, Ginger, Sugars, Indigo, Rice, and the reft of the Plantation Goods have brought us (befides what was neceffary for our own Confumption) a Ballance from *France*, *Flanders*, *Hamborough*, *Holland* and the Eaft Countries of above fix hundred thoufand Pounds a Year.

Our Traffick with the *Eaft-Indies* for Callicoes, wrought Silks, Drugs, Salt-petre,

## ( 6 )

raw Silk, Tea, Coffee, and Cottons, Cotton Yarn, *Carmania* Wool, *&c.* is, over and above our own Ufe, a great Gain to us.

If the Value fent to *Eaft - India* be 500, 000. Pounds *per An.* their Sales have been many years for above 2, 200, 000 *per An* of which 'tis fuppofed one Million may be confumed at home, the reft exported, ont of this we muft deduct about 400, 000 for the draw back, then the Balance of the Account will be above 300, 000 Pounds *per An.* clear Profit. But then as this Trade has maintain'd fo many people befides, and furnifh'd us with what otherways we muft have bought of the *Hollanders*, as well as brought down the Price of other *European* Commodities we made ufe of before our entring into this Trade, it muft be faid the Nation's Profit is annually above a Million : It is not to be underftood, that on the Balance of this Account we receive above a Million of Specie; but if thefe *Indian* Commodities pay for Goods in thefe feveral Parts for which we muft have otherways fent Gold or Silver, it is in effect the fame thing

I fhall not contend with thofe that fay that this Commerce is not carried without a Lofs of Silver to us; but then it muft be confidered too that we only lofe in Proportion

## ( 7 )

portion to the reft of *Europe*, every Nation bearing fome fhare in the general Lofs, and ours perhaps lefs than any other

It is not unlikely but that of the Silver that has been brought into *Europe* fince 1602, there has been above one hundred and fifty Millions buried in the *Eaft-Indies*. Had that Money been proportionably difperfed over the feveral Countries of this Part of the World, and our Share treble what it is now, if Commodities and Labour too had rifen in a treble Proportion, 'tis no Paradox to affirm that in effect we are as rich now as we fhould have been under thofe Circumftances, Gold and Silver being only valuable as they relate to other Commodities.

But as the Riches of a Country does not confift in any Quantity of Gold and Silver, if it cannot keep them, or acquire more; fo our utmoft Attention fhou'd be to preferve thofe Methods; and I believe I may with Certainty affirm that one way to effect this is to leffen the Price of our Labour, which only can be done by employing the Poor, I mean erecting Work-houfes in every Parifh, and obliging them that are able to maintain themfelves.

It has been computed that above 600, 000 Pounds are rais'd annually for the Subfiftence of the Poor in *England*, by which

B 4          Account

( 8 )

Account, at the Allowance of eighteen Pence *per* Week to each Perfon, we may reckon an hundred and fifty thoufand Poor that live by Alms, the Labour of thefe Perfons, one with another, at Six-pence *per Diem* wou'd be worth to the Nation about 1,350,000 Pounds *per Ap.* and how fuch a Quantity of Labour would operate on the Woolen Manufa-cture (Spinning and Carding being the chief Employment of thefe poor People) I leave to every body's Confideration.

Next to the leffening the Price of La-bour is to bring down the Price of Wool; it has been in a great meafure owing to the Dearnefs of our Woolen Manufacture, that both *Holland* and *France* have thought it worth their Care to fet up Looms of their own, to our great, if not irreparable Detriment, and *France* has fo far fucceed-ed, that fhe feems to have no farther Oc-cafion for our Cloths at all.

And *Holland* has found out this Secret of Trade, to buy up our raw Cloths (if I may be allow'd the Expreffion) and dye and nap them fo much cheaper than we, that they are able to under-fell us in Goods of our own Produce.

The Prohibition of the Export of the *Irifh* woolen Manufacture abroad, and the Duty on *Irifh* Wool imported in *England,*

has

# ( 9 )

has in a great Meafure contributed to this; and *Ireland* has for many Years run all Hazards, and fent an annual Supply of Wool to *France*, which has enabled her to carry on this profitable Employ.

We cannot wonder that fo neceffary a Branch of Trade fhould not efcape the Obfervation of fo wife a Minifter as *Colbert,* or the indefatigable *Hollanders*; but why fo much Remiffnefs on our Part is unaccountable? And, perhaps, it would not be Prudence to give the Reafons. But we are not to wonder that any Nation takes the Advantage of our Negligence; nor is it impoffible that *Spain* her felf, may, in fome time, fet up a woolen Manufacture of her own; fo that if we are cut out of this Trade from *Holland, France* and *Spain,* in all Probability, they may, in time, fupply *Denmark, Norway, Sweden, Ruffia,* and *Germany,* with what they want, as well as furnifh a finer fort of fcarlet Drapery for the *Levant* Trade, by which means we fhould lofe the Vent of feveral Millions *per Annum*, * for fo much the Export of our woolen Manufacture from his Majefty's Dominions have been computed at, over and above the Cloaths fent to *America.* Though this Pro-

---

* Sir *William Petty,* p 83. has computed it at 5 Millions, but I believe he has over-rated it.

fpect

§( **10** )

spect is at a great Diftance, yet certainly it is worth our Attention, the Poffibility of the Event alone might alarm us.

Our Plantation Trade has been a conftant Source of Wealth to us, and might yet be improved to a much greater Advantage ; our naval Stores might in a great Meafure be fupplied from *New England*, and we might fave a great Part of four or five hundred thoufand Pounds *per Annum* in thefe Commodities, which we bring from *Denmark*, *Sweden*, and the Eaft-Countries. To preferve this valuable Commerce, we ought to have a vigilant Eye on *France*, who has made great Encroachments fince our firft Settlements there, and watches an Opportunity to diveft us of our Properties in that Part of the World.

Perhaps it might be advifable to give fome additional Strength to our Forts and Places, to prevent any Surprize that may arife from any Rupture with an Enemy ; it being much eafier to keep Poffeffion, than to regain it after it is loft.

Our Trade to *Turkey*, which once was efteemed among the beft Branches, becaufe it took off fo much of our woolen Manufacture, is in a great Meafure gone, and, it is thought, we are obliged to fend Money every Year to pay the Balance of our Accounts there.

*Italy*

## ( 11 )

*Italy* and *Spain* have paid us a constant Tribute; and *Portugal* for many Years has opened her Treasures with a liberal Hand to us. *France* has enjoyed a long Advantage of us in point of Commerce, but the Necessities of the Government obliging them to raise the Value of their Money so often, has cost them very dear, and it may be a Question, whether some Years the Difference of the Exchange did not pay the Balance of the Trade.

*Holland,* no doubt, takes off many of our *East-India* Goods, and a great deal of our coarser woolen Manufacture; but, I am afraid, they do us more Hurt in the Markets where they carry them, than Good in the buying them here.

*Hamborough* and the East-Countries take off the same Commodities, and, no doubt, return Gold and Silver to balance.

*Ireland* for what she has, or can get out of other Countries, is a constant Stream running into this great Lake.

As for *Newfoundland* and *Greenland* they have been long neglected, but might prove of the greatest Consequence to us.

The *African* Trade might be improved to a great Heighth, and is a most beneficial Traffick, forasmuch as it takes off chiefly our Manufacture; and except their Gold Dust, the Commodities brought from thence

are

( 12 )

are but of little Value in that Country. The Contract made in favour of this Company with the King of *Spain* in 1713, see in the *Appendix*.

But before I quit this Subject of Trade I shall speak a little more largely of that of *France*; and I rather choose to do it, because there is no Traffick looked upon with a more malignant Eye than this, by many People. Some have affirmed, that the Goods imported out of *France* have amounted yearly to two Millions six hundred thousand Pounds Sir *William Petty* on the contrary says, that they cannot come to five hundred thousand Pounds *per Annum*. I shall not enter farther into this Dispute, than to declare my Opinion for the latter. But perhaps I may be thought very singular, when I affirm, that I believe, had the Treaty of Commerce, which was ratified at U-trecht the 31st of *March* 1713, been the Rule of our Trade with *France*, our Affairs, in respect to that Nation, had been in a better Condition now than they are, or are likely to be; for by the 20th Article of that Treaty, we had Liberty to import in *France* every thing but warlike Instruments, subject only to the Duties they were wont to pay by the Tariff of 1664, except the following Goods, *viz* the Product of Whales, Woolen Manufactures, Salt Fish, and Su-

gars,

## ( 13 )

gars, which were provided for in a separate Inftrument, *viz.*

The Product of Whales were to pay the Duties appointed by the Tariff of 1699.

The Woolen Manufacture the fame.

Salt Fifh, the Duties appointed before 1664, and befides 40 Livres *per* Laft.

All refined Sugars by the Tariff of 1699, as you may fee more particularly in the Treaty itfelf, which I have fubjoin'd in the *Appendix.*

Had we gone on this Plan, we might have better fupported that luxurious Traffick, and our Woolen Manufacture muft have found Vent in that Country. But high Duties and Prohibitions on our fide, beget high Duties and Prohibitions on theirs ; but there is this Difference between us, that large Impofts deter them from the Ufe of thofe Commodities ; but on the contrary, our Affectation makes us run the more greedily after them, notwithftanding the great Improvements we have made in a few Years in the Manufacture of Silks, yet we fee nothing elfe in a Drawing-Room but prohibited *French* Silks Vaft Quantities of *French* Wine and Brandies come into our Cuftom-Houfes; for all the great Duties, and perhaps as much more is run in upon us, fo that I don't find that our high Impofts and Prohibitions fave us any thing at Home, the

Damage

**( 14 )**

Damage they have done us Abroad is but too well known.

The Policy of *Holland* might inſtruct us not to prohibit Commerce of any Kind, or load any Branch of it with Duties which makes it impracticable. A trading Nation ſhould be an open Ware-Houſe, where the Merchant may either buy what he pleaſes, or ſell what he can. Whatever is brought to you, if you want it not, you will not purchaſe it; if you do want it, the Large-neſs of the Impoſt does not keep it from you. However, this is certain, that a pru-dent People will always keep thoſe Gates open, that let out their Manufactures or native Commodities. But to do any Act which may draw upon you the Loſs of the beſt Branch of your Manufacture, is wretch-ed Policy. If this has not been our Caſe, I wiſh it never may; but this one Thing I am ſure of, that there hardly ever was a more critical Juncture in *England*, to look into the ſeveral Branches of our Trade, than the preſent.

ↄ

( 39 )

## CHAP. IV.

## *Of the Circulation of Money.*

THERE is hardly any one will doubt, but the firſt Traffick in the World was carried on by bartering of Commodities one with another, and in the Infancy of the World, where Peoples Wants were few, and their Ideas narrow, and confin'd to the Objects around them, this ſort of Commerce was ſufficient for the Neceſſities and Comforts of human Life ; but when the Inſolence of Power diveſted Men of their Properties, when the Eſtates of Millions came into a few hands, then Induſtry and Invention by degrees found out all the Conveniencies and Delicacies of Life, the lazy Uſurper parted with his Eſtate to gratify his Appetites, and in a ſeries of Time the Succeſſors of thoſe very People who had been ſpoil'd of their Properties were reſtor'd to them again. But this Circulation could never have been in this manner, but for the Invention of Money,

D 4 whereby

( 40 )

whereby the Induſtrious Man is enabled to lay by ſo much of his Gains as in time a-riſes to the purchaſe of a great Eſtate.

When Commerce came to be more extended, the Difficulties that aroſe from Bartering made People agree to fix a certain Value upon Gold and Silver, and theſe Mettals (being ſcarce, lying in a little Compaſs, and not being much ſubject to Ruſt and Diminution by uſe) became the Standard of the Value of other Commodities

For Inſtance, if ſo much Cloth is worth ſo much Gold or Silver in *Smyrna* or *Liſbon*, and ſo much Silk, or ſo much Wine, is worth the ſame Quantity of Gold or Silver, then the Merchant in *Smyrna* or *Liſbon* will exchange ſo much Silk or Wine for ſo much Cloth, becauſe there is a greater demand for Cloth in *Smyrna* or *Lisbon*, than for Silk or Wine , but if the ſame Quantity of Silk or Wine was worth more Gold and Silver than the ſame Cloth, the Demand for the Cloth would be no Temptation to him to purchaſe it at that Rate.

All Commodities have their Value from the Demand for them. A Scarcity of any one Commodity and a Demand for it will raiſe the Value even where there is a Scarcity of Gold and Silver But though Gold and Silver be the Meaſure of Goods, yet they have often varied according to their Quantity. Thus

## ( 41 )

Thus tho' in proportion to the People the Demand for Wheat might be the same in Queen *Mary*'s Time that it is now, yet then Wheat was at 7 s. and 6 d. *per* Quarter, which is is now above four times as much. This Difference can only arise from the Quantity of Gold and Silver which has lessen'd the Demand for them.

And this Difference does not only relate between them and other Commodities, but also to one another. The Quantity of Silver by the opening of the Mines of *Peru* and *Mexico*, being greater than Gold, gave an extraordinary Value to Gold ; and hence it was that in the eleventh of King *James* I. the Unity-piece of Gold was rais'd from 20 to 23 s. On the contrary, a few Years ago the Demand for Silver was so great, that we were oblig'd to lower the Value of Gold ; and in all Probability in a little time we shall think a farther Diminution absolutely necessary. But it is not alone the Quantity of Gold and Silver that lessens the Demand for them, but the Circulation too, a great Trade making a greater Demand for Industry and Commodities than Money, lessens its Value, and consequently raises the Price of the other two.

Trade and Credit, as they are inseparable in themselves, so they are the Parents of Circulation : Money without these would

be

### ( 42 )

be but a dead Treaſure in few Peoples hands, and conſequently the Community little the better for it. *France* is to *England* as eight to three, their Specie perhaps proportionable, yet there is a greater Shew of Money in *England* than in *France*; but if the Circulation of *France* were equal to that of *England*, then ſhe would appear of courſe ſo much richer than *England*.

'Tis a ſtupendious thought to conſider the Money-Tranſaction of this Kingdom, perhaps it may not be unacceptable to give ſome Account of it. I believe I ſhall be allow'd to compute the Rents of this Kingdom at     20, 000, 000

And upon the ſuppoſition that the Lands of *England* are not tax'd at half the Value, this Account may be near the Truth

The Duties on the Cuſtoms produce *per Annum* about     1, 600, 000

Which upon an Average of 30 *l. per Cent. ad Valorem* ſhows our Imports to be for about     5, 300, 000

Beſides

# ( 43 )

Befides our Re-export which
may be about    } 1,500,000

The reft of the Duties and
Funds    } 2,199,328

If it is allow'd me that there
are Eight Millions of People
in this Nation, I believe I fhall
not exceed if I reckon the Manufactures confum'd at Home
to amount to *per Ann.*    } 16,000,000

I fhall not mention the Intereft arifing from mortgag'd
Land, that being computed before in the Rental, but I muft
take notice of the Mortgages
themfelves, becaufe they are
often transferr'd, and may be
reckon'd Money in Circulation ; and thefe have been
computed at a fifteenth part
of the Land, which will come
to about    } 26,000,000
Principal Money.

The next thing I fhall mention is the great
National Debt ;

And this is about    53,000,000

The

## ( ⁺44 )

*l.*

The Malt produces more a-⎫
bout        ⎭ 600,000

So that the whole Money-⎫
Tranfaction of this Nation ⎬126,199,328
feems to be for about  ⎭

And all this is carried on ⎫ 15,000,000
with no more than   ⎭ Specie.

And perhaps I may be particular in faying, the Reafon of this prodigious Circulation is the Debt itfelf, for the large and regular Intereft that has been paid on thefe State - Actions have exhaufted all private Hoards, and made thefe Securities become like a new Species of Money, current in every body's hands.

People are by this means enabled to make a greater Expence, and as the Fafhion of Life extends itfelf, and affects mediately or immediately almoft every Branch of Trade, 'tis not wonderful to fee that Increafe of it. A great Confumption of Commodities generally attends Affluence, and a loofe Oeconomy is often the Effect of great Plenty.

This large and regular Intereft has not only made a Circulation amongft one another, but has drawn great Sums from Foreigners, which has help'd to balance the

4         Loffes

( 45 )

Loffes of our Specie, we fuftain'd in the two laft Wars with *France*.

It muft be admitted we owe this Money, and the Intereft is an annual Lofs, as well as the Principal will be a real one when paid off.

But fuppofing we fhould ftate this Account at Six Millions, which is about the ninth part of our Debt, the Intereft of this Sum, 300,000 *l. per Ann.* yet I will not allow this is all loft to us : On the contrary the Difadvantage may not be half fo much as it appears to be ; for if A. the Government, borrows of B. C. D. 100 *l.* a piece, at 5 *per Cent.* Intereft ; if A in Trade employs 100 *l.* and gains 16 *per Cent.* this Loan is an Advantage to him ; and tho' this Employment cannot be fuppos'd to be made of all the Money lent to us, yet if a fixth part could be thus us'd, it would reduce our Lofs from 300,000 *l.* to 140,000 *l. per Annum.* Which, confidering our vaft Traffick, is inconfiderable.

Again, this large and regular Intereft has made a Paper - Coin current amongft us, which ferves the Office of twenty times the Specie; that is, an Annuity of 5 *l. per An.* is generally taken for 100 *l.* for though no body is oblig'd to take Annuities in Payments for Money, yet they are feldom refus'd; and if they are, and Money requir'd,

this

**( 46 )**

this Money comes at laſt to Market to purchaſe ſuch Securities, and it is by this means
the money'd Man always finds a ready Intereſt, and conſequently is enabled to live at
greater Expence, which muſt neceſſarily o-
perate an Advantage to all that part of the
Society that have to deal with him, a Demand riſing from the Conſumption of Goods
certainly raiſing the Price of them.

And this is likewiſe a great Advantage to
the trading Part of the Nation, who have
an Opportunity of immediate Intereſt for
their Money 'till they can employ it in Traffick.

This quick Circulation of ſo many Millions gives the Profits of our Trade and Induſtry to the whole Society; for the Duties
on the Goods of B. C. D. Merchants, go
towards paying the Intereſt of Money due
to F. G. H. who have Occaſion for the Product J. K. L. Landed Men, which puts a
greater Value on their Eſtates, and conſequently the Tenants of J K. L are Gainers
too in their Proportion, which enables them
to give their Labourers a Part of their Profit.

And thus it is, the Price of Labour is
rais'd, the Demand for Goods being great,
the Dealers ſtrive to excel in Quality or
Quantity, and conſequently out bid one another in the Price of Labour.

And

( 47 )

And by this means we may account for the Difference of thefe Times, and what they might be a Hundred Years ago, becaufe an Addition only of Four Pence a Day Expence to every Individual, reckoning Eight Millions of Souls in *England* and *Wales*, amounts to above Forty eight Millions *per Ann.* fpent now more than at that time. But without doubt the Increafe of People in this Series of Years has been very much; for in the ordinary way of Reckoning it is judg'd that in one hundred Years a Nation increafes one half in Number  And it is to this as well as to the Quantity of Gold and Silver, that the Lands of this Kingdom have increas'd fo much in Value, Numbers of People making great Demands for the Product of the Earth, and putting Men upon the Neceffity of cultivating and improving for their Suftenance

But 'tis obfervable that Corn has not rifen in proportion to the Price of Land, or other Commodities, within thefe fifty Years, a Bufhel of Wheat being near the fame Value now, it was then : But by a new-fafhion'd Induftry the fame Quantity of Ground is more productive, and the Tenant has his Advantage in fomething elfe.

And had this Nation double the Riches they have, the Demand for Corn might not be greater than it is now, and confe-

I  quently

## ( 48 )

quently not of more Value, nor indeed can it be of more Value, unlefs in Times of Famine, becaufe the Eaft Countries would furnifh you with any Quantity at a little more than the prefent Price.

| | *l.* |
|---|---|
| Numbers of People always make a great Expence; a great Expence of courfe a great Circulation; but when you add Credit to them there is no End of the Account; thus we fee in *England* Fifteen Millions of Specie ferve to anfwer a Debt of Seventy nine Millions, and perform the Office of | 47,399,328 more. |

And I am inclin'd to think from what has been expended in the two laft Wars, there is no more than 15,000,000 *l.* For the Coinage fince Queen *Anne*'s Time has been for above Ten Millions Gold, and not much above 500,000 *l.* Silver, as may be feen in the following Account of the Quantities of Gold and Silver that have been coin'd in the Mints from 1701 to 1724 inclufive.

GOLD

## ( 49 )

GOLD and SILVER Coin'd between 1701 and 1724 inclusive.

| | GOLD | SILVER |
|---|---|---|
| | ℔ | ℔ |
| 1701 | 26742 | 37477 |
| 1702 | 3642 | 114 |
| 1703 | 34 | 718 |
| 1704 | | 4007 |
| 1705 | 104 | 429 |
| 1706 | 537 | 932 |
| 1707 | 607 | 1174 |
| 1708 | 1010 | 3751 |
| 1709 | 2468 | 25423 |
| 1710 | 3716 | 817 |
| 1711 | 9324 | 24768 |
| 1712 | 2855 | 1784 |
| 1713 | 13137 | 2333 |
| 1714 | 29526 | 1566 |
| 1715 | 39090 | 1643 |
| 1716 | 23765 | 1650 |
| 1717 | 15186 | 948 |
| 1718 | 3010 | 2295 |
| 1719 | 14745 | 1756 |
| 1720 | 18959 | 7832 |
| 1721 | 5832 | 2313 |
| 1722 | 12728 | 1983 |
| 1723 | 8306 | 48099 |
| 1724 | 5860 | 1652 |

Total ℔ 241183     ℔ 175464

E                                    And

## ( 50 )

And tho' in a Nation of great Commerce the Fabrication of Gold and Silver in the Mints may not be an exact Rule to measure those Commodities by, because the Difficulties that attend the Exportation of coined Money make People to keep Bullion for their Traffick; yet it may be allow'd me, that were there more Silver or Gold Metal than cou'd be us'd in Traffick, they wou'd naturally be brought to the Mints; so without doubt we may conclude a Nation gains by Trade, when we see a great Stock of Specie in Currency; on the contrary we may conclude there is something wrong in that Oeconomy which makes a Scarcity of Money, especially Silver, which is the Measure of the Commerce of almost the whole World.

The great Scarcity of this Commodity we laboured under a few Years since, was owing to the too great Value we put on Gold in Proportion to Silver, and not so much to the Exportation of that Metal for the *East-India* Trade, as some have imagin'd

And the great Coinage of Gold about that time makes it apparent that Foreigners gain'd by the Exchange of Gold for Silver. The Cessation of that quick Coinage and the Currency of Silver since, will enforce this Truth

# JACOB HENRIQUES, WHEN TRADE INCREASES

Jacob Henriques, *When Trade Increases, Riches will Improve* (London: n.p., 1755). Cornell University, NY, shelfmark HJ8623.H51 W5.

This one-page text, dated as late as 1755, argues for the opening up of the East India trade to private traders. It is by no means a plea for free trade. To speak of freer trade during this period implied in effect a critique of the monopoly of chartered companies.[1] It is here stipulated that the chartered East India Company should still have a monopoly of certain goods, but at the same time admit competition with regard to other goods. Moreover, the author is old fashioned enough to still think that the export of gold and silver should be regulated, and to speak in favour of the protectionist navigation laws. He sounds like a practical man, not a theoretician. More than anything his scheme shows the importance of the discussions on the East India Company, the Merchant Adventurers and other privileged companies in the economic discussion of the seventeenth and eighteenth centuries.

Nothing is known of the author except that he had been a merchant since he was fifteen years old, and obviously had first-hand experience trading with the East Indies. According to his signature on this text, he was born in 1683.

---

1   See the Introduction to Volume 2 of this edition.

## When Trade Increases, Riches will Improve.

A Worthy Scheme (humbly Submitted to better judgment) for to grant by Act of Parliament, a free private Trade to the East-India Colonies, and as I was a Merchant from 15 Years Old, I had much Expence in Trade and Navigation, and observed that Trading Companies (were are excluded private Traders) was a detriment to the Public, ruinous and to the Subjects in General. And as I hope that for the good of the Public, and honour of the Nation, the honourable Parliament the worthy East-India Company, and all loyal Subjects will soon take Notice and Encourage the Merrits of this Important Scheme, therefore and for many other good Reasons, I humbly propose that the East-India Company, and the private Traders ( the sooner the better) should seperately deliver to the honourabe Parliament their Proposals for that Important Purposes, upon the Settling of the following Preliminary Articles for it, &c.

First, That no Gold, or Silver Coin, or Bullion, should be Exported above a reasonable Stipulated Quantity Yearly, to avoid the ill Consequences of the great Exportation of it, and should be with a permit from the Goverment, and if proper to Pay a particular reasonable Duty for it.

2d, That no foreign Manufactories should be Exported, but only those of the Fabricks of this Kingdom, except such as cannot be avoided for carrying on the said Trade.

3d, That no Foreigners direct or indirect, should be permitted to have a Share in this Trade.

4th, That the private Traders should pay a reasonable per Cent. (as shall be agreed of the Value of all their Exports and Imports to the Government, as also to the East India Company, as a perticular Duty for to Consent them to the said Trade.

5th, That no Freight should be paid for the Goods, which the private Traders should be willing for to Leaden in any of the East India Company's Ships.

6th, That the East India Company, in Consideration of their Charter, should be prefered to Export and Import some perticular Commodity, as shall be agreed, which the private Traders should not have the Liberty to do.

7th, That the Government should be at the Expences to Support the Forts and Colonies, in those parts of the East Indies; and in Time of War to provide sufficient Convoies to secure the said Trade.

8th, That all the Goods that shall be Imported by private Traders, shall be free Lodged in the Company's Warehouses, and there to be disposed by the owners.

9th, That the East-India Company and the private Traders should Support one another, so as to promote their Credit, Trade, and Advantages.

10th, That the East India Companys Charter should be continued perpetually, or for 99 Years, upon the settling of the new Agreement, and should moderate them on Necessary Expences, and give yearly a Ballance of their Trade to their Proprietors.

11th, That when I shall be informed of some perticular Matters in Relation to Agreement, I shall shew Ways and Means to Settle the Duties, and Drawbacks upon the East-India Goods, in such a manner that the Returns will be greater, the Profits for the Company and Traders also, and Commodities Cheaper.

12th, That the East India Company and the private Traders should Support the Government in all Events, to be a Terror for their Enemies and for the honour, welfare and glory of their King and Country.

Note, I offer to remove all Objections if any, and this Proposal and Scheme will be Yearly be offered till it is established, and I also offer a Lottery Scheme all Prizes and no Blanks, to sink part of the National Debt, which may serve as a prudent Patron to shew the Probability of my Annual Sinking Fund Lottery, for the Benefit and Glory of this Kingdom ; but as what is Good seems to be little encouraged, it is a misfortune for the Community and a great discouragement for People to Study for it, therefore let the noble Authority Encourage, and prudent People will Study and then both will Comply with their Duty for their own, and for the Public Welfare.

*。* My deceased honourable Father was the Promoter of the Bank of England, he was very Rich, he never desired any reward for it, and I have had the promise of my offered Matters, which I have attaind with long Study, great Fatigue, vast Expences, good and loyal Intention, honest Industry ; and what I deserve for it? I humbly Submit to Justice and Reason, &c.

JACOB HENRIQUES.

London, January, 1755.          Born Anno, 1683.

# EDITORIAL NOTES

## Thomas Milles, The Customers Replie (1604)

p. 3, l. 9: *Midlebourghe*: Middelburg, an important trading town in Zeeland, the Netherlands. It played a leading role in the wool trade during the medieval and early modern period between England and Flanders.

p. 6, ll. 39–40: Societie of the *Merchants-Adventurers*: The Company of Merchant Adventurers was first founded in 1407, and received its charter from Elizabeth I in 1581. For a long period the Company held a monopoly of the cloth trade with north-western Europe from England. This was temporarily withdrawn by the Crown in 1614. See G. D. Ramsay, 'Clothworkers, Merchants Adventurers and Richard Hakluyt', *English Historical Review*, 92:364 (July 1977), pp. 504–21.

p. 9, l. 40: *Counsailes*: i.e. counsels in the Counsel Chamber of the English monarch during the Tudor and Stuart period.

p. 17, ll. 1–2: *Ciuill Lawes*: Civil or 'common' law governs the relations between private individuals, as opposed to canon laws.

p. 17, ll. 6–7: *Tables of* Exchange: lists of exchange rates of different monies; initially actual tables at ports such as Dover for the exchange of foreign coinage, giving way to a schedule or table of rates of exchange. The tables were aimed at preventing the export of English coin in favour of negotiable paper.

p. 17, l. 8: Edward *the third*: Edward III (1312–77), King of England, who passed a statute on money in 1335 instituting the Tables of Exchange. It was repealed in 1344 on the issue of a new gold coinage.

p. 17, l. 18: Cambios *and* Rancos: exchange places for money where Lombard or Jewish money dealers met their customers.

p. 17, l. 23: *Cambiadors*: money dealers.

p. 20, l. 27: at Usance: the length of time, established by custom and varying between countries, that is allowed for payment of a foreign bill of exchange.

p 27, l. 39: Usuries: usury was a common term used to condemn taking interest on money lending during this period.

p. 30, ll. 14–15: Societies *of* Merchants Staplerers *and* Adventurers: see G. F. Ward, 'The Early History of the Merchants Staplers', *English Historical Review*, 33:131 (July 1918), pp. 297–319.

p. 30, l. 37: *Edward* the fourth: Edward IV (1442–83), King of England.

## Milles, The Custumers Alphabet and Primer (1608)

p. 49, ll. 2–4: *ALPHABET and Primer*: the basic tools for the education of young people at this time.

p. 53, sidenote, l. 6: *Treaty at* Barwick, 1586: also known as the Peace of Berwick. The treaty was signed between Elizabeth I of England and James VI of Scotland on 6 July 1586, ending a period of religious wars between the countries.

p. 64, 2nd sidenote, l. 1: *SIBILLA CUMANA*: According to legend the sibyl at Cumae offered nine of her prophetic books for sale to Tarquinius Superbus, the last king of Rome. When Tarquinius refused to pay the sibyl burned three of the books, then demanded the same price for the remaining six books. Tarquninius still refused, so the sibyl burned another three books. Tarquinius finally relented and had to pay as much for the remaining three as the sibyl had demanded for the original nine.

p. 70, l. 35: *CASTOR and POLLUX*: In Roman mythology Castor and Pollux were the twin sons of Zeus and Leda. In astronomy they are the two brightest stars in the constellation Gemini.

p. 72, sidenote, l. 1: *Constantinus Magnus*: Constantine I (Ceasar Augustus 305–6 AD), father of Constantine the Great.

p. 74, 2nd sidenote, l. 1: Lapis Phylosophicus: *Lapis Philosophicus*, an exposition of Aristotle's physics, was written by John Case in 1599.

p. 74, 3rd sidenote, l. 1: Universalia Medecina: Possibly *Lapis metaphysicus, aut philosophicus qui universalis medicina vera fuit patrum antiquorum, ad omnes indifferenter morbos: etiam eos quos incurabiles vocarunt illi qui curare non potuerunt, et ad metallorum tollendam lepram, fabricandos lapides preciosos, &c ...* (Gerard Dorn, 1570).

p. 77, l. 7: Cotsall: an archaic form of the Cotswolds, the hill country in Gloucestershire historically noted for its sheep rearing.

p. 77, l. 8: Cheuiat-hills and Barham-downes: The Cheviot Hills in Northumberland, on the border between Scotland and England, was a sheep rearing area, giving its name to a breed of sheep. Barham Downs, another sheep rearing area, is in Kent, England.

p. 77, ll. 11–12: Tenterden-Steeple ... Sandwich-Haven: Tenterden is a small town in Kent, England, which during the medieval period held a monopoly on the wool trade from England to Flanders. The Tenterden Steeple was proverbially said to be the cause of the Goodwin Sands, as money destined for the maintenance of Sandwich Haven was diverted to the building of the tower of St Mildred's parish church. Sandwich Haven was one of England's major ports between the eleventh and thirteenth centuries but declined as its natural harbour silted up.

p. 82, l. 41: Cesternes: cisterns of fresh water, of which the ones from Alexandria were the most famous at this time.

p. 84, sidenote, l. 9: *Cicero offic: Lib: 2*: Cicero, *De Officiis* (On Duty).

p. 85, 2nd sidenote, l. 8: *Offic: Lib: 3*: ibid.

p. 89, ll. 7–8: *THESEUS ... ARIADNE*: In Greek mythology, Theseus, son of King Aegeus, was sent as one of seven young Athenian men for sacrifice to the Minotaur on the island of Crete at the demand of its king, Minos. Minos's daughter Ariadne provided Theseus with a ball of red fleece to enable him to find his way through the Minotaur's labyrinth to destroy him.

p. 89, 5th sidnote, l. 1: *Sir* Tho: Moores *Epigram*: see S. H. Atkins, 'Certain of Sir Thomas More's Epigrams Translated by Stanihurst', *Modern Language Review*, 26:3 (July 1931), pp. 338–40.

p. 91, l. 25: *King JAMES*: James I (1566–1625), King of England, and King of Scotland as James VI. His ascension to the English throne in 1603 united the two kingdoms.

p. 91, ll. 35–6: *Queen ANNE, Prince HENRIE*: Anne of Denmark (1574–1619), wife of James I of England. Their eldest child and heir to the throne was Henry (1594–1612), Prince of Wales from 1610 until his death. He predeceased his father, who was succeeded instead by his second son Charles I.

## Henry Robinson, England's Safety in Trades Encrease (1641)

p. 99, l. 20: Grand Duke of Florence: Ferdinand II, who ruled Florence as Grand Duke under the auspicies of the Austrian Habsburgs from 1621 to 1670.

p. 112, l. 27: Lex talionis: the law of retribution, as in the law of Moses.

p. 112, l. 32: *Legorne*: Leghorn or Livorno, the principal port of the Dukedom of Tuscany.

p. 117, sidenote, ll. 1–3: *2* Kin. *5, ll, 12, 13*: 2 Kings 5:11–13: 'But Naaman was wroth, and went away, and said, Behold, I thought, He will surely come out to me, and stand, and call on the name of the LORD his God, and strike his hand over the place, and recover the leper. Are not Abana and Pharpar, rivers of Damascus, better than all the waters of Israel? may I not wash in them, and be clean? So he turned and went away in a rage.'

p. 121, l. 21: *Algier Pyrates*: also called Barbary pirates and Ottoman corsairs, the Algier pirates attacked shipping and were responsible for raids on European costal settlements, capturing and selling their inhabitants into slavery.

p. 122, l. 4: Amboina *businesse*: in present-day Indonesia. The Portuguese discovered the so-called Spice Islands in the early sixteenth century, giving them a monopoly on the trade in cloves. However in 1605 the Dutch captured Amboyna, and with it the monopoly.

p. 129, l. 9: Medici: The Medici were the most prominent family in Florence from the thirteenth to the seventeenth centuries, becoming dukes of Florence and Tuscany. Their bank was one of the wealthiest and most influential throughout Europe.

p. 131, l. 26: Perpetuana's: a durable woollen twill fabric which was exported from England to West Africa.

p. 133, l. 21: Placentia: Placentia, or Piacenza, is situated in northern Italy on the great plain, between the rivers Po and Trebia.

p. 134, l. 20: Luke *6. 35*: Luke 6:35: 'But love ye your enemies, and do good, and lend, hoping for nothing again; and your reward shall be great, and ye shall be the children of the Highest: for he is kind unto the unthankful and to the evil'.

## Henry Robinson, Briefe Considerations, Concerning the Advancement of Trade and Navigation (1649)

p. 171, l. 24: Guiney: a reference to the Dutch trade to what is presently New Guinea. Guinea's principal trade was slaves, although there was also significant trade in gold and ivory.

## Decay of Trade. A Treatise against the Abating of Interest (1641)

p. 186, l. 14: *Company of Merchant Adventurers*: see note to p. 6, ll. 39–40, above.

p. 186, ll. 26–7: *King* Henry *the seventh, and Queene* Mary: Henry VII (1457–1509), was the first Tudor on the English throne, ruling from 1485 until his death. His granddaughter,

Mary I (1516–58), became Queen of England in 1553. She was married to Phillip II of Spain.

## Thomas Violet, An Humble Declaration ... Touching the Transportation of Gold and Silver (1643)

p. 194, ll. 17–18: *Court of* Star-chamber: The Star Chamber (Latin *Camera stellata*) was an English court of law named after the location of its sessions in the Palace of Westminster. In operation from 1487 until 1641, the court heard political libel and treason cases.

p. 195, ll. 7–8: *Ninth, Tenth and Eleventh year of his now Majesties Reigne*: i.e. 1642–4.

p. 197, l. 15: *Lords of the Privie-Councell*: The Privy Council was the English monarch's private council during the sixteenth and seventeenth centuries, which met in secrecy during the Tudor period. It was responsible for general administration of the country, and its members were the richest and most powerful noblemen in the country.

p. 197, l. 17: *S*ʳ. John Bankes: John Bankes (1589–1644), Attorney General and Chief Justice to Charles I from 1634.

p. 197, l. 18: *M*ʳ. Diconson and *M*ʳ. Trumball: John Dickenson, Clerk of the Privy Council from 1618 until his death in 1636; William Trumball, Clerk of the Privy Council from 1614 until his death in 1634.

p. 199, ll. 5–6: *Lord Keeper* Coventry: Thomas Coventy (1578–1640), first Baron Coventry. He was made Lord Keeper of the Great Seal in 1625.

p. 199, l. 6: *M*ʳ. *Secretary* Cooke: John Cook (1608–60), Solicitor General who drafted the indictment against Charles I which led to the King's execution.

p. 201, l. 21–p. 202, l. 1: Hillary *Terme*: formerly one of the four terms of the common law courts in England, running 11–31 January.

p. 202, ll. 16–17: *S*ʳ. John Wollaston *Knight, and* William Gibs: Sir John Wollaston (1585/6–1658), Mayor of London. William Gibbs was an alderman from 1634. See M. C. Wren, 'The Disputed Elections in London in 1641', *English Historical Review*, 64:250 (January 1949), pp. 34–52.

p. 203, ll. 9–10: Peter Fountarne: untraced.

p. 204, ll. 12–13: *Earle of* Holland: the title was created in 1624 for Henry Rich (1590–1649), first Earl of Holland.

p. 205, l. 7: John Parrat: untraced.

p. 212, l. 5: *Chapman*: small trader.

## [John Houghton], England's Great Happiness (1677)

p. 242, l. 14: *his Majesties Happy Restauration*: Charles II was crowned monarch in 1661.

p. 244, ll. 29–31: *Mr.* Mun's ... East-India *trade*: Thomas Mun (1571–1641), author of *A Discourse of Trade from England unto the East Indies* (London: Pyper, 1621), a defence of East India Company practices.

p. 245, l. 15: *Mr.* Fortrey: Samuel Fortrey (1567–1643), merchant and author.

p. 249, l. 10: *Duke of* Lorrain: Charles Léopold Nicolas Sixte (1643–90) became Duke of Lorraine in 1675 as Charles V of the House of Vaudemont. He enjoyed a distinguished military career.

p. 249, ll. 19–21: *S*. Walter Raleigh's ... *opulency of Cities*: the famous soldier, adventurer and rich Irish landowner Sir Walter Raleigh (1552–1618). He published *Causes of the Magnificency and Opulence of Cities* in 1651.

p. 249, l. 23: Tamerlan the great: Tamerlane (1336–1405), Mongolian warrior-king and emperor, also known as the 'conquerer of the world'.

p. 258, l. 16: Corah: Corah led a revolt against Moses following his appointment of Aaron and his sons to the priesthood.

## William Carter, An Alarum to England to Prevent its Destruction by the Loss of Trade and Navigation (1700)

p. 267, ll. 1–2: *TO THE KING'S*: William III of Orange (1650–1702), King of England.

p. 269, ll. 12–13: I did in the Year, *1669.* express my Fears: William Carter, *England's Interest Asserted in the Improvement of its Native Commodities and more especially its Manufacture of Wool, plainly shewing its Exportation Un-manufactured, Amounting unto Millions of Loss to His Majesty, and Kingdom. With some brief Observations of ... Sir W. Rawley, Touching the Same ... By a True Lover of His Majesty and Native Country* (London: Francis Smith, 1669).

p. 270, l. 22: Mr. *T. Smith*: untraced.

p. 277, l. 9: late War: the invasion of William of Orange (the Glorious Revolution) and the upheaval of the Stuart monarchy in Scotland (James VII of Scotland).

p. 281, l. 22: *the* French *King*: Louis XIV (1638–1715), King of France.

p. 282, ll. 22–3: Callice *and* Diep: the two Flanders harbour towns in present-day France, Calais and Dieppe.

p. 283, l. 8: *End of the Reign of King* James: King James II of England reigned between 1660 and 1688.

p. 283, l. 15: *Sir* Matthew Hale: Sir Matthew Hale (1609–76), Lord Chief Justice of England from 1671 until his death. Hale was the best-known judge of the Commonwealth under Oliver Cromwell, and a great scholar on the history of English common law.

p. 283, l. 26: *15th* Carol. *2*: probably *By the King. A Proclamation concerning the Acts of Navigation, and Encouragement of Trade* (26 August 1663).

p. 284, l. 1: *Act against importing Cattle from* Ireland: probably *By the King. A Proclamation, for due Execution of the late Act of Parliament against Importing of Cattel from Ireland, and other parts Beyond the Seas* (30 September 1667).

p. 289, ll. 28–9: *Discourse writ by Mr.* Andrew Marvyl: Andrew Marvell, *An Account of the Growth of Popery and Arbitrary Government in England* ([London], 1677).

p. 296, ll. 14–16: *Tract ... to a* Parliament *Man*: *A Letter to a Member of Parliament: shewing how probably the Credit of the Nation may be Speedily Raised* (London: T. Cockerill, 1697).

p. 299, ll. 21–2: *1669 ... Account*: unidentified.

p. 309, l. 28: *Sir* Josiah Child: Sir Josiah Child (1630–99), Governor of the East India Company. See the headnote to Josiah Child, Charles Davenant and William Wood, *Select Dissertations on Colonies and Plantations* (1775), in Volume 3 of this edition, pp. 253–4.

p. 310, l. 5 *Discourse of Trade*: Josiah Child, *A New Discourse of Trade* (London: John Everingham, 1693).

p. 310, l. 32: the author of the *Essay* on *Ways* and *Means*: Charles Davenant, *An Essay upon the Probable Methods of Making a People Gainers in the Ballance of Trade* (1699), see Volume 2 of this edition, pp. 157–292.

p. 311, l. 1: Hans *Towns*: towns of the Hanseatic League.

## Richard Welton, The Great Advantages of Navigation and Commerce to any Nation or People (1710)

p. 319: 1.8: *City of* Tyrus: Tyre, in present-day Lebanon.

p. 320, l. 18: *my last Discourse*: not identified.

## Erasmus Philips, The State of Nation, in Respect to her Commerce, Debts and Money (1725)

p. 371, ll. 1–2: *War with* France: Between 1688 and 1697 France was at war with the League of Augsburg, which included England, the United Provinces (Dutch Netherlands), Spain, the Holy Roman Empire, Sweden, Brandenburg-Prussia, Saxony, Bavaria and Savoy.

p. 371, ll. 3–4: *last war with* France: the War of the Spanish Succession (1701–14).

p. 377, l. 8: Colbert: François Colbert, the French finance minister.

p. 377, footnote, l. 1: William Petty: Sir William Petty (1623–87), political economist, philosopher and scientist. He is often cited as the founder of the school of political arithmetic.

p. 379, l. 18: Hamborough: Hamburgh in Germany, with access to the North Sea rather than the Baltic, was an important outlet for many North European goods.

p. 380, ll. 1–3: *Contract ... with King of* Spain: the peace treaty between Spain and England, finalized in Utrecht 1713.

p. 380, ll. 19–21: *Treaty of Commerce ...* Utrecht: A number of peace agreements were signed in Utrecht in 1713 between the major powers of Europe. In addition a commercial agreement was made between France and England which was later attacked, especially by proponents of the Whig party, who described it as too generous towards French trade interests.

p. 384, l. 13: Smyrna: Smyrna was an important trading route into the Ottoman Empire, with substantial settlements of English, French, Dutch and Italian merchants.

p. 385, l. 15: King *James* I: see note to p. 91, l. 25.

p. 392, l. 20: Queen Anne's time: Anne I (1665–1714), Queen of Enlgand, Scotland and Ireland. Anne succeeded to the throne in 1702.

## Jacob Henriques, When Trade Increases, Riches will Improve (1755)

p. 397, l. 48: *Lottery Scheme*: The first lottery occurred in Italy in 1530. Elizabeth I established the first English lottery. James I established a lottery to fund the establishment of the Jamestown settlement in America.

For Product Safety Concerns and Information please contact our EU
representative GPSR@taylorandfrancis.com Taylor & Francis Verlag GmbH,
Kaufingerstraße 24, 80331 München, Germany

Printed and bound by CPI Group (UK) Ltd, Croydon, CR0 4YY
08/05/2025
01864487-0001